BOMBS GONE

BOMBS GONE

The development and use of British air-dropped weapons from 1912 to the present day

Wing Commander John A. MacBean
and Major Arthur S. Hogben
Forewords by Marshal of the RAF Sir Michael Beetham
and Air Vice-Marshal W.K. MacTaggart

Patrick Stephens Limited

First published in 1990

British Library Cataloguing in Publication Data

MacBean, John A.
Bombs gone : the development and use of
British air-dropped weapons from 1912 to
the present day.
1. Air-operations by Great Britain.
Military Equipment. Weapons 1912–1988
I. Title II. Hogben, Arthur S.
355.8'2'0941

ISBN 1-85260-060-8

Patrick Stephens Limited is part of the Thorsons Publishing Group,
Wellingborough, Northamptonshire NN8 2RQ, England.

Typeset by Burns & Smith, Derby

Printed in Great Britain by Bath Press, Bath, Avon

2 4 6 8 10 9 7 5 3 1

CONTENTS

'The present is always taken by surprise because we do not sufficiently know and consider the past.'

G. M. Trevelyan

FOREWORDS

A number of books have been written about aerial bombing and in particular the bombing operations of World War 2. When bombing can arouse such emotion and controversy in some quarters the subject certainly merits careful study, the more so because, so far as warfare is concerned, it is certainly the most significant product of the air age.

This book is unique in that it covers comprehensively the story of the actual weapons which were employed right from World War 1 through to the present day. We are told how they were conceived and designed, how they functioned and how effective they were, and the whole story is put in context with the operations of the time. There is enough detail for the historian and the technical specialist but plenty to interest the layman too.

The authors know their weaponry as well as anyone. John MacBean has been closely associated with RAF bombs for more than forty years having dropped them, serviced them, loaded them and on occasions recovered some that had not exploded. Arthur Hogben has wide experience as a bomb disposal expert in the Royal Engineers. Together they have combined to give us a fascinating story and an invaluable contribution to the history of air warfare.

Marshal of the Royal Air Force
Sir Michael Beetham GCB, CBE, DFC, AFC, FRAeS

The authors have amassed an incredible amount of technical data and operational information, which they have arranged into a fascinating tale of technical brilliance and bumbling laced with operational derring-do.

Neither history book, technical manual nor novel, *Bombs Gone* encapsulates the development and use of aircraft bombs from the earliest days of flying, to the atomic age, in an easy flowing style and although apparently tightly structured, the text follows related events as the need arises. This makes for a readable book, redolent with facts for historian, technician and layman alike. Perhaps one day a companion volume could tell more of the armourers themselves, without whom neither weapon nor aircrew could function; also the place of the gun and the guilded missile in aerial warfare.

Marshal of the Royal Air Force, Lord Trenchard, coined the original armourers' commercial, 'Without armament there is no need for an Air Force', a statement as true today as ever was. *Bombs Gone* is an object lesson in how this was essentially ignored prior to World War 2. In peace-time, 'flying-hours' inevitably tend to be used as a measure of Squadron ability, but unless these flights are made using aircraft with fully operable weapon systems the figures are self-deluding: they merely count time spent 'boring holes in the sky'. Perhaps *Bombs Gone* should be mandatory reading for all those concerned with aerial warfare.

Wing Commander MacBean and Major Hogben are much to be congratulated on such an attractive solution to their mammoth task of collecting the history of aerial bombing and recording it in readable fashion.

Air Vice-Marshal W. K. MacTaggart, CBE, BSc, CEng, RAF (Retd.)
Past Director of Air Armament MOD(PE) and President of the Ordnance
Board

ACKNOWLEDGEMENTS

In attempting, within the scope of one book, to provide an account of the development of British aerial delivered weapons since before 1914 up to modern times, including the changes in strategy and tactics brought about by the progressive introduction of new weaponry, it is clear that we required help from a wide range of sources. It is practically impossible to name all the organizations and individuals, both in this country and elsewhere, who have in one way or another provided information, photographs or illustrations to supplement that already held, thus adding to our individual knowledge of a wide array of aerial weapons.

However, we are particularly indebted to a number of Service Libraries, including those in the Air and Naval Historical Branches of the Ministry of Defence, the Royal Air Force and Fleet Air Arm Museums, the Public Records Office in London and later Kew, the Bomber Command Scientific Branch (that was), whose records were sifted over many years. We are also indebted to the excellent archives maintained by a number of West German towns and cities, and to the owners of private collections which we were privileged to see or receive extracts from, like those of Mr N A Bonney of Brunel University, Mr G Quick, an ex-employee of Vickers, and Herr Manfred Rauschert, an ex-member of the German bomb disposal organization, who saw the results of British bomber raids from the receiving end.

Acknowledgement is made of the photographs provided by the Imperial War Museum, Her Majesty's Stationery Office, Hunting Engineering Limited and a number of private individuals who have already been thanked for what we believe to be unique photographs, some of which have not been published previously. Efforts to prove other copyright holders have been unsuccessful; anyone having a claim should contact the publishers.

We are also indebted to Marshal of the Royal Air Force, Sir Michael Beetham GCB, CBE, DFC, AFC, FRAeS, himself a Bomber Command Lancaster pilot with Nos 50 and 57 Squadrons, and Air Vice-Marshal W. K.

MacTaggart, CBE, BSc, C Eng, a past Director of Air Armaments MOD, who have kindly provided the Foreword. Nor must we forget the contribution of four ladies who made the writing of the book possible, namely Miss Debbie Parkinson, who drew the vast majority of the line drawings, Mrs Anne Ord, who gave up much of her spare time in immaculately typing up the original scripts, and finally our respective wives, who patiently bore with us in the course of our endeavours.

INTRODUCTION

'An Air Service can be used as an independent means of war. As far as can at present be foreseen, there is no limit to the scale of its independent use. The day may not be far off when aerial operations with their devastation of enemy lands and destruction of industrial and populous centres on a wide scale, may become the principal operations of war to which older forms of Military and Naval operations may become secondary and subordinate.'

Thus wrote General Jan Smuts in 1917, when he was strongly recommending to the British Government the formation of an 'Independent Force'. Independent, that is, from the jurisdiction of the Admiralty and the War Office, who between them at that time jealously controlled the operations of the Royal Naval Air Service and the Royal Flying Corps, in the interests of their own specific requirements. Smuts wrote this in support of arguments he produced for instituting an independent flying force with the specific task of bombing German industrial targets during the latter months of the First World War.

Some claim this was a political rather than a strategic move because, in Britain at that time, there was public clamour for vigorous retaliation against Germany in response to a series of Gotha bomber raids launched on London and elsewhere during that year. Whatever the spur, it triggered the first real pressure to form a strategic air arm. The short-lived Independent Force (RAF) formed in June 1918 as a result of Smuts's deliberations was the forerunner of Royal Air Force Bomber Command, whose stated aim during the latter half of the Second World War was 'the progressive destruction of the enemy's military, industrial and economic systems, and the undermining of civilian moral to a point when their capacity for armed resistance was fatally weakened.'

General Smuts's vision of possible future bomber operations was recorded just six years after the very first bombs had been dropped in anger from a heavier than air machine, during the Turkish–Italian War. This dubious honour went to Lieutenant Guilio Gavoti of the Italian Air Service, when on 1 November 1911 he dropped primitive bombs on Turks and Arabs in the towns of Tagura and Zara in North Africa. Like some of his contemporaries, and many famous men to follow, General Smuts optimistically assumed that when a bomber dropped its load over a target, that target would most likely be hit and destroyed. In the years to come, this assumption was frequently proved wrong on both counts.

As late as 1937 when air plans were being formulated at the Air Ministry, there were those who thought that, in the right conditions (whatever those were), Bomber Command might bring the German war machine to a standstill in just 14 days, in the course of 3,000 sorties directed at 19 power stations and 26 coking plants in the Ruhr. In fact during the Second World War, Bomber Command undertook some 380,000 sorties and dropped 657,674 tons of bombs on Germany, along with 297,370 tons elsewhere. The cost was high: 8,953 aircraft were lost and 55,000 aircrew were killed and a further 8,400 wounded. This, augmented by the United States of America's contribution of a further 621,830 tons, just about brought Germany's industry, oil production and supply, and communications to a grinding halt by March 1945.

Much has been said and written about that bombing campaign, some of it ill-founded or even derogatory. Nevertheless, the bombers did force the Germans (not to mention the Italians) to divert a million men from the front line and to convert something like 50,000 anti-tank guns for anti-aircraft use to protect important industrial centres. The Luftwaffe, short of aircraft because of the everlasting attack on components factories and main plants, was also forced to leave the front line and concentrate on home defence, thus losing command of the air on various fronts, and eventually their own air space. Futhermore, the relentless bombing attacks contributed significantly to decreasing U-boat production and to the rapid progress of the Allied Armies across Europe after D-Day with fewer casualties than might otherwise have been the case. A number of officers in the Nazi hierarchy later freely admitted that the Allied bombing offensive was Germany's greatest lost battle.

Thanks to the 'Trenchard Doctrine', which was very similar to the ideas expressed by General Smuts back in 1917, Britain entered the Second World War with the Royal Air Force determined to demonstrate that the air-dropped bomb was a weapon of unique potential. This doctrine unfortunately was based on somewhat limited strategic bombing experience gained during the last year of the First World War, and with many of the lessons learnt during that period forgotten. Initially it was still extremely difficult to navigate a bomber above cloud or on a dark night halfway across Europe and find a specific industrial complex in a huge built-up area. Even with all the technology embodied in the later bombers, the load once released was an astonishingly crude and imprecise weapon.

Consequently Bomber Command and others found it almost impossible to distinguish between incidental damage to German cities, from that claimed by some, mostly with masterly hindsight, to be barbarous and deliberate destruction for destruction's sake. It may be that from late 1943 onwards, the force unleashed to pound industrial cities already critically damaged, was somewhat overdone. It may be that economically and strategically a greater proportion of the effort should have been directed at knocking out electrical power and oil stores, along with communications, at a much earlier date than actually was the case.

However, it is not proposed in this book to argue the rights and wrongs of a policy which was generally applauded at the time and, in the main, only produced misgivings in the light of hindsight and years later, away from the traumatic events of the war. Much has already been written about policies, politics and morality relating to air operations as a whole, as well as, quite rightly, the dedication and heroism of the aircrews involved in the two major wars. Comprehensive information on the aircraft deployed, ranging from the flimsy Avro 504 carrying up to four 20 lb Hales bombs, up to the mighty Avro Lancaster capable of carrying the 22,000 lb Grand Slam has also been published.

Yet little or nothing has been said about the weapons deployed, thus leaving many questions unasked, for instance, after the cry of 'Bombs gone!' how did the falling weapons perform? Whether they were primitive devices, little more than hand grenades, or sophisticated weapons with complex fuzing systems, just how effective were they? How were they conceived and designed? Were they the best available? Did they function as designed, and perhaps most important were they destroying or at least grievously damaging the targets for which they were intended?

The object of this book is to try and answer these questions and to describe the range of air-dropped weapons produced for use by the fliers of the First World War and by the Royal Air Force and the Royal Navy before, during and after the Second World War. The best aircraft in the world, crewed by the most courageous and well-trained men, count for little if the weapons they carry are ineffective. Conversely, well designed weapons, deployed and functioning as intended, can be battle winners. This book is concerned not only with the battle winners, but also with those that were less than adequate, the specials and the also-rans, some of which were overtaken by events before their true worth could be established.

Lack of space and the need to avoid repetition prevents this from being an exhaustive account of each and every mark of the bombs and other weapons mentioned. Hopefully, however, it provides adequate details of the main types deployed. Much of the book is devoted to the roles played by Bomber and Coastal Commands. This can hardly be avoided, as they were the main users of the various weapons described and illustrated. Nevertheless the role played by other Royal Air Force commands and the Fleet Air Arm of the Royal Navy must not be forgotten. As will be seen, they too used the same or similiar weapons.

The brief outline of the development of air power and associated weaponry during the early days of the First World War and the inter-war years has been included, as it forms a part of the story and the progressive (and sometimes moribund) developments had a considerable bearing on things to come.

CHAPTER ONE

THE GENESIS OF BRITISH BOMBING 1912-18

The early development of British air-dropped weapons is closely linked to the development of the aircraft, the formations and organizations who flew the aircraft, and perhaps most importantly, to the then current thinking in respect of the tactical and strategic deployment of the then brand new weapon system.

Perhaps to use the modern term 'weapon system' is inappropriate, as it infers a design relationship between the aircraft and the bomb such as to permit them to operate as a single system, and in many cases this was far from true. As will be seen, the naval and military aviation services largely proceeded independently in the design of aircraft and bombs. In both cases a considerable amount of private enterprise took place, with the development of numerous designs of air-dropped missiles, over and above approved systems.

British military aeronautics can be said to have developed from the Royal Engineer Balloon School founded in 1888 at Chatham, Kent following the use of balloons as aerial observation posts in the Sudan and Bechuanaland Campaigns. In 1892 the Balloon School and the Army Balloon Factory were established at Laffan's Plain near Aldershot, moving in 1905 to Farnborough, Hampshire. Six years later, in 1911, the Balloon School was renamed the Air Battalion Royal Engineers, and the Balloon Factory the Army Aircraft Factory. The Air Battalion consisted of two companies, one equipped with airships and the other with aircraft.

During this period the Royal Navy, too, was interested in flying and as early as 1908 proposals were put forward by Admiral Bacon, Director of Naval Ordnance, for the design and construction of a rigid airship (those in service in 1911 were still of the non-rigid variety). It was not, however, until March 1911 that naval officers became interested in flying heavier-than-air machines, and by December that year a Naval Flying School was established at Eastchurch on the Isle of Sheppey, Kent.

The British Government, mindful of the aviation progress being made by other European countries, and in particular the growing strength of the German Zeppelin fleet, formed the Royal Flying Corps (RFC) on 13 May 1912. The Corps consisted of a Naval and a Military Wing, maintained and administered by the Admiralty and the War Office respectively, a Central Flying School and the Royal Aircraft Factory (previously the Army Aircraft Factory, and later to become the Royal Aircraft Establishment, a title retained until quite recently). To ensure co-operation between the two Services, a Joint Air Committee was established. During the early years this committee proved to be unworkable, as its members polarized to their respective Service viewpoints. The military view was that aircraft should be an extension of the ground forces and so become their long distance 'eyes and ears' and, when required, be able to give tactical support to the ground troops. The Navy, however, recognized that the aeroplane was capable of use as an instrument for bombardment, and that in this context Britain, and particularly the naval establishments, were very vunerable to attack. The Naval Wing clearly saw the need for bombs and defensive armaments, and between 1912 and 1914 carried out a variety of experiments to improve both its aircraft and their armaments. This divergence of views within the RFC clearly could not continue, and in July 1914 the Naval Wing, with the connivance of Winston Churchill, the First Sea Lord and a great believer in air warfare, detached itself from the RFC and became known as the Royal Naval Air Service (RNAS). The two air services functioned separately throughout the First World War, but the RNAS often supplemented the RFC on the Western Front in times of dire need.

At the outbreak of war the RNAS consisted of one airship section (having become responsible for all airships within the RFC at the end of 1913) with stations at Kingsnorth on the Isle of Grain and at Farnborough, and seven aeroplane and seaplane stations. In all the RNAS had seven airships and 70 aeroplanes. The Military Wing consisted of four squadrons and an aircraft park consisting of a total of 179 machines. With the onset of hostilities, the numbers of machines and personnel were hastily increased, the RNAS instituted coastal patrols, and the RFC moved *en masse* to France where it worked in close co-operation with the British Expeditionary Force.

Initially the War Office was responsible for the air defence of Britain, but with the RFC deployed in France it was unable to fulfil this role, and at General Kitchener's request the Admiralty assumed this responsibility on 3 September 1914. A RNAS station was established at Dunkirk, tasked with preventing aerial attacks on Britain. It was hoped to achieve this by attacking airborne Zeppelins and those in their sheds in Germany and Belgium. Responsibility for air defence was not resumed by the War Office until February 1916.

The military activities on the Western Front in France and Belgium fell into three main phases. First, the open warfare of August and September 1914, culminating in the German advance to the Marne and the development of siege warfare. Secondly, the siege-like operations which lasted until March 1918, interspersed by ferocious and bloody battles such as those in the Somme, Loos, Arras, Paschendaele and Ypres, when the opposing armies made vigorous efforts to break-out or alternatively wear down their opponents by a war of attrition. Finally, the break-out by the Germans in March 1918, which achieved considerable initial success but led to their final defeat in November.

Throughout the various phases, tactical bombing took place, although, with some exceptions, it was ineffectual compared with the casualties and damage caused by the ground forces. As the war progressed, improvements were made to aircraft, bombs, and in bombing techniques. The RNAS concentrated mainly on the Belgian coast, attacking enemy naval bases housing destroyers, U-boats and seaplanes, and in both the air defence role and support to the field armies, attacked enemy airfields and Zeppelin sheds in the Belgian coastal zone and in Germany itself. It also attacked enemy U-boats wherever they could be found.

The RFC directed its entire effort at targets in the general battle area and immediately behind the enemy lines. These included enemy troops, airfields, ammunition dumps and lines of communication. Such attacks were considered particularly important during a ground assault as a means of preventing enemy reinforcements from moving forward. Later it will be seen that the results were far from effective. Because of the emphasis on reconnaissance and artillery spotting, with bombing a very secondary consideration, the RFC found itself at a considerable disadvantage compared with the RNAS when it came to bombing, particularly in the early war years. Indeed it undertook no systematic bombing until the spring of 1915, and even then had to rely heavily upon naval airmen for details of technical innovation in the bombing role.

Things began to improve progressively from 1916 onwards. By the time the RNAS and the RFC amalgamated to form the Royal Air Force on 1 April 1918, during the lead up to the final battle on the Western Front, tactical bombing began to produce results more commensurate with the bomber force deployed. The siege mentality had to a large extent been broken, the enemy troops were mobile and in the open, and offered better targets, whether on the march, in vehicles, or using railways. Aircraft carrying fragmentation and blast bombs were able to cause both damage and casualties.

Strategic bombing, that is the attacking of enemy war industries, communications and civil industrial population, as opposed to attacks on military equipment and personnel in the battle area, was never more than a minor facet of the air war. Its influence on the outcome of the First World War was negligible, coming too late, in too small numbers and probably without enough whole-hearted enthusiasm from some in authority. Indeed, this form of bombing was not fully developed as a possible battle-winning tactic until well into the Second World War, when Bomber Command turned it into a weapon of great power and destruction.

Probably the first-ever strategic bombing attack was carried out by the RNAS on 21 November 1914 when, as an extension to its tactical attacks on military Zeppelin sheds in Belgium and others in Düsseldorf and Cologne, it turned its attention to the Zeppelin works at Friedrichshaven on Lake Constance. The details of this raid are described later in the chapter. Apart from isolated attacks upon Germany, there was no strong body of opinion which supported the establishment of a strategic bomber force. Indeed, there were viable arguments against it, as every available aircraft was required on the Western Front and elsewhere. However, the Admiralty was facing serious U-boat threats and although some were being sunk, the air lobby at least considered it was a reasonable and viable policy to prevent their production at source, rather than trying to find and sink them once they put to sea.

Consequently, despite some diehard opposition within the Admiralty, 3 Wing RNAS was formed in 1916 with the main objective of inflicting damage, with French Air Force co-operation, on German industry in the Saar area, thought to be making steel for U-boats. Despite strong military opposition, the naval airmen firmly believed that the bombing of industrial towns in South West Germany was not only possible, but highly desirable. Not only would it slow down U-boat and other armament production, but it would also provide an effective response to the Zeppelin raids on Britain. They anticipated that sufficient aircraft would be made available for this purpose without detriment to military needs; how wrong they were! Right from the initial formation of the Wing, the incessant demands for aircraft made by Major-General H M Trenchard, then General Officer Commanding RFC Western Front, restricted 3 Wing's anticipated build up.

It was not surprising that General Trenchard wanted replacement aircraft urgently, because at the time he was heavily engaged in the bloody battle of the Somme. Between 1 July and 17 November 1916 the RFC lost 782 aircraft and 499 pilots and observers killed, wounded or missing. Compared to the slaughter taking place at ground level, 500 aircrew might not seem excessive, but it took far longer to train aircrew than to replace infantrymen. The early replacement of nearly 800 aircraft was of paramount importance to the RFC, so perhaps it can be appreciated why during its short life 3 Wing RNAS never bettered a strength of 74 aircraft including its fighter escorts, many unsuitable for the task required of them. Nevertheless, from its French base at Luxeil, 3 Wing undertook 13 raids during the period October 1916 to April 1917, dropping a total of 15 tons of high explosive, until lack of logistic support and other priorities finally resulted in its disbandment on 14 April 1917. Considering the small tonnage of bombs dropped and the robustness of most of the industrial complexes attacked, it is not surprising, with hindsight, that the attacks did not cause the severe damage or disruption to German industry which had been anticipated.

Just a year after the first raid by 3 Wing RNAS, and six months after its disbandment, Major-General H M Trenchard was ordered to start a bombing campaign against German industrial targets. It is perhaps ironic that the one airman who, together with his military chief General Douglas Haig, had been so much against the formation of 3 Wing RNAS was now ordered to form and command a strategic bomber force – a form of operation he eventually came to support enthusiastically. Although attacking German industry was in itself desirable, the Government order was prompted very much by a need to assuage British public anger and Government consternation stemming from a sustained bombing campaign on southern England mounted by German bombers operating from bases in Belgium.

The German onslaught started in May 1917 and continued until May 1918.

In all, eight daylight and 19 night raids were mounted, deploying 297 Gothas and at least 28 giant Staaken aircraft. Approximately 100 tons of bombs were dropped, including the German 1,000 kg (2,205 lb) bomb, the heaviest used by either side during the war. Two daylight raids on London on 13 June and 7 July 1917, killing 219 people and injuring 625, had a most dramatic effect on public and political opinion.

The outraged public demanded adequate counter-measures leading in the first instance to the formation of 41 Wing RFC in October 1917, enlarged into VIII Brigade RFC in February 1918 and ultimately to the Independent Force RAF on 6 June 1918 – the forerunner of Bomber Command. Each of these formations operated from bases in Eastern France to bring targets in the Saar and Rhineland within range of the bombers available.

Except in isolated cases, like its predecessors, the Independent Force caused no major damage to German industry, but production was significantly reduced in some areas by constant air raid warnings and the need for workers to take shelter. Apart from interruption to industrial production, the workers, like their British counterparts, demanded protection, and the Germans were forced to divert considerable numbers of aircraft, guns and men to defend the Fatherland – resources which could be ill-spared from the Western Front at a time when things were beginning to go badly for them. The indifferent results were not caused entirely by the relatively small and ineffectual bombs (the Independent Force dropped over 330 tons of high explosive and incendiaries on German soil) but by the conditions under which the aircrew operated.

The bomber crews were seriously handicapped by lack of even the most rudimentary navigational and bombing equipment and, perhaps with the exception of some ex-RNAS veterans, much was left to be desired in the training of pilots and observers in the elementary art of aerial map reading and navigation – which in any case was not much good to them at night or above cloud. Thus, often beset by enemy harassment, darkness or heavy cloud obscuring the landmarks, briefed only with suspect weather and wind forecasts, many crews failed to find the target area, let alone the precise objective – others were completely lost. This was equally true during the early days of the Second World War, in that the Air Staff underestimated the problems of long distance flights over hostile territory. In daylight, enemy fighter aircraft and ground defenders prevented many bombers reaching the target, and at night it was almost impossible, considering the state of the art, to find even largish towns in perverse weather conditions. The only real assistance were Germany's belching foundries, which made good secondary targets for First World War fliers when all else failed.

So much for the Air Services deployed during the First World War, the bombing philosophy employed by the individual services and the difficulties they encountered. It would now be appropriate to consider the bombs they used, because they were forerunners of those which three decades later were to bring havoc to so many of the towns and cities of Europe.

Having established their own flying school at Eastchurch on the Isle of Sheppey, the naval airmen immediately took considerable interest in evolving bombing techniques and in the development of bombs. At this time, when it was an achievement in itself to get a flimsy aircraft into the air, their first experiments in early 1912 were ambitious in the extreme. They set out to determine if indeed an aircraft could lift a bomb and, just as important, the effect upon the aircraft of suddenly releasing it. At that time most aircraft were designed to carry only a pilot and in some cases an observer, and that with some difficulty. In the opinion of many, additional weight could adversely affect the exceedingly flimsy structure. Nevertheless, Commander Samson RN, flying a Short Pusher biplane powered by a 50 hp Gnome engine, lifted off from Eastchurch with a dummy 100 lb bomb constructed on the base. Despite fears to the contrary, the trial indicated not only that it was possible to carry such an 'exhorbitant' load, but also that its carriage and release had little effect upon the flying characteristics or aircraft structure.

Resulting from this experiment, in May 1912, the Admiralty requested the

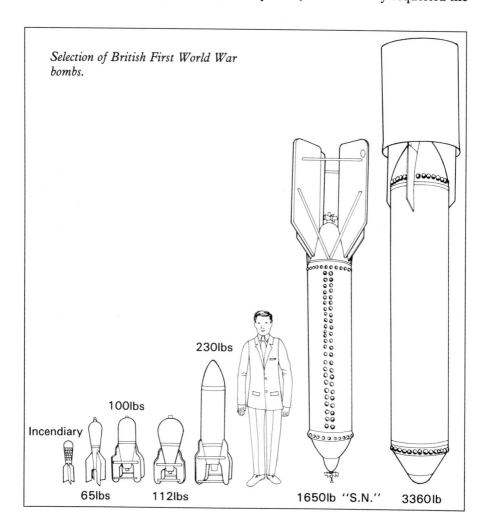

Selection of British First World War bombs.

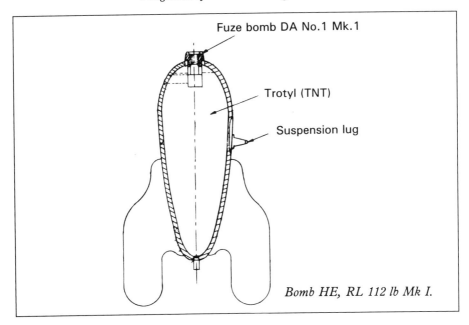

Fuze bomb DA No.1 Mk.1

Trotyl (TNT)

Suspension lug

Bomb HE, RL 112 lb Mk I.

Ordnance Board (familiar up to that time only with land projectiles) to co-operate in designing a 100 lb bomb for use against submarines and to co-ordinate the production of suitable equipment for its carriage and release. It was mutually agreed that a bomb having a large blast effect would be most suitable, and the explosive should be carried in a relatively light case to ensure the largest possible proportion of explosive. Such a bomb was eventually produced by the Royal Laboratory (RL), Woolwich Arsenal in time for the first World War. It was known as the Bomb, HE RL 100 lb Light Case, Mark I. It was produced only after a number of traumatic experiments designed to prevent it somersaulting through the air and to make its fuze sensitive enough to ensure detonation when hitting the target and yet safe enough to be handled and transported.

Parallel to the development of the 100 lb bomb, a heavy-cased type of the same size and general design was developed. This was the Bomb, HE, RL, 112 lb Mark I Cast Steel. The light-cased bomb contained 60 lb of explosive, and the heavier thick-cased bomb contained just 35 lb. The additional steel making up the total weight of the 112 lb bomb made it most suitable for all sorts of general bombardment purposes requiring penetration or fragmentation effects.

With the build up of the Zeppelin force in Germany, the Naval Wing at Eastchurch also set about evolving some method of dealing with them. A variety of *ad hoc* methods were evolved, including the use of rifle grenades and incendiary darts. Some of these will be described later. However, the most favoured method postulated was to fly over the Zeppelin and drop bombs on it. As it happened, Mr Martin F Hale, well known to naval aviators from 1913 onwards, had designed a 20 lb aerial bomb containing 4.5 lb of explosive, which it

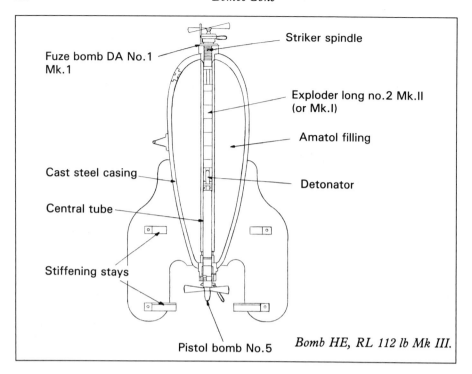

Striker spindle

Fuze bomb DA No.1
Mk.1

Exploder long no.2 Mk.II
(or Mk.I)

Amatol filling

Cast steel casing

Detonator

Central tube

Stiffening stays

Pistol bomb No.5

Bomb HE, RL 112 lb Mk III.

was thought could be dropped singly or in sticks (several bombs at spaced intervals) on to airborne or grounded airships. Subsequently, in 1914/15 the confidence in Hale's bomb was justified by the destruction of a number of
Zeppelins.

The development of the Hales and the two larger bombs prompted more experimentation at Eastchurch, for nobody was sure of the effect of a bomb
detonation immediately below a flying aircraft. The whole subject was a matter
of much debate. In December 1913 no high explosive bombs were available for
experimental purposes. However, it was clearly necessary to determine the
minimum safe height at which a bomb could be released, and consequently a
series of explosive charges floating on the sea surface were detonated elec-
tronically as aircraft flew overhead.

As a result it was concluded that a machine flying at 500 ft suffered little or
no damage from a 30 lb charge. With hindsight, one wonders if the charge was
large enough and, being uncased, whether the problems of fragmentation were
overlooked. Certainly three years later Captain P Huskinson RFC released two
112 lb bombs from 200 ft, perhaps foolishly if they were not fitted with delayed
action fuzes, and graphically described the outcome as follows:

' ...they flung me high like a jack-in-the-box. My wings, when I collected myself
sufficiently to look at them, were nothing but a blur of flapping fabric and what I
could see of the fuselage too closely resembled a sieve to be encouraging ... . My
aircraft when I landed, fell gently to pieces.' (*Vision Ahead* by Air Commodore P
Huskinson, CBE, MC).

He was one of many to suffer self-inflicted damage from their own bombs. To ensure a hit, however, airmen had often to fly exceedingly low, and as recounted later, Lieutenant Rhodes-Moorhouse who won a posthumous Victoria Cross in April 1915 was a case in point.

At the outbreak of war, due largely to the efforts of the Naval Wing, now the RNAS, three types of bomb were available in small quantities, the Hales 20 lb and the RL 100 and 112 lb, mentioned earlier. The Hales was manufactured by the Powder Company at Faversham, Kent, some ten miles from Eastchurch. During the early years of the war it was used extensively by the RNAS, and from 1915 by the RFC.

As the war progressed, a considerable range of bombs and other missiles was produced to meet the specific needs of the two air services. Some, like the Hales (10, 20 and 100 lb), the Cooper 20 lb and the Ranken Baby Incendiary, were designed by private venture. The majority, however, were designed and produced by the Royal Laboratory and the Royal Aircraft Factory. Usually the RNAS favoured the former and the RFC the latter.

By August 1916 there were over 20 main types of bomb in use, and in an effort towards standardization the range was reduced by May 1917 to approximately ten. The vital statistics of the bombs developed are tabulated in Appendix 1. In this chapter the bombs referred to will be illustrated in the text, but little further technical detail provided.

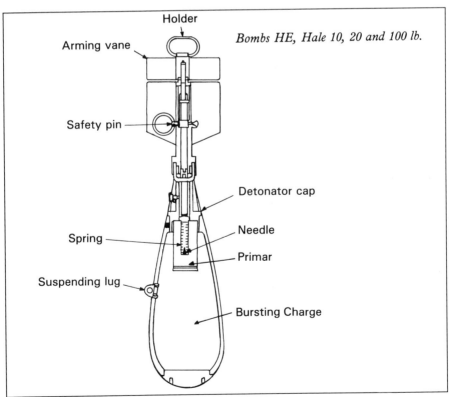

Bombs HE, Hale 10, 20 and 100 lb.

It is not surprising that because of its pre-war preparations and general readiness for bomber operations the first bombing attacks of the war were carried out by the RNAS. Mindful of the threat posed by Zeppelins, and since September its responsibility for the air defence of Britain, it quickly set about attacking Zeppelins wherever they could be found. The Germans had often boasted they they would make use of their airships to destroy the British fleet and its people. Consequently the naval airmen, encouraged by Flight Lieutenant R L S Marix's destruction of Zeppelin Z-9 in its shed at Düsseldorf on 9 October 1914 with two Hales bombs dropped from a Sopwith Tabloid, decided to strike at the heart of the threat. Three 1 Squadron Avro 504s, with a top speed of 62 mph at 6,000 ft, carrying four 20 lb Hales bombs apiece, set out across the Rhine valley on 21 November 1914 from France's eastern fortress town of Belfort to bomb the Zeppelin Works at Friedrichshaven on Lake Constance. The aircraft were piloted by Squadron Commander E S Briggs and Flight Lieutenants S V Sippe and J F Barington. Briggs was shot down over the target, and, slightly wounded, taken prisoner. In all, nine bombs fell in the immediate target area. One hit a Zeppelin shed, destroying the airship inside, and another a gasometer, which exploded violently. This was indeed an epic flight, possibly having the distinction of being the first-ever real strategic bombing raid. It is interesting to note that the aircraft involved were designed by Alliott Vernon Roe (AVRO), born in 1877, whose Lancasters were to become the star bombers of the Second World War.

The RNAS scored another first, on Christmas Day 1914, when a number of Short Seaplanes were transported to the Heligoland Bight, by ships converted as aircraft carriers, and used to attack the Zeppelin sheds at Nordholz, between the Rivers Weser and Elbe near Cuxhaven. Eleven 20 lb Hales bombs were dropped, without causing any significant damage. It was, however, the first air attack launched from British aircraft carriers.

Airborne airships, too, were not immune from bomber attack. Late on 7 June 1915, 1 Wing RNAS, based in the Dunkirk area, was alerted that three airships were returning to their sheds in Belgium, following an attack on England. Immediately, Flight Sub-Lieutenants Rose and Warneford, flying Saulnier Moranes, were ordered to attempt an interception and failing that, as a last resort, to attack the sheds at Berchem St Agathe. At about 2.00 a.m. on the 8th, Warneford intercepted Zeppelin LZ-37, and was having an exciting close-quarter duel with it over Bruges, having caught up with it near Ostende. Gradually he managed to outclimb the airship, and at about 11,000 ft, 150 ft above LZ-37, he released six 20 lb Hales bombs from a crude improvised bomb rack. A violent explosion threw the aircraft over on its back, and the flaming airship spiralled earthwards, where it fell on a convent, killing a nun and two men. Flight Sub-Lieutenant R A J Warneford was awarded an immediate Victoria Cross, but died in an aircraft accident in Paris ten days later.

Dropping bombs on airships and observation balloons was not the only means of dealing with them. During 1914 and 1915 a variety of incendiary devices were designed for the same purpose, and additionally to deal with stockpiles of animal fodder and other 'warlike' stores. In most cases they were

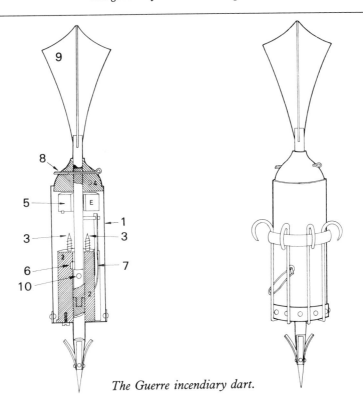

The Guerre incendiary dart.

This device invented by M Henri Guerre consists of a steel cylinder (1) to which is secured a central block (2) fitted with two sharp spikes (3). A circular wood block (4) which is free to slide easily within the cylinder (1) closes the top of the cylinder and carries a small annular tank (5) containing an inflamable spirit. A central spindle passes through the device and is secured to the top block (4) by a split pin (8). A shoulder and key (6) prevents the block (2) from sliding down the spindle but leaves it and its attached cylinder (1) free to slide up the spindle. A rod (7) is attached to the spindle and rests in a slot on the side of block (2).

The method of operation is as follows:
The bomb, in falling through the air is kept point downwards by the tail fin (9) attached to the end of the spindle. When the bomb strikes a balloon or airship the barbed point pierces the outer skin and passes through it, but the bottom of the cylinder is stopped by the fabric. This movement drives the annular tank (5) hard against the spikes (3) releasing the spirit onto the block (2). The same movement causes the rod (7) to slide in the slot in the block (2) striking a Vestas compound which ignites the spirit. A safety pin (10) passes through the cylinder and the spindle locking their relative movement and preventing a misfire. This safety pin is removed before dropping the bomb.

Should the bomb strike its target obliquely the hooks catch into the fabric thus stopping the movement of the cylinder and causing the bomb to function as previously described.

fitted with hooks to ensure that, having pierced a Zeppelin or balloon, they remained in position until the inflammable gas in the target was ignited. One of the first of these darts was demonstrated by one Henri Guerre of Lyons in early 1914, when he dropped some of his darts from the first platform of the Eiffel Tower on to targets of straw and wood. Although effective in igniting the target, his design suffered from the fact that it had to be dropped by hand, a method with little appeal to pilots. A year later Engineer Lieutenant-Commander F Ranken of the RNAS perfected the Ranken Dart, which had the advantage of being launched via a tube from an armour-plated carrying box. The dart was an inch in diameter and 5.25 in long, and designed to pierce the airship or balloon fabric and ignite the hydrogen and air mixture formed as the hydrogen escaped through the hole made by the dart.

Another device was the 3.45 in diameter, 8 in long Bomb Incendiary 3.45 in. Two designs were produced, one with hooks for use against airborne targets, and the other hookless, for attacking ground targets. Both were released through a tube fitted in the aircraft's fuselage, but uniquely for the period they were ignited electrically on passing down the tube. After falling about 20 ft, both ends of the hooked version were blown off, freeing two triple hooks attached to the bomb by wire. At the same time, the incendiary composition was ignited and burnt fiercely for about 40 sec. Colloquially it was known as the 'Fiery Grapnel'. The hookless version was similar, except that it ignited 20 seconds after leaving the launch tube, and burnt itself out on the ground, as did the other if it missed the intended target.

Whilst the RNAS was pioneering British aerial bombing, the RFC was unable to carry out anything like systematic bombing, until March 1915. However, this did not stop the military airmen from doing some 'do it yourself' bombing. It was mostly ineffective, but did assuage their enthusiasm, fighting spirit and undoubted courage. Some merely lobbed hand grenades over the side, but a number of serious attempts were made to use improvised missiles. These included rifle grenades, from which the stick was removed and replaced with a fabric streamer to provide flight stability. Later the Hales rifle grenade was fitted with fins and converted to a small aerial bomb. Other improvisations included the fitting of a bomb fuze and tail fins to French artillery shells. The *ad hoc* missile load carried by Lieutenant Conran of 3 Squadron RFC in early September 1914 gives some idea of the private enterprise adopted by individual squadrons. He set off in his Bleriot Parasol from Fère-en-Tardenis to attack Laon railway station, carrying sixteen hand grenades in the cockpit, two French shrapnel shells stowed in racks outside the fuselage for hand launching, and two 26 lb modified French shells tied to the aircraft, to be released when a length of string was cut by a knife. History does not record what havoc this mixed bag caused the Germans, but it quickly became clear to the RFC that improvised weapons posed a very real hazard to their own men, especially during loading and launching. On a number of occasions shells were inadvertently released during loading, resulting in death and injury to ground and air crew as they detonated.

The need to use improvised missiles gradually diminished, and by spring

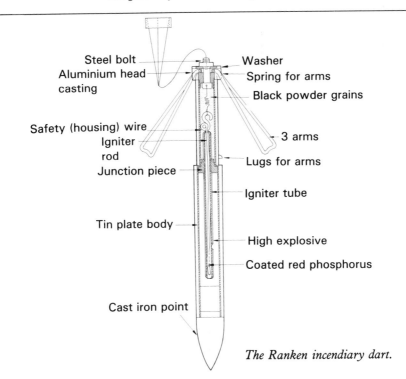

Steel bolt
Aluminium head casting
Safety (housing) wire
Igniter rod
Junction piece
Tin plate body
Cast iron point

Washer
Spring for arms
Black powder grains
3 arms
Lugs for arms
Igniter tube
High explosive
Coated red phosphorus

The Ranken incendiary dart.

The Ranken Dart invented by Engineer Lieutenant Commander F Ranken RN is similar in many ways to the French Guerre Device. It has the advantage, however, of being launched via a tube from an armour plated carrying box. The dart consists of a tin plated cylinder 1 in/25.4 mm in diameter and approximately 5.25 in/133 mm long. At one end is a cast iron point and at the other a junction piece which joins the cylinder to a smaller diameter tin plated cylinder approximately 3 in/76 mm long. Running through the junction piece into the larger cylinder is an igniter tube containing an igniter rod. The end of the igniter rod is coated with friction sensitive red phosphorus. The top of the igniter rod, clear of the tube, is formed into an S shape and attached by wire to a bolt through the aluminium head casting which closes the top of the smaller cylinder. The aluminium head is fitted with three spring loaded arms held in the closed position by a securing cap whilst in transit and by the launching tube when on the aircraft. The rubber securing cap is attached to the top of the dart by a short wire.

On release from the aircraft the dart falls point first because of the weight of the cast iron point and the drogue effect of the cap. When the dart strikes the surface of a balloon or airship the point penetrates the skin and continues through, the rear section of the dart is stopped by the arms acting as a grapnel. The main body of the dart continues, pulling the igniter tube past the now stationary igniter rod causing the main charge of the dart to explode. At the same time the black powder is ignited and blown backwards by the main charge. These sparks ignite the hydrogen and air mixture which has been formed as the hydogen escapes through the hole made by the dart.

The only safety device is a pin (not shown in the sketch) which passes through the side of the smaller cylinder and the S bend in the igniter rod.

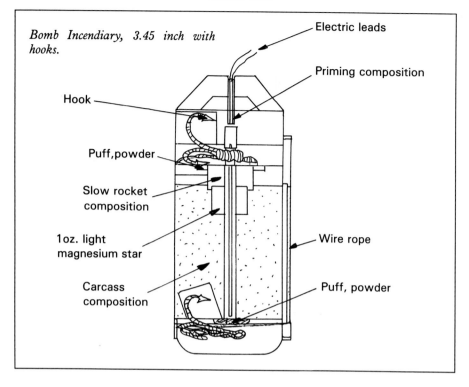

Bomb Incendiary, 3.45 inch with hooks.

Electric leads

Priming composition

Hook

Puff,powder

Slow rocket composition

1oz. light magnesium star

Carcass composition

Wire rope

Puff, powder

1915 the RFC was progressively using standard issue bombs. Flight Sub-Lieutenant Warneford RNAS, referred to earlier, was not the first airman to win the Victoria Cross. This distinction fell to Lieutenant W B Rhodes-Moorhouse of 2 Squadron RFC, based at Merville. Along with other members of his squadron, he was briefed to harass the railway system carrying German reinforcements from Ghent to the Ypres salient. Taking off in a BE 2b at 3.05 p.m. on 26 April 1915, armed with a single 100 lb RL bomb, he set out to attack the rail junction at Courtrai. In the face of fierce rifle and machine-gun fire he flew over the target at 30 ft and dropped his bomb plumb on the railway track. The aircraft's fuselage was perforated by bomb splinters and bullets, and Rhodes Moorhouse was badly injured in the thigh, stomach and hand. He finally landed back at Merville at 4.15 p.m., barely conscious, reported his action and died two days later, unaware that he was to become the first airman holder of the Victoria Cross.

As the war on the Western Front progressed, or stagnated, more and more bombs were being dropped by the RFC. For instance, in the period 23-28 September 1915, the total included 82 100 lb RL, 163 20 lb Hales and 26 petrol and carcass incendiaries. The latter contained a complex mixture of saltpetre, resin, aluminium powder, turpentine and other ingredients. By the end of 1915, day bombing had become a costly activity and consequently bombers were forced to fly in formation, supported wherever possible by a fighter escort. Operations were mainly limited to objectives in or not too far

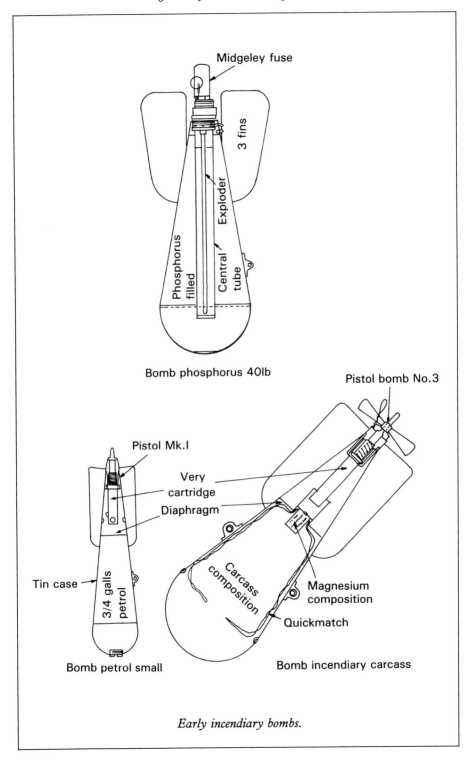

Bomb phosphorus 40lb

Early incendiary bombs.

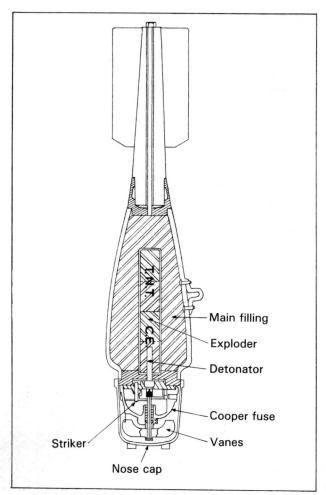

Left *Bomb HE, Cooper 20 lb.*

Main filling

Exploder

Detonator

Cooper fuse

Striker

Vanes

Nose cap

Right *Germans look at dud 112 lb RL bombs.*

beyond the front lines. As a result, safety and bombing results improved marginally.

Up to that time, the effects of tactical bombing did not live up to expectations, as demonstrated by a report sponsored by the RFC in July 1915. The statistics produced indicated that between 1 March and 20 June of that year, the RFC, RNAS and French Air Force had carried out 483 attacks using 4,062 bombs. Of 35 attacks on ammunition depots, factories, power stations and dockyards, only four were considered to have been successful. The results against railway stations and rail junctions, receiving by far the most bombs, were even worse: out of 41, only three were judged successful. The failure of tactical bombing to cause the destruction expected was to prove, perhaps with the exception of operations in 1918, a common theme throughout the remainder of the war. In evidence of this, Major-General Sir John Salmond, General Officer Commanding RAF Western Front (although the RAF was formed on 1 April 1918, distinctive RAF ranks were not adopted until July

1919) reported to 'Higher Authority' on 20 June 1918 that:

> 'Material damage from daylight bombing is, I am afraid, very small and must remain so as long as it is necessary to bomb from great heights (losses are severe at lower level) at which an error of 1,000 yd is not at all excessive. Material damage from night bombing is undoubtedly greater on suitable nights, but all experience shows it is seldom vital.'

These sentiments applied equally to Bomber Command in the early years of the Second World War, before more sophisticated navigation and bombing aids were provided. General Salmond went on to outline some of the shortcomings experienced; one such was:

> 'Before the battle of the Somme (1 July–21 November 1916) we selected six points, the destruction of which would have isolated the battle area from German reinforcements. At only one did we have any marked success. That was at St Quentin where infantry were caught entraining and an ammunition train was blown up. The total effect, as regarding holding up reinforcements, was practically nil as far as we know.'

The successful attack quoted was carried out on the day the battle opened by four BE 2cs of 7 Squadron RFC, each carrying two 112 lb RL bombs. None of the aircraft returned, but the pilots survived and became prisoners of war. A German report of the incident stated that a single bomb hit an ammunition

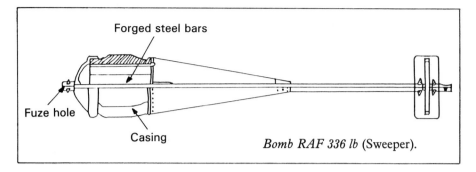

Forged steel bars

Fuze hole

Casing

Bomb RAF 336 lb (Sweeper).

shed, causing about 60 tons of explosive out of 300 to explode, killing and wounding 180 men and severely damaging the station.

In all, during the battle of the Somme, the RFC expended about 17,600 bombs (292 tons approximately) including a large number of 20 lb Hales, and 100 and 112 lb RL bombs. The battle also saw the introduction of two new types, the 40 lb phosphorus incendiary and the 336 lb 'sweeper' bomb designed by the Royal Aircraft Factory. Both bombs were innovative for their time.

The 40 lb phosphorus bomb was designed mainly for attacking airborne airships and captive observation balloons, and replaced the hooked Bomb Incendiary 3.45 in. It was fitted with a variable time fuze designed by Mr Albert Midgeley, who was still successfully designing bomb fuzes and pistols during the Second World War. The fuze was timed so that the bomb would function in the air as near as possible to the target, spreading a shower of burning phosphorus over a circle of about 750 ft in diameter. Thus, if it burst within 125 yd of the target in any direction, it was certain of a hit, with a high probability that the airship or balloon would catch fire. If initiated directly overhead, the distance could be increased, as the burning phosphorus continued to burn for about 1,000 ft as it fell. When incendiary bullets were introduced for use against airships and balloons, the 40 lb incendiary was subsequently utilized for more conventional incendiary purposes and ground marking. The Midgeley fuze was replaced by a direct impact type.

The 336 lb HE bomb was produced by the Royal Aircraft Factory after considerable experimentation. The basic concept was for the explosive charge to be surrounded by manganese steel bars, which would be propelled outwards at speeds of approximately 2,000 ft per second, capable of penetrating steel plate of up to 2 in thick over a wide area. Theoretically this type of bomb detonating on a workshop or factory floor would destroy or damage machinery over a considerable distance (hence the title sweeper), and in the case of a railway station would severely damage buildings and rolling stock. Initial experiments were made with bombs weighing 580 and 380 lb. The first proved too heavy for existing aircraft, and the second, without the manganese steel bars, did not meet the 'sweeper' concept. Finally a bomb containing about 70 lb of explosive and ten manganese steel bars was accepted. Two versions were produced, fitted with either a long or short tail to enable its carriage on a variety of bomb racks. Final operational trials were conducted on the eve of the Battle of the Somme, when at least one was dropped on St Saveur railway station near Lille by RE 7 aircraft of 21 Squadron RFC. Later it was reported that serious damage had been inflicted on the station. Despite all the work expended on the 336 lb bomb, it gained little distinction, mainly because it was too ponderous and specialized for general use.

The RFC almost doubled its strength between July 1916 and April 1917, in time for the third battle of Ypres, which opened on 31 July 1917. By that time the veteran all-purpose 20 lb Hales bomb was supplanted by the more robust and efficient 25 lb Cooper bomb, later to be classified as a 20 lb bomb. This new bomb was ideally suited for attacking aircraft on the ground, and vehicles and troops, and was widely used throughout the remainder of the war. For instance 102 Squadron RFC flying FE 2bs claimed to have dropped 18,912 of them, along with 2,826 112 lb RL and 110 230 lb RFC bombs; both the RFC and later the RAF considered the last two to be the most efficient general bombardment bombs available.

It is interesting to note that 102 Squadron dropped 365 tons of bombs in the First World War, and 14,118 tons during the Second, typifying the ever-increasing scale of air bombardment.

As the third phase of the battle on the Western Front reached its climax in September/October 1918, the then Royal Air Force showered high explosive bombs of every shape and size, ranging from 20 to 1,650 lb, upon the closely

Officers of 207 Squadron on 29 August 1918 with the 1,650 lb SN bomb. Behind is the HP 0/400 aircraft that carried it. Two 20 lb Cooper bombs are also in view – the largest and smallest HE bombs used by the Royal Air Force in 1918. (IWM)

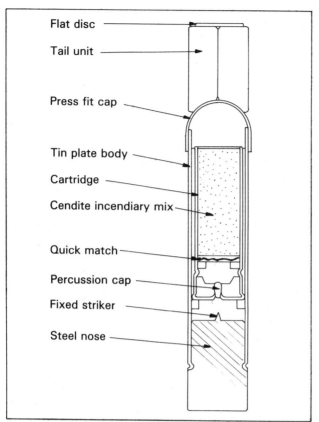

Flat disc

Tail unit

Press fit cap

Tin plate body

Cartridge

Cendite incendiary mix

Quick match

Percussion cap

Fixed striker

Steel nose

Left *Bomb, Incendiary, Baby 6½ oz.*

Below *Baby bomb container and release gear.*

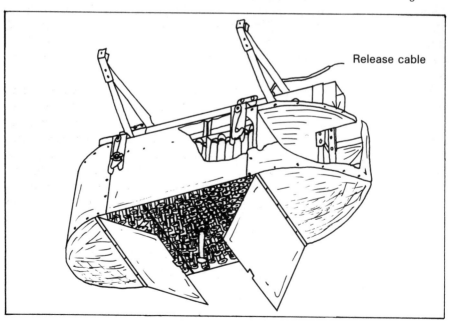

Release cable

packed and fleeing enemy. The bulk of the junctions and roads in the general battle area were attacked by all available bombing aircraft, including the new Handley Page 0/400 capable of delivering the heavier 250 and 550 lb RL and RAF bombs, and the mighty 1,650 lb SN blockbuster. This thin-cased bomb contained approximately 800 lb of explosive which, detonating immediately on impact, produced high blast effects. It was designed with German industrial targets in mind, such as Essen – hence the designation SN.

In addition to the air battles over the Western Front, the work of the RNAS in their tireless bombing campaign against U-boats must not be forgotten, nor their continuous campaign against the Belgian coastal ports. Ever since the Germans occupied the coast in 1914, the strategic and tactical value of Ostende and Zeebrugge, which offered facilities for warships and U-boats, and the inland port of Bruges capable of housing, assembling and servicing U-boats, was not underestimated. Each received its share of attacks by the RNAS and latterly the RAF. For example, during 1917 the RNAS squadrons based at Dunkirk expended 344 tons of bombs, including 80 on Bruges, 30 on Zeebrugge and 20 on Ostende. Coastal airfields in Belgium also received 114 tons, at a time when Gotha bombers were attacking South East England, and the railways a further 90 tons. An additional 622 tons were expended in 1918, but this figure includes the heavy bombing support given to the Royal Navy Assault on Zeebrugge during the night of 22/23 April. (This compared very favourably with the 6,400 tons dropped elsewhere along the Western Front during that year.)

There is no doubt that the naval bombing of the Belgian ports throughout the war years delayed and interrupted German naval operations and progressively forced them to strengthen the port installations. To this extent the bombing could be considered effective, but, as the buildings, including U-boat shelters, were reinforced, even the larger calibre bombs becoming available in 1917-18 were incapable of inflicting significant damage. The same problem was faced by Bomber Command when dealing with the V sites and U-boat pens of the Second World War.

Turning to the U-boats at sea, bombs ranging from 16 to 520 lb were used by the RNAS and later the RAF against them, but with limited success. The most commonly-used bombs were the 65 and 100 lb RL, and a flat-nosed version of the 230 lb RFC bomb. These weapons were deployed by seaplanes, flying boats, airships and land-based aircraft. A number of U-boats were sunk in co-operation with surface craft, but as far as can be ascertained, only one, the *UB-32*, was sunk by aircraft alone. The success went to Flight Sub-Lieutenant N Magor RNAS and crew flying a Curtiss H-12 flying boat out of Felixstowe on 22 September 1917. Found on the surface East of Harwich, the U-boat was sunk by two 230 lb RFC bombs detonating alongside.

The Naval-Military controversy over strategic bombing versus the use of aircraft to support the Western Front has already been discussed, as have the shortcomings of much of the equipment used. However, notwithstanding the epic raid on Friedrichshaven in 1914, it is worth recounting some details of the first strategic raid carried out by a strategic bomber force as such. This was mounted on 12 October 1916 by a combined British and French Force from Luxeil in Eastern France against the Mauser factory at Oberndorf some 100 miles distant. In all, 55 aircraft took part, No 3 Wing RNAS providing 15 bombers (six Bregeuts and nine Sopwith single-seater 1½ Strutters), and six escort two-seater Sopwith 1½ Strutter fighters. The French provided nine bombers and 25 fighters. The Sopwith bombers carried four 65 lb bombs apiece, and the others a variety of bombs.

The various formations set off in waves just after 1.00 p.m. Unfortunately, heavy cloud intervened just as the last Sopwith flight was taking off; failing to achieve any sort of formation, they aborted the sortie before reaching the lines. However, the rest pressed on, despite isolated heavy anti-aircraft fire and enemy fighter attacks. Flight Commander R H Jones and his gunner Flight Sub-Lieutenant C N Downes shot down one enemy attacker, and another Sopwith fighter claimed a second probable. The French claimed four shot down. Three RNAS bombers piloted by Flight Sub-Lieutenants Butterworth, Newman and Rockey, were reported missing, together with six French aircraft. The British claimed that their 3,867 lb of bombs caused considerable damage in Oberndorf, whilst subsequent German reports indicated that 60 bombs fell in the town, causing slight material damage, and many fell in open country. They also claimed their fighters shot down Rockey's Breguet near Oberezen and Butterworth's Sopwith over Freiburg, whilst Newman's Breguet was shot down by ground fire near Mülheim. All survived and became prisoners of war. Final reports indicate that twelve aircraft bombed the town and possibly others bombed the wrong town. If this was true, it was to become not a rare occurrence during the course of the First and Second World Wars.

Nevertheless this was an historic raid, and some of the difficulties encountered can be judged by this abridged extract from the operational report submitted by Breguet pilot Flight Sub-Lieutenant H E Wigglesworth:

> 'I left the aerodrome at 1.50 pm and crossed the lines in squadron formation at 8,000 ft ... speed indicator defective and rev counter broken ... shelled on way out and attacked by Fokker monoplane ... we opened fire at 50 yd but gun jammed after one round. Top left hand plane torn apart and riddled by enemy bullets. I reached objective after heavy bombardment and dropped two bombs (65 lb RLs) successfully but the wire release cable for the remaining four broke, and the bombs dropped between Oberndorf and home. After recrossing the lines I was attacked by two monoplanes ... one was seen to spiral down after a short engagement with one of our fighters. ... I landed safely at 5.40 pm ... I submit that Breguets could be more safely used in night raids instead of during the day where they require almost a fighter escort each.'

This strategic bombing raid in 1916, and many others during the course of the war, did little to affect the final outcome, but it sowed the seeds which led to the devastation of Germany's industrial areas during the Second World War with high explosive and incendiary bombs. The forerunner of the mass-dropped, efficient stick-like incendiary bomb, used widely by both sides throughout the Second World War, was the Baby Incendiary Bomb (BIB) invented by Engineer Commander F Ranken (of incendiary dart fame) during the year of the Oberndorf raid. Typical of all RNAS private enterprise he not only designed the small 6.5 oz bomb, but also organized a special incendiary filling factory at Roslin Castle near Edinburgh. During 1918 the Independent Force showered his 'Babies' down on to the targets, mostly from HP 0/400s fitted with containers holding 198 or 272 bombs. A container load dropped from about 3,000 ft gave a ground spread of approximately 80 × 30 yd. This spread gave more chance of causing a conflagration than did single fire bombs. On impact, each BIB ejected a burning thermit cartridge from its 6 in long casing. This cartridge burned fiercely, until all that remained was a small pile of white hot slag.

These small bombs reached their terminal velocity after falling about 2,500 ft, and at that velocity were capable of penetrating any normal roof covering. They came into their own, however, in the latter months of the war when used in conjunction with high explosive bombs, which damaged roofs and blew out doors and windows, thus creating a free flow of air to encourage the spread of fire caused by the BIB. During the last 13 months of the war, the strategic bombers of 41 Wing, 8 Brigade and the Independent Force (RAF) dropped approximately 665 tons of bombs on industrial targets, communications and airfields. Between 6 June and 11 November 1918, the Independent Force dropped 550 tons of that total on targets in the Rhineland and Alsace–Lorraine, and 220 tons were directed at enemy airfields. The total figure was made up as follows:

Bombs	Nos	Bombs	Nos
1,650 lb SN	11	50 lb RL	21
550 lb RL/RAF	54	40 lb Phos Incendiary	266
250 lb RL	Not known	20 lb Cooper	3,820
112 lb RL	9,902	BIB	816,000 approximately

Bombing during 1914-18, whether tactical or strategic, was only a very small part of air operations as a whole, and almost negligible compared with the numberless thousands of tons of high explosive thrown at each other by the protagonists during the bloody ground fighting.

Nevertheless it would seem that as much was done as could be done with the meagre resources provided to the Independent Bombing Force. Many of the industrial towns of the Rhine area felt its bite, and no doubt cursed the ever-present threat to their well-being. The threat might have become reality if the 60 squadrons planned, equipped with sufficient HP 0/400s supplemented by the bigger still V/1500s capable of carrying two 3,300 lb bombs (available in November 1918, but never dropped in anger) or 30 250 lb bombs, had been produced according to plan. Instead the Independent Force had to make do with nine squadrons, some of them operating with obsolescent bombers incapable of delivering cost-effective bomb loads.

Perhaps it should be said that some of the bombs available in 1918 were probably much more effective than those supplied in the early days of the Second
World War. Like a number of other lessons learned between 1916 and 1918,
many were forgotten or ignored before the onset of the next major conflict.

Bearing in mind that a bomb can only be planted accurately on a selected
target if everything is just right, it must be emphasized that the gallant airmen
of 1914-18 did their best, and often much more, with the primitive machines
and equipment provided. In criticizing their effectiveness or otherwise; it must
be remembered that they flew mostly in wooden-framed structures covered in
dope-coated fabric, usually in open cockpits lacking efficient navigational
equipment and bombsights, subject to extreme cold at heights up to 18,000 ft
and generally without additional oxygen or heating, at the mercy of unpredictable engines and with no parachutes. Their attacks were conducted with
variable efficiency, depending upon the skill of the crew, their navigational prowess and the bombsight available to them. There was always a measure of
unavoidable error in hitting a precise target using a fallible bomb aimer (or
pilot) who, in a moving platform, often under stress imposed by enemy fire,
aided only by his naked eye and a rudimentary bombsight, had to aim at a point
several miles ahead and several thousands of feet below. He must then judge the
precise moment to release a bomb or bombs having ballistic qualities of a very
imprecise nature.

Despite such vexing problems, many lessons were learned, both in the design
of bombs and fuzes, and perhaps most importantly by those controlling bombing operations. The latter learnt that day bombing was hazardous, targets were
difficult to hit from high levels, and that by night landmarks were practically
non-existent. All reasonably self-evident, but suprisingly some members of the
Air Staff, both in 1918 and later in the mid 1930s, continued to regard bomber
aircraft as precision delivery vehicles, and their bomb loads a weapon of assured
destruction.

CHAPTER TWO

BOMB DEVELOPMENT: THE BARREN YEARS 1918–39

In the two years following the Armistice of 1918, the Royal Air Force, like the other armed services, underwent swingeing cuts as the revulsion at the bloody slaughter of the 'war to end all wars' was felt throughout the British Empire. Of the 95 squadrons deployed on the European mainland in 1918, only one remained in 1920. The strength of 304,000 men was reduced to 29,730 and the total order of battle was reduced to eight squadrons in India, seven in the Middle East and one at home, equipped with a motley selection of aircraft and bombs, some slightly updated, but mostly left-overs from the war years. This situation remained largely unchanged until the great rearmament drive in the mid-thirties which ended a period of forced stagnation, which was perhaps understandable considering the climate of opinion militated against all forms of armament.

Contrary to popular belief, when bombing inadequacies became apparent in the early days of the Second World War, this was not the result of earlier Air Chiefs entirely lacking foresight; indeed they had been well aware that tactical and strategic bombers were likely to play a major part in any future wars. It will be seen later that, they were pressing for new designs of bombs, and aircraft to carry them, as early as 1921. However, Government policy was 'no war for ten years', and this policy continued well into the 1930s. This dictum did not mean that the Government expected a war in ten years' time, but rather that they could be assured of at least ten years warning of such a possibility. Consequently, little money for armament research and development was made available.

During these barren years the Royal Air Force developed a number of very limited bombing techniques in undertaking an Imperial Policing role in the wilder and remoter corners of the British Empire. This role took the form of punitive raids against rebellious tribesmen and ambitious chieftains. The Government considered it more cost effective to bomb tribal areas and villages than to send a punitive land force, which could take months to reach the scene of the 'crime', only to find the rebels gone or unworthy of large-scale operations.

Some substantial attacks were directed against the tribesmen of India's North West province, now Pakistan, during the 1920s and right up to the onset of the Second World War. For example in July 1924, 27 and 60 Squadron dropped 87 230 lb, 68 112 lb and 113 20 lb bombs on the Shaba Khel tribe. Similar operations were mounted in Mesopotamia (Iraq), Aden, and indeed wherever the need arose. The Royal Air Force assumed responsibility for the defence of Palestine and Transjordan in 1924, and four year later Aden and its surrounds. This latter area was under the continued threat of invasion by Yemeni tribesmen, whose leaders wished to annex Aden's valuable harbour facilities as well as settle old scores. During a six-year period, 8 Squadron dropped over 50 tons of bombs on these tribesmen, killing many hundreds and staving off what was considered a very real threat.

As was the case elsewhere, the bombs used were of First World War vintage, in some cases updated with minor modifications. Some lessons were undoubtedly learnt, but operations of this nature provided little foretaste of what it would be like to fight a modern air war against an equal or better-armed adversary. In short, the experience gained fell far short of that achieved by the *Luftwaffe* during the Spanish Civil War, and little progress was made in evolving better navigational and bombing equipment and techniques. Indeed many of the lessons learned during the First World War were unfortunately all too soon forgotten or ignored.

However, the inter-war operations did produce some capable and prominent leaders of middle rank. These men not only influenced the Royal Air Force build-up in the late 1930s, when the bombing threat to great cities became a matter of growing concern and public debate, they also practically dominated air force thinking during the 1939–45 war years. Those like Portal, Slessor, Harris and Cochrane played a vital role in the gruelling bombing campaign against Nazi Germany and her allies.

Despite insufficiency of funds, and in some cases a lack of motivation, some thought was being directed towards the design and testing of a new range of bombs, albeit without any sense of urgency. In considering inter-war bomb development and that undertaken during the war years, it would be appropriate first to broadly describe what an aircraft bomb is and how its major components relate one to another.

In broad terms a bomb is a container for high explosive, or incendiary/pyrotechnic substances, usually made of metal. Other payloads may be included, ranging from propaganda leaflets to war gases or nuclear materials. The container is equipped with a pistol or fuze, which enables the bomb to be safely carried, handled (or inadvertently mishandled) and yet cause it to detonate efficiently at the appointed time.

The container is usually fitted with one or more suspension lugs enabling its carriage on, and release from, an aircraft bomb rack. A tail unit is also fitted, to provide ballistic stability. In the case of First World War bombs and some of the Second, the tail was an integral part of the bomb, being bolted or screwed to the main container. However, it was found that rough handling during the transportation of the heavier bombs damaged their relatively fragile tails, adversely affecting their ballistic properties. Therefore tails for these were supplied in specially designed transportation and storage containers, and were unpacked and clipped on to the bombs during preparation for actual operational sorties. The tails had to be bolted on to some of the larger high explosive blast bombs, while in the case of the smallest bombs, many retained an integral tail which was protected by a type-designed container during transportation.

High explosives were known about for hundreds of years, some being more stable and therefore safer to handle than others. Some examples are ammonium nitrate (1650), picric acid (1771), fulminate of mercury (1799) and trinitrotoluene (1863). Initially the latter was known as trotyl, and more commonly as TNT. Most of these explosives were used in unaltered form both long before and well after 1914. In that year, when aircraft bombs were being produced in quantity for the first time, picric acid (sometimes known as Lyddite in recognition of experimental work done at Lydd in Kent) was used as the main explosive filling in artillery shells and other projectiles, and consequently was in short supply. TNT, made from coal tar, was therefore used for early bomb fillings, but it was expensive to produce in quantity so it became necessary to mix TNT with ammonium nitrate to form a new filling, Amatol.

Fortuitously, Amatol turned out to be more disruptive, less costly and far superior to pure Lyddite or TNT. Subsequently it was used as a high explosive bomb filling from 1916 right up to the early years of the Second World War, with periodical variations in the percentages of ammonium nitrate and TNT to suit particular requirements. From the results achieved, many at the 'sharp end' considered that Amatol had more than outlived its useful life when it became apparent during the Second World War that it was considerably less effective than its German counterparts. This was clearly manifested during the 1940–41 Blitz on London and elsewhere. Static trials in late 1941 demonstrated that, weight for weight, the Luftwaffe bombs were about twice as effective against built-up areas, bridges, railways and public service installations as the general purpose (GP) types used by the Royal Air Force. Consequently, Amatol was progressively ousted by much more powerful explosives such as Cyclonite (RDX/TNT), Torpex, Amatex and Minol. By late 1943 it was realized that high-explosive power could be further enhanced by adding aluminium powder. Trials quickly demonstrated that effectiveness could be increased by as much as 40 to 100 per cent. The advent of the new explosive substances, and bomb cases to carry them, ensured that British bombs not only vied with the German types, but outstripped them in power and effectiveness, both in size and range available.

A number of essential bomb components are required to ensure efficient detonation of these high explosives at the appropriate time, and among these is the bomb pistol. This is a mechanical strikered device, used either to initiate the practically instantaneous detonation of the bomb, or to set in train a delayed action. It is fitted with a number of safety devices to prevent accidental detonation. The various safety devices are too numerous to describe, but chief amongst them is a safety pin which is removed from the striker mechanism at the last moment before take-off, and a safety clip which is automatically withdrawn as the bomb is released from the aircraft, thus preventing any possibility of striker operation until the bomb has cleared the aircraft. Safety is further enhanced by the use of arming vanes or safety caps which supplement the safety pins and clips. In any event, the striker is normally freed after a fall of about 30 ft, and on impact it impinges on and fires the percussion cap of a detonator. The detonator usually contains a small amount of highly sensitive explosive, such as fulminate of mercury or lead styphnate. Detonators are designed to function immediately the percussion cap is struck; alternatively, delay compositions may be built in to provide delays ranging from micro seconds up to 11 seconds for bombs used for general bombardment purposes. More complex mechanisms were incorporated to produce longer delays and booby traps. Detonators by themselves are incapable of detonating the main explosive charge, so an intermediary is incorporated. This is the exploder, consisting of a few ounces of an explosive with a sensitivity between that of the detonator and the main charge, Tetryl (also known as composition exploding (CE)) was the substance usually employed.

The detonation process can best be described as follows; on impact the pistol (or fuze) striker initiates detonation through the medium of the detonator (or fuze magazine), exploder and main high explosive filling. Detonation of the latter instantly produces an exceedingly large volume of expanding incandescent gas at high temperature which shatters the metal container, in turn producing high blast or fragmentation effects dependent on the amount of high explosive content and the case thickness. As already mentioned, the sequence can be delayed to the required extent by incorporating a delay substance between the detonator percussion cap and its sensitive filling.

Some bombs could be fuzed, that is fitted with the appropriate components, at either the nose or the tail end, or both. Those intended for instantaneous action were normally fuzed at the nose end, but backed up by the tail fuze to provide some sort of assurance in the event of nose defects. Delayed-action bombs were only fuzed at the tail end. Earlier bombs, such as those used up until 1939, were fitted with a central longitudinal tube through the bomb to take the required pistols/fuzes, detonators and exploders, whereas the more modern large bombs had a pocket at one end or the other, or both, to take the aforementioned components, less the exploder, which now formed an integral part of the bomb construction.

Obviously, it was vitally important that the appropriate components were selected and fitted to the bomb to suit specific targets. For instance, the Germans might have destroyed more British aircraft on the ground during the Battle of Britain if more bombs had detonated on the surface, rather than digging themselves in because of fractional delays in detonation.

Before leaving bomb components, it is worthwhile saying something more about bomb fuzes, which unlike bomb pistols had their own integral striker and detonator mechanism. Fuzes, too, tended to be more complex, often incorporating barometric, clockwork, pyrotechnic or hydrostatic processes, but in each case the initiating flash passed from the fuze magazine to the exploder at the appointed time and without the need for an additional detonator. Fuzes were a mixed blessing, in that their very complexity produced more defects than the direct action mechanical pistols. However, they provided many varied options, such as those for airburst or underwater deployment.

Examples of typical bomb fuzes and pistols are shown in Appendix 2, together with some of the more complex models designed to produce long delays or booby traps for the unwary.

Bombs fall into two main categories, the incendiary and the high explosive. The purpose of the incendiary is self evident, it is designed to set its target alight. It will be seen from later descriptions that there were a number of different types of incendiary bomb. Some were little better than damp squibs, others were highly efficient. The older inhabitants of many towns and cities across Europe could certainly vouch for their destructive fire-raising qualities.

High explosive bombs were categorized and designated in accordance with particular roles. Thus for general bombardment there were general purpose (GP), medium capacity (MC) and high capacity (HC) types. The GP, as its name implies, was designed with the widest range of objectives in mind (based on optimism rather than pertinent trials); consequently, as with most compromises, it tended to be relatively ineffective for most specific purposes. The term 'capacity' in the MC and HC ranges did not relate to total weight or internal capacity, but to the percentage weight of explosive compared with the overall weight of each size of bomb (and even these were nominal to the nearest round figure). This is known as the charge weight ratio (CWR). In this context, an MC bomb had a CWR of approximately 50 per cent, whereas an HC had one in excess of 70 per cent. Clearly, to obtain such a high percentage of explosive, the casing must be relatively thin, consequently HC bombs were high blast-producers, fuzed to detonate instantaneously on impact. Delayed detonation, inadvertent or otherwise, was usually sufficient to cause the less than robust casing to break up, or at the best to produce much diminished detonation effects.

GP bombs, constructed with relatively thick cases, had CWRs well below 30 per cent and in the very early days as low as 23, and consequently they were largely ineffectual, producing minimal damage from either blast or fragments. The better-shaped MC bomb was a vastly improved version of the GP, and came to be Bomber Command's first choice as a general bombardment weapon against targets where the use of HC and incendiary bombs was not deemed suitable. In the main, the MC range was used against precision targets, as opposed to the saturation of industrial centres.

A number of special-purpose bombs were introduced, such as the 20lb anti-personnel fragmentation bomb, anti-submarine (AS), armour-piercing (AP) and semi armour-piercing (SAP) bombs, together with other specials such as those designed by Barnes Wallis to destroy dams and other specialist targets. Many of the Second World War bombs were designed with much forethought and alacrity, but sadly this did not always apply during the inter-war years.

Because they have some bearing on the shortcomings suffered by the Royal Air Force at the outset of the Second World War, the problems experienced with the development of the GP series, which are outlined in some detail, will give an idea of the frustrations and delays which brought a less than adequate range of bombs to fruition. Despite nearly 17 years spent on development, those available by 1939 were still largely untested against representative targets, and by 1941 had been shown to be vastly inferior to German bombs of a similar size. Their inadequacy largely stemmed from a lack of development funds, and other causes which will become apparent as the story unfolds.

An Air Staff requirement for a GP bomb or series of bombs was first presented in 1921 and, in April 1922, a development programme was approved for a range of this type. It was stated that a provisional range of 50, 120, 250 and 500 lb bombs would help to standardize type and shape, simplify design and manufacture, and provide a reasonably efficient weapon against all types of unarmoured or lightly protected targets. The size and weight of the bombs was strictly limited by the types of future aircraft likely to be available to carry them. The concept was certainly realistic, because the Royal Air Force was then using a motley collection of First World War left-overs in support of their overseas operational commitments. Unfortunately no mention of performance requirements was stipulated at that stage, other than that they should be reasonably efficient.

In 1925 a small number of 250 and 500 lb bombs existed, albeit inert-filled. Dropping trials showed that their trajectory and stability in flight was superior to existing war-time bombs of similar weight. This is hardly surprising, since the designers took some three years in which to perfect the shape!

Without further testing, the Chief of Air Staff agreed in July of that year that the lower priority 50 lb bomb should be redesigned and the 120, 250 and 500 lb bombs should be produced for service use. Thus the Mark I range of GP bombs went into production, with a puny CWR of approximately 23 per cent. Almost immediately, design changes were introduced to boost the CWR, but at this stage no live GP bombs had been dropped, nor were they for some years to come; certainly not in 1927, when penetration trials were carried out. These consisted of firing inert bombs from a test gun into a series of vertical concrete walls designed to represent building floors. This was the standard method of checking penetration at Shoeburyness on the Essex coast, where the majority of trials were associated with the design of artillery shells, and knowledge of aircraft bombs was minimal.

The first trial using a 500 lb bomb was only partially successful. The bomb broke up in flight, but its front three-quarters penetrated all four walls (floors). Although inconclusive, this trial was deemed (optimistically) to have 'indicated the improbability of such a target resisting a bomb of such type and weight'. Bombs, however, are not artillery projectiles, and do not always strike the target nose first, and certainly not at right-angles to the floor. First they have to penetrate the roof, and then depending upon the type of building construction, might possibly be deflected on hitting main beams and girders, before hitting subsequent floors sideways or even breaking up, before detonation.

In 1928 two new concrete targets similar to that already used were constructed, except that each simulated six rather than four floors. One was tilted back at an angle of 20 degrees to the vertical, and the other at 10 degrees, in an attempt to simulate the effect of a bomb dropped from 2,000 and 10,000 ft respectively, thus taking into account the likely strike angles from these heights.

Again the results were inconclusive, and suggested that, although floors could be penetrated, problems still existed if a bomb fouled toughened floor supports. Indeed, one of the trial 500 lb bombs was damaged on impacting a wooden strut. This did not augur well for the future, and certainly no live drops were directed at typical targets, toughened or otherwise.

Concurrently, to meet a stated requirement, designs were drawn up for 1,000 and 2,000 lb bombs. These were scaled-up versions of the 500 lb bomb. By 1928 a small number of experimental 1,000 pounders existed, but like the smaller versions were never test dropped. One, however, was fired out to sea from a gun, to confirm that it had a stable trajectory. In the absence of Air Staff pressure, the bomb and its design remained in limbo until 1932, when it was decided not to proceed with development.

It was not until 1935, with the war clouds gathering, that an Aircraft Bomb Sub-Committee was formed to determine whether the necessary and appropriate types of bombs and components existed for efficient attack on potential enemy targets. Its limited recommendations included the need for a new 20 lb anti-personnel bomb to replace the aged Cooper bomb, and a GP bomb of between 30 lb and 50 lb for use against vehicles, houses and aircraft on the

Street scene in Cologne during 1940. The 250 lb GP bomb, tail fuzed, has failed to detonate. Between 10 and 15 per cent continued to do so throughout the war. (Lurz/Collection Rauschert)

ground. Finding no use for the 120 lb GP, the Committee recommended its demise.

The Air Staff agreed, and priority was given to the development of a 30-50 lb bomb, which finally entered service in December 1938 weighing 38 lb and nominated the 40 lb GP. The 20 lb anti-personnel fragmentation bomb developed concurrently was introduced at about the same time and designated the 20 lb (F). Both were extensively deployed during the coming war.

In June 1938 the need for a 1,000 lb GP was resurrected, and with heavier bombers on order, it was decided to go ahead with development along with a 2,000 pounder, and if necessary an even larger 4,000 lb GP. The requirement for the 1,000 pounder design posed few problems, it was just a question of altering the 1928 design in line with current GP modifications. By then the 250 and 500 lb range had been modified up to Mark IV standard, which included the fitting of clip-on tails. Large-scale production of this range started late in 1939. None of the larger GP bombs were available to the Royal Air Force, or aircraft large enough to carry them, during the early days of the Second World War. Consequently, the airmen were stuck with various marks of the suspect and unproven 250/500 lb GP range, supplemented by 20 lb (F) and 40 lb GP bombs suitable only for the fragmentation role against troops and vehicles.

By 1941 both the 1,000 and 1,900 lb GP (meeting the 2,000 lb requirement) were in service. During trials, the latter provided less effective than the smaller 1,000 pounder. Despite this, trials continued with the still larger 4,000 lb bomb, which eventually entered service in early 1943.

All GP bombs suffered from the same deficiency, too much metal, too little explosive. With some exceptions, most failed to distinguish themselves, and were largely discredited by Bomber Command. In all, the Command dropped some 800,000 GP bombs (listed by type later in the chapter). With few exceptions their effectiveness was disappointing across the entire range and failed to distinguish themselves, the larger 1,900 and 4,000 pounders in particular. Fortunately, the MC range was superior in every respect.

Air Commodore P Huskinson MC (late Captain RFC), mentioned in the previous chapter, arrived too late to have much influence on GP bomb effectiveness when he was appointed Royal Air Force Member to the Ordnance Board on the outbreak of war. However, he was distinctly doubtful about the effectiveness of the bombs currently available, and decided that all new bomb designs should be fully tested against realistic targets before they were approved for operational use. With hindsight, one wonders why such a logical decision was not implemented earlier. In any event, as an emergency stop gap, he arranged for a trials target to be set up in an abandoned ammunition filling factory near Gretna Green on the Scottish border.

Some of the existing bombs were subjected to trial, and much to his and the other observers' horror, many if not the majority failed to function. Either their fuzes were torn from the bomb before detonation, or the bombs themselves sustained damage which prevented their functioning. Wasted time and labour was expended in bomb rectification which might have been avoided had meaningful trials taken place at earlier stages of development. Many of the faults

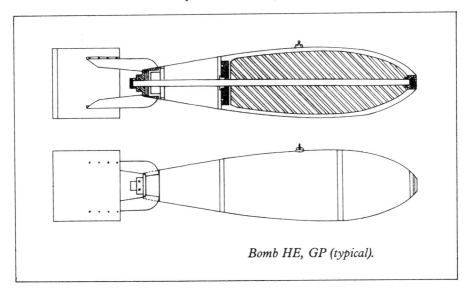

Bomb HE, GP (typical).

might have been eradicated during the leisurely days of peace, rather than in the early days of a war for which most of the country was unprepared and could ill spare the time to rectify past development lapses.

With people like Huskinson around, lessons were quickly learnt, and with commendable urgency, and with the release of money for operational research and development, a plan dormant in the Air Ministry files since 1938 was resurrected. As a result, a bombing target was designed and built at Braid Fell near West Freugh on the west coast of Scotland. It was ready for use by late 1941 and helped to perfect a range of bombs which eventually destroyed Germany's industrial heartland and much besides.

This then was the story of the prolonged and sometimes futile development of the GP range of bombs. It would not be entirely true to say that the GP series was a complete failure; some successes were achieved, and in any event no bombs dropped over enemy territory are completely valueless, but in no way did they distinguish themselves, unlike those who delivered them at considerable cost in men and machines.

During the first two war years, GP bombs predominated in the Royal Air Force armoury, where hugh stocks had accumulated. Ironically, the much superior MC bomb range, which began to become available towards the end of 1941, was seldom available in adequate numbers. The number of GP bombs dropped by Bomber Command is tabulated overleaf. The huge number of 500 lb bombs was mostly deployed after the D-Day landings (6 June 1944), when the largely discredited obsolescent stocks were used to offset MC bomb shortages when Bomber Command concentrated an all-out attack on both the German Army in Normandy and the V-Weapon sites in Northern France.

Numerous 250 lb and 500 lb GP bombs were showered down on the Pas de Calais V-sites during the Summer of 1944. The smaller bomb in particular produced disappointing results, as it had some four years earlier when the Bristol

German Feuerwerker (bomb disposal technician) stands by a recovered and mounted 500 lb GP bomb. (Stadt Bonn Bildarchiv)

Loading a mixture of 500 lb MC and GPs into a Lancaster for an attack on the Pas de Calais V-weapon sites, 10 July 1944.

GP bombs dropped annually by Bomber Command

Year	40lb	250lb	500lb	1,000lb	1,900lb	4,000lb
1939	—	50	29	—	—	
1940	26,179	61,572	20,106	153	—	—
1941	4,650	34,692	65,341	10,447	482	—
1942	6,938	15,206	29,482	14,409	1,241	1
1943	5,172	3,188	13,659	36,182	28	40
1944	—	7,768	395,641	20,845	366	176
1945	—	27,180	27,076	128	24	—
TOTAL	42,939	149,656	551,334	82,164	2,141	217

Blenheims and Fairey Battles of the Advanced Air Striking Force attempted to stem the powerful German threat westwards into France and Belgium from 10 May 1940 onwards. At this time, both aircraft carried a maximum of four 250 lb GP bombs, or a mixture of 250 lb and 40 lb GPs.

Many near-suicidal attacks were made, especially against bridges, with catastrophic results to aircraft and crews. None were more so than those against the 370 ft long and 30 ft wide bridges over the Albert Canal at Veldwezelt (metal) and Vroenhoven (concrete) two miles west of Maastricht. On 12 May 1940 it was believed that two Motorized Panzer Divisions were using these bridges in an attempt to break through to Brussels and split the Belgian and British Armies. Along with a number of other squadrons, successive waves of high-flying Blenheims and low-flying Battles of 139 and 12 Squadrons RAF attacked in a futile attempt to stem the advance.

During the morning, nine Blenheims of 139 Squadron led the way in an attempt to destroy the bridges with 250 lb GP bombs. Eight were shot down by enemy fighters, and one escaped with wings and fuselage riddled with bullet holes. Later in the day, the attack was taken up by five Battles of 12 Squadron based at Amifontaine, near Rheims, each carrying four 250 lb bombs fitted with 11 second delay pistols. The crews were chosen by lots, since everyone had volunteered. They attacked the bridges at low level, disregarding the fighters above and the anti-aircraft fire below, both by now at full alert. All five Battles were shot down, and four crews killed or captured. Both bridges were damaged and temporarily put out of commission, but unknown to the British the Panzer Divisions had already crossed and advanced 15 miles beyond the bridges, well on their way to Brussels – the sacrifice had been in vain.

Flight Lieutenant D E Garland in his Battle pressed home a determined attack on the Veldwezelt bridge with such vigour that even the defenders were impressed with his courage and apparent foolhardiness. This did not, however, prevent he and his crew from perishing in the withering gun fire. Twenty-year-old Donald Garland and his observer/bomb-aimer Sergeant Tom Gray were both awarded posthumous Victoria Crosses – the first Royal Air Force VCs of the war. For some inexplicable reason the wireless operator/air gunner, Leading Aircraftsman L R Reynolds, was overlooked, although he too went to his death, blazing away from his exposed gun position.

In terms of casualties alone, the Bomber Command raid on 30 March 1944, when 95 heavy bombers failed to return from Nuremburg, proved to be the most disastrous ever sustained, but in percentage terms the greatest losses were suffered by the Fairey Battles during May 1940. For example on the afternoon of 14 May, 39 out of 61 aircraft were lost (64 per cent) attacking bridges at Sedan with 250 lb GPs, with little to show other than wreckage strewn around the valleys of the Ardennes. Few of those involved survived the war to see their aircraft and bombs deemed ineffectual, but on the day, the members of the nine squadrons involved (12, 103, 105, 114, 139, 142, 150, 218 and 226) considered they were doing their very best with what was available, and paid scant attention to the rights and wrongs of aircraft and bomb development. In any case, few had ever seen a live bomb till a few months earlier, much less dropped one. Most experience in the pre-war bomber squadrons was limited to 11.5 lb smoke training bombs. So there was no evidence to either inspire or undermine confidence at squadron level in the available high explosive bombs – and most were loyal to their own particular aircraft type.

Among the other high explosive bombs developed during the inter-war years

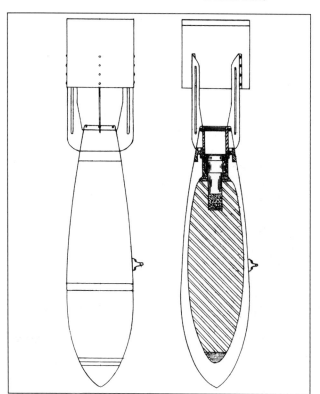

Left *Bomb HE, SAP* (typical).

Below *Bomb HE, AP 2,000 lb.*

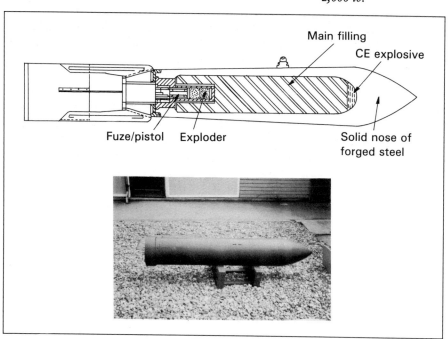

Main filling

CE explosive

Fuze/pistol   Exploder

Solid nose of forged steel

was the semi armour-piercing (SAP) and armour-piercing (AP) range. Designed to attack warships, they were both conceived, like the GP range, in 1921 and went through a similar gestation period. After many policy and design changes, both types were finally tested by firing at a series of near vertical sheets of armoured plate representing ship decks. When live dropping trials against *HMS Marlborough,* a naval target ship, were proposed in 1930, this was opposed by the Admiralty, who feared the target might be sunk, preventing further trials. Again money, or the lack of it, was the overriding consideration. With hindsight and much greater experience, it is now known that the chance of Marlborough being sunk was somewhat remote. In any event, a compromise solution was adopted: one bomb was detonated at rest between the decks of the warship, which appears to have caused no major damage. Nevertheless, production went ahead, and by the onset of the Second World War, stocks of the 250 and 500 lb SAP and the 2,000 lb AP bombs were available with robust bodies and charge/weight ratios of 17, 18 and 8.8 per cent respectively.

Each type was well shaped for the task envisaged, but suffered a number of disadvantages. The prime need to provide a heavy metal toughened case to penetrate hardened targets without breaking up left little room for the high explosive filling. So little in fact that, assuming adequate penetration, the damage done by the detonation was likely to be relatively insignificant.

Furthermore, as enemy warship armour improved in quality and thickness, the chances of achieving penetration except from high altitude decreased even further. Consequently these bombs tended to be ineffectual when dropped from low level, and at medium and high levels it was extremely difficult to hit a ship at anchor; under way, the chances of a hit were practically negligible, depending very much on luck. So it cannot be said that either the SAP or AP bombs were successful. Perhaps the design, along the lines of a naval shell, failed to take into account the difficulty of trying to hit a ship from the air. Nevertheless, a modicum of success was achieved against German warships in port. Just how much, can be determined from Chapter Eight.

The 250 lb and 500 lb SAP bombs were deployed from the first days of the War, and the first 2,000 lb AP made its debut on 7 May 1940 when a Coastal Command Bristol Beaufort unsuccessfully aimed one at a German cruiser anchored off the Frisian island of Norderney. That still to become famous bomber pilot, Flying Officer Guy Gibson, serving with 83 Hampden Squadron at Scampton, Lincolnshire, inadvertently dropped the first of this type to fall on Germany proper on the night of 1-2 July 1940. Having aimed at the battle cruiser *Scharnhorst* in Kiel dockyard, and failing to release the bomb after six attempts, it finally fell free, overshot the target and landed in the town, killing ten people.

It is difficult to pinpoint with certainty many successes for the 2,000 lb AP bomb, although along with other types it did an excellent job in crippling the battle cruiser *Gneisenau* docked in Kiel on the night of 26–27 February 1942. The 250 lb and 500 lb SAP bombs too scored at least two notable victories, one by the Fleet Air Arm and the other the Royal Air Force. The former sank the German cruiser *Königsberg* moored near Bergen in Norway, and the latter seriously damaged the *Scharnhorst* at anchor in the French naval harbour at La Pallice. These attacks are described in more detail in the relevent chapter.

One other AP bomb was added to the range in the dying days of the war. Code named 'Disney', it was a 4,500 lb rocket-assisted AP bomb, capable of penetrating 14 ft of reinforced concrete like that used in the construction of E-boat and U-boat pens. These pens were practically immune to the standard general bombardment and AP bombs. Indeed, reports indicated that they did little more than dent the surface. Disney was very similar to the smaller German rocket-assisted 500 kg (1,100 lb) bomb used to penetrate the natural underground shelters on Malta during 1942. Disney's body/warhead was a scaled-up version of the 2,000 lb AP bomb, containing 520 lb of Shellite high explosive, and was driven through the air by a 950 lb rocket motor attached as a tail assembly. It was intended that the 19 separate rockets forming the rocket motor would fire simultaneously just after the weapon fell away from the carrying aircraft, giving it a smooth and accelerating trajectory to the target, and sufficient energy to penetrate the concrete roof without disintegrating.

Great difficulty was experienced in trying to get simultaneous rocket ignition, consequently an erratic flight path produced more misses than hits. In fairness the bomb, developed in haste during 1944, was still undergoing operational trials against live enemy targets when the war ended. It was hoped that two, at least, might be carried in the Lancaster bomb-bay. Plans to carry Disneys on British aircraft came to naught, consequently use was made of American Flying Fortresses to deliver attacks against German targets. Two bombs were slung under the wings. Serious consideration was given to using these bombs against the Japanese fleet. However, it is doubtful whether 520 lb of high explosive would have been adequate, even assuming that the top deck armour plate was penetrated. In the case of the heavy concrete bunkers, it is now known that the charge was insufficient. In all, 149 Disney bombs were deployed between February and April 1945, when the E-boat pens at IJmuiden in the Netherlands and the U-boats pens at Farge (near Bremen) and Hamburg were attacked. Those that penetrated did little damage, or failed to detonate. The Germans found a number unexploded at each site, six entry holes were investigated at Hamburg as late as 1980, and it is likely that more may still be discovered. These weapons posed little threat on the day they were launched and today, lying at a considerable depth, they pose even less, providing they remain undisturbed.

As recounted in Chapter One, RNAS and latterly Royal Air Force aircraft were doing their best to defeat the U-boat during the First World War. The need was great because during April 1917, for instance, enemy submarines were sinking Allied shipping at an average rate of 28,000 tons per day. However, once the U-boats put to sea, air attacks alone had only very limited success. In that same year, RNAS flying boats, aeroplanes, seaplanes and airships sighted 168 U-boats and bombed 105, mostly with 65 and 100 lb RL bombs and the 230 lb RFC (flat-nosed version). This modification to the 230 lb bomb prevented it from sinking too fast, permitting the delay mechanism to initiate detonation at a depth of between 60 and 70 ft. The sinking of a number of

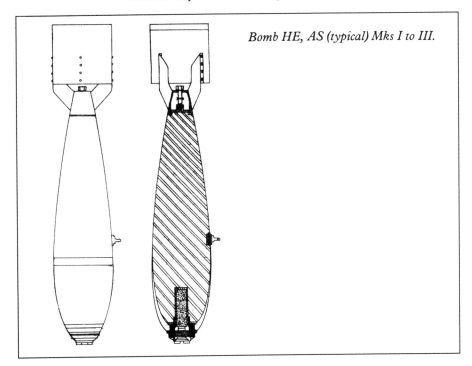

Bomb HE, AS (typical) Mks I to III.

U-boats by aircraft on their own was claimed, but as far as can be ascertained, only *UB-32*, as recounted in Chapter One, can be confirmed. However, a number of sinkings were confirmed following combined air and surface attacks.

Very early in the 1914–18 war it had been appreciated that a bomb required minimum metal and maximum explosive to achieve maximum underwater effectiveness, hence the use of thin-cased bombs. High blast underwater detonations, compounded by water pressure, close to a submarine's vulnerable hull caused considerable internal damage, as well as leakage due to sprung rivetting. To cater for lucky direct hits, or the more likely near misses, bombs were fuzed to detonate either on impact or after a short delay to enable sinkage beneath the hull before detonation.

During the earlier First World War anti-submarine campaigns, the use of bombs ranging from 16 to 230 lb was not uncommon. However, by the time the Royal Air Force was formed in 1918, only the 230 lb and a new thin-cased 520 lb RL were deployed specifically for the purpose. These were the forerunners of the new designs introduced during the inter-war years.

The Admiralty agreed the need for two new anti-submarine bombs weighing 250 and 500 lb in 1924, but contrary to Air Ministry requirements, amended its decision in the following year by excluding the 250 lb and including one of 100 lb. This conflict was triggered by the need to have at least two sizes of anti-submarine bomb available. One, big enough, which if circumstances permitted could be accurately dropped on or alongside a submarine with the expectation of a single bomb making a kill. In these circumstances, both establishments opted for the 500 lb bomb. Recognizing that assurance of a strike might only be guaranteed by dropping sticks of bombs, to compensate for the difficulty of hitting a relatively small and elusive target from anything but suicidal heights, the question arose as to which was the smallest bomb worth using. The smallest viable bomb had to be selected, because contemporary aircraft had a limited ability to carry large multiple loads. The Admiralty supported the use of the 100 lb and the Air Ministry the 250 lb version; both views based more on conjecture than experimental evidence. To satisfy both egos, and with true British compromise, it was mutually agreed to simultaneously develop 100, 250 and 500 lb AS bombs.

The initial design was based on the shape developed for the new GP range, but with a thinner-walled body. No trials were conducted to determine the thickness of wall required to withstand impact on water from varying release heights. Instead, the thickness was selected arbitrarily to give a CWR of just over 50 per cent.

By late 1926 five 100 lb AS bombs had been dropped and four were considered satisfactory, since they did not break up on impact and detonated below the surface. To conclude the trial, a sixth was detonated statically underwater to determine fragmentation effectiveness. The spread was considered satisfactory. Thus by early 1928 the Bomb AS 100 lb Mark I was declared fit for service, despite never having been tested against a realistic target such as a simulated submarine hull or indeed any other type of ship.

Almost immediately it was decided to replace the steel tail with one made of a light metal. This upset the bomb's ballistic performance, necessitating a body change to reduce the weight of the nose. Of course this delayed production and caused a certain amount of retooling on the production line. Having just started, it was realized that aluminium would be in short supply in wartime, so yet another change of design was made, to introduce a light steel tail. After these setbacks the redesigned bomb became the Mark II, with one saving grace, the reduction in nose and tail metal weight resulted in the all important explosive ratio rising to 62 per cent.

This design was drop-tested in 1930 and, based on the 1926 criteria, was judged satisfactory. By 1931 the Mark I and II 100 lb AS bombs were introduced into service, nearly six years after first conception. The Mark III quickly followed, but this modification involved only the strengthening of the suspension lug fastening to enable the carrying aircraft to be catapulted from a flight deck without fear of leaving its bomb load behind.

However, further problems had still to be confronted, not the least being those in the fuzing mechanisms of the 250 and 500 lb bombs (scaled-up versions of the 100 pounder) experienced in 1934 during trials to determine the underwater behaviour of the entire anti-submarine range. The results of these tests were most alarming, disclosing not only that the nose fuze functioned erractically, but its very presence in the bomb nose caused the underwater trajectory to be almost totally unpredictable. This led, some two years later, to a fresh requirement for a new range of AS bombs constructed with solid noses and tail fuzing.

Above *Four 250 lb AS bombs (nose fuzed) being checked before being pushed out from the Sunderland flying boat hull to the wing position.* (IWM)

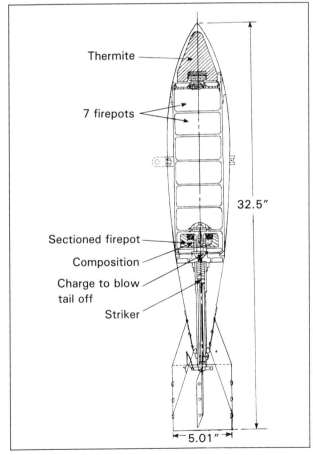

Thermite

7 firepots

32.5″

Sectioned firepot

Composition

Charge to blow tail off

Striker

5.01″

Right *Bomb Incendiary 25 lb Mk I.*

Die Wirkung der Britischen Brandbombe inc 25 lb

German view of 25 lb incendiary's mode of action.

The design of the modified bombs, nominated the Mark IV range, threw up new problems associated with the revised fuzing system, which included the use of a No 30 pistol. The problem was only partially resolved when operational stocks finally became available in late 1939. Many of the earlier suspect marks were held in war reserve against urgent contingency plans pending a build-up of the somewhat more reliable Mark IVs.

For better or for worse, the Fleet Air Arm and Coastal Command RAF entered the Second World War with a range of anti-submarine bombs designed to attack a well-defined threat, but which had never been tested against realistic targets. Consequently no one knew for sure how they would perform when confronted by the real thing. A 40 per cent failure rate due to malfunction of the tail pistol, and in some cases the older nose fuze, did little to establish confidence among the Air Staffs and operational airmen when they were used for real in the early days of the war.

An example of the poor underwater trajectory of the nose-fuzed bombs occurred on 14 September 1939. Two 803 Squadron Blackburn Skuas flying from the aircraft carrier HMS *Ark Royal* spotted a surfaced U-boat, and flying low over it released their 250 lb Mark III AS bombs. To their everlasting embarrassment one of the bombs skipped out of the water and detonated beneath them, forcing both splinter-damaged aircraft to ditch adjacent to their intended victim, which was undamaged. The well-disposed Kapitän Lemp of the 770 ton Type VII C, *U-30,* who a few days earlier had sunk the liner *Athenia,* picked up the dejected airmen and made them prisoners. Remarkably, the *U-30* survived the war, only to be scuttled in Flensburg in 1945.

The Royal Air Force, too, experienced some traumas, not least of which was experienced on 5 September 1939 by the crew of a 233 Squadron Avro Anson from Leuchars, Fife. The aircraft succumbed to splinters from two 100 lb bombs dropped on an 'enemy' submarine off the Scottish West Coast. Nearly home, the Anson had to ditch in St Andrews Bay, leaving behind the very shaken but otherwise unharmed submariners of HMS *Snapper*, wondering no doubt who the enemy was in the two-day-old war.

The much maligned AS bombs did not entirely lack success, indeed two 100 lb bombs achieved the first Fleet Air Arm U-boat sinking of the war on 13 April 1940. This was accomplished by Petty Officer Airman F C Rice accompanied by Observer Lieutenant-Commander W Brown and Leading Telegraphist M Pacey flying in a Swordfish floatplane from HMS *Warspite*. They found the brand-new 1,100 ton Type 1XB, *U-64* in Herjangs Fjord near Narvik, and promptly dropped the two bombs from 200 ft. One detonated alongside, and the other near the conning tower. The U-boat sank, with 12 of the 48 crew lost.

Coastal Command too had some early partial and shared successes with AS bombs. For example, a 228 Squadron Sunderland flying boat from Pembroke Dock, captained by Flight Lieutenant Brooks, assisted two destroyers in 'persuading' Kapitänleutnant Heidel to scuttle *U-55* in the Western Channel on 30 January 1940. Then, just after dawn on 1 July 1940, Flight Lieutenant W N G Gibson in a Sunderland of 10 Squadron Royal Australian Air Force based at Mount Batten in Plymouth Sound, Devon, assisted HMS *Gladiolus* in the sinking of *U-26* with eight 250 pounders. HMS *Rochester* picked up 41 survivors off Bishop Rock. Some four months later, on 25 October, Flying Officer Maudsley in a 233 Squadron Hudson from Leuchars seriously damaged *U-46* with four 100 lb bombs whilst she was under way in Norwegian waters.

Any success achieved by the largely discredited pre-war range of AS bombs was far outweighed by the failures, causing considerable concern at all levels, and considerable pressure was soon exerted to design and produce more adequate weapons to tackle the ever-increasing U-boat menace at sea. These included air-dropped depth charges – a concept not previously considered, and a number of custom-built anti-submarine bombs. The development and deployment of these weapons is described in Chapter Eleven, which covers the battle with the U-boats more comprehensively.

Having now broadly outlined the story of the design, development and deployment of the high explosive bombs produced during the inter-war years, one comes to the story of the design and development of that other main category, the incendiary bomb, evolved during the same period.

During and after the First World War, the incendiary bomb's potential for destruction was never fully appreciated. The effects of combined high explosive and mass bombing with the Baby Incendiary Bomb (BIB) during the closing months of the war had, however, given some indication of things to come in the next major conflict.

The post-war development of incendiary bombs was given very low priority compared with the effort, little as it was, expended on high explosive bombs, at least until the mid-1930s. As already recounted, any form of bomb development was hindered by the constant lack of funds, among other factors. During the early 1920s when bomb requirements were being considered by the Ordnance Committee and requirements for such as the GP, AP, SAP, and AS high explosive types were formulated, it asked the Director of Operational Requirements if it was necessary to investigate incendiary fillings and bomb types. The reply was certainly not encouraging. It merely summarized the operational advantages and disadvantages of using many small incendiary bombs, compared to a smaller number of large ones, and asked the Committee to consider trials of both kinds of bomb but 'without great expense'. This virtually stopped any development work on new incendiary designs during the twenties and early thirties. The small amount of incendiary work which was done was merely to improve the ballistic properties and terminal velocity of the BIB, a bomb which, despite its unsuitability for modern warfare, remained in service until early 1939.

Following ballistic trials of the BIB in 1931, and the realization that some problems had still not been fully solved, the need for a heavier bomb was tabled. The requirement was put to the Ordnance Committee, who decided to proceed with the design of a bomb of approximately 20 lb which, on functioning, would eject a number of thermite-filled firepots. Its development followed the now familiar pattern of traumas pervading armament and weapon development during this period, with constant changes in design detail, including an increase in weight to 25 lb.

As European relationships deteriorated and the war clouds gathered once more, the Cabinet approved a succession of Royal Air Force rearmament programmes beneficial to the production of bombs and bombers to carry them; the period of inertia was ending. In this climate it cannot be said that the contemporary quality of bombs improved to any large extent, but at least a 25 lb Mark I incendiary bomb was put into production by August 1937, after six years' design and development. It had a fine streamlined body accommodating seven magnesium-alloy firepots holding in all 1 lb of thermite and 5.25 lb of magnesium. On impact, the firepots were progressively ejected to a distance of 10 to 15 yd through the rear end. The bomb nose also contained a charge of thermite, so in theory each bomb produced eight point-sources of fire. Ballistic trials on the production bomb were still taking place in 1938. Undoubtedly, it was tested from every aspect and its qualities and limitations had been accurately quantified, with one major exception. Surprisingly, it was not tested to evaluate its ability to start a fire in a respresentative target until April 1939, when dropping and functioning trials were conducted at the disused filling factory near Gretna Green, referred to earlier.

Here, to everyone's dismay, the bombs proved a total failure. On hitting the roof, concrete floors or hard standings, they broke up and failed to function. On hitting softer ground they tended to bury themselves, again preventing satisfactory functioning. The outcome was that the Ordnance Board recommended that the bomb should not be regarded as suitable for attacking a land target from any height. The Director of Operational Requirements wrote '... it is clear that no modification will make this bomb entirely satisfactory'. Unfortunately, by then some 660,000 bombs had been manufactured.

Clearly, from an economic and operational viewpoint it was undesirable that these should be abandoned without a determined effort to either modify the design or recover the material used. Three options were considered, the first was to modify and strengthen the bomb body to prevent break-up on impact, and to fit a three-way acting pistol, thus improving the chances of functioning, whatever the impact attitude. These modifications would increase the weight of the bomb to just over 40 lb, but it had the advantage that the firepots could be extracted from the discarded 25 lb bombs and used.

The second option was to fit the three-way acting pistol and modify the tail design. The third was to fit the original 25 lb bomb with a small drogue parachute and use it only against targets which required no penetration – standing crops and forests for example.

Like all compromises, none of these options was really satisfactory, although all were implemented to a lesser or greater degree and all three versions were deployed in significant numbers, with diverse and unremarkable results. After several attempts, a modified bomb, the Bomb 40 lb Incendiary (option one) was successfully demonstrated in early 1940. An order for 500,000 was placed, together with one for special machinery to recover the firepots from the original 25 lb bombs. Production was expected to start on the first 100,000 by December 1940. In October of that year it was decided that the project should be discontinued, but the order for the first 100,000 was to stand because it was then too late to cancel it. However, by June 1941 wiser council prevailed and production was finally stopped. A succinct opinion expressed in an Air Ministry file of the period stated, 'It seems to be a very bad business to carry all the way to Germany 35 lb of good steel in order to deliver 5 lb of magnesium.'

A second version of the 25 pounder, the Mark II (option two) fared no better than its predecessor. Likewise failing to surmount rigorous trials and operational use, it was abandoned and finally withdrawn from service in early 1942 after Bomber Command had dropped some 20,000 – break up on impact was the cardinal fault which sealed its fate.

At about the same time, a small number of the original Mark Is, fitted with parachutes (option three) to soften impact shocks, were abandoned as not worth the effort put into delivering them to distant targets.

In the wake of this chain of dismal failures and mini-disasters, and at a time when every bomb counted, approximately 400,000 25 lb incendiaries had to be scrapped. In retrospect, much time, money and effort could have been saved if the 25 lb incendiary had been subjected to realistic trials during the early days of its life, before the pressures of war forced compromises on an already discredited design.

Perhaps now it would be appropriate to turn to a success story which started during the inter-war years with the design and development of the 4 lb incendiary bomb. During the course of the Second World War, Bomber Command dropped nearly 80 million of these small hexagonal stick-shaped bombs.

The 4 lb incendiary was first conceived in 1934, probably sparked off by a demonstration of a number of incendiary devices in December 1933, one of which, ironically, was a German electron-cased bomb. Electron is an alloy of magnesium and zinc, with other trace elements. The German bomb burned fiercely, throwing out showers of burning particles which could not be readily extinguished, or even approached safely — the perfect incendiary device.

Ballistic trials were completed by July 1936 on a number of variously shaped electron-cased bombs, including pointed-nose streamlined bombs with drum tails, flat-nosed cylindrical, and even hexagonal cross-sectioned blunt-nosed stick-like bombs.

It was concluded that the latter were the most acceptable. Their hexagonal shape made for ease of packing in the containers being designed for the carriage of incendiaries and very small high explosive bombs, they separated well after release in batches from the container, and did not jostle each other unduly as they fell. They were simple in design, consequently they generally functioned satisfactorily on impacting hard or soft targets. In outline the bomb was a hexagonal cylinder of electron, filled with thermite which was easily ignited by a simple internal striker. The tail was a tin plate continuation of the main body. The arming device consisted of a spring loaded plunger, retained in each bomb by its neighbour packed in the container. On release from the container, the bomb plunger sprung out, freeing the striker thus arming the bomb.

Much of the development was carried out by Imperial Chemical Industries in conjunction with the Royal Aircraft Establishment. By September 1936 live bombs had been successfully dropped from various altitudes, all functioning well, in that they ignited and did not break up on impact. In common with all other bombs developed during this period, none were dropped on representative targets. Following limited but successful trials, an order for four and a half million bombs was placed in October, and the Bomb Incendiary Aircraft

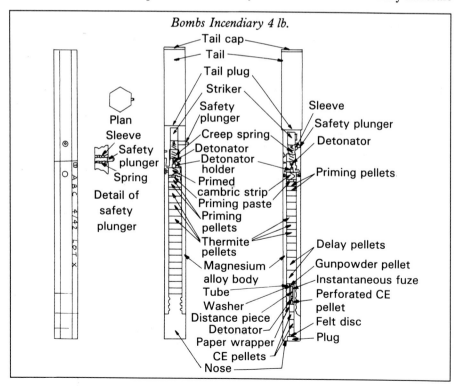

Bombs Incendiary 4 lb.

4 lb Mark I was well and truly launched. The first instalments left the production line in March 1937, and by June 4,000 had been produced. Three months
later the bomb was formally introduced into service.

At this stage, no tests had been conducted against buildings, so the Ordnance
Committee, perhaps late in the day, recommended a series of trials using
representative targets. These facilities were not readily available, consequently
the final trials consisted of firing inert bombs at targets designed to represent
typical roofs. From the results it was concluded that the 4 lb bomb would
penetrate an 'average' roof, reaching the top floor and perhaps even the one
below, before igniting. This was accepted by the Air Staff, and no further trials
were carried out. Subsequently German reports indicated that the 4 lb incendiary bomb frequently penetrated several floors before igniting.

It was agreed in March 1938 that some bombs (15 per cent of output) should
contain a small explosive charge to deter fire-fighters from approaching them
whilst they were still burning. These bombs, known as the Mark I E, functioned most satisfactorily when dropped on the target near Gretna Green during
April 1939, penetrating, burning and detonating just as expected.

When the Second World War broke out on 3 September 1939, some five
million 4 lb incendiary bombs were available, supplemented by a weekly output from the factories of 60,000. Thus, the Royal Air Force was in an excellent
position in respect of this bomb, if not so well supplied with other types of
bomb developed during the same period. Operationally, if aimed well, and this
was not always the case, the two initial designs of the 4 lb incendiary bomb performed admirably, but for a number of reasons slight modifications were progressively incorporated. For example, the Mark II bomb introduced in early
1940 differed from the Mark I only in having a slightly shorter tail to enable its
carriage in the then-current Small Bomb Container. In an effort to economize
on the expenditure of magnesium, which was at a premium in 1941, the internal bomb bore was increased by an eighth of an inch, resulting in the saving of
2.5 oz of magnesium per bomb, now nominated the Mark III. Futher paring off
of the internal magnesium raised the status to Mark IV, without seriously
affecting the fire-raising qualities. Later still the E range, containing a small explosive charge, was supplemented by the development of the X range. This
incorporated a much more powerful explosive charge, located adjacent to the
bomb's steel nose. The fragmentation emanating from this source after selected
periods of burning time, provided a considerable deterrent to the enemy fire-
fighters.

First World War experience clearly indicated that smaller bombs
(250–550 lb) were notably ineffective against specially hardened targets such as
the German naval installations on the Belgian coast, and inflicted little damage
on Germany's industrial complexes. Nevertheless, in the earlier post-war years
the Air Staff concentrated its requirements on a 250–500 lb range of 'modern'
general bombardment bombs, in the belief that a goodly number of smaller
bombs was better than fewer large ones. Of course, the decision was tempered
by the fact that the existing or planned bombers would mostly be incapable of
carrying larger bombs.

The momentum established in bomb design and development during 1917–18 quite naturally fizzled out, and did not return until the late thirties. In the mean time, with low priorities, few incentives, a certain lack of direction among those who might have influenced events, not to mention a serious lack of funding, design and development just drifted in the general apathy towards all warlike projects. Weapon development progressed tardily, and in the absence of detailed scientific studies and pertinent trials, bomb designs were often outdated or inadequate before coming to fruition years later. Consequently, substandard bombs just had to be accepted, either to justify money already spent, or because the increasing threat of a new war precluded turning back the development clock. Of course, much of this can be said with the luxury of hindsight, as well as the information culled from contemporary reports. It would be true to say, however, that the shortcomings of many of the pre-war range of bombs soon became apparent in the heat of battle, thus justifying a lack of confidence expressed earlier at various levels.

Nevertheless, once the heat was really on in the late thirties, the Air Staff did at last forcefully specify and monitor realistic revised operational requirements for bigger and better bombs, and bombers to carry them. Although these did not make an appearance until the Second World War was well underway, there is little doubt that the initial designs, development, trials and production were handled enthusiastically, with considerable alacrity and no mean success. Thus the 'barren years' were transformed, with some hiccups, to those of sufficiency.

CHAPTER THREE

THE ADVENT AND USE OF THE BATTLE WINNERS

The three types of major battle-winning bombs of the Second World War, excluding the specialist types developed for specific purposes, were the incendiary and the medium and high-capacity high explosive bombs. Each type is described later in the chapter, and examples are given of their operational deployment. It should be borne in mind, however, that although each more than fulfilled its potential, success was not initially achieved, for reasons other than the effectiveness or not of individual bombs. Success depended upon bombs being released accurately over the intended target, but as will be seen later in Chapter Four, this criterion was not always met during the early war years.

In 1939, high explosive bombs were considered the primary weapon, and incendiaries as just a useful adjunct for harassment. In 1940, bomb loads included no more than six per cent by weight of incendiaries, mostly four and 25 lb types. As the weight of Bomber Command attacks increased, so did the proportion of incendiaries, reaching 40 per cent by mid 1942. Later, during the battles of the Ruhr and Berlin, up to two-thirds of the loads were composed of incendiaries, mostly of the smaller types, the four pounder, the 30 lb Phosphorus, and the 30 lb 'J', the latter producing a jet something like a flame-thrower.

However, the two most notorious attacks, those on Hamburg in July 1943 and Dresden in February 1945, in which freak fire-storms raged, causing enormous casualties, were triggered with a percentage of incendiaries somewhat below 50 per cent. For example, on the night of 13–14 February 1945, Dresden received 1,478 tons of high explosive bombs and 1,182 of incendiaries, including 650,000 four pounders.

The backgrounds of these particular raids are dealt with in some detail later, because they both have points of historical significance unrelated to the vast devastation inflicted. Whatever the rights and wrongs of this form of warfare, there is no doubt that cities like Hamburg, Kassel, Darmstadt and Dresden have every reason never to forget the tragic conflagrations stemming from the effectiveness of incendiaries used in conjunction with high blast bombs.

Kassel, like Dresden and Hamburg, suffered from ferocious typhoon-like fire-storms which could not be controlled, Its worst attack, or perhaps from the Bomber Command point of view, the most successful, occurred on the night of 22–23 October 1943, when over 500 bombers dropped 1,800 tons of bombs, including 190,000 incendiaries. The devastation was widespread, over 63 per cent of the living accommodation being made unusable, and German records indicate that over 160 industrial and military buildings were destroyed, together with 63 schools and churches. Photographic reconnaissance after the attack showed that the railway system and associated installations had been severely damaged, as were all three Henschel aircraft factories. These three were manufacturing V-1 flying bombs, so the raid undoubtedly had a major detrimental effect on the starting date and scale of the V-1 campaign yet to be mounted against Britain. An estimated 8,000 people were killed in Kassel that night, and many more would have died but for the fact that many residents were still evacuated following the breaching of the Eder Dam in May, which had partially flooded the town. Bomber Command did not escape unscathed; a total of 43 aircraft, 25 Halifaxes and 18 Lancasters, were reported missing.

During interrogation, Generalmajor W Linder, responsible for German civil defence counter measures, confirmed that fire-storm conflagrations had caused many deaths by scorching, carbon monoxide poisoning, or by suffocation in air-raid shelters. In some cities, the inrush of air was so fierce that victims' clothes were torn off, firemen were hurled from their ladders, and many people were sucked into the fires. Not only was suction felt in the immediate vicinity, but great tongues of flame were sucked in from outlying areas to produce a gigantic blowlamp effect directed towards the major fire area. He went on to say that fire breaks as wide as 50 m (164 ft) failed to stop the rapidly spreading conflagration, which was further ventilated by high explosive detonations.

In retrospect, the Hamburg, Kassel and Dresden fire-storms are thought of with awe and a sense of pure horror, and no wonder; 40,000 died in Hamburg and over 50,000 in Dresden. However, the freak fire-storms were not planned as such. In any case, 'all-out-war' decisions should be studied in the context in which they were taken. This point is considered in more detail in Chapter Four.

So far, consideration has been given only to four and 25 lb incendiary bombs, both conceived and developed prior to 1939. During the war, however, ten other incendiary bombs or devices were developed, to meet diverse purposes. With some exceptions, the incendiary range of bombs performed well; naturally, some were much more efficient than others. For instance, there was a most significant efficiency gap if one compares the performance of the four pounder with that of the erratic and inefficient 25 pounder. The smallest incendiary devices developed and deployed operationally were those codenamed 'Razzle' and 'Decker'. They were also probably the least successful.

Both depended upon phosphorus pellets drying out and igniting spontaneously. 'Razzle', a sandwich of celluloid strips and pellets 3 in by 1 in, was

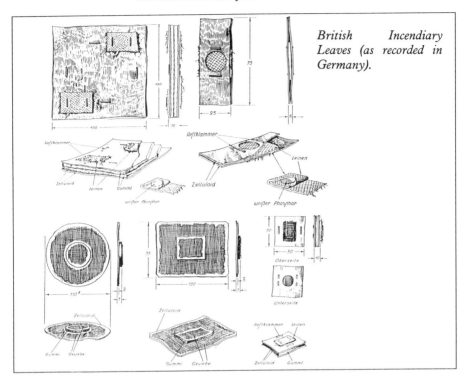

British Incendiary Leaves (as recorded in Germany).

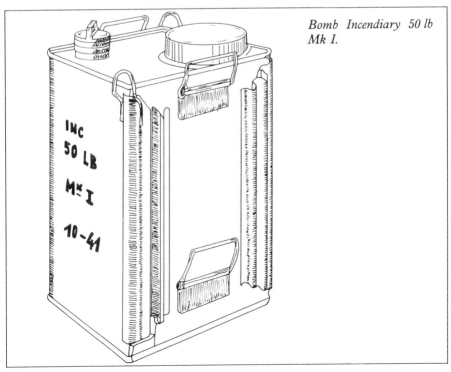

Bomb Incendiary 50 lb Mk I.

rushed into production during the summer of 1940 in time to attack the German harvest. Burning time was increased in 'Decker' by introducing latex rubber into the sandwich and increasing the surface area to 4 in by 4 in. Bomber Command aircraft dropped a considerable number during the summer and autumn, but despite reasonably dry conditions the Germans found them to be no more than a minor nuisance – except for those who foolishly put them in their trouser pockets as souvenirs, and suffered some private embarrassment. Occasionally these incendiary leaves also caused small fires in and around the aircraft during loading, if inadvertently exposed.

They were carried to the target in tins of alcohol and water, each containing about 500 leaves, and poured down the aircraft flare chutes. German reports indicated that 'Razzle' burnt out very quickly, if it got going at all. They were more concerned by 'Decker', which burnt fiercely for about 15 minutes once the phosphorus dried out. However, the drying out took time, and once the warning was given, the entire rural population, including children, was recruited to make thorough searches to ensure that the offending leaves were collected before they had time to ignite. Apart from isolated field and barn fires, little damage was done, and certainly no forest fires were started, despite attacks made by a number of squadrons, including the Wellingtons of 37 and 75 (RNZAF), Feltwell. These two showered the Black Forest, the Thüringen and Grünwald Forests, and the wooded slopes of the Harz Mountains, but with little effect. Indeed, German reports boasted that their war effort benefited from the salvaged latex rubber. Among other raids, 49 Squadron Hampdens from Scampton dropped a considerable number in the Lüneburg-Soltau-Celle area during September 1940.

However, with higher priorities, and in the absence of any significant success even under the most favourable conditions, Bomber Command turned elsewhere to make better use of less gimmicky weapons. Only slightly less so were the 45 and 50 lb incendiary bombs. The 45 pounder was essentially a five-gallon petrol can holding 4.5 gallons of petrol and 2 pints of a special ignition fuel. Its purpose was the ignition of oil patches on water, subsequent to high explosive attacks on oil tankers or oil installations along a waterfront. On release, a fabric streamer gave some sort of stability before impact, when the can shattered and the ignition fuel reacted with the water and set alight the petrol and hopefully whatever spillage was already on the surface. Experience indicated that it served no useful purpose, and further comment is unnecessary.

The 50 lb incendiary was very similar to the 45 lb version, except that it was filled with a rubber-phosphorus solution which ignited spontaneously when the can shattered. Hopefully, it was going to cause conflagrations in selected German forests and scrubland hiding ammunition dumps etc, but it did not live up to expectations, despite reasonably successful trials conducted in a wood near Burford, Surrey, during July 1941. By the time 10,000 were produced in late summer, it became clear that whilst they might do the job under ideal tinder-dry conditions, green or wet forests were a totally different proposition. Shortly afterwards, this type of operation was abandoned and Bomber Command turned its attention to more worthwhile targets. However, rather than

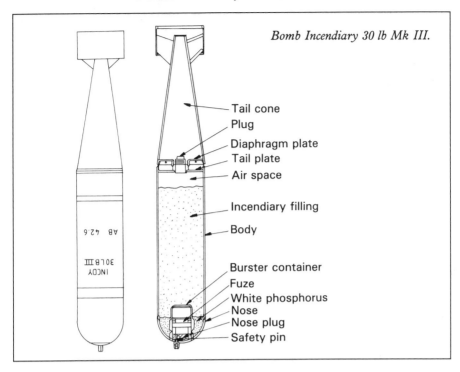

Bomb Incendiary 30 lb Mk III.

Tail cone
Plug
Diaphragm plate
Tail plate
Air space

Incendiary filling

Body

Burster container
Fuze
White phosphorus
Nose
Nose plug
Safety pin

AB 42.6

30LB III
INCDY

waste the left-over 50 lb bombs, they were dropped on built-up areas, where they were more effective than against growing trees. Considerable numbers were dropped on Berlin during the night 7-8 September 1941, when a total of 197 aircraft attacked the city carrying both 50 lb incendiaries and a full range of GP bombs. The Lichtenburg and Pankow districts of the city were destroyed, but at a cost of 15 bombers lost.

Second only to the prolific four pounder, the 30 lb Phosphorus incendiary bomb was produced and deployed in vast numbers. It was conceived in 1940, as a liquid-filled incendiary, to offset the short-comings of the 25 pounder and a possible future shortage of magnesium which might have serious effects on production of the four pounder. Fortuitously, some 250,000 30 lb light-cased bomb bodies, intended to accommodate a chemical (gas) filling but not now operationally required, could be adapted, providing a suitable incendiary mixture was found. Experience indicated that rapidly-burning petrol or benzol alone were practically useless. What was needed was a slow-burning mixture, because most targets took some time to set ablaze; a moderately viscous fluid served best, in that loss by evaporation was kept to a minimum.

The filling selected was one-and-a-half pounds of liquid phosphorus and six pounds of rubber-benzol mixture. An initial order for 400,000 such bombs was placed in June 1941, and a month later they were being produced at a rate of between 4,000 and 5,000 per week. Designated the 30 lb Phosphorus Incendiary Mark I, the bomb used the original light-cased bomb fuze, No 38. On impact, the fuze ignited a burster, blowing off the tail and base plate, and ejecting the fiercely-burning contents over an area of 60 × 40 yd. Production had barely started when the filling was changed to white phosphorus and 6.5 lb of a rubber-petrol mixture; during the filling process the former was easier to handle, and benzol was dispensed with because its toxicity was affecting the workers.

By the end of the year the Mark I (revised fill) was in full production and in use by Bomber Command. At the same time, a Mark II version was beginning to come off the production lies, with a type-designed drawn steel body (the original empty light-cased bombs having been expended) and fitted with a new fuze, No 846. The Mark III appeared later, differing only from the Mark II in that it had a welded body. Ultimately, a thinner-cased Mark IV was produced, filled with cellulose acetate manufactured initially from scrap perspex. The changes were introduced to save steel and to compensate for an acute shortage of rubber, arising from the Japanese occupation of the Far East rubber plantation areas.

The 30 lb incendiary was undoubtedly a very effective weapon, especially when dropped in conjunction with high explosive bombs. The general opinion amongst Germans interrogated at the end of the war was that there was very little to choose between the fire-raising qualities of the four and 30 lb incendiary bombs. If this were true it meant that, weight-for-weight, the four pounder had a seven-to-one advantage. In fact earlier in 1944, the Air Ministry Incendiary Panel expounded the view that weight-for-weight the 30 pounder was four times less efficient than the four pounder, and had the added disadvantage of producing clouds of dense black smoke, which tended to obscure the target, thus necessitating its use at the tail end of a raid. Despite this view, the 30 lb Phosphorus incendiary filled an important slot in the incendiary inventory, and gave added insurance against the possibility of magnesium shortages. Fortunately, these never became really acute, so general use of the 30 pounder was abandoned towards the end of 1944. By then, Bomber Command had dropped over three million.

A goodly proportion of this total was successfully directed at the Baltic ports of Lübeck and Rostock in March and April 1942. Being relatively easy to find, Lübeck received its one and only major attack on the night of 28-29 March (Palm Sunday). After some very mixed and disappointing results, Bomber Command considered the raid to be one of its first major successes. Over 200 aircraft took part and dropped more than 400 tons of bombs, 60 per cent being incendiaries, mainly the 30 lb type. The main aiming mark was the Altstadt (old town) consisting of very old half-timbered houses which caught fire easily. This attack was a simple case of fire raising on the grand scale, and one of the first area-bombing attacks. Industrial premises destroyed included a factory manufacturing oxygen equipment for U-boats, but by far the greatest damage was caused to residential property. Aerial photographs taken after the attack indicated that some 30 per cent of Lübeck's built-up area was destroyed, mainly by fire. As it turned out, this was the first and almost the last attack made by Bomber Command against that ancient city. The President of the International Red Cross later negotiated a secret agreement with Britain that the port would

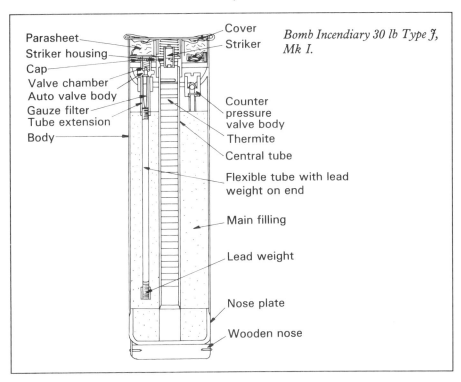

Parasheet
Striker housing
Cap
Valve chamber
Auto valve body
Gauze filter
Tube extension
Body

Cover
Striker

Counter pressure valve body
Thermite
Central tube

Flexible tube with lead weight on end

Main filling

Lead weight

Nose plate

Wooden nose

Bomb Incendiary 30 lb Type J, Mk I.

not be a major target again, because it was being used for the shipment of Red Cross supplies to British prisoners of war, among others. In fact two other minor attacks took place some months later. Eight bombers attacked on 16 July, and 25 Stirlings from 3 Group delivered a sporadic raid on the night of 1–2 October. No serious damage ensued and it is not certain if the Red Cross agreement had been mutually confirmed by that stage. Some relatively insignificant Mosquito diversionary attacks were made in July 1942, July 1943 and another in April 1945, to draw the defenders' attention away from the main bomber force's primary objectives.

Rostock's turn came on four successive nights, the 23-24, 24-25, 25-26 and 26-27 April, and like Lübeck these were combined high explosive and incendiary attacks, with the centre of the old part of the town as the main aiming mark. Unlike Lübeck, however, on each night a proportion of the bomber aircraft was specifically tasked to attack a particular industrial target, namely the Heinkel aircraft factory situated on the southern edge of the town. In all, a total of 520 aircraft took part, with the loss of eight. Reconnaissance photographic evidence indicated that the aircraft factory and 60 per cent of the main town area was seriously damaged. Over 200 people were killed, and the casualty rate would have been higher had the vast majority of the population not fled from the town after the first attack.

Another 30 pounder mentioned earlier was the 30 lb 'J' (Jet) Incendiary Bomb. It was first conceived in 1942, but it suffered a long and difficult gestation period. Among other problems encountered, some senior Air Staff sang its praises, whilst others condemned the project as a waste of time and money. Who was correct will become apparent as the story unfolds. Once it got going, if it did, it produced a spectacular 60 sec two-ft-wide jet of flame to a distance of 15 ft. The mechanism to accomplish this was somewhat complex, consequently a considerable percentage failed to function. It was another case of the weapon looking fine in the laboratory, but being suspect on the battlefield. Like the ordinary 30 lb bomb, it was developed to make an incendiary largely independent of materials in short supply, namely magnesium and rubber, by burning liquid hydrocarbons. The designers settled on a solution of methane in 1.3 gallon of petrol under a pressure of between 90 to 110 psi in a light cylindrical case. The diagram illustrates what the bomb looked like and how the jet of flame was initiated.

Finally, by 1944, the bomb became available for a full-scale operational trial, with the proviso that it should be used against a town not previously attacked by incendiary bombs. For one reason or another, a suitable 'virgin' target could not be found, so Brunswick was selected as the next best option. Subsequently, some 250 bombers delivered an attack on the night of 22-23 April, dropping 32,256 J bombs (432 tons). Many failed to function, and others fell far wide of the mark, due in part either to a failure in target-marking, or to the presence of German spoof markers. In any event, the raid was far from successful, and as an operational try-out the results were, to say the least, inconclusive. With less confidence, J bombs were also dropped on Kiel on the night of 23-24 July, Stuttgart on the nights of 24-25, 25-26 and 28-29 July, Stettin on 16-17 August, and Königsberg on 29-30 August. All four towns were partially damaged, but no clear worth of the J bomb was determined. More were dropped in mixed loads against Kaiserslautern during the night of 27-28 September 1944, and Nuremberg on 19-20 October. The attack on Nuremberg was not a great success, but that on Kaiserslautern caused widespread damage, some 36 per cent of the built-up area being destroyed, mainly by fire.

Under interrogation, a German prisoner-of-war said he had been engaged in salvage work in Kaiserslautern after the raid, and that many dud 30 lb J bombs were recovered and the fuel emptied into vehicle fuel tanks. At this time Bomber Command were lambasting many oil and other fuel complexes, so perhaps ironically, it could be said that it was giving with one hand and taking away with the other. Ultimately it was decided that the J bomb was inferior to the tried and true four lb incendiary. Consequently Bomber Command retained them in the stockpile, but did not deploy them again, having expended a total of 413,165 on the targets mentioned. Of course, by this time in 1944 there was little left to burn, in any case. Unlike the ordinary 30 pounders, which were carried and released from Small bomb containers, the J bomb was supplied in and dropped in Aimable Clusters (14 bombs each), which disintegrated at a lower level.

So much for the smaller incendiaries, what of the larger sizes? There were four in all, the 250, 400, 500 and 2,700 pounders. The 250 lb bomb, like the initial 30 pounder, utilized a redundant light case originally designed for

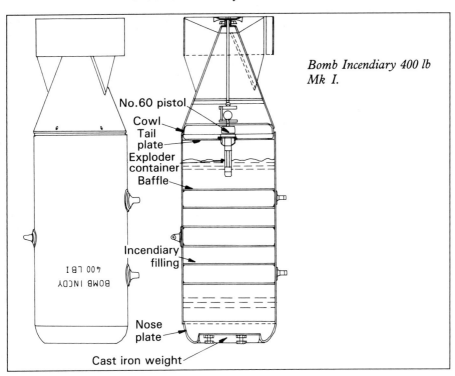

Bomb Incendiary 400 lb Mk I.

No.60 pistol
Cowl
Tail plate
Exploder container
Baffle
Incendiary filling
Nose plate
Cast iron weight

BOMB INCDY
400 LB I

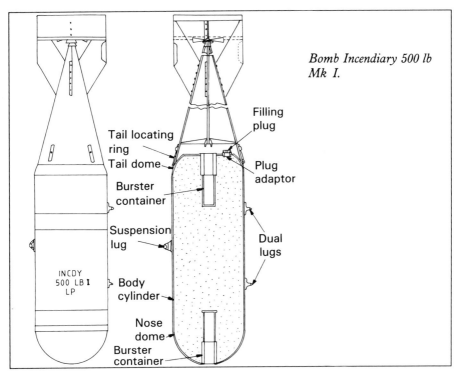

Bomb Incendiary 500 lb Mk I.

Filling plug
Tail locating ring
Tail dome
Plug adaptor
Burster container
Suspension lug
Dual lugs
Body cylinder
Nose dome
Burster container

INCDY
500 LB I
LP

chemical warfare. During its useful life it underwent several conversions in the incendiary role, and finally ended its days as a target-marker, filled with coloured pyrotechnic substances.

It started its operational life in 1940 filled with a mixture of paraffin and rags, the hopes being that it would set alight German standing crops and forests suspected of screening hidden dumps of ammunition and fuel. On impact, a burster charge ejected the incendiary contents through the tail end. Like most of the incendiaries intended for forest fire-raising, it failed and was soon abandoned. It was carried by a number of the contemporary bombers, for instance the 214 Squadron Wellingtons from Stradishall began their wartime operations when two dropped their 250 pounders on the Black Forest during the night of 14/15 June 1940.

The bomb made another comeback in 1941, filled with a rubber-benzol mixture for use against industrial targets, warehouses and dock gates, and had some limited success during the Spring of 1942 and later in Hamburg in 1943, but it was never more than a make-weight bomb.

The superiority of larger numbers of smaller bombs, the four and 30 pounders in particular, was self-evident. Some continued to be used, but no more were produced after mid 1942. Bomber Command dropped 7,000 in all, and the balance of some 9,000 was converted to target markers.

The 400 lb incendiary bomb was specially developed in 1944 for attacking small craft, such as Sampans in Japanese-controlled Far Eastern harbours. It was a cylindrical, drum-shaped bomb in two sections, the main front part contained petrol and the smaller rear portion a cellulose-acetate mixture ignited by a detonator/burster charge in the tail. The Napalm-like effects were the most vicious produced up to that time. About 400 were sent to South East Asia Command in December 1944 for advanced operational trials but little, if any, use was made of them by the time the war in that theatre had ended in August 1945.

The 500 pounder was a scaled-up version of the 250 lb bomb already described, but containing 16 gallons of liquid phosphorus and designed primarily for special low-level missions. For instance, 617 Squadron's Mosquitoes used a few to mark, and set alight, a marshalling yard at La Chapelle just North of Paris during the night of 20–21 April 1944. The bomb casing was shattered by a standard tail-pistol/detonator/exploder combination, liberating the phosphorus which spontaneously produced significant incendiary effects and a dense smoke screen for up to two hours. Otherwise, its use was mainly limited to battlefield targets in daylight, and then by the light tactical bombers of the Second Tactical Air Force on the European mainland after D-Day.

Perhaps the least well-known bomb in the incendiary range, and the largest, was the 2,700 pounder, a 4,000 lb HC bomb case filled with incendiary substance. The same case was also used in 1942 to accommodate a pyrotechnic composition for the target marker 'Pink Pansy', described in more detail in Chapter Four. When it appeared in the incendiary role in 1944 it was little-used, being specifically earmarked for low-level attacks on special targets. It was never fully developed, and by July of that year no further need was seen for it. Nevertheless, the Mosquitoes of 139 Squadron, Upwood, dropped at least

Above *A 2,000 lb HC Mk III about to be loaded into a Lancaster in November 1943.*

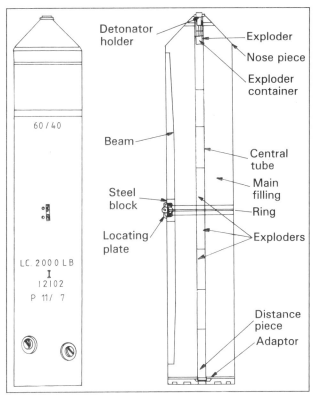

Detonator holder

Exploder

Nose piece

Exploder container

Beam

Central tube

Main filling

Steel block

Ring

Locating plate

Exploders

Distance piece

Adaptor

60/40

LC. 2000 LB
I
12102
P 11/ 7

Right *Bomb HC 2,000 lb Mk I.*

four on Berlin on the night of 12–13 April 1945. At that stage of the war, almost any weapon to hand was being dropped on the devastated cities of Germany.

Turning from incendiaries to the main bombardment weapons of the Second World War, the high and medium capacity high explosive bombs, it should be noted that whilst each category performed admirably, some of the individual types stood out as much more effective and reliable than others – these were the real battle winners.

The HC bombs were a modernized version of the 1,650 lb SN high explosive blast bombs, deployed reasonably effectively during 1918. They were designed like their successors, to flatten German industrial complexes. Consideration had been given to developing bombs up to 4,000 lb in the late 1930s, along with suitable aircraft to carry them, but neither was available until the war was well underway.

The devastation caused by, and the general effectiveness of the German parachute G mines, first dropped on land inadvertently, and then deliberately on London, Coventry and Birmingham during the 'Blitz', did much to concentrate the minds of those responsible for bomb design and development. It provided the spur which resulted in the placement in Autumn 1940 of a firm requirement for a so-called 'Blockbuster', the 4,000 lb HC bomb, and its first appearance in spring 1941. From then on, supplemented with four and 30 lb incendiaries, mostly the former, it became, with some exceptions, the standard load for the Bomber Command heavy bombers.

The lack of a powerful high explosive for use in the bombs produced during 1940 and 1941 posed a problem. Amatol, developed during the First World War, was the only substance readily available. However, it was being progressively supplanted by Cyclonite (RDX/TNT), Torpex, Amatex and Minol. The real virtue of the HC range was the high CWR, of over 70 per cent; naturally, the enormous quantities of explosive required placed a severe strain on production facilities and on other military weapons competing for a share of the available stocks. These problems were largely overcome, and without much doubt, the HC bombs were those which in combination with incendiaries laid waste to Germany's main industrial areas in North-Rhine Westphalia and elsewhere during the latter half of the war. The power and effectiveness of the HC bomb increased significantly in 1943 when aluminium powder was added to the main filling, forming the new high explosive, Minol. Not only did this increase the blast effects, it also boosted the incendiary side effects.

Initially the requirement was for a 4,000 lb bomb only, but within weeks this was followed by a call for a 2,000 lb and later still for 8,000 and 12,000 lb versions. The story of the development and deployment of these bombs will be described in ascending weight order, but the most interesting aspect of the development related to the 8,000 and 12,000 lb bombs, which involved what was at that time a unique principle in bomb design – modular construction, each being made up of 4,000 lb sections.

The design criteria for the HC range was that the bombs should be cylindrical in shape and have the highest-possible explosive content. The implications were that the casing must be of light construction, but sufficiently robust

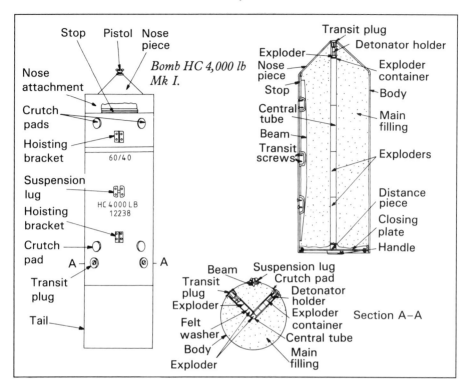

Bomb HC 4,000 lb Mk I.

Labels (left diagram): Stop, Pistol, Nose piece, Nose attachment, Crutch pads, Hoisting bracket, Suspension lug, Hoisting bracket, Crutch pad, A, Transit plug, Tail, 60/40, HC 4000 LB 12238, A

Labels (right diagram): Transit plug, Detonator holder, Exploder, Nose piece, Exploder container, Stop, Body, Central tube, Main filling, Beam, Transit screws, Exploders, Distance piece, Closing plate, Handle

Section A–A labels: Beam, Suspension lug, Transit plug, Crutch pad, Exploder, Detonator holder, Felt washer, Exploder container, Body, Central tube, Exploder, Main filling

not to break up on impact. Therefore initially both the 2,000 lb and the 4,000 lb bombs were designed with drogue parachutes, to lessen impact shocks. To permit release from low altitude it was also deemed necessary to incorporate delay fuzing in addition to the parachute, to allow the aircraft adequate escape time before detonation. However, trials indicated that sheet metal drum tails, conforming with the general bomb shape, provided more efficient ballistics for general use at high level. Parachutes and long delay fuzing would only be required on bombs earmarked for special operations. By the time the 8,000 and 12,000 lb bombs became available, in September 1942 and February 1944 respectively, most of the ballistic and fuzing problems were resolved and all HC bombs, less the 12,000 pounder were fitted with cylindrical drum tails conforming to the shape of the bomb. The monster 12,000 lb was found to be unstable with anything other than a conventional ballistic cone and fin tail supported by a drum strut.

Production of the 2,000 lb bomb started in the latter half of 1941 and continued until late 1943. Unlike its successors, which were constructed with domed noses, the Mark I had a conical-shaped nose, and the earliest models were designed with parachutes and alternative options for direct impact or delay action fuzing. Most of the 97 dropped during the year, none from low level, were of this early type. For preparation and ballistic reasons the parachute system proved unsatisfactory, so, whilst still remaining the Mark I, it was fitted with a cylindrical tail. In conjunction with incendiaries it played a major role in the devastation of Lübeck and Rostock in the Spring of 1942, as already re-counted. By that time, plans for dropping large blast bombs from low level were largely abandoned, although some hazardous low-level attacks were undertaken with the mighty 12,000 pounder in 1943.

The domed nose, 2,000 lb Marks II and III were in service by 1943. Neither had side fuze-pockets for delay fuzing, and each now had three bomb pistol pockets in the nose. These were to provide insurance against possible pistol defects. Perhaps with over confidence, two were permanently plugged in the Mark II, one being deemed adequate. Bomber Command dissented, so the Mark III reverted to the three-pistol system. In all 28,633 bombs of this size were expended, the Marks I and II forming a very small percentage of the overall total.

The 4,000 lb HC bomb, known within the Royal Air Force as the 'Cookie' was the first of the large blast bombs to be designed, just beating the 2,000 pounder by a matter of weeks. It was also the first of the really large bombs to be dropped, although the 4,000 lb GP was not far behind. The Mark I version, like the 2,000 lb Mark I, was constructed with a conical-shaped nose with a single nose pistol pocket and two side pockets for delayed-action fuzing. It was formally introduced into service in January 1942, despite the fact that 402 had already been dropped on German targets during the previous nine months. Reports on what appeared to be extended operational trials officially recorded the damage done as 'satisfactory ... they created a tremendous impression on the population.' This must be considered one of the understatements of the war, if one happened to live in Emden, Berlin, Kiel, Wilhelmshaven, Cologne, Hamburg, Essen or Norderney, which received these 'trial' offerings.

The 'Cookie' made its operational debut on the night of 31 March–1 April 1941, when Squadron Leader K Wass, of 149 Squadron, Mildenhall, and Pilot Officer Franks, of 9 Squadron, Honington dropped one each on Emden from their Wellingtons. These were the first of 68,000 expended operationally throughout the war years. Progressively, more and more 'Cookies' were deployed on individual operations, until up to 200 became the norm. An example was the attack upon Darmstadt on the night of 11–12 September 1944, when over 200 4,000 lb HC and 286,000 four lb incendiary bombs were released, devastating the city by blast and fire-storm. A current city guide indicates that 12,300 people were killed and 70,000 made homeless on that fateful night. At the time the Germans saw this as an extreme example of British 'terror bombing'. To many, this is certainly as sensitive a subject as the bombing of Dresden, perhaps more so when one considers there were no major industries in Darmstadt. Like Dresden, its misfortune lay in being a major rail communications centre, at a stage of the war when paralysis of communications was given high priority, with the intention of speedily ending the war.

By this time, the 4,000 lb HC Mark I was supplemented by dome-nosed types up to the Mark IV. Like the 2,000 lb HC, the Mark II had a redesigned nose fitted with three pistol-pockets, but unlike the 2,000 lb bomb it retained its side fuze-pockets for delayed-action fuzing. It was not until the Mark III appeared with minor structural changes that the side pockets were omitted as

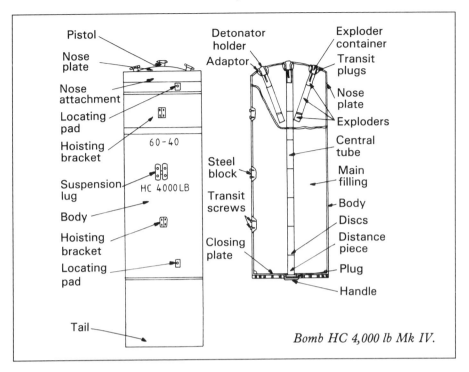

Pistol
Nose plate
Nose attachment
Locating pad
Hoisting bracket
Suspension lug
Body
Hoisting bracket
Locating pad

Tail

60-40

HC 4000LB

Detonator holder
Adaptor

Steel block
Transit screws

Closing plate

Exploder container
Transit plugs
Nose plate
Exploders
Central tube
Main filling
Body
Discs
Distance piece
Plug
Handle

Bomb HC 4,000 lb Mk IV.

redundant. For the record, the Mark IV, produced in October 1942, incorporated some minor internal structural changes, and was very similar to the Marks V and VI manufactured in America, except that the latter were fitted with two suspension lugs for carriage on American aircraft, and additionally the Mark VI was filled with a different high explosive.

As far as the British were concerned, these bombs were carried singly by Wellington, Halifax and Lancaster aircraft. However, by 1944 the nimble Mosquito began to play a significant role when at precisely 8.45 pm on 23 February, Squadron Leader S D Watts of 692 Squadron, Graveley, struck Düsseldorf with the first Mosquito-delivered 'Cookie'. Within minutes, Flight Lieutenant T V S Moore added a second, and the Mosquito onslaught had begun. The Mosquitoes really went to town, or perhaps more accurately went to Berlin, when between 1 January and 21 April 1945 they dropped about 1,500 'Cookies' on the city, attacking it on 36 consecutive nights. During this period they dropped 1,572 more on other targets, with a total loss of 26 aircraft. These bomb totals include a number of 2,700 lb incendiaries (with 'Cookie' cases) dropped on Berlin and mentioned earlier.

With a crew of two (pilot and navigator) the twin-engine, unarmed Mosquito, carrying 4,000 lb and flying the 600 miles to Berlin in two hours at 27,000 ft, compared most favourably with the seven-crew Lancaster carrying 8,800 lb (less for the Halifax), flying at less than 20,000 ft and taking four hours on the outward journey, thus increasing their exposure time to enemy defenders.

Even when the heavy Main Force bombers were not operating, Mosquitoes

Top *A 4,000 lb HC Mk I on a British airfield.*

Above *A 4,000 lb HC Mk I 'Cookie' which failed to function – recovered in Cologne, early 1942. (Stadt Bonn Bildarchiv)*

of the Light Night Striking Force kept the Germans awake night after night. The defenders never quite knew where they would turn up next, often in small numbers just adequate to cause the maximum confusion among the radar trackers and defenders. Apart from the significant damage they caused in their own right, on numerous occasions they diverted attention from the more vulnerable 'heavies' by making spoof attacks far from Bomber Command's main target for the night.

With the possible exception of 'Tallboy', dealt with in Chapter Six, the 4,000 lb HC bomb was probably the Royal Air Force's most effective weapon.

Certainly the citizens of most German cities would not disagree, nor for that matter would the citizens of Naples, Genoa and other Italian towns and cities.

The 'Super Cookie', or 8,000 lb HC (3.57 ton) bomb was first conceived in early 1941, the intention being to carry this huge weapon on a modified ex-troop-carrying glider as part of a project to produce a pilotless winged-bomb, something considerably less ambitious than the German V-1 flying bomb. However, for a variety of reasons nothing came of this project, or of another to drop it by parachute. The bomb in its final configuration consisted of two 4,000 lb cylindrical sections bolted together and fitted with a drum tail. Contrary to popular belief these were not the body sections of two 4,000 lb HC bombs. The 4,000 lb bomb had a diameter of 30 in, whereas the 8,000 and 12,000 lb bombs were of 38 in. It was delivered to Bomber Command early in 1942 for carriage on the Halifax and Lancaster only, neither the Wellington nor the Stirling having large enough bomb-bays. By the end of the year, 28 had been dropped on Germany and the occupied territories, a further 1,060 being deployed in the following years.

The first Super Cookie was aimed at Essen on the night of 10–11 April 1942 by Pilot Officer M Renault and his crew of 76 Halifax Squadron, Middleton St George, the squadron providing eight of the 250 aircraft taking part in the raid, which proved unsuccessful. The target was covered by cloud and the bombing force scattered by heavy anti-aircraft fire over the Ruhr. Although many claimed to have bombed Essen, later reports indicated that not more than six aircraft loads actually landed in the target area. The aircraft carrying the 'Super Cookie' was badly damaged and there is no record of where the bomb actually landed. It certainly did not hit Essen.

The first Super Cookie to hit an Italian city was delivered on the night of 28–29 November 1942 during a 200-plus aircraft attack on Turin. Wing Commander G P Gibson and Flight Lieutenant W N Whamond, both of 106 Lancaster Squadron, Coningsby each dropped one on to the city. Wing Commander Gibson was later to be remembered for his dam-busting exploits

Another 'Cookie' recovered near Düren. The tail has broken away, revealing the HE filling. (Stadt Bonn Bildarchiv)

with 617 Squadron rather than this first with the Super Cookie.

Apart from the considerable damage caused to Turin, the raid is also remembered because on the return journey Flight Sergeant R H Middleton, a young Australian, who was the skipper of a 149 Squadron Stirling, gave his life to save the majority of his crew. He was subsequently awarded a posthumous Victoria Cross.

The 12,000 lb HC bomb can hardly be called a 'Super Super Cookie', but that is exactly what it was. Whereas the 8,000 lb HC had two 4,000 lb sections bolted together, the ponderous 12,000 lb HC was an 8,000 lb bomb with a third section bolted to the rear of the body. This monster was seen as an ideal bomb for blasting canal banks and viaducts as well as built-up targets. Containing over 8,000 lb of high explosive, the potential for devastation was enormous. However, its very size did create problems, especially during ground carriage and aircraft loading.

To ensure ballistic stability it had to be fitted with a six-finned ballistic tail some two ft longer than the cylindrical drum tail of the 8,000 lb bomb. Thus with the longer tail and an additional bomb section, it could only be carried on specially modified Lancasters. It took a minimum of 35 mins to load the weapon into the aircraft, and its specially-designed bomb trolley had a ground clearance of only 4.5 in, thus great care was needed in moving it around the airfield. These factors caused problems when time was of the essence.

The first bombs were delivered to 617 Squadron (the Dambusters) Coningsby in September 1943. This was the only squadron with modified Lancasters, and the only one to carry the 12,000 lb HC bomb. Almost immediately, the first attacks were launched against the Dortmund-Ems Canal near Ladbergen. Surprisingly, earlier trials indicated that the bomb could be safely dropped with adequate fuzing delays, from heights of only 300 ft into 12 ft of water, and consequently these were the parameters adopted.

On the night of 14–15 September 1943, eight Lancasters took off from Woodhall Spa, each carrying the massive bomb. However, whilst still over the North Sea, the attack was aborted because heavy fog was reported over the target. During the return flight the aircraft of Flight Lieutenant D J H Maltby (who earlier, in May, had breached the Möhne Dam) crashed into the sea and the crew perished. The operation was repeated on the following night, and

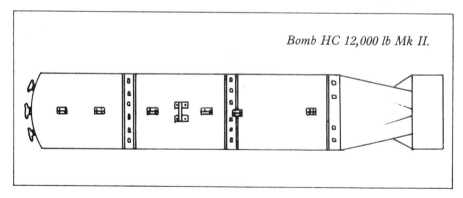

Bomb HC 12,000 lb Mk II.

although the eight aircraft reached and bombed the canal, in misty conditions, it was not breached. Only three aircraft returned, amongst those killed being Pilot Officer L G Knight, another of the Dams Raid survivors. These heavy losses, compounding those associated with the Dams Raid on 16–17 May, confirmed that low-level attacks on German targets using a combination of heavy bombers and ponderous bombs were both hazardous and less than fruitful. Subsequently 617 Squadron became a specialist high-altitude bombing unit, although low-level target-marking operations were frequently undertaken using Lancasters, Mosquitoes and also a Mustang.

Despite the lack of evidence that the 12,000 lb bombs were really effective, the Air Staff was asked to formally approve their introduction into service. They declined to do so until further operational trials were completed, but finally gave the go-ahead in March 1944. Possibly satisfaction with the results achieved during two specialist attacks during February and March 1944 had something to do with this stamp of approval.

Whether true or not, twelve Lancasters of 617 Squadron, led by the Squadron Commander, Wing Commander Leonard Cheshire, attacked the German-controlled Gnome and Rhône aero-engine factory at Limoges, 200 miles South West of Paris on the night of 8–9 February 1944. The intention was to drop the 12,000 lb 'blockbusters' from high level on to target markers placed by Cheshire from extremely low level. Great care and precise bombing was required, because the factory was surrounded on three sides by French civilian houses. Cheshire made three low level passes to warn the factory workers to take shelter or flee. On the fourth pass, flying at between 50 and 100 ft, he dropped a full load of 30 lb incendiaries and Red Spot Fires. Luckily the target was undefended, otherwise such heroics in a Lancaster could have proved suicidal, as was demonstrated earlier at the Dortmund-Ems Canal.

The remaining bombers each dropped their 12,000 lb blockbusters on to the fires with great accuracy; ten hit the factory and one fell into the river running alongside the perimeter. As might be expected, production was brought to a standstill in the devastated ruins of the once highly productive factory.

This low-level target-marking technique was to become the trade mark of 617 Squadron. Later, however, the target-marking was more normally undertaken by Mosquito aircraft, rather than the less nimble Lancaster.

Just over a month later the Michelin tyre factory at Clermont-Ferrand met a similar fate when it was devastated by six 12,000 lb HC bombs. This was more than enough to convince the Air Staff of the 12,000 lb HC's prowess, enabling all concerned to legitimize its existence.

In all, 193 were dropped, with mixed success. They did well against conventional buildings, but less so against canals and viaducts – blast without penetration was inadequate in coping with larger and stronger structures. To be fair, the HC range were designed purely as blast bombs, and there was no initial intention that they should be used against hardened targets. In any event, in June 1944 they were overtaken by the 12,000 lb Tallboy, supplemented in March 1945 by the even larger 22,000 lb Grand Slam. Both bombs were initially designated DP (Deep Penetration), but subsequently and more accur-

Top *A range of HC and MC bombs. (IWM)*
Above *German bomb disposal team in 1943 with a recovered 1,000 lb MC and 500 lb GP.*

ately they were redesignated MC (Medium Capacity). Both did well against heavy concrete structures, bridges, viaducts and canals, as outlined in Chapter Six.

Overall the high capacity blockbuster range of bombs more than proved its worth. Most were eminently successful, particularly so when supplemented by incendiaries.

Leaving aside the Tallboy and Grand Slam, which were specialist weapons, what of the main range of smaller general bombardment MC bombs? They, like the HCs, found their inspiration from a German weapon. In this case it was the SC (Spreng Cylindrisch) range of bombs, which produced surprisingly good results when dropped on British towns during 1940. Surprisingly good, that is, when compared with the British equivalent, which at that time was the somewhat discredited GP range.

In early December 1940 a meeting chaired by the Deputy Chief of Air Staff considered the question of whether the GP range was adequate. Intelligence reports produced at the meeting clearly indicated that it was not, mainly because of its low ratio of explosive, and also because for one reason or another many bombs failed to detonate on impact. The meeting decided that the HC range, the design of which was just beginning, had only a limited application, and what was needed to replace the streamlined GP range was a British version of the German SC range. That was a bomb with a parallel-sided case, a pointed nose and clip-on or bolt-on tail unit. It was decided that the CWR should be as high as possible, consistent with the need for the bomb to be sufficiently robust to withstand impact stresses on all types of structure other than reinforced concrete, including metalled roads and the deep penetration of multi-storey buildings.

A specific requirement was passed to the Ordnance Board before the end of the year, and work started immediately on the first of the range, the Bomb HE 500 lb MC. The fabrication, trials and production of the initial design posed a number of difficulties; in all, three designs were produced, the fabricated (welded) type and those with forged or cast steel cases. The bomb bodies produced in the first instance, because the work could be produced that much more quickly, were welded together (the fabricated bomb). However, many production prob-

German bomb disposal team removing a 1,000 lb GP bomb.

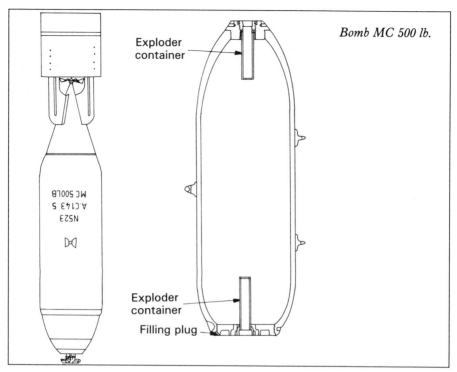

Exploder container

Exploder container

Filling plug

N523
A.C143 5
MC 500LB

Bomb MC 500 lb.

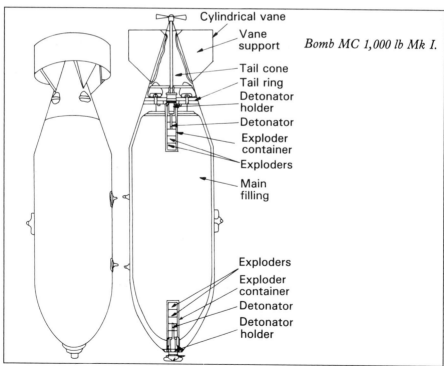

Cylindrical vane

Vane support

Tail cone

Tail ring

Detonator holder

Detonator

Exploder container

Exploders

Main filling

Exploders

Exploder container

Detonator

Detonator holder

Bomb MC 1,000 lb Mk I.

lems were encountered, because of the varying welding standards at manufacturers throughout the country. As a result these bombs tended, when fitted with delay fuzing, to break up during penetration of multi-storey buildings. As might be expected, bombs with forged cases gave the best results; however, they took longer to produce, and consequently output was not as high as that for the fabricated body. Both the fabricated and forged bomb had a CWR of 50 to 51 per cent.

The third method of construction was straight-forward casting, which produced a robust body but used more metal, thus lowering the CWR to 42 per cent. In all, during the war years, 15 different Marks of the 500 lb MC bomb were designed, although only 12 including one or other of the above processes, were actually produced in any quantity. Marks I to IV were all approved for service use by the end of 1942, and Marks VI to IX were the same bombs fitted with American suspension lugs. The Mark V was a Mark III which, due to a manufacturing fault, had its centre of gravity outside the limit specified. Rather than waste these 6,000 bombs, they were segregated for use with long tail-units to restore stability, and designated the Mark V.

With the advent of heavier bombers and increased commitments, in 1942 the Air Staff voiced the need for a 1,000 lb MC. By February 1943, 18,000 a month were being produced; no mean feat! However, there were some production advantages, in that it was only a scaled-up 500 pounder constructed in cast and forged steel. By then, too, the pitfalls in the manufacturing processes were largely corrected. Normally, forged steel bombs were used to deal with heavily-girdered buildings, and the somewhat less-effective fabricated bombs were restricted to targets demanding instantaneous detonation. When long delays of six to 144 hr were needed, forged bombs were used if available, otherwise, one-piece cast steel types were used in lieu.

The 500 and 1,000 pounder out-performed all the other general bombardment bombs, indeed after its introduction in 1943 the latter became Bomber Command's first choice. It dropped 17,500 in 1943, 203,000 in 1944, and 36,000 in 1945, whilst the Second Tactical Air Force on the Continent expended at least 30,000. There is no doubt that the figures would have been much greater but for the shortages which caused the GP range to be resurrected, and increased use made of 500 and 1,000 lb American bombs. The later bombs of both countries were designed for carriage on the aircraft of either, the main difference being that the British used one suspension lug and the Americans two.

The 4,000 lb MC was hastily produced in 1943 at Bomber Command's insistence to oust its suspect GP counterpart. Although diminishing, there was still a need for a large, robust bomb to attack substantially-constructed industrial complexes and shipyards from low level. Trials indicated that it had good penetrative qualities even from 100 ft, achieving craters 14 ft deep and 54 ft wide.

However, by the time the bomb became available in adequate numbers, the Commander-in-Chief of Bomber Command, Air Marshal Sir Arthur Harris, was reluctant to put his valuable four-engined aircraft at the mercy of the very efficient German anti-aircraft fire at point blank range, as would be the case in a low-level attack. In any event, he was beginning to have considerable success from high level with the advent of the professional pathfinding and target-marking force and the use of HC blockbusters in conjunction with incendiaries. Consequently there were no specific targets for the new bomb and, as far as the main bomber force was concerned, the 4,000 lb MC was relegated to general bombardment from high level. However, the 8 Group Mosquitoes used them most effectively at low level during 1944–45 fitted with 11 second delays to permit an adequate escape time. The Mark IV Mosquito was capable of carrying a single 4,000 pounder in the modified bomb-bay or four 500 lb MC bombs, or a load of target-markers.

In all, Bomber Command expended 21,000 4000 lb MCs, 13,000 of them in 1944. Some were used in the bomber blitzes on German industrial areas, but the Mosquitoes delivered their quota in a more clinical fashion. For example, to prevent vital supplies reaching Von Runstedt's sorely pressed armies, 16 aircraft of Nos 128, 571 and 692 Squadrons from Wyton, Oakington and Graveley set out on New Year's Day 1945 to hurl their loads into the mouths of vital road and rail tunnels in the Mosel/Rhine valleys near Koblenz. Bombs successfully entered those at Mayen and Scheven, and at least one other was seen to erupt and collapse.

Among the smaller bombs in the MC range, the 500 pounder played a significant tactical role, the 1,000 lb less so and the 250, not big enough for the job, hardly figured at all except on the light fighter-bombers such as the Hurricane, Spitfire and Mustang. The 500 pounder was deployed effectively on many well-publicized raids, and no more so than those briefly described below.

In early February 1944, the execution of many members of the French resistance movement was thought to be imminent within the walls of Amiens prison. One of the movement's leaders, Dominique Ponchardier, postulated that with Royal Air Force help some might just escape this cruel fate. To permit escape, the 22 ft high perimeter wall and the three ft-thick prison wall would have to be breached. With political backing, the Royal Air Force decided the job might be done with 500 lb MCs, tail-fuzed with 11 second delays, dropped at very low level to skip along the ground and detonate against the outer and inner walls. On 18 February the job was entrusted to 18 Mosquitoes of 140 Wing, Hunsdon, Herts (21, 464 (RAAF) and 487 (RNZAF) Squadrons), led by Group Captain C Pickard and carrying two bombs apiece. The New Zealanders led the way and from a height of 10-15 ft breached the outer wall, followed by the Australians who dealt with the prison wall. 21 Squadron was not required. Belief has it that at least 150 of the 700 prisoners escaped; unfortunately 37, along with about 50 Germans, were killed, as were two of the Mosquito crews. The leader was shot down by a FW 190 and the other, piloted by Squadron Leader I R McRitchie, by ground fire. Controversy has continued as to the real purpose of this attack and who actually ordered it, but no criticism can be aimed at the crews, who undertook the operation with remarkable skill and accuracy in very hazardous circumstances, believing it to be a poignant errand of mercy.

Just about a month later, on 21 March, 18 Mosquitoes of the same wing, led by Wing-Commander P A Kleboe, of 21 Squadron, with similar bomb loads, attacked Gestapo Headquarters in the six storey Shellhaus building in Copenhagen, where Danish resistance leaders feared plans were being drawn up for the arrest of their members. Direct hits were achieved as the aircraft roared in at 100 ft in broad daylight – the hazards were reflected in the loss of the wing leader and three other aircraft. Many Gestapo officials were killed or wounded, but more importantly, vital records were destroyed.

Both the above operations were more successful than that carried out on 25 September 1942 when the Gestapo Headquarters in Oslo was attacked with some of the earliest 500 lb MC bombs. Four Mosquitoes of 105 Squadron, Marham, Norfolk detached to Leuchars, Scotland, timed the attack to coincide with a Quisling rally (Norwegian pro-Germans). Unfortunately, as the aircraft made their low-level bombing run they were intercepted by FW 190s, one Mosquito being shot down and the others severely harassed.

Despite these distractions, four bombs struck the Headquarters; three passed right through the building and failed to detonate, and the fourth which remained in the building also failed to detonate. This attack showed remarkable accuracy and courage under the most difficult conditions, and was spoiled only by the total failure of the bombs. It seems unlikely that all four would fail to function because of technical defects, therefore it is open to speculation that the bombs were released from such low level that the safety devices did not have time to free the pistol strikers. Nevertheless, the locals were impressed, and the Nazis and their collaborators became aware that they could no longer bank on immunity in their distant headquarters.

Just over two months later the 500 lb MC more than vindicated itself when deployed against the Phillips radio and valve factory in the centre of the Dutch town of Eindhoven. The importance placed on this factory, which was producing large amounts of vital electrical equipment for the German forces, can be estimated by the number of aircraft deployed both on the main attack and the operations carried out to divert Luftwaffe fighters. This latter consideration was important, because the aircraft would be attacking at low level in daylight, on a town well beyond the range of available British fighter escorts.

On Sunday 6 December 1942, 93 light bombers of 2 Group, Bomber Command, took part: 47 Venturas (21, 464 and 487 Squadrons), 36 Bostons (88,107 and 226 Squadrons) and 10 Mosquitoes (105 and 139 Squadrons). One of the Mosquitoes was a photographic aircraft, which returned with some spectacular photographs. The bombers carried a mixture of 500 lb MC and 250 lb GP bombs, some of the latter being fitted with long-delay pistols (to delay and hamper debris clearance) but the majority of the bombs were fitted with 0.025 second delays, just enough to get them through the roofing on to the factory floor before detonation. The attack took place in clear weather and the bombing was remarkably accurate, causing severe damage. The factory did not resume production until six months later.

Sunday was deliberately selected, to avoid casualties among Dutch factory workers. This was largely achieved, there being few casualties within the factory. Unfortunately some bombs fell wide, and local reports indicate that 148

Winter scene 1944-5. Preparing 4 lb incendiary clusters in a Yorkshire bomb dump. (IWM)

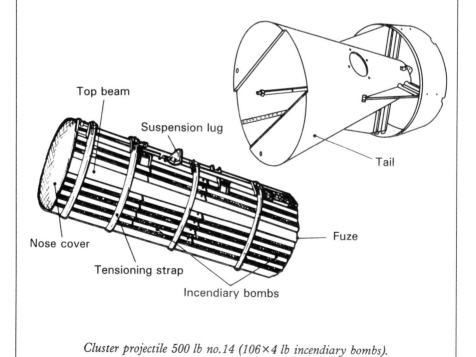

Cluster projectile 500 lb no.14 (106×4 lb incendiary bombs).

Dutch civilians and some German soldiers were killed outside the factory perimeter.

Two diversionary attacks were undertaken: 84 American B-17s, escorted by Fighter Command Spitfires, attacked Lille, and a Mustang Squadron flew offensive sweeps along the Dutch coast. Despite these complementary operations, the losses among the Eindhoven attackers were heavy, a total of 15 aircraft being lost over the Netherlands and three others crashing in England.

Fighter bombers too made sound clinical use of MC bombs, particularly on the Continent after D-Day, harassing the retreating German armies, striking strong-points and V-sites in France and the Netherlands. From late 1944 to March 1945 the enemy was launching V-2 rockets at the United Kingdom from launching pads around the Hague and Leiden areas. To get at the root of the problem, the Spitfire XIVs of 229, 453 (RAAF) and 602 Squadrons made a spectacular low level attack on Christmas Eve, shattering a block of flats housing the headquarters of the rocket-firing troops at Haagsche Bosche in the Rotterdam area. The well-aimed 250 and 500 lb MC bombs ensured evacuation of the buildings, and a considerable decrease in the daily firings directed towards London and South East England.

Perhaps a greater menace to German troops and vehicles were the three-inch rocket-firing, bomb-carrying, Hawker Typhoons, known as the Bomphoons, also armed with four 20 mm cannons. With eight 60 lb high-explosive rocket heads, or two 500/1,000 lb MCs underwing, they caused considerable havoc, and not a little fear, among the enemy troops from D-Day onwards – even Erwin Rommel felt their sting when 193 Squadron struck his staff car in July 1944, seriously wounding Germany's eminent Field Marshal. Later in October, accompanied by 197, 257, 263 and 266 Squadrons, they went one better in undermining the Wehrmacht hierarchy, when they destroyed 15 Army Headquarters at Dordrecht in the Netherlands. The 500 and 1,000 lb MCs killed over 70 staff officers, wounding many more. By February 1945, during the final push on the Rhine they were supplementing their bomb loads with two Cluster Projectiles, each carrying 26 20 lb 'F' bombs.

Although in all, over three-quarters of a million MC bombs were dropped, it has been impossible in this chapter to do more than mention a few of the varied uses they were put to. Like the other ranges, they suffered a proportion of failures, the 'dud' rate being between 12 and 15 per cent, some due to straightforward technical defects, others to cockpit trouble, in that they were inadvertently dropped 'safe'. This latter fault could be caused by an electrical defect in the release gear, or even failure by the crew at a moment of great stress to make the appropriate switches.

Nevertheless, it can be said with confidence that these were the most effective and reliable general bombardment bombs employed by either side, as also were most of the HC range, and particularly the 4,000 lb HC backed up by the ever-efficient four lb incendiary. The latter's effectiveness improved enormously in 1944, when it was dropped in aimable bomb clusters. These disintegrated at low-level altitude, permitting greater concentrations of the contained bombs (child stores), rather than showering them down from small bomb containers (attached to the aircraft) from high altitude. The advent of the clusters also largely circumvented the possibility of a bomber at higher level inadvertently hitting his colleagues flying below with, in the case of the Lancaster, something like 3,000 four pounders.

Bomb design and development in wartime, especially during the birth pangs of a completely new bomb or range of bombs, was beset with problems of priority and the need to meet urgent and often conflicting demands in the shortest possible time. At the same time, tactics and strategic requirements changed rapidly. Indeed, some projects were outdated before they came to fruition, and one was left with bombs which were no longer suitable or required for their original purpose. The 4,000 lb MC was a good example, athough it redeemed itself to some extent in the final months of the war.

Successes far outmatched the failures and, in looking back, one can only admire the work achieved by so many unsung designers, developers and producers of the weapons provided to the 'sharp end', very often under the most trying conditions. Of course, those conditions were considerably less trying and stressful than those faced by the men who prepared and delivered them to their appointed target.

Having recounted some of the problems associated with bomb development, and briefly indicated how the finished products were used, it would be appropriate to outline the policies governing their strategic use by Bomber Command. It is also appropriate to consider the many problems encountered (and mostly overcome) in delivering them to an exact spot on the ground in the middle of the darkened Continent of Europe. Undoubtedly, not doing so often led to bombing ineffectiveness and considerable wastage of valuable effort, material and men; consequently, Chapter Four is devoted to these aspects.

CHAPTER FOUR

STRATEGIC BOMBING POLICY, TARGET IDENTIFICATION AND MARKING

The strategic bombing policy adopted by Bomber Command throughout the Second World War was governed by four main considerations: directives from higher authority, types of weapons available, weapon effectiveness, and navigational capability. As stated previously, the effectiveness of many of the early war weapons was far from adequate. Only when bigger, better, more powerful bombers, and special to-purpose bombs were developed, was it possible to effectively attack the wide range of targets demanded by the strategic bombing policy. This was based on a progressive series of directives issued by the War Cabinet and Air Ministry. The frequent changes in operational requirements stemming from such directives not only caused problems for the senior staff officers at Bomber Command, who did not always see eye to eye with them, but also among the operational air crew who, having begun to perfect a particular bombing technique, were at times required to change it at short notice to cater for a totally different type of target.

The all-pervading, intractable difficulty in the early war years was that of locating and attempting to strike accurately at pin-point targets. Recognition of the inability to do so forced a change of policy, whereby target areas were saturated with bombs to try and ensure that so-called pin-point targets would be caught in the general mayhem. This came to be known as area bombing, and it was of some comfort to the Royal Air Force that for similar reasons the Luftwaffe employed the same tactic.

Despite some early setbacks, by late 1943 Bomber Command had become a well-organized and well-equipped force, capable of hitting hard at the German industrial heartland. As will be seen, the path from ineffectiveness to comparative success was not without its traumas, drama and controversy. At times, the Command was even required to fight with one hand tied behind its back. Although not intended as such, the very first directive, based on a statement made by the Prime Minister, Mr Neville Chamberlain in the House of Commons, had very much this effect. He said that 'only military targets would be bombed by the Royal Air Force and that every possible care would be taken to avoid civilian casualties'. The Air Staff interpreted this to mean that no attack could be made against targets on German soil.

Consequently, right from the start, knowing that it was virtually impossible to bomb without causing civilian casualties, the Royal Air Force complied by restricting bombing attacks to those on enemy warships and otherwise gaining operational experience by dropping countless propaganda leaflets far and wide over Europe. The stifling restrictions imposed by Chamberlain's edict, no doubt uttered with the best of intentions, prevented Bomber Command striking at naval targets close to German naval towns, at a time when U-boats and other warships posed considerable problems for British warships and merchantmen. There were other implications too, for instance reconnaissance aircraft took photographs of German preparations being made to invade its western neighbours, but no action was taken against the massing forces, who ultimately launched their planned invasion on 10 May 1940.

The Royal Air Force responded by bombing the advancing German forces and their lines of communication, but no attacks were directed at targets East of the Rhine. However, in response to the Luftwaffe's heavy bombing of Rotterdam on 15 May, the War Cabinet on the same day authorized Bomber Command attacks on mainland Germany. That same night the Command took off the kid gloves by deploying 99 bombers to 16 targets in the Ruhr area, and keeping up the momentum on the following night when 37 aircraft attacked the Münchengladbach area – two Hampdens and a Whitley failing to return. From these small beginnings began the most incessant and comprehensive strategic bombing campaign of modern times.

The embargo on bombing Germany was not total, as it had been broken earlier, on the night of 19–20 March in response to a German bombing raid on the naval base at Scapa Flow in the Orkney Islands two nights before, which had killed a British civilian and injured several others. Incensed, the Government had authorized a reprisal attack. So, the Hörnum Seaplane Base on the Island of Sylt was attacked by 20 Hampdens and 30 Whitleys carrying 20 tons of high explosive bombs and about 1,000 incendiaries, on this the first offensive raid against naval forces on German territory. Historical it may have been, but it did highlight some of the problems lying ahead, in that photographic reconnaissance revealed no damage, although 41 aircraft crews claimed to have inflicted various amounts of damage.

Prior to the bombing of Germany proper on 15 May 1940, Bomber Command's 4 Group Whitleys had gained considerable night flying experience dropping propaganda leaflets far and wide over Germany, ranging from Hamburg to the Ruhr and even to Berlin. Benefiting from refuelling facilities at British bases in France, they even showered their messages as far afield as Prague (12–13 January 1940) and Warsaw two months later. These epic flights did much to highlight the navigational and technical problems experienced in traversing much of blacked-out Europe. The flights, often in appalling weather, with only rudimentary navigational aids, and suspect weather forecasts, made a nonsense of dead reckoning navigation.

Back in May 1939, the Air Officer Commanding 3 Group reported to Head-quarters Bomber Command that 'Dead reckoning navigation by day above cloud can only be expected to get aircraft within 50 miles of the target.' A year later, when the widespread scattering of leaflets was supplanted by the need to direct real bomb loads on to pin-point targets, the shortcomings in navigational techniques and equipment, particularly at night, were clearly demonstrated.

With a number of disastrous daylight experiences against the German fleet in December 1939, the bombers were forced, by German fighters, to operate only during the hours of darkness. Then more often than not they flew in conditions previously experienced by the Whitley leaflet raiders, which caused them to drift miles off the selected course to the target with little hope of even getting within miles of the objective. Crews who reduced height, and many did, to try and identify their true position by scanning the ground features, put themselves in considerable danger from the ground defences. This was par-ticularly true in the vicinity of large industrial conurbations and sensitive military installations.

Whilst fine moonlight nights, showing up coastlines and other ground features, made target location relatively much easier from heights up to about 12,000 ft, it also eased the task of the enemy fighters and anti-aircraft batteries, adding to the many other hazards faced by the bombers. Larger towns could be picked out from 4,000 to 6,000 ft, but bombing strongly-defended locations from these heights was foolhardy, even suicidal. Consequently, it was recogniz-ed that for all practical purposes only large targets such as dimly-lit marshalling yards could be located and possibly hit from a safe altitude, and then only on fine moonlight nights. These were rarely found in the Ruhr, where industrial haze tended to cover the great sprawl of this area.

From the foregoing it can be seen that no matter how effective or ineffective the bombs, they had little bearing on the outcome if they could not be dropped on the appropriate targets. It mattered not whether this was because of political restrictions or the inability to deliver them to the precise target location.

By the end of October 1940, Air Marshal Sir Richard Peirse had been ap-pointed Commander-in-Chief Bomber Command to replace Sir Charles Portal, who became Chief of the Air Staff and effectively overall Commander of the Royal Air Force. His first directive, issued that month, instructed Peirse primarily to concentrate bombing attacks on German oil targets, and as a sec-ond priority other named industries and lines of communication. At this stage any suggestion of area attacks to offset bombing inaccuracy was firmly rejected. So, small numbers of bombers were sent to various oil targets throughout Ger-many with little chance of success, though this was not fully recognized at the time. Losses were high and effectiveness left much to be desired. Again, this was not fully appreciated, just suspected by some. Obviously, little could be done in the short term to remedy the basic shortcomings, but it would seem that a number of directives continued to place confidence in the bombers' ability to produce the desired effects.

In any event, Peirse was instructed during January 1941 that 'the sole primary aim of your bomber offensive, until further orders, should be the destruction of the German synthetic oil plants'. The directive listed the plants to be attacked, and indeed some were. However, before the offensive really got underway it was supplanted by a new directive, dated 9 March 1941 and bearing the signature of the Vice-Chief of the Air Staff, but like some of its predecessors reflecting the strong views of the Prime Minister, Winston Churchill. Perforce of circumstances, Churchill had often to vacillate from day to day to confront an ever-growing number of complex priorities, thus putting considerable strain on the recipients of directives stemming from that source.

This time Bomber Command was directed to attack installations related in any way to U-boats, including dockyards like Kiel, Hamburg and Bremen, and marine diesel engine plants in towns like Mannheim and Stuttgart. Perhaps the most important and far-reaching clause in this directive was that it indicated that area bombing would be appropriate. It read as follows: 'Priority of selection should be given to those targets which lie in congested areas where the greatest morale effect is likely to result.' An amendment issued nine days later in respect of Mannheim and Stuttgart stated: 'Both are suitable as area objectives and their attack should have high morale value.' Thus for the first time a policy to break civilian morale in addition to destroying strategic targets was introduced. Perhaps it was significant that the amending directive was signed by the Deputy Chief of the Air Staff, Air Vice-Marshal Arthur Harris, later a great protagonist of area bombing; perhaps too, it was now accepted that Bomber Command was unable to hit precision targets.

In any event, in better weather and with more to aim at, the results from April onwards improved marginally. Some quite successful attacks were directed at Hamburg, Bremen, Kiel, Brest and elsewhere. The German battleships *Gneisenau* and *Scharnhorst* were bottled up in Brest during April, giving added incentive to attacks on its dockyards. Other attacks during this phase were not so successful; for example, on the night of 5–6 May, Mannheim was the target for 141 aircraft, and 121 claimed to have hit the town. Yet, German contemporary reports indicated that only 25 bombed the town, killing four people, but causing no damage to industrial plant. Things were different four nights later when 146 aircraft launched a further attack. On this occasion the German records reported that 22 large and medium industrial plants were badly damaged, 64 people killed and 2,134 rendered homeless.

Four months after the attack on dockyards and other related naval targets began, the bombers were once more directed elsewhere by the Air Ministry in a directive dated 9 July 1941. It emphasized that it was now considered that Germany's weakest points were the morale of its civil population and its inland transportation system, and included a most important sentence '... you will direct the main effort of the bomber force, until further instructions, towards dislocating the German transportation system and to destroying the morale of the civil population as a whole and of the industrial workers in particular.' The directive continued by listing towns and cities considered suitable for attack. Among these were places like Hamm, Osnabrück and Düsseldorf, the destruction of whose railway sidings and junctions would cause major disruption to the distribution of industrial output from the Ruhr area. Also included were cities suitable for general attack on moonless nights, not only because they contained vital targets but they also had the misfortune to sit astride the relatively easily-found landmark of the River Rhine. Among these were Cologne, Duisburg, and once again Düsseldorf. The list was by no means exhaustive and also suggested that targets like Hannover, Hamburg and Stuttgart should also be considered. For the first time, wide scope was given to the Command in terms of target selection and form of attack. Subsequently, many of the targets mentioned were attacked with ever-increasing numbers of aircraft, but losses too went up alarmingly. Aircraft were still flying individually or in small groups spread over a large area of sky and by now the German night fighter aircraft, under command of General Josef Kammhuber, were becoming battle-experienced and efficient, supported by a well-organized ground control system making full use of radar stations established along the main bomber routes.

The larger numbers of aircraft flying almost nightly to Germany with increasing losses could only be justified if the results showed increased damage and destruction. Unfortunately, although maximum effort was exerted, this was not the case. Despite crew reports to the contrary, intelligence reports indicated that many aircraft were bombing wrong targets or none at all. In an effort to substantiate successful claims, Bomber Command had a large number of photographs taken by bombing aircraft and the War Cabinet, or rather Lord Cherwell, scientific adviser to both the Prime Minister and the Cabinet, decided that they should be scientifically analysed.

Some 4,000 photographs shot during 100 raids in June and July 1941 were analysed and the results published in the 'Butt Report' (the analyst and writer of the report was Mr D M Butt). To say the least, they were alarming. Despite crew reports generally given in good faith, it was shown that on a moonlit night only 1 in 3 aircraft were bombing within 5 miles of their German targets, and on moonless nights the ratio was as low as 1 in 20. In the main, this was due to the lack of any but the most primitive navigational aids, and to some extent to the German practice of lighting decoy fires many miles clear of obvious targets, to attract the attention of unsuspecting bomber crews.

The implications of Butt's findings in August 1941 were clear to all. The Commander-in-Chief Bomber Command could do little other than admit that with the contemporary navigational equipment and expertise, his force could not hope to strike targets with any greater degree of accuracy, even on a moonlit summer night. For the next few months Bomber Command went through a vexatious phase, but there was no real evidence to suggest that the 'press on' attitude of the air crews was beginning to wane, although morale had taken some nasty knocks. This was hardly surprising considering the Command lost over 520 aircraft between July and November 1941, representing a percentage loss of over 7 per cent by day and 3.5 per cent by night.

In judging cost effectiveness, perhaps the raid on Berlin, when 169 aircraft took part on the night of 7–8 November 1941, gives some idea of what the bombers were up against. Of course this was far from being a typical target. In any event, 73 reached Berlin and reported bombing the general area, 21 were lost (12.4 per cent) and the meticulous German reports indicate that 14 houses were destroyed and 11 people killed. This was indeed a poor return for the enormous resources put into the effort.

Arising from the Butt Report and marginal results thereafter, the Air Ministry advised Sir Richard Peirse on 13 November that only essential operations were to be undertaken during the coming months, and that the future of Bomber Command was under consideration. Despite this restriction and lack of confidence, the Command operated over Germany on just over half the nights available between 13 November 1941 and 22 February 1942, undertaking over 5,000 sorties with a loss of 125 aircraft (2.5 per cent), perhaps an indication that 'softer' targets, if there was such a thing, were deliberately selected during this period.

During this relatively quiet period when the future of Bomber Command was being decided at Cabinet and Air Ministry level, events elsewhere were far from quiet. The British public was being overwhelmed by a spate of bad news. The campaign in the Western Desert was not prospering well, the Japanese were overrunning the Far East and were about to capture Singapore, and on 10 December had sunk the battleships HMS *Prince of Wales* and *Repulse*. However, the British public felt that, 'at least our bombers are giving the Germans some stick', and this they were, even if the results did not always come up to expectations.

As a result of the Cabinet/Air Ministry deliberations, Sir Charles Portal managed to convince Winston Churchill, and thus the War Cabinet, that Bomber Command had a vital and major role to play. That was, given more heavy bombers and most importantly adequate navigational and bombing equipment, along with suitable bombs, and not least resolute leadership. Subsequently, Sir Richard Peirse was removed from his post on 8 January 1942 and replaced temporarily by Air Vice-Marshal J E A Baldwin. Some say Peirse was sacked, others that he was promoted sideways, but there is no doubt whatever about the reason, he was in charge when Bomber Command went through a period of extremely poor bombing results, very high casualties and a perceptible reduction in Command morale. Not so much that enthusiasm for operations deteriorated but that it was felt that too little was being done to provide adequate facilities for the task. Peirse eventually became the Supremo of Allied Air Forces in India and South East Asia, so he was certainly not relegated to the wilderness or thought of too badly.

Baldwin received his first directive on 14 February 1942. It was certainly no valentine, it was the famous or notorious 'area bombing directive' which after the war became so controversial and generated so much discussion both by those who understood the contemporary problems and others who certainly did not. It was clear that the Butt Report had confirmed what many suspected, namely that rarely was it possible to obtain accurate bombing of individual industrial complexes by night and from high altitudes. Subjecting an entire town or city and its people to the bombs was more likely to achieve the objective by destroying individual plants and the public services which kept them in operation, whilst at the same time undermining civilian morale.

To this end the directive read: 'It has been decided that the primary objective of your operations should now be focused on the morale of the enemy civil population and in particular of the industrial workers.' It will be noted that this was not a new Air Ministry concept, having many similarities to the requirements of the directive issued in July 1941.

Just eight days after the new directive was issued, Air Marshal Arthur Harris, 'Bert' to his peers and later 'Bomber' or 'Butch' to others, was transferred from his post of Deputy Chief of the Air Staff to that of Commander-in-Chief, Bomber Command, an appointment he was to retain until the end of the war. One suspects that he had a hand in confirming the area bombing policy whilst serving in his previous post. However, contrary to popular belief he was not the main instigator. The policy was drawn up with the approval of the Chief of Air Staff (Portal) and supported by the Prime Minister, even though in later years, for his own reasons Churchill tended to distance himself from the decision. Later it will be seen that the area bombing policy was fully supported at even higher level.

Harris was indeed fortunate to take over when he did, although much still remained to be done to turn Bomber Command into an effective strategic bomber force. However, the long awaited four-engined bombers were being produced in ever greater numbers, the Stirlings and Halifaxes were being supplemented by the Lancaster, and the shorter-range smaller load carriers like the Hampden, Whitley and Wellington were gradually being phased out. At this time he had 469 bombers under command, although not all of them were available for operations on a day-to-day basis. The force comprised of 29 Stirlings, 29 Halifaxes, and four Lancasters, the remainder being mostly Wellingtons.

Yet only three months later he launched a 1,000 bomber raid on Cologne to demonstrate his resolution and the Command's potential. Not all came from first-line operational squadrons, a large proportion was provided by the operational training units and crewed by instructional staff and students (for further details see Chapter Five). Though Harris, or rather Sir Arthur Harris as he now was, having been awarded the KCB following the successful 1,000 bomber attack on Cologne, was more than able to get his own way and greatly influence operational action both at higher and lower levels, there was little further he could do to speed production of the heavy bombers and ancilliary equipment. Nevertheless, although his first-line operational aircraft numbers increased little by the end of 1942, the load-carrying capacity increased dramatically with the advent of more and more 'heavies'.

GEE, for its time an advanced navigational aid, was making an appearance, and trials were being conducted on H2S, a raidar navigational aid, as they were on OBOE, another sophisticated bombing aid. Their capabilities and value to Bomber Command are considered later.

A policy Sir Arthur quickly eradicated was that where the bombing crews selected their own route to the target/targets, more than one might be attacked on a single night, and consequently, no concentration was achieved and attacks were sporadic, with aircraft arriving over a target with anything up to three hours between the first and last, thus exposing the raiders for far too long and giving the defenders more time to retaliate. His revised policy, in the main, restricted the bombers to only one prime target per night. At the same time, by more careful planning and briefing, the timing of the force over the target was concentrated into the shortest possible time. This increased the risk of collision over the target, but greatly reduced the time during which the aircraft were exposed to flak defences.

At the same time, making use of experienced incendiary-carrying crews in the vanguard of the attack did much to 'blaze' the trail for following crews. Sir Arthur also increased the percentage of incendiaries making up the overall bomb loads, in the belief that it might be easier to burn down an industrial or urban target than to blow it up. Undoubtedly he proved the point with a combination of HC and incendiary bombs when, within a few weeks of assuming command, he launched his bombers on Lübeck and Rostock, as described in Chapter Three.

Perhaps it said something for Harris that directions from 'on high' dried up somewhat in 1942. However, in early January 1943 no less than two directives were received in quick succession at Harris's Headquarters. One stemmed from the Casablanca high-level conference attended by President Roosevelt, Prime Minister Churchill and the Combined Chiefs of Staff. It stated bluntly that the task of Bomber Command (and the American Eighth Air Force) was: 'The progressive destruction and dislocation of the German military, industrial and economic system and the undermining of the morale of the German people to a point where their capacity for armed resistance is fatally weakened.' Within that general concept, priority was to be given to German submarine construction and other facilities, aircraft manufacturing and oil plants, and transportation systems.

The other directive, from the Air Ministry taking the Casablanca agreement into consideration, stated among other things '... the War Cabinet has given approval to a policy of area bombing against the U-boat operational bases on the West Coast of France. A decision has accordingly been made to subject the following bases to a maximum scale attack by your Command at night with the object of effectively devastating the whole area in which are located submarines and their maintenance facilities ...' The bases in order of priority were listed as Lorient, St Nazaire, Brest and La Pallice. This was a major change of direction, as it was the first time that area bombing had been suggested or approved against a target in an occupied country.

As far as Harris was concerned, the key sentence in the Casablanca directive was the undermining of the morale of the German people, which he firmly believed could best be achieved by continuing the massive area attacks on German cities started somewhat hesitantly in 1942. However, he did not entirely ignore the priority targets specified in the directives, and regularly attacked them, but only when he thought fit much to the chagrin of his Air Ministry superiors. Perhaps this accounted, at least in part, for the cold shouldering he received when the war was won.

Nevertheless he responded immediately to the second directive, delivering his first attack on Lorient on the night of 14–15 January, using 122 aircraft. This was the first of nine such raids undertaken during the next five weeks, the scale of the attacks ranging from 75 to 466 aircraft. After the last raid on the night of 16–17 February almost 4,000 tons of bombs had been dropped on the town and it was reported to be completely ruined and deserted. Bomber Command then moved on to the next target, St Nazaire, and on the night of 28 February–1 March, 437 aircraft bombed the town, destroying some 60 per cent of its built-up area and as at Lorient, scoring many hits in the port area.

These attacks, a tragedy for the French, were undoubtedly a success in respect of target marking , navigation and bomb aiming, but in respect of their main purpose proved a total failure. Having learnt from previous raids in 1941, the Germans had constructed massive pens (reinforced concrete shelters in which U-boats hid whilst being provisioned and serviced) which were virtually immune from conventional bombs. Thus the U-boats suffered only minor inconvenience and no real disruption to their operations. Once the impotency of these particular operations was appreciated, the attacks were abandoned and Brest and La Pallice spared, at least until the 12,000 lb Tallboy appeared on the scene in 1944.

With this task out of the way, Bomber Command once more took up what it considered to be its main objective, namely the destruction of German industrial areas. To this end the battles of the Ruhr, Hamburg and Berlin were bloodily fought between March 1943 and March 1944. The details of these battles are given in Chapter Five.

German industrial targets received some respite during June to August 1944 whilst Bomber Command was heavily involved supporting the Allied invasion forces and attacking V-Weapon sites in France and elswhere. At the same time, a number of attacks were mounted against Germany itself, but not with the frequency of earlier months. This was quickly to change, as a new directive required Bomber Command to give priority to oil targets and all forms of communication and transportation systems. Harris thoroughly disagreed with this, being firmly convinced (probably wrongly) that the best role for his bombers was the total destruction of German industrial cities and the morale of their inhabitants. Nevertheless, despite his misgivings, the largest proportion of the now huge bomber force was involved from the last quarter of 1944 until the very last days of the war in 1945 in the destruction of those targets quoted in the directive.

During this phase the bomber force was operating at peak strength; indeed, the numbers available were putting considerable strain on the bomb production and supply systems, although the figures altered day by day, dependent on losses and serviceability. Harris now had 84 bomber squadrons available (56 with Lancasters – 1,340 aircraft; 17 with Halifaxes – 500 aircraft; 11 with Mosquitoes – 260 aircraft). He now had the ability to strike at a number of targets on any one night, or even by day. With this huge force under his command, during the last eight months of the war in Europe the tonnage of bombs expended was almost as much as that dropped in all the preceding war years put together.

In post-war years, this fact alone prompted charges of needless killing and wanton destruction. Yet at the time, the Allied and national leaders, the Commander-in-Chief Bomber Command in particular, were fighting for what they believed to be right, and although opinions often differed on the most appropriate course of action, all were dedicated to bringing the war to a quick end using the most effective weapons available. Although much of the criticism for the mass destruction of German cities has been levelled at Air Chief Marshal Sir Arthur Harris, it can be clearly seen from the Casablanca directive in particular that, although perhaps with some over-enthusiasm, he was carrying out the instructions of the Allied political and military leaders and the British War Cabinet.

Although the various directives were couched in broad terms, some of the demands placed on Bomber Command were more explicit. Two examples are those directives associated with the raids on Duisburg, Dresden and Chemnitz, codenamed Hurricane and Thunderclap.

The orders for Operation Hurricane (Duisburg) were received by Bomber Command on 13 October 1944, but judging from the speed of reaction, prior warning may have been given. The directive indicated that it was necessary to demonstrate to Germany the overwhelming superiority of the Allied Air Forces in the theatre by applying in the shortest practical period the maximum effort of Royal Air Force Bomber Command and the American 8th Air Force upon targets in the Ruhr. Duisburg was selected as the target for the RAF, and Cologne for the USAF.

At dawn on 14 October over 1,000 Lancasters and Halifaxes, plus 20 Mosquitoes, set out for Duisburg together with a large fighter escort and dropped over 4,000 tons of bombs, some 20 per cent of which were incendiaries. Fourteen aircraft–13 Lancasters and a Halifax–failed to return. That night (14–15 October) another 1,000 plus bombers attacked the still-smoking ruins, adding a further 4,540 tons of bombs, 90 per cent being high explosive. Seven aircraft failed to return.

Thus within 24 hours Bomber Command had flown over 2,000 sorties and dropped almost 9,000 tons of bombs on this single target. Reports later indicated that Duisburg was virtually destroyed, and its coal mines and coke ovens stilled. By comparison, when Coventry was attacked on the night of 14–15 November 1940, 437 aircraft dropped 450 tons of bombs, destroying five per cent of its built-up area. The American contribution to Operation Hurricane was a daylight attack on Cologne on 14 October, when 1,250 heavy bombers took part, escorted by 750 fighters. It is perhaps interesting to note that, although the directive required the maximum effort from Bomber Command, on the same night that Duisburg was attacked, some 200 Lancasters with Mosquito target-markers were also deployed to Brunswick where they destroyed the centre of the old town, an area of 370 acres. If any proof was needed, these raids were an ample demonstration of the force wielded by Bomber Command in the autumn of 1944.

Operation Thunderclap was executed exactly four months later, in accordance with Air Ministry exigency plans drawn up towards the end of 1944 requiring concentrated attacks on a number of German cities considered to be important centres of communication. The aim was to strike hard at several vital locations, to cause the final breakdown of the civil administration and hopefully prevent the movement of reinforcements towards the advancing Allies, and of refugees fleeing from the fighting zones. Refugees can, as was shown in France during 1940, provide most effective road-blocks. The timing of this plan was vital and it was decided that it could not be implemented until the military situation in Germany was critical.

This state of affairs was deemed to exist at the end of January 1945. Russia had crossed the Eastern German border and the British and Americans were rapidly advancing into Western Germany. Thus, German forces were fighting on two fronts within the Fatherland, and their continued ability to reinforce and move troops was of vital importance to them. Consequently, it was decided that Dresden, Leipzig and Chemnitz (now Karl-Marx-Stadt), all communications centres immediately behind the German Eastern Front, were vital and legitimate targets. By the end of January Bomber Command was provided with details of the proposed three-pronged air attack, codenamed Operation Thunderclap.

Thus at the Yalta Conference a few days later (attended by Churchill, Stalin and Roosevelt) when Stalin requested that air attacks be made against those towns and cities behind the German lines on the Eastern Front, he was advised that plans existed, and in due course Bomber Command would implement them. The Americans too agreed to provide assistance.

So the die was cast, and nine days later on the night of 13–14 February 1945, 796 Lancasters and nine Mosquitoes bombed Dresden. In all, 1,478 tons of high explosive and 1,182 tons of incendiary bombs were directed at the doomed city. The effects of this particular raid have been well publicized; it is sufficient to say that a devastating fire-storm, similar to that experienced by Hamburg in July 1943 and Kassel three months later, developed, resulting in horrific loss of civilian life. Exact figures are not known, but most agree that the death toll was in excess of 50,000.

When the Lancasters left, 300 American B-17s added another 800 tons of bombs during the morning, using the smoking remains of the railway yards as their aiming mark. They repeated the attack on the following day and again on 2 March, but by that stage there was little left to destroy.

In years to follow, albeit with the wisdom of hindsight, the Dresden raid by Bomber Command, with its massive death toll, did much to detract from the well-deserved British goodwill extended to the Command.

In compliance with the Operation Thunderclap requirements, Bomber Command then turned its attention to Chemnitz on the night following the Dresden raid. A mixed force of 717 Lancasters and Halifaxes bombed the city through thick cloud, making use of sky markers as aiming points. (This technique is described later in the chapter.) Photographic reconnaissance indicated that many bombs had fallen in the city, but the largest proportion fell wide, in open country, a disappointing result at that stage of experience and technological advance. A follow-up attack was directed at Chemnitz on the night of 5–6 March, when 760 bombers set out to attack the city. Nine crashed near their bases due to severe icing problems, and a further 22 failed to return. Large areas of the city were destroyed by fire, including the industrial area

Above *Chemnitz (now Karl-Marx Stadt) before the Bomber Command attacks of March 1945.*

Below *Chemnitz after the attack. As is clearly seen, much of the city has been gutted by fire.*

which housed the Siegmar tank-engine factory.

By the time the remaining city on the Thunderclap list, Leipzig, was dealt with, the war was in its dying days, like the target itself. With less than a month to go, 230 aircraft struck the railway yards in daylight on 10 April, followed up by a night raid of 95 bombers. A small force for the time, but perhaps indicative of the numbers needed to finish the task. In any event, satisfactory results were achieved, for the loss of nine bombers.

The foregoing gives a general idea of the policies governing the British strategic bombing campaign and of a few of the raids undertaken in accordance with their requirements. Consideration must now be given to the various types of equipment which were progressively introduced to ensure that the bomb loads were utilized in the most effective fashion. Apart from improvements made to the bombs themselves, the most striking advances were made in the navigational/bombing aids and in the development of special pyrotechnics, the first to guide the bombers to the target area and the second to clearly mark the selected aiming points.

Among others, three main navigational/bombing aids took pride of place, namely GEE, OBOE, and H2S. The first of these, GEE was a synchronized pulse aircraft navigational aid. Pulses were transmitted from three ground stations, Daventry, Ventnor and Stenigot Hill, and received on a cathode-ray tube in the aircraft. The navigator was able to plot the phased difference of each pulse and theoretically fix his position to within about four miles, at an extreme range of 400 miles, even on the darkest night. This was the breakthrough Bomber Command was fervently seeking – and navigators in particular, who could now stop wrestling with their sextants, astrographs and other questionable aids.

The first operational trial of this equipment took place on the night of 11–12 August 1941, when a number of aircraft attacked rail sidings at Mönchengladbach. Two GEE-equipped Wellingtons of 115 Squadron, Marham took part by guiding others to the target, which was obscured by thick cloud. Nevertheless, the raid proved relatively successful, giving hope that with experience better results could be achieved. Next night the two GEE-equipped Wellingtons, accompanied by 76 others, successfully found and bombed Hanover. Four Wellingtons, including one of the GEE aircraft, failed to return, but the secret equipment was destroyed either by accident or deliberately and, luckily for Bomber Command, the technical details did not fall into German hands.

Owing partly to the successful operational trials, and to some extent to the fear of compromising the equipment, no further 'live' trials were undertaken. Instead, a manufacturing programme was instigated to build several hundred GEE sets to equip a large proportion of the existing bomber force. Within seven months, at least 150 aircraft were fitted with GEE, ensuring that more bombers would at least find the general target area, if not the precise aiming point.

GEE got its first full outing on the night of 8–9 March 1942 when over 200 aircraft attacked Essen, one of the main centres of armament design and production. The raid was not a success; unfortunately, as frequently occurred, the whole Ruhr area was covered with industrial haze. Whilst GEE could, within its limits, point in the general direction, it was not sufficiently accurate to pinpoint the particular target area, much less the aiming point.

However, it did prove its worth when Cologne was successfully attacked five nights later, and went on to be a valuable navigational aid throughout the war years. In the closing war years this equipment was supplemented by G-H, a super GEE, which was a highly accurate blind-bombing system, in which the bomber transmitted pulse signals to two ground stations which received the pulses and transmitted them back. This enabled the navigator to measure continuously the bomber's distance from the two known points, and so track it over any target within range of the system, and determine the bomb release point. Any number of aircraft could latch on to the ground stations at any one time.

With increasing use, it was inevitable that a GEE set would fall into German hands. Consequently within five months of its operational début the Germans started to jam transmissions. Jamming was first experienced during a raid on Essen on the night of 4–5 August. However, the British scientists soon came up with an anti-jamming device, which eradicated this problem.

OBOE came along four months later during the last days of 1942. This was a ground-controlled radio navigational and blind bombing system of unique accuracy – arguably the most precise of the whole war on either side. From 30,000 ft, the average aiming error was something like 300 yd, even less at lower altitudes. The marker/bomber aircraft was controlled by two ground stations, one at Trimingham, Norfolk, the other at Walmer, Kent. As time went on, other ground stations were set up to control more aircraft and, after D-Day, mobile caravans were deployed to the Continent to extend OBOE range beyond the Ruhr. The high-flying Mosquito provided the best platform for the airborne equipment, because earth curvature imposed unacceptable range limitations on the lower-flying heavier bombers. The first ground station automatically informed the bomber crew whether or not they were on the correct course and corrected deviations. The second kept check of the aircraft's distance from the target and instructed the aircrew when to drop the target markers or bombs. Results, even on the darkest nights and through the thickest cloud, were equally as good as visual daylight bombing with a bombsight. OBOE Mosquitoes predominately led Main Force raids, particularly to the Ruhr, but after D-Day (6 June 1944) they were supplemented by a small number of OBOE Lancasters. Other than range limitations in the early days, OBOE had no overriding disadvantages, and reduced the possibility of human error to a minimum.

OBOE was first used over enemy territory on the night of 20–21 December 1942, heralding a month of experimental raids. The first OBOE-directed bombs were released by Squadron Leader H F Bufton and his navigator Flight Lieutenant E L Ifould, when three Mosquitoes of 109 Squadron each dropped three 500 lb MC bombs at a power station at Lutterade in the Netherlands, close to the German border. The nine bombs formed a perfect group, but were some two km from the target. With further experience this could certainly be improved on, and indeed it was. The accuracy of OBOE was convincingly demonstrated on a number of small Mosquitio attacks between that time and the end of the month when the Krupps armament complex in Essen, the main target, was successfully attacked.

This phase of trial raids was completed on the night of 29–30 December, when three OBOE-directed Mosquitoes again successfully attacked Essen. It was thus clearly demonstrated that, despite cloud and haze, industrial targets in the Ruhr could be found and bombed with reasonable accuracy from high level, i.e. 18,000 ft.

Next it was necessary to demonstrate that Mosquitoes fitted with OBOE could adequately locate and mark a target, in turn enabling non-OBOE heavy bombers to place their bomb loads on the markers (the types of markers employed are described later in the chapter). Therefore, a series of ever-larger experimental raids was undertaken to the targets specified below.

31 December–	
1 January 1943	– 2 OBOE Mosquitoes + 8 Lancasters to Düsseldorf
3– 4 January	– 3 OBOE Mosquitoes + 19 Lancasters to Essen
4– 5 January	– 4 OBOE Mosquitoes + 29 Lancasters to Essen
7– 8 January	– 3 OBOE Mosquitoes + 19 Lancasters to Essen
12–13 January	– 4 OBOE Mosquitoes + 55 Lancasters to Essen
13–14 January	– 3 OBOE Mosquitoes + 66 Lancasters to Essen

These raids produced diverse results, for a variety of reasons unrelated to OBOE. For example on the night of 13–14 January, two OBOE Mosquitoes had to return without marking the target, and the markers of the third Mosquito failed to ignite above the clouds. Despite these problems, OBOE clearly proved itself, and the stage was set for the first battle of the Ruhr, due to start on the night of 5–6 March 1943.

Almost concurrently with the OBOE trials, the third aid which was to enhance navigational and hence bombing effectiveness was introduced and began operational trials. This was H2S, a primitive form of airborne ground-scanning radar. It presented the navigator with a flickering indeterminate picture of coastlines, wide rivers and canals, and the outline of large built up areas. These details could be obtained despite cloud and darkness, so that apart from its value for blind marking/bombing, it solved many of the navigation problems. Its efficiency depended largely on a high quality of servicing and the skill of the operator, often in very difficult circumstances. It never achieved anything like OBOE accuracy, and clutter over large conurbations like Berlin and the Ruhr reduced its efficiency markedly. One of its main advantages was that, being totally airborne it had no fixed range, unlike OBOE, and could be used wherever the parent aircraft flew. Consequently, the general policy was to use OBOE over the Ruhr and H2S elsewhere. Unfortunately, in the early days before OBOE caravans were deployed to the continental mainland, Berlin for instance was beyond OBOE range. Despite its limitations, H2S enabled both the Pathfinder Force – of which more later – and Bomber Command as a whole, to operate over enemy territory in the poorest visibility.

To prove its operational worth, H2S went into action on the night of 30–31 January 1943 when a small number of 7 Squadron Stirlings and 35 Squadron

Halifaxes led an attack on Hamburg, Germany's second largest city, where the coastline, the River Elbe, the dock area and Lake Alster provided some outstanding identification landmarks for the H2S operators. These were to prove the city's undoing during the full-scale four raid battle which took place on the nights of 24–25, 27–28, 29–30 July and 2–3 August 1943 under the codename Operation Gomorrah, details of which are recounted in Chapter Five.

A second operational trial was conducted on the night of 2–3 February, when OBOE Mosquitoes and H2S Stirlings of 7 Squadron were deployed to guide and mark Cologne for some 150 bombers, mainly Lancasters and Stirlings carrying a mixture of incendiaries and 4,000 lb HCs. Unfortunately one of the H2S-equipped Stirlings was damaged by a night fighter and crashed in the Netherlands, and the secret equipment fell into German hands. This resulted in the rapid German development of a device known as Naxos which enabled their night fighters to home in to H2S pulses. Consequently, from then on, sets were only switched on for limited periods, to check expected landmarks.

A number of bomber losses were directly attributable to the efficiency of German scientists and the accuracy of German counter-measures in the shape of Naxos. Despite these frustrating setbacks, every Pathfinder aircraft carried H2S by the end of 1943, and later in 1944 most aircraft of the Main Force were similarly equipped.

With the advent of GEE, the role of raid leaders or pathfinders (not to be confused with the professional Pathfinding Force established later) became easier, but no less hazardous. Supported by GEE the raid leaders, normally experienced aircrew from within the Squadrons, flew ahead to illuminate and mark the target for their colleagues. Whereas previously success depended largely on the experience and expertise of individual navigators, GEE at least helped them into the general target area. The task of some of the aircraft in the vanguard was to illumiate and identify the target using 4.5 in Reconnaissance Parachute Flares, then others marked it with incendiaries to provide an aiming point for the followers. Should the target be obscured by cloud cover or ground haze, the leading aircraft dropped the recce flares only as sky markers, in the hope that GEE and a modicum of dead reckoning had brought them to within striking distance of the target. This second technique was far from fruitful. Nevertheless, with better concentrations, results were improving, and with further experience they continued to do so.

When GEE made an appearance in August 1941, proposals were submitted to the Air Ministry suggesting that aircrew of above average professional skill with the ability to consistently find selected targets should form a 'Target Finding Force' within Bomber Command. The instigator was Group Captain S O Bufton who earlier commanded 10 Whitley Squadron in 4 Group. He claimed (quite rightly) that the proposed technique had been developed on a small scale at squadron level, with some success.

The proposal was put to Air Marshal Arthur Harris when he was appointed to Bomber Command in February 1942. At that time he would have none of it, spurning the formation of an élite force. He preferred to keep the experienced crews within their squadrons, hoping that by example all-round standards would be enhanced. Eventually, however, Sir Charles Portal, Chief of the Air Staff, instructed him to form such a force. This he did, somewhat reluctantly, by allocating a number of squadrons from his various Groups manned by the average crewman, rather than selecting those with outstanding ability. Furthermore, not liking the title 'Target Finding Force' he renamed the motley embryo force the 'Pathfinder Force' (PFF), a title which became synonymous with skill, courage and daring of the highest order.

Thus the PFF came into being on 15 August 1942 consisting of 156 Wellington Squadron (Ex 1 Group), 7 Stirling Squadron (Ex 3 Group), 35 Halifax Squadron (Ex 4 Group) and 83 Lancaster Squadron (Ex 5 Group), based at Warboys, Oakington, Gravely and Wyton respectively. They were joined at Wyton by 109 Wellington/Mosquito Squadron, until then a radio countermeasures unit, and in May 1943 by 105 Mosquito Squadron from 2 Group. The PFF was commanded by the newly promoted Group Captain D C T Bennet, also ex-10 Halifax Squadron, who had recently returned to England via Sweden, having been shot down on 27 April whilst attacking the *Tirpitz* in a Norwegian fjord (see Chapter Twelve). As the PFF commitments grew and the size of the force expanded, Bennet's command was raised to Group status on 13 January 1943, and nominated 8 (PFF) Group. Until then it operated as a direct adjunct to Harris's staff at Bomber Command. Bennet, as the first and only Air Officer Commanding 8 (PFF) Group, at last achieved a measure of independence and was promoted Air Commodore and later in the year Air Vice-Marshal. Thus in less than a year he had risen from Wing Commander to Air Vice-Marshal, and never was promotion more deserved.

Donald Bennet, an experienced pilot and noted navigation and wireless specialist, in true Australian fashion was extremely critical of the shortcomings imposed on dedicated aircrews by inadequate navigational and bombing aids. Like many at the sharp end, he recognized that the excellent bombs, then becoming more readily available, were likely to be ineffectual, like their predecessors, unless precisely directed on to targets in great numbers over a short period of time to ensure the bombers were not exposed to the defenders for longer than necessary.

In any event, Bennet soon made his presence felt, hastening the development and production of the new sophisticated navigational and bombing aids, along with a new range of pyrotechnics for illuminating and marking targets. Initially, however, he did not find it easy to meet the prodigious task of ensuring a greater and more accurate concentration of bombs on area targets, or on individual precision targets when the need arose. Pathfinding experience was inadequate, and this was reflected in some inconclusive results. Indeed, the first PFF-led raid on the night of 18–19 August against the North German port of Flensberg went badly wrong, due to atrocious weather and poor visibility – something often endured by the long-suffering Main Force. Nevertheless, the PFF crews soon got a grip on things, making the best use of concentrated on-the-job training. Rudimentary techniques were evolved for blind ground-marking and sky marking, along with visual ground marking using a bombsight when the actual aiming point could be seen, by the light of flares if need be.

Later, these techniques were codenamed Parramatta, Wanganui and Newhaven respectively – the hometowns of the PFF staff in Australia, New Zealand and England.

Having broken much new ground, as far as pathfinding techniques were concerned, during the first five months as something of a cuckoo force in the Bomber Command nest, the fully-fledged 8 (PFF) Group came into its own at the beginning of 1943. It had already led the Main Force squadrons to numerous targets in Germany and Italy, flying some 1,100 sorties and losing 50 aircraft and experienced crews in the process. This was not surprising because the PFF aircraft were particularly vulnerable in the early stages of a raid, before the Main Force saturated the target encouraging the defenders to keep their heads down. Not surprisingly, the slower Wellingtons and Stirlings suffered most.

Nevertheless, even in the absence of the more sophisticated blind bombing aids and target-marking pyrotechnics yet to come, the PFF made a significant contribution to the much improved bomber concentrations and bombing effectiveness. At the same time, the techniques to be used henceforth by PFF 'Illuminators', 'Supporters', 'Backers-up' and 'Primary Visual Markers' were firmly established. 'Supporters', carrying bombs only, were used to make the defenders keep their heads down when the all-important marking was proceeding in the early stages of the attack. 'Backers-up' replenished flares and markers as required, and 'Primary Visual Markers' were called in when aiming points could actually be identified and the bombsight used to drop the markers accurately, rather than blindly.

Up until early 1943 when OBOE and H2S became available, along with an adequate range of type-designed target markers, the PFF was forced to operate with little or no specialist aircraft equipment, other than GEE in conjunction with a range of improvised target markers. Consequently, although they could guide the Main Force to the target area, the limitations of GEE meant that precise aiming points could not always be defined. From 1943 onwards there were three methods of establishing aiming points: seeing them visually, determining where they lay using OBOE or H2S, or a combination of both.

Establishing the location of the target, and if possible precise aiming points, was a prime PFF task. This was all-important to the success of the entire operation. Equally important was the ability of the pathfinders to guide the main bomber force to the target area, to illuminate it when necessary and clearly mark the selected aiming points so that the bomb aimers made the best use of the bomb loads. This demanded the expenditure of large amounts of various pyrotechnics to suit particular purposes. Some were relatively simple, but as the enemy became more adept at laying spoof fires and ground markers, the British countered by developing even more complex target markers.

Before type-designed pyrotechnics became available, the pathfinders used makeshift incendiary target markers to define aiming points pinpointed by 'Illuminators' and 'Finders'. Two in particular, the 250 lb Red Blob and the 2,700 lb Pink Pansy (4,000 lb HC bomb-case adapted) were filled with benzol-rubber-phosphorus mixtures, suitably coloured to stand out amidst other incendiary fires. The Red Blob, in a converted 250 lb incendiary carcass, burned for some considerable time, but the Pink Pansy flash was instantaneous, although it often caused fires. Visible for miles around, the flash was too short for the crews to latch on to, but it did indicate the general target location. The first was dropped by an 83 Squadron Lancaster at Düsseldorf on the night of 10–11 September 1942. Red Blob had already proved its value during a successful attack on Nuremberg 14 days earlier. Successful, that is, in respect of damage done and the accuracy of the marking, but achieved at considerable expense in that 23 of the 159 bombers taking part failed to return, representing a 14.5 per cent loss rate. The Wellingtons suffered most, with a loss rate of 34 per cent, 14 out of 41 failing to return, once again emphasizing the vulnerability of this relatively slow-moving robust aircraft which did such staunch work from 3 September 1939 until October 1943, when the last was phased out of Bomber Command.

During the PFF work-up period, the standard 33 lb 4.5 in Reconnaissance Flare, 33 in long and 4.5 in diameter was used for illumination purposes. Once the candle on its parachute was ejected from the tubular tin-plate container, at the appropriate height selected on the fuze (mechanical /pyrotechnic), it burned for three to four minutes with a yellowish/white flame of 750,000 candlepower. By early 1944, it was supplemented by an 85 lb, 7 in Hooded Flare, 63 × 7 in. The hood focused the light downwards and reduced the dazzle effect on the aircrew inherent in the smaller flare. Both could be dropped in clusters of four and seven respectively, in single clusters or in sticks, whilst a number of the candles fitted with phased delays provided continuity of burning time, with something like 500-600 ft between bunches.

Variations of the 4.5 in flare were introduced for sky-marking purposes. Initially, those with red or green candles were used as route markers, or to define demarcation lines in the target area. To counter enemy decoys, coloured candles were themselves fitted with coloured stars – red with yellow stars, green with yellow stars, red with green stars and green with red stars. The candles burned for about three minutes and the stars were ejected at 20 second intervals, burning for 10 seconds. These were known as Target Flares. Towards the end of 1942, the 4.5 in 28 lb Skymarker Whitedrip Flare made an appearance. It contained a magnesium alloy candle which burned for up to two minutes. As it burned, pieces fell away, giving the appearance of a vertical chain of light in the sky; often the tail stretched for as much as 1,000 ft. The first of these was used on the night of 31 December 1942–1 January 1943, when a 109 Squadron Mosquito lit up the night sky over Düsseldorf guided by OBOE, itself undergoing final operational trials.

The 19 lb, 4.5 in Photographic Flash Bomb (Photoflash) was used throughout most of the war years to determine night bombing results – or lack of them. Detonating at the appropriate height, a quantity of magnesium flash powder produced a one million candlepower flash, timed to coincide with the impact of the accompanying bombs.

A Target Indicator (TI Bomb) introduced in 1943 went one step further. In addition to 40 coloured pyrotechnic candles, it contained a photoflash element so that the accuracy of the aiming points could be established at later inquests into the effectiveness of particular bombing raids. It produced fine results from 29,000 ft when first used during October of that year. It is believed that the record goes to Flight Lieutenant J W Jordan, 105 Mosquito Squadron who, when accompanied by other Mosquitoes on a bombing sortie, snapped Osnabrück from 36,000 ft on the night of 18–19 April 1944.

The TI mentioned was but one of over 40 different types of pyrotechnic device produced. They included both ground and sky markers, but by far the most prolific were the TIs. These bombs were developed during the latter half of 1942 by Dr Coxon and his colleagues at the Ministry of Aircraft Production. Two sizes were produced, 250 and 1,000 lb, the smaller being the most commonly used. The 8 (PFF) Group aircraft rarely used the 1,000 pounder, however the rival 5 Group pathfinders made good use of it in their low-flying Mosquitoes when leading this élite Lancaster bomber Group on special operations. Dr Coxon's main task was to design efficient markers with high light intensity and a range of colours to suit myriad purposes. They also had to defeat enemy counterfeits; the Germans, like ourselves, were adept at producing decoys to hoodwink unwary bomber crews. Indeed, before and after the advent of TIs, many bomb loads were launched on what looked like genuine target markers. For instance, a raid on Magdeburg on the night of 21–22 January 1944 was ruined mainly because many of the 645 bombers dropped their loads on German decoy red and green markers, or on incendiary fires started by early arrivals among the Main Force who beat the PFF to the general area. As sometimes happened, many of the following bomb loads were dropped in open country on what was assumed to be the genuine target, particularly if the decoy markers (or incendiary fires) were sighted from great height in the general location the crews expected to see the real thing.

One of the main needs was for TIs with good ballistic qualities for carriage on the PFF heavies and Mosquitoes. For instance, the Lancaster could carry 20, although it was usually used in mixed loads, supported perhaps by Illuminating Flares or even bombs. The Mosquito carried four. Before type-designed TI Bombs were produced in their own right, redundant 250 lb incendiary cases were employed to fill the gap. Packed with 60 nine-inch coloured candles, the improvised model differed little from the 'real thing'. The 1,000 pounder was type-designed right from the start and contained 200 candles. Both sizes included a three-ounce ejection charge. Functioning was simplicity itself; when the fuze functioned it ignited the bursting charge, which ejected the candles through the tail end. The point at which this occurred depended on the marking technique adopted, ground marking or sky marking. In the case of small precision targets, ejection was timed to take place on impact, whereas the normal practice was to make the candles cascade down from something like 1,500 ft, which gave a candle spread some 60–100 yd diameter on the ground. More often than not, the TIs were released in salvoes of four to provide a tight and distinctive pattern on the aiming point. For sky marking purposes, ejection took place at heights of 9,000 ft or more, depending on the cloud ceiling.

Nose and tail fuzes, like the No 860 and 867 Barometric type, were fitted to

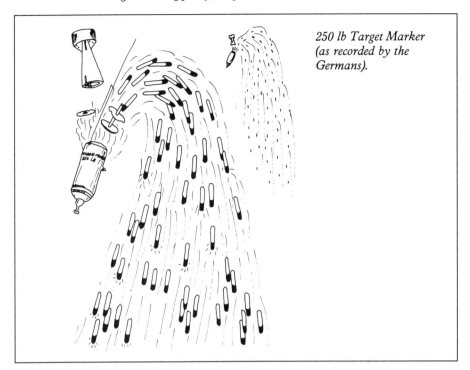

250 lb Target Marker (as recorded by the Germans).

suit particular circumstances, as were a number of mechanical/pyrotechnic delay and clockwork types. The barometric fuzes were more flexible, in that they functioned at a fixed height above the aiming point independent of aircraft height, whereas the others were fitted with pre-selected delays, requiring the pathfinder to fly at the briefed altitude. Neither the TIs nor their fuzes proved absolutely reliable, but considering wartime conditions and the efforts that went into their development, it would be churlish to decry their performance. In any case, salvoes and backers-up covered individual failures.

In early 1943, when Berlin became the first target to be marked by TIs on the night of 16–17 January, the coloured candles, red, green, or yellow, as selected, simply cascaded down burning, and continued to do so on the ground for a total of about three minutes. To obviate marking gaps, candles in later TIs were provided with phased delays to increase overall burning time to 7 or 12 min. These were known as TI Long Burning (TILB) and TI Very Long Burning (TIVLB). Some of the candles in the 1,000 pounder were programmed to burn for a phased period of 20 minutes. A proportion of all candles were fitted with explosive charges which detonated intermittently to deter enemy fire-fighters from dousing them. Other TIs were filled with 210 flash units (red, green or yellow) which initiated coloured flashes at intervals of 1.5 sec during a five minute period. Yet another produced a series of short and long flashes representing morse letters at intervals of 20 seconds over a period of 24 minutes.

A further development was the 250 lb Spotfire (Red, Green, or Yellow). It

Top *250 lb Target Marker fitted with a barometric fuze – recovered in Bonn, 1944.* (Rauschert)

Above *250 lb TI on display, 1988.*

contained a cotton bale saturated in a solution of metallic perchlorate dissolved in alcohol. When initiated, it produced a single spot of colour on the ground for 15-20 minutes. It was first used on the night of 17–18 August 1943, when 571 bombers dropped nearly 2,000 tons of high explosive and incendiary on the German experimental rocket establishment at Peenemünde on the Baltic. Considerable damage was done to the V2 rocket assembly lines, the experimental station and the scientists' living accommodation, setting back development by some months and causing the authorities to disperse much of the work. Normally used as an aiming point for precision targets, the Spotfire was also used for route-marking – it had to be used sparingly, because it also attracted German nightfighters who waited, ready to pounce on the unwary. Indeed, route markers of any sort fell out of favour in 1944.

Three other 250 lb TIs are worthy of mention. The first was the Skymarker Floater, used for the first time on the night of 20–21 January 1944, during the Battle of Berlin. It contained 27 candles (red, green or yellow), each with its own parachute. The contents were ejected at high altitude, above cloud level, where they remained suspended burning for about three minutes. Heavy cloud over Berlin during the winter of 1943–44 practically precluded the use of ground markers, so the PFF crews usually adopted the Wanganui technique (referred to earlier), marking blind on H2S fixes. This technique rarely proved entirely satisfactory over large conurbations like Berlin. To compound the problem the Floater (and illuminating) flares were inclined to drift away from the selected aiming points, in strong winds. Consequently when used that first January night in 1944, there was some doubt whether any bombs actually fell on the city, or at best anywhere inside the outer fringes.

The second and third were developed for daylight use after D-Day (6 June 1944). The first of these contained coloured smoke for battlefield use. Standard TIs were often obscured by smoke and dust, whereas the coloured smoke (yellow, blue or green) rising with the dust and high explosive smoke was easily discernible. The other produced large coloured puffs in the air which were remarkably distinctive and lasted for about two minutes. They were excellent for visual bombing, and also as a guide for blind bombing. This was the case on 11 March 1945, when 32 PFF Mosquitoes, carrying two smoke-puff TIs each, led and marked Essen for the 1,100 bombers which attacked the already derelict town for the very last time in the war.

Many other TI Bombs were produced to meet specific operational requirements, some of which were just permutations of others. However, it would not be practicable to describe each and every type of the comprehensive range, all of which were produced to enhance bombing effectiveness.

As already inferred, not all target marking was done by 8 (PFF) Group or its embryo force, although undoubtedly from mid 1942 to May 1945 it provided the chief raid leaders and markers who did the job from high level. From April 1944 onwards, 5 Group formed its own pathfinding element, and used some revolutionary marking techniques, not always to 8 Group's liking. One of these, called the Controlled Visual Technique, was the dropping of proximity TI bombs and flares to guide Mosquitoes, which then came in to mark the precise aiming point at very low level, perhaps with a Red Spot, backed up with coloured TIs. The Master Bomber, if satisified with the positioning of the various markers, then called in the heavily-loaded 5 Group Lancasters, which were often deployed when a high degree of skill was required.

Group Captain Leonard Cheshire, Commander, 617 Squadron (the Dambusters) led a number of raids, sometimes in a Mosquito, occasionally a Mustang. He marked the Saumur Tunnel on 8–9 June 1944 (see Chapter Six). Later, on the night of 24–25 April 1944, Cheshire acted as Master Bomber when a force of Mosquitoes and Lancasters attacked the marshalling yards in Munich with 8,000 lb HCs and incendiaries. He flew over the yards repeatedly at about 700 ft directing operations and ensuring that the Red Spots and other TIs were accurately placed. During the work-up phase 617, normally a Lancaster Squadron, acquired a small number of Mosquitoes to prove the 5 Group target-marking techniques. Having done so to Sir Arthur Harris's satisfaction, he let the Group have 627 Mosquito Squadron and 83 and 97 Lancaster Squadrons on permanent loan from 8 (PFF) Group. The Lancasters were normally used from higher level to illuminate targets and provide general support to the Mosquitoes by backing up with TIs, or even to bomb, to make the defenders keep their heads down during the initial marking process.

Cheshire, a veteran of a 100 bomber operations starting back in 1940, was awarded the Victoria Cross subsequent to his success as Master Bomber at Munich. The role of Master Bomber ('Master of Ceremonies') became a regular feature in 1944–45; however, it was not an entirely new idea. To some extent Wing Commander Guy Gibson had pioneered the idea over the Ruhr Dams on the night of 16–17 May 1943 (see Chapter Seven). It evolved somewhat more when 8 (PFF) Group first deployed a Master Bomber on the night of 20–21 June 1943, when 97 Squadron Lancasters led, marked and controlled a force of 56 Lancasters from 5 Group who attacked the former Friedrichshaven Zeppelin works on Lake Constance where radar sets for German night fighters and V-1 Flying Bomb components were being manufactured. The Master Bomber on this occasion was Group Captain L C Slee, although due to engine trouble he was forced to hand over to his deputy, Wing Commander G L Gomm of 467 Squadron. The method was really perfected when Group Captain J Searby, 83 (PFF) Squadron led and controlled the first full-scale attack on 17–18 August 1943 when, as already related, the target was Peenemünde. Henceforth the job became firmly established, and most attacks large and small were controlled by a Master Bomber – not always of senior rank, but the most skilled. Success or failure depended on his expertise, and a calm experienced voice passing instructions over the target did much to cool many a fevered brow to ensure that all the expensive machinery and bombs – not to mention exceptionally valuable manpower – were used as effectively as possible.

Bombing raids like that at Peenemünde and other targets mentioned both in this chapter and the next, show in some measure how Bomber Command translated fulsome wording from directives into direct action at the sharp end. Hopefully they also show how organizations, procedures and techniques were progressively introduced to improve bombing effectiveness, after a poor start. This was done by making the best use of technological advances in bombs and pyrotechnics, the load-carrying capacity of aircraft to carry them and above all in the navigational and bomb aiming equipment which ensured the loads were effectively released on the targets selected.

CHAPTER FIVE

STRATEGIC BOMBING – MAJOR ATTACKS AND WEAPONS DEPLOYED

Previous chapters have covered the development of bombs from the small, insignificant, and largely ineffectual, to the massive and efficient high capacity types of up to 12,000 lb capable, in conjunction with incendiaries, of devastating entire cities. Details have also been provided regarding development of strategy, tactics and navigational/bombing aids to enable the weapons of mass destruction to be delivered with considerable accuracy to the intended target. This chapter enlarges on British strategic bombing by providing details of one spectacular raid and three major battles fought over Europe during the last three years of the Second World War. By necessity, the emphasis is placed on the activities of Bomber Command. However, this being so, it should not be forgotten that other Royal Air Force Commands at home and overseas played a significant role in the various bombing campaigns throughout the war years. In comparison with the enormous bomb tonnages expended by Bomber Command, those dropped by other Commands were relatively small. Between them, Coastal and Fighter Commands and the Second Tactical Air Force (2 TAF) expended something like 70,000 tons, whilst the Middle East/Mediterranean and Far East Air Forces dropped some 76,000 and 4,000 tons respectively. With the arrival of Air Marshal Harris at Bomber Command in February 1942, followed by successful raids like those on Lübeck and Rostock during March and April, the Command's reputation improved significantly, indeed its standing was progressively improving. However, he still did not have the resources to mount and maintain a decisive bombing offensive, with at most 400 bombers available daily, some unsuitable for long-range bombing.

At the same time, he was being badgered by certain elements in the Naval Lobby to provide aircraft and aircrew to Coastal Command to do battle against the ever-increasing scourge of the U-boats. Indeed it was being suggested that entire Lancaster Squadrons should be transferred because, it was said, they would be more effectively employed over sea, rather than wasting their effort over Germany.

In the face of such a possibility, by early May 1942, Harris was convinced that he would have to mount a really spectacular series of operations to influence the War Cabinet and the Chiefs of Staff that, given adequate resources, the Command could knock out a single large industrial/commerical target in the course of one night. He was undoubtedly influenced in his thinking by views expressed to Prime Minister Churchill by his Scientific Advisor Lord Cherwell, proposing that a clear policy of mass bombing on 60 German cities could cause inestimable damage. He opined that this might be achieved using 1,600 to 1,800 tons of bombs per city, assuming that 50 per cent at least fell in the target area.

Harris's main problem was to find sufficient bombers to carry such large tonnages, but, with Churchill's tacit blessing, he set about the task. He concluded that it could be done by borrowing aircraft from Coastal and other Home Commands, and using others from his own training resources in 91 and 92 Groups (recently 6 and 7 Groups), and indeed this is where they came from in the main. Next he had to select targets that might be within the capacity of the somewhat motley force he was employing. They had to be such that they were easily identifiable during the full moon perod, or within GEE range. He subtly settled on Hamburg, Germany's second largest city, because not only was it reasonably easy to find, it was also an important centre for repairing and building U-boats, so his choice might appeal to the Admiralty who had operational control over Coastal Command in the U-boat war. In the event of bad weather on the night, he nominated Cologne as the secondary target. Standing on the banks of the River Rhine, and within GEE range, it was also relatively easy to find during a moon period in good weather. As luck would have it, bad weather over Hamburg destined that on the night of 30–31 May 1942, Cologne would be attacked by a force at least twice the size of any previous one, with a bomb-carrying capacity four times that of the largest bombing fleet ever before directed at one objective. This raid, the first of three, was mounted by the Air Marshal to prove that, given sufficient resources the possibility of destroying 60 industrial/commercial centres was no pipe dream; nor was it. This group of attacks, commencing with the raid on Cologne, was to be known as Operation Millenium.

Accounts of the raid on Cologne have already been widely publicized, consequently this narrative will be restricted to a number of salient points perhaps not so well known. Perhaps not surprisingly, in view of the U-boat war, the Admiralty vetoed the use of Coastal Command aircraft on this, the first leg of Operation Millenium. Nevertheless, Harris scraped together the required numbers. The front line operational squadrons of 1, 3, 4 and 5 Groups managed to provide 678, 91 and 92 (Operational Training Unit) Groups provided 365 and Flying Training Command a further four, making in all 1,047 aircraft. Those not from operational squadrons were crewed by instructors, and in some cases students.

All aircraft were ordered to carry the maximum economical load of 4, 30 and 250 lb incendiaries, made up as necessary with high explosive bombs. Where the latter were used to make up loads, large HCs and GPs were to be given preference, but in any event, none were to be less than 500 lb. As many 4 lb

'X' explosive incendiaries as possible were to be carried by aircraft of 3, 4 and 5 Groups, and most by aircraft in the first wave. Because the raid was being carried out in moonlight, no reconnaissance flares were to be dropped.

The bombers were channelled out through a 20-mile wide corridor between Southwold and Orfordness on the East Anglian coast on a direct route to Cologne crossing the least amount of enemy territory. The intention was to attack the target in a period of just 90 min. This was to ensure that the bombers passed over the German air and ground defences in the shortest possible time, to minimize losses. Obviously such a concentration increased the danger of mid-air collision, but it was felt that this would be more than offset by providing less opportunity for the enemy night fighters. It was known that the German Würzburg Radar Centre could deal with only one bomber at a time. Consequently, concentrated streaming and bombing would provide the fighters with fewer targets.

Of the 1,047 bombers that took off (602 Wellingtons, 131 Halifaxes, 88 Stirlings, 79 Hampdens, 73 Lancasters, 46 Manchesters and 28 Whitleys), 40 failed to return (four collided), 19 crashed, and 113 were damaged by flak or fighters. As to the raid itself, all went very much to plan and, as expected, the raiding force approaching Cologne after skirting the heavy flak defences at Mönchen-Gladbach found the Rhine-side city bathed in moonlight. Enemy fighters were active *en route*, and crews began to notice flaming bombers plunging earthwards. The raid was led by the GEE-equipped 1 Group Wellingtons and 3 Group Stirlings which dropped their 4, 30 and 250 lb incendiary markers on the city about 36 min after midnight, in the face of desultory flak. The incendiary fires quickly took hold, as more and more bombers added to what was becoming a raging inferno. As the flak intensified somewhat, following aircraft had no difficulty in identifying the target as they flew in at bombing heights of between 9,000 and 18,000 ft and saw flames rising to hundreds of feet, giving the appearance that Cologne was burning to the ground. By the time the last Lancaster left the city, just after 3 am, some three quarters of an hour after the deadline, it did indeed seem that the whole of the old part of the city was burning from end to end. The damage, by fire in particular, was substantial, although it was not the mortal blow anticipated. Miraculously, only 469 people were killed and just over 5,000 injured. About 12,840 residential buildings were made uninhabitable, about a quarter being totally destroyed. Some 2,560 industrial and commercial premises were devastated and 630 badly damaged. Extensive damage was done to the gas, electricity and telephone systems and to communications in general, which added to the plight of about 45,000 people made homeless. Some 20 per cent of the 700,000 population wisely fled the city temporarily, in the wake of an horrendous night.

It is believed the damage was inflicted by 868 of the bombers who claimed to have attacked the primary target. However, taking into account the aircraft that may have bombed but did not return, or crashed in England before reaching base, it is difficult to say precisely what bomb tonnage fell on Cologne, but it has been recorded as 533 tons of high explosive and 920 tons of incendiary, made up of the bombs tabulated in the table below.

Aircraft type	No of air-craft	Bombs – No carried and overall weight in tons						
		4,000 lb HC	2,000 lb HC	1,000 lb GP	500 lb GP	250 lb INC	30 lb INC	4 lb INC
(a)	*(b)*	*(c)*	*(d)*	*(e)*	*(f)*	*(g)*	*(h)*	*(i)*
Wellington	496	20 (35.7)	—	44 (19.6)	575 (128.3)	38 (4.2)	488 (6.5)	213,250 (380.8)
Halifax	105	—	—	302 (134.8)	—	—	2,504 (33.5)	81,270 (145.1)
Stirling	71	—	32 (28.6)	35 (15.6)	143 (31.9)	—	3,016 (40.4)	61,280 (109.4)
Hampden	71	—	—	—	50 (11.2)	2 (0.2)	—	25,470 (45.5)
Lancaster	67	66 (117.9)	—	—	—	—	112 (1.5)	41,550 (74.2)
Manchester	35	—	—	—	—	—	1,364 (18.3)	25,470 (45.5)
Whitley	23	—	—	—	42 (9.4)	—	32 (0.4)	7,940 (14.2)
Totals	868	86 (153.6)	32 (28.6)	381 (170)	810 (180.8)	40 (4.4)	7,516 (100.6)	456,230 (814.7)

Cologne will forever be associated with the very first 'Thousand' bomber raid but this, although the heaviest so far, was neither its first nor its last attack. It had the dubious honour of another first, when a RNAS pilot, failing to find Zeppelin sheds in the area, dropped some 20 lb Hales bombs on the railway station in October 1914. It had the even more dubious honour on 15–16 May 1940 of being a target on the first night of strategic bombing of German industry during the Second World War. On that night Cologne had suffered its first bombing casualty from a total of over 20,000 to die in the city during the war. Just over a year after Operation Millenium, when the Battle of the Ruhr was at its height, Cologne suffered its worst raid of the war, when over 4,000 people were killed in one night. The city continued to be a target throughout the war, and its last Bomber Command attack occurred on 2 March 1945, just four days before its capture by American troops. The photographs show what effect prolonged bombing can have on a city.

As a continuation of Operation Millenium, Harris mounted two further 'Thousand' bomber raids, one on Essen and the other on Bremen on the nights of 1–2 and 25–26 June 1942 respectively. Neither was anywhere near so successful as that on Cologne. Bombing of Essen lacked concentration and was widespread – bad weather was the main obstacle and GEE was operating at its extreme range. In any event, damage to Essen was slight, although the surrounding towns like Oberhausen, Mülheim and Duisburg received some

Above *Cologne after prolonged bombing. The cathedral is damaged but standing.*

Above *Cologne's road and rail bridge over the Rhine in 1945.*

Below *A mixture of 500 lb MC and GP bombs being pushed under a Lancaster at Linton-on-Ouse for a raid on Cologne, 24 April 1944.*

damage. If for no other reason, the Bremen raid was distinguished because 102
Hudsons and Wellingtons from Coastal Command took part, giving them an
opportunity to dump a fair number of badly-discredited 250 and 500 lb anti-
submarine bombs on the naval orientated city. It also boosted the number of
aircraft taking part to 1,067, 20 more than the Cologne raid. Damage generally
was limited, although comprehensive damage was inflicted on the Focke-Wolf
aircraft plant. Because of a lack of front-line bombers, Harris's intention to
mount similar raids during every full moon period foundered. With tardy production and aircraft wastage, the time when he could again mount a 'Thousand' bomber raid was some time off.

These raids, although spectacular in their size, are more remarkable in that
they proved the advantages of using bomber streams and the technique of concentration. In later years, 500 to 700 aircraft would regularly bomb a target in
less than half an hour. Thus a turning point in tactics was achieved, morale
within Bomber Command was boosted, and the British people felt that they
were fighting back. Air Marshal Sir Arthur Harris earned his nickname
'Bomber' Harris, and the German people had a foretaste of what was yet to
come as Bomber Command grew in strength, experience and weaponry.

However, by Spring 1943, supported by the 8 Group Pathfinder Force (PFF)
and the new navigational/bombing aids H2S and OBOE, together with
something like 850 heavy bombers, 240 Wellingtons and a goodly number of
Mosquitoes, Bomber Harris felt strong enough to mount a sustained offensive
on specific industrial targets. The aircraft available on any particular day did
not increase dramatically but, boosted by the increasing number of 'heavies',
the average bomb tonnage per aircraft certainly did. Back in May 1942 this
amounted to about a ton, but now it was upped to something like two and a
quarter tons. Later the figure rose further, but for the time being, bomb expenditure of 1,000 tons per raid was becoming commonplace.

In any event, Harris decided that he was going to mount his main offensive at
targets in the Ruhr, Hamburg and Berlin, interjected by raids elsewhere. The
series of attacks on these specific targets later became known as the Battles of
the Ruhr, Hamburg and Berlin, and indeed they were just that as the aircrews
battled their way across enemy territory, and sometimes even friendly territory,
often in the most adverse weather conditions and constantly harried by night
fighters and large flak concentrations. Truly, it can be said that almost nightly,
a bloody battle of nerves, courage and technology was fought over Europe by
the protagonist on both sides. The mounting losses suffered by Bomber Command reflect some of the ferocity of these particular battles, but of course give
only a sparse indication of the trauma and suffering of many crews. They survived long periods of intense danger, not to mention the anxiety brought about
by technical failures and extreme cold, compounded by wondering if once
again they would have to face East Anglian, Lincolnshire and Yorkshire
blanket fogs on return after eight hours or so in the dangerous night skies.

Before turning to his planned offensive against the Ruhr, Harris did not completely ignore the terms of the Casablanca directive insisting that high priority
be given to action against the U-boat bases in the French Bay of Biscay ports.

Between mid-January and mid-February 1943, he launched some 2,000 sorties against Lorient and 400 to St Nazaire on 28 February. (These are covered in Chapter Eleven). In any event, Admiral Dönitz, the U-boat Chief, ironically supported Harris's contention that the British bombs then available were not man enough for the substantially built U-boat shelters, when he wrote, 'the towns of St Nazaire and Lorient have been rubbed out ... nothing but the submarine shelters remain.'

In the battles to come, Harris now gave top priority to industrial targets in the Ruhr, and with good reason; this was the largest centre of heavy industry and coal mining in all Europe. Not only did it provide finished products of all kinds, but also the raw materials needed for the production of war material elsewhere in other Ruhr towns, like Duisburg, Oberhausen and Mülheim, all associated with heavy engineering. Essen, one of the prime targets, was the business and commercial centre of the coal and iron industry, and also contained the vast Krupps complex producing iron, steel, coke, tractors, locomotives, mining machinery and above all armaments of every kind. In opening the Ruhr campaign on the night of 5–6 March 1943, Essen was the target he was going to strike hard; it was also to be the first full-scale raid led by OBOE-equipped Mosquitoes. The Main Force aircraft carried loads of one-third high explosive, two-thirds incendiary. Some 30 per cent of the former was fitted with long delay pistols (No 37) and anti-disturbance fuzes (No 845).

The raid was planned to start over Essen at 9.15 p.m. and finish within the hour. Eight PFF OBOE Mosquitoes dropped yellow flares to guide the main force along the route into Essen, and went on to mark the aiming points, the centre of the Krupps complex, with salvoes of red TIs. Meanwhile, 22 heavy PFF aircraft supported by adding to the flare path and supplementing the red TIs with salvoes of greens and bombs to encourage the defenders to keep their heads down. The 412 Main Force aircraft, made up of Wellingtons, Stirlings, Halifaxes and Lancasters, attacked in three waves, briefed to bomb the red TIs or the greens if the reds could not be seen. An area of approximately 160 acres was laid waste and 450 extensively damaged. In the main group of Krupps buildings, 53 workshops were severely damaged and 13 were put out of action permanently. Three coal-mines, a sawmill, a foundry and an important and vital screw works suffered most severely. Some power stations, gasworks, railway and tram depots were gutted, along with many commercial undertakings. In addition, over 5,000 houses were destroyed or seriously damaged. Four bombers fell to flak, and five to fighters. The fate of another five was unknown. The raid was notable not only because it was an OBOE full-scale first, but because it was assessed from photographic evidence that at least 153 bomb loads fell within three miles of the aiming point, by far the most accurate so far, this being some 37 per cent of those which set out. Considering the unpredictability of bomb loads once they left the aircraft, and that they were being released from over three miles up, this was considered a good effort. Undoubtedly target marking was beginning to pay off, and supplemented by GEE (and later G–H), OBOE, H2S and the stabilized automatic bomb sight which replaced the rather primitive Mark IX course-setting type, things looked black for the victims of Harris's night raiders. Raids like this came as a considerable shock to the German leadership and the population as a whole.

By the end of May 1943, 2,070 sorties (five raids) had been despatched to Essen, at a cost of 92 bombers. Goebbels, visiting the city on 5 April, in mid campaign, said, 'The damage is colossal and indeed ghastly, it will take twelve years to repair', and this at a time when there was much more to come, both during this particular phase and later. On the night of 25–26 July (during the Battle of Hamburg) when 704 crews pounded Essen, 368 salvoes fell within three miles of the aiming points (52 per cent). Fire-storms swept through the city, causing more damage than all the previous raids put together. Krupps lost 110 out of 190 workshops. Goebbels wrote in his diary 'The last raid in Essen caused a complete stoppage of production in Krupps. Speer (Minister of Munitions and War Production) is much concerned and worried.'

Earlier, back in May, when the Battle of the Ruhr was reaching a climax, places like Duisburg, Dortmund, and Düsseldorf came in for savage treatment, but none more so than Wüppertal-Barmen on the night of 29–30 when 611 aircraft claimed to have bombed this, the primary target. 475 crews dropped their loads within three miles of the aiming points, 33 failed to return and 71 were damaged. 76 were attacked by night fighters, who claimed 22 victims. The bombs caused general havoc in an area extending to 1,000 acres; 90 per cent of the built-up area was wrecked, and the remainder severely damaged to a lesser or greater degree. 118,000 people were made homeless and about 3,400 were killed. The main railway station was immobilized, two power stations, the

101 Squadron Lancaster dropping a 4,000 lb HC and 30 lb Incendiaries on Duisburg, 14 October 1944. (IWM)

gasworks and waterworks were completely wrecked. Five vital factories and 108 other industrial establishments were severely damaged.

By the end of the Battle of the Ruhr in June 1943, Bomber Command had dropped 34,705 tons of bombs on this vital area. Coupled with 617 Squadron's breaching of the Ruhr dams on the night of 16–17 May (see Chapter Seven), the damage caused serious problems for the industrial chiefs in the region. They had quickly to start dispersing vital industries as far as possible beyond the bombers' reach. Later, in the last quarter of 1944, Bomber Command fought the Second Battle of the Ruhr, dropping 163,000 tons of bombs on 16 towns and cities. Duisburg, for instance, suffered 7,907 tons of high explosive and 1,442 tons of incendiary bombs in 24 hours during 14–15 October, 1,945 bombers taking part. By that time, when Germany's fighter strength had diminished alarmingly (for them), daylight raids were becoming more commonplace. Dortmund, for instance, received 1,584 tons on 29 November 1944. Full details of these attacks during the Second Battle of the Ruhr are shown on Page 124.

One other Ruhr raid is worth mentioning, although it falls between the First and Second Battles. This was the first full-scale attack using the Super GEE navigational equipment (G–H), directed at the Mannesmann Tubular Steel Works in Düsseldorf on the night of 3–4 November 1943.

Turning again to the First Battle of the Ruhr, by the end of June 1943, Harris was beginning to think that enough was enough, and in any case the loss of 628 aircraft during the Battle on this, the best-defended target in Germany, was extremely worrying for him. So now he switched attention to Hamburg in the hope that it would be an 'easier nut to crack', being relatively easy to find on the River Elbe and showing up well on the H2S monitor screens. This apart, not only was it a great general industrial/commercial city, but it also included, as the largest port in Europe, huge port facilities and ship-building yards, many concentrating on U-boat building and repair. Undoubtedly, attacks on these would vastly please the Admiralty who, in conjunction with Royal Air Force Coastal Command had just got the upper hand in the U-boat battle at sea (see Chapter Eleven).

The Battle of Hamburg, prophetically code-named Operation Gomorrah, which opened on the night of 24–25 July 1943, consisted of four night attacks by Bomber Command and two daylight ones by the American Eighth Air Force over a period of ten days. The former launched some 3,000 night sorties, expending 10,000 tons of high explosive and incendiary bombs; the latter flew just over 250 B-17 (Flying Fortress) daylight sorties on 25 and 26 July, dropping just enough bombs to keep going the fires started by the night raiders. The Main Force Lancasters carried maximum loads of 4, 30 and 250 lb incendiaries, in conjunction with 4,000 and 8,000 lb HC bombs. The Wellingtons, Stirlings and Halifaxes carried one-third incendiaries and two-thirds high explosive bombs, including 2,000 and 8,000 lb HCs and many GP bombs fitted with long-delay anti-removal bomb pistols. Many of the incendiary loads contained the maximum number of four lb 'X' incendiaries. In all, some 4,200 of the huge HC bombs and 25,000 high explosive bombs of smaller calibre were

Date	Target	No of bombers	Missing	Tonnages HE	Tonnages Incdy
9–10 OCT	Bochum	404	6	1,717	276
4–5 NOV	Bochum	705	25	2,743	589
6–7 OCT	Dortmund	483	5	1,900	560
29 NOV	Dortmund	291	6	1,370	214
14 OCT	Duisburg	1007	15	3,867	915
14–15 OCT	Duisburg	938	6	4,040	507
30 NOV–1 DEC	Duisburg	553	3	2,030	75
17–18 DEC	Duisburg	486	3	1,430	378
23–24 OCT	Essen	955	8	4,130	409
25 OCT	Essen	740	4	3,200	490
28–29 NOV	Essen	308	—	1,025	175
12–13 DEC	Essen	529	6	2,260	118
6 NOV	Gelsenkirchen	693	5	2,780	490
2–3 DEC	Hagen	465	1	1,540	280
5 DEC	Hamm	91	1	400	58
26 OCT	Leverkusen	102	—	490	22
18 NOV	Munster	444	—	1,590	100
22 OCT	Neuss/Düsseldorf	97	—	450	75
27–28 NOV	Neuss/Düsseldorf	297	1	1,090	105
28–29 NOV	Neuss/Düsseldorf	147	—	624	108
1–2 NOV	Oberhausen	282	6	1,023	163
4 NOV	Solingen	174	4	820	125
5 NOV	Solingen	170	1	770	115

Notes:
1. A total of 16 Ruhr centres were attacked during this period; those not shown above received slightly less than 20,000 tons, making a total tonnage of approximately 66,000 in all.
2. Other attacks were directed at targets outside the Ruhr during this same period.
3. Double dates indicate a night attack, and a single date a day attack.

expended, along with 3,000,000 incendiaries, causing unspeakable damage to people and property alike. Much of Hamburg was shattered by blast or gutted by fire. A fifth of the dock installations were destroyed or seriously damaged, and repair or production of U-boats at the Blohm und Voss shipyard was seriously disrupted by physical damage and a subsequent lack of labour. 183 major factories and 150 industrial plants were devastated, as were some 4,000 smaller commercial concerns. The civil population, however, bore the brunt of the attack; nearly 20,000 multi-storey apartment buildings were destroyed, representing at a conservative estimate a quarter of a million homes. The numbers killed could not be accurately assessed — figures ranged from 40,000 to just under 50,000.

Hamburg's burnt-out residential and industrial areas.

From the word go, on the night of 24–25 July these particular operations certainly lived up to their gruesome codename. That first night 791 Main Force bombers, 347 Lancasters, 246 Halifaxes, 125 Stirlings and 73 Wellingtons dropped 2,284 tons of bombs in less than an hour on to the markers accurately placed by the PFF elements. In itself, target marking was no simple task – the complexity can be appreciated by studying the Marking Instructions for the attack on 24–25 July in Appendix 3. Sir Arthur Harris mounted his second attack on the night of 27–28 July (729 aircraft and 2,326 tons of bombs), the third on 29–30 (707 aircraft and 2,318 tons of bombs) and the fourth and last in this battle on 2–3 August (740 aircraft, tonnage not known).

The first three attacks caused serious damage to the target, but the fourth was far from successful. Of the 740 aircraft despatched, very few reached their target. There was a huge thunderstorm area over Germany, producing atrocious flying conditions. The PFF could not mark the target and the attack was an undoubted failure. Many aircraft turned back, some bombed alternative targets, and only a small amount of scattered bombing of Hamburg took place. Thirty aircraft failed to return, a number of which were lost due to severe icing problems, turbulence, and at least two by lightning strikes.

Despite this and the other more successful attacks, no damage can compare to that stemming from the attack on the night of 27–28 July, which incidentally was Bomber Command's hundredth attack upon the city. On that particular night Hamburg experienced a horrendous and totally unexpected fire-storm, precipitated by the large blast bombs abetted by incendiaries, and to some extent by the prevailing weather conditions. In any event, unfettered raging fires swept tornado-like through a number of city areas that fire brigades could not reach, hampered by road obstructions, unexploded bombs and exploding four lb incendiaries. Suddenly, the fires in the densely-populated Hammerbrook district joined up into one huge inferno which extracted oxygen from surrounding areas to sustain the fires, thus generating storm-force winds. Temperatures in excess of 1,000 degrees centigrade were experienced and many people, lacking oxygen in shelters and elsewhere, died from suffocation, not to mention heat exhaustion and severe burns. Many others survived with dreadful injuries caused during the five hours when the fires grew from nothing to an awesome intensity in the absence of any emergency action which could be taken to quell them.

Brigadier-General F Anderson, Commander American Eighth Air Force, who flew in an 83 Squadron Lancaster to observe Bomber Command's target marking and bombing techniques must have been impressed with what he saw, or perhaps horrified. This was his second night out with the Royal Air Force, for on the night of 25–26 July he had also travelled in a Lancaster of 83 Squadron to observe the bombing of Essen, a raid mounted right in the middle of the Battle of Hamburg, whilst Window was still confusing the German defences.

Sir Arthur Harris lost 87 bombers in the battle, just under three per cent of the force deployed. Losses were largely mitigated by the first use of Window on the 24/25 July. It consisted of metalized strips of paper tied into bundles of

Above *The World Trade Fair Centre at Leipzig used for the construction and repair of Ju 88 night fighters.*

Below *Leipzig, the same site after the Bomber Command raid of 3–4 December 1943.*

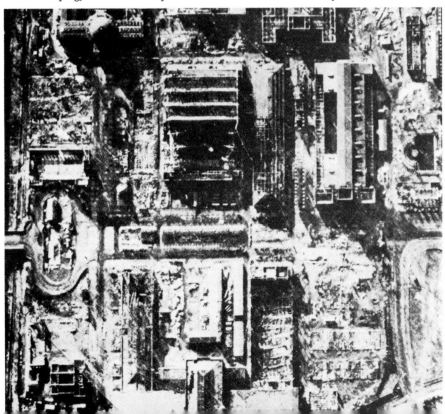

2,000. The contents were laboriously pushed out through the aircraft launching chutes from a point near Heligoland on the inward (to Hamburg) and outward flights, to blanket the German Würzburg ground radars which plotted the bomber stream, and the night fighters' Lichtenstein radars which homed them on to individual bombers. Not surprisingly, the contents of 112,000 bundles (50 tons) certainly caused considerable consternation to ground gunners and night-fighter crews alike, as well as minimizing the bomber losses.

Armed with an ever-increasing heavy bomber force and an extraordinarily wide range of technology and tactics, Bomber Harris (now well-known to one and all, some even referring to him as 'Butch', perhaps unkindly with reference to the large expenditure of men and machines) felt confident that he could inflict a catastrophe on Berlin to match that of Hamburg. Perhaps it would even be a decisive blow against the Nazi regime. He fought the Battle of Berlin for these reasons between 18 November 1943 and the end of March 1944, mounting 16 major attacks (9,100 sorties) on Berlin, interjected by some 11,110 sorties against other cities, among them Nuremburg and Leipzig. During these operations about 1,100 bombers failed to return, and it became clear in the early phases of the Battle that the Stirlings and Halifaxes were not up to the task. Consequently, the Battle of Berlin itself was over-whelmingly fought by Lancasters and Mosquitoes, whilst the others were diverted to targets nearer home.

However, despite the removal of the slower and lower-ceiling aircraft, losses continued to grow thoughout the Battle of Berlin. The first attack on Berlin on the night of 18–19 November resulted in two per cent of the aircraft failing to return, and by the last attack on the 24–25 March 1944 losses had risen to 8.9 per cent. Six nights later the losses at Nuremburg were a staggering 11.9 per cent. The period of the Battle of Berlin was undoubtedly the period when German night fighters were at their peak; rather surprisingly, since it was only four months since the introduction of Window, which had clearly defeated the night fighter guidance system. However, released from the closely-controlled box system, the fighters were now given much wider freedom of action and made full use of it.

For most crews the 1,150 mile round trip to Berlin was something of a nightmare in mid-winter, beset by snow, icing problems and freak winds, on top of the increasing hazards posed by night fighters and flak. However, the direct route to and from Berlin was, as the Battle progressed, far from the norm. To confuse the German defences the bomber force frequently detoured either northwards over Denmark, or southwards between the Ruhr area and Frankfurt, thus adding to the distance travelled and the time the crews were exposed to the natural hazards, but marginally reducing those posed by the enemy. Yet morale stood up well, if somewhat shaken in some instances. However, it never became a major problem such as that experienced at the American Eighth Air Force bases during their terrible losses in 1943. To add to the many other problems, Berlin was beyond OBOE range, and the H2S operators found it particularly difficult to pick out specific locations in the vast city sprawl. The 'Big City', as it was known to the aircrews, was too far inside Germany to sustain high bomber concentrations and, more often than not, the

PFF had to mark blind using Skymarker Flares or TI 'Floaters' above heavy cloud, where they soon drifted out of sight. Red and green ground TI markers were also dropped, just in case some of the Main Force might sight the ground. Due to suspect H2S fixes, compounded by blind target marking, bombing effectiveness never reached the high standard achieved elsewhere.

On the first night of the Battle (18–19 November 1943), 402 heavy bombers dropped 1,590 tons of bombs, mostly 4,000 lb HC 'Cookies' and four lb incendiaries. That same night a further 320 bombers off-loaded 850 tons on Mannheim, the first time two major attacks were delivered on the same night. Frostbite was not uncommon, particularly among the rear gunners, as the crews faced fog, severe icing, and towering cumulo-nimbus cloud. Such a night was 'Black Thursday', 16–17 December 1943, when 25 aircraft failed to return and another 30 crashed in swirling fog on return to their bases. The PFF lost six in this way, ten others crashed, two of which were abandoned when their crews baled out, and No 1 Group lost a further 14. As to the raid itself, Wing-Commander J N Northrop, 83 (PFF) Squadron, a 'backer-up' on this occasion, often recounted how he led 482 Lancasters and dropped his TIs and five 2,000 lb HC bombs into Berlin's raging fires, only to run into fog which reduced visibility to 200 ft at his home base of Wyton. As he landed, with considerable trepidation, another flak-damaged Lancaster flew across his path and crashed into trees on the airfield perimeter; his traumatic experience was by no means unique.

Berlin's heaviest raid took place on the night of 15–16 February 1944, when 771 bombers led by 120 Pathfinders unloaded 2,600 tons of high explosive and incendiaries, at a cost of 43 aircraft. The initial aiming-points were marked with red and green Sky Marker Flares dropped by nine Lancasters and six Halifaxes, and replenished periodically by 'Backers-up', whilst 'Illuminators' did their best to light up the scene with 7 in Hooded Flares for the Main Force, which attacked in five waves, approximately 140 bombers in each. The heavy bombers did not return to Berlin after a final raid on the night of 24/25 March, but the Mosquitoes of Bomber Command's Light Night Striking Force saw to it that the Berliners got little or no rest from then on.

The Battle of Berlin was far from cost effective, and certainly Berlin was not on the point of surrender as had been predicted by Sir Arthur Harris at the beginning of the battle. Nervertheless, 33 per cent of its built-up area, some 6,430 acres, was devastated, particularly in the western sectors of the city. The photographs taken after the Battle of Berlin give an indication of the vast amount of damage done by the combination of high explosives and incendiary bombs. Throughout the war it suffered 45,517 tons of British bombs*, followed closely by Essen (36,420 tons), Cologne (34,711 tons) and Duisburg (30,025 tons). The damage to the city included many industrial plants, for example, on the night of 22–23 November 1943, five factories of the Siemens Group and the Alkett Tank Factory were destroyed together with 20 other largish industrial

---

* In 19 attacks between 23–24 August 1943 and 24–25 March 1944, the bomb loads included approximately 6,800 4,000 lb HC, 53 8,000 lb HC and in excess of five million 4 lb incendiary bombs.

Berlin's burnt-out centre.

premises. Four nights later, German reports indicated the destruction of another 38 war industry factories. Perhaps on the lighter side, the Zoo fencing was breached and hungry leopards, panthers and jaguars roamed the streets, adding to the general confusion, before they were hunted down and shot. On a sadder note, some 9,000 to 10,000 people were killed during Bomber Command's Battle of Berlin, but few in relation to the casualties inflicted during the final Russian ground onslaught in early 1945.

As mentioned earlier, some 11,100 sorties were launched elsewhere during the Battle of Berlin, some no less difficult than Berlin itself, some more so. See table below for details.

Main targets other than Berlin attacked during the Battle of Berlin 18 November 1943–31 March 1944

Date	Target	Aircraft despatched	Percentage missing
18–19 Nov 1943	Mannheim	395	5.8
19–20 Nov	Leverkusen	266	1.9
25–26 Nov	Frankfurt	262	4.6
26–27 Nov	Stuttgart	178	3.4
3– 4 Dec	Leipzig	527	4.6
20–21 Dec	Frankfurt	650	6.3
5– 6 Jan 1944	Stettin	358	4.5
14–15 Jan	Brunswick	498	7.6
21–22 Jan	Magdeburg	648	8.8
19–20 Feb	Leipzig	823	9.5
20–21 Feb	Stuttgart	598	1.5
24–25 Feb	Schweinfurt	734	4.5
25–26 Feb	Augsburg	594	3.6
1– 2 Mar	Stuttgart	557	0.7
15–16 Mar	Stuttgart	863	4.3
18–19 Mar	Frankfurt	846	2.6
22–23 Mar	Frankfurt	816	4.0
26–27 Mar	Essen	705	1.3
30–31 Mar	Nuremburg	795	11.9

The raids on Nuremburg and Leipzig were significant, apart from the heavy damage inflicted, because of the heavy losses suffered by the raiders. The loss of 96 aircraft – 65 Lancasters and 31 Halifaxes – at the former on 30–31 March 1944, and 78 at the latter on 19–20 February exceeded the 73 which failed to return from Berlin on the 24–25 March. Many were claimed by night fighters, which at this stage of the war, as mentioned earlier, were, back in the ascendancy. Perhaps it was no wonder that aircrew morale was somewhat edgy, and many wondered about the wisdom of attacking these far-flung targets, outgunned by the fighters and often operating in the most appalling weather conditions.

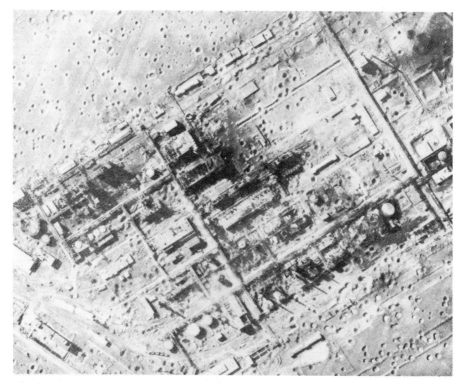

Above *Magdeburg synthetic oil plant, showing its total destruction.*

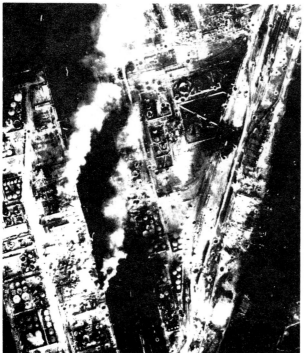

Left *Hamburg oil storage and refineries showing the damage following the Bomber Command attack of 9 April 1945.*

Needless to say Bomber Command directed its attention to many other targets, far too many to describe, and the description of which would add nothing to the story of the weapons dropped. The aircrew got some respite from the long-haul targets when the Command supported the D-day landings and subsequent land battle, necessitating very accurate bombing indeed. Similarly it helped to counter the V-weapon threat during the summer months of 1944.

However, this change of tactics did not last long and by the last quarter of 1944 the Second Battle of the Ruhr was underway and went on to devastate much of Germany's oil resources, so vital to the Luftwaffe and the mobility of the German land forces. The directive issued to Bomber Command in September 1944 made it quite clear that the top priority was the German oil industry, followed by any target connected with communications, whether it be railways, viaducts, canals, marshalling yards or large cities at the conjunction of land or water routes. As recounted in Chapter Four, nearly half the total bomb tonnage dropped by Bomber Command throughout the war was dropped in these last nine months.

By the time Bomber Command called a halt, in the very last days of the war, some 60 towns and cities were cruelly disabled, if not totally destroyed. Subsequently, during interrogation, the German Air Chief, Reichsmarshal Hermann Goering, said 'The Allied bombing attacks on synthetic oil were the most decisive in Germany's defeat.' Similarly, Field Marshal Von Rundstedt, Commander-in-Chief of the German Army admitted that 'Allied strategic bombing behind the German lines was the main factor in Germany's defeat, together with the destruction of German cities.' Thus two German leaders, although agreeing that the bombing campaigns were a decisive factor in Germany's defeat, could not agree which was the most decisive. However, there have been a number of British historians who, with academic hindsight, have taken the view that Bomber Command might have done more to bring about the Third Reich's earlier demise. They, perhaps with some justification, expressed the view that it would have been better to have concentrated more on communications and the dwindling oil stocks earlier, rather than continually pounding devastated urban industrial areas long after the more important industries were dispersed. Perhaps this aspect, along with the controversial bombing of Dresden and certain other cities, was Bomber Command's 'Belgrano'? Nevertheless, there can be little doubt that Sir Arthur Harris faithfully carried out the Churchill-Roosevelt Casablanca directive of 1 January 1943, and set about the progressive destruction of the German military, industrial and economic systems.

Mostly while under Harris's command, Bomber Command despatched 389,809 sorties, dropped 955,044 tons of bombs, of which 35 per cent was directed at industrial and commercial areas. This vast tonnage was made up of the bombs listed on page 135.

It is hoped that this chapter, dealing with some of the largest and heaviest attacks carried out by Bomber Command, together with the information in the foregoing chapters, will provide some of the answers to those questions posed

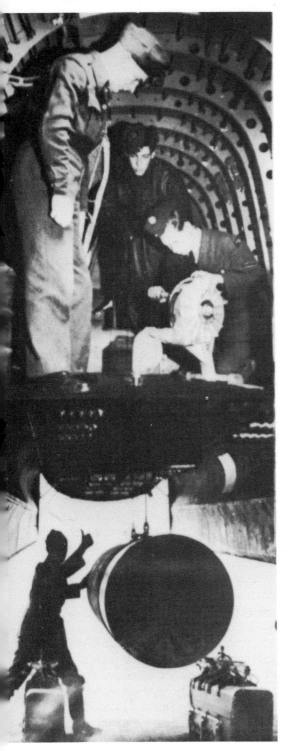

Above *Typical bomb dump scene, 1943. Armourers loading Small Bomb Containers with 4 lb incendiaries.* (IWM)

Left *Composite photograph showing a 4,000 lb HC and Small Bomb Containers (150 4 lb Incendiaries each) being loaded into a 57 Squadron Lancaster at East Kirkby on 26 January 1944.*

Below *German drawing of a Small Bomb Container showing bombs dropping away when electric release unit is freed.*

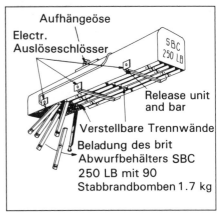

Aufhängeöse

Electr. Auslöseschlösser

SBC 250 LB

Release unit and bar

Verstellbare Trennwände

Beladung des brit Abwurfbehälters SBC 250 LB mit 90 Stabbrandbomben 1.7 kg

Type	Total no	Type	Total no
Fragmentation (F)		High Capacity (HC)	
20 lb	5,000	2,000 lb	28,633
		4,000 lb	68,000
General Purpose		8,000 lb	1,088
(GP)		12,000 lb	193
40 lb	42,939		
250 lb	149,656	Medium Capacity	
500 lb	531,334	(MC)	
1,000 lb	82,164	500 lb	403,000
1,900 lb	2,141	1,000 lb	253,800
4,000 lb	217	4,000 lb	21,000
		12,000 lb Tallboy†	854
Semi-Armour-		22,000 lb Grand	
Piercing (SAP)*		Slam†	41
500 lb	11,600		
		Incendiaries	
Armour-Piercing	Exact figure is not	4 lb	80,000,000
(AP)*	known but less	25 lb	20,000
2,000 lb	than 10,000	30 lb (Phosphorus)	3,000,000
		30 lb 'J'	413,000
		250 lb	7,000

†* The use of these bombs is described in Chapters Six and Eight respectively

in the introduction regarding the effectiveness of the general bombardment bombs and their methods of delivery. The same questions in respect of specialist weapons will be considered in the following chapters.

However, before leaving general bombardment bombs, it is appropriate just briefly to mention some of the people who handled the huge tonnages of bombs involved at dozens of bomber bases. The aircrew, of whom, quite rightly, much has been written both here and elsewhere, were ably supported by thousands of well-motivated and skilled ground personnel. Everyone on a bomber base worked exceedingly hard to support the usual complement of two squadrons, between them putting up 35 to 40 four-engined bombers on a regular basis. None worked harder than the armament staff. East Kirkby, a 5 Group Lancaster station in Lincolnshire was typical of most. There the armament staff laboured at all hours, seven days a week, summer or winter, preparing bomb loads, loading the aircraft, replenishing the bomb dump stocks, servicing the aircraft bomb carriers, turrets and their guns.

During the peak period in 1944–45, it was not unusual to prepare and load 190 tons of bombs per day on a two squadron station, East Kirkby supported 57 and 630 Squadrons. This figure of 190 tons takes no account of load changes occasioned by a change of target at short notice. Incendiary loads produced the greatest work load, many hours being expended in unboxing well-sealed four pounders and restowing them in Small Bomb Containers for carriage on the aircraft. The advent of made-up clusters of incendiaries in 1944 eased that burden

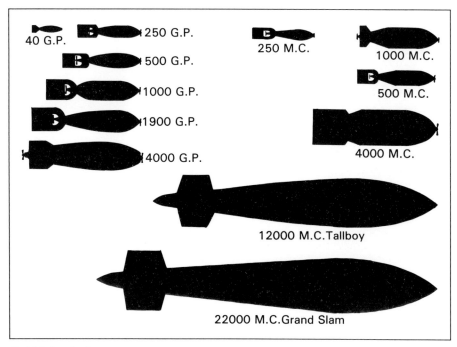

British bomb shapes.

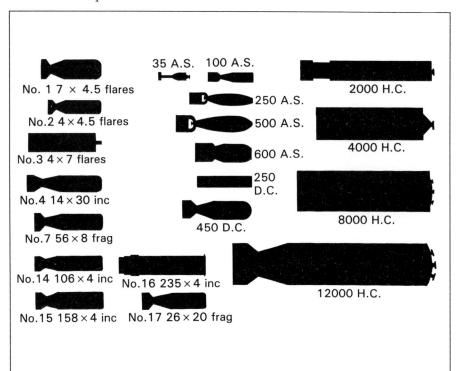

somewhat. Furthermore, no two days were the same. As an example, shown below are the bomb loads of the Lancasters of 57 Squadron for four days in early January 1945:

Date	Target	Load
4/5 Jan	Ladbergen (canal viaduct)	1 × 4,000 lb HC + 16 × 500 lb MC
5/6 Jan	Oil targets	13 × 1,000 lb MC
6/7 Jan	Mining	6 × A Mark I–IV Mines
7/8 Jan	Munich (Area bombing)	1 × 4,000 lb HC + 10 Incendiary clusters (1,060 × 4 lb Incendiaries)

Working hastily among explosives of all shapes and sizes, more often than not against the clock, could be hazardous, and no more so than when high explosive bombs were being fuzed with long delay anti-removal bomb pistols and anti-disturbance fuzes. Not a few armourers lost their lives, as did others around them due to accidents.

Thus it was that the effectiveness of a bomb depended not only upon its design and that of its fuze or pistol, the technology to guide and carry it accurately to its target, but also upon the skill and training of both the aircrew and the ground crew, working as a team.

CHAPTER SIX

EARTHQUAKE BOMBS

As has already been seen, the bombs used during the early years of the Second World War were of the relatively small and often ineffectual General Purpose and Armour Piercing categories. These were later supplemented by a much improved Medium Capacity range and the larger High Capacity blast bombs. By the end of 1943 the latter bombs ranged from 2,000 lb to 12,000 lb, and were extremely efficient destroyers of normal industrial buildings and domestic properties. The damage to a number of German towns and cities was testimony to their power and efficiency. None of these weapons, however, was capable of destroying or even seriously damaging deep underground or heavily-reinforced surface installations.

These shortcomings were foreseen as early as 1940 by at least one person, namely Mr Barnes Wallis, then the Assistant Chief Designer at Vickers Armstrong Ltd (Aircraft) based at Weybridge, Surrey. Between July 1940 and March 1941 he wrote a technical paper entitled '*A Note on a Method of Attacking the Axis Powers*'. This 100 page document, half of it made up of technical appendices, was based on the following premise:

> Modern warfare is entirely dependent upon industry. Industry is dependent upon adequate supplies of power. Power is dependent upon the availability of natural stores of energy such as coal, oil and water. Thus if the current bombing stalemate is to be overcome a method must be found to destroy the stores and sources of energy.

The paper reviewed all current methods of attack against targets such as mines, underground fuel storage, earth dams and the means of distribution of resources. The latter category included subterranean targets, such as bridge and viaduct foundations. He concluded that these pin-point targets were not only difficult to hit, but that current weapons were totally inadequate and the solution demanded a new technique. This he suggested, required the use of a far larger bomb than currently in use, or foreseen, with the capability of penetrating deep into the ground before detonation. The effects of such a bomb would depend upon utilizing the shock waves set up by detonation in the surrounding medium, whether ground or water, to destroy the target at its foundations, rather than relying upon surface destruction, which required a direct hit; even then, success could not be guaranteed. His mathematical calculations led him to recommend the construction of a bomb with sound ballistic properties, weighing ten tons, for release from a height of 40,000 ft. At that time no bomb of that weight had been designed, nor had any aircraft capable of carrying it to that height and with sufficient range to reach targets in Germany been produced or even contemplated.

Wallis's paper was considered by a special committee under the Chairmanship of Sir Henry Tizard, Scientific Adviser to the Chief of Air Staff. This committee of scientists and representatives of both the Air Council and the Ministry of Aircraft Production concluded that there was 'something in the idea', and accepted the general premise of deep penetration followed by earth shock as a sound method of attacking certain targets. However, the Director of Scientific Research (Dr Pye) expressed the view that there was 'no case on scientific grounds in favour of a bomb larger than could be carried on existing aeroplanes'. This opinion, together with the fact that there was no aircraft capable of carrying such a bomb to the required height, led to a recommendation to the Air Staff that no development of the ten ton bomb should be initiated. As far as the Air Ministry was concerned, the possible project was abandoned, for the time being.

Nevertheless it was not entirely forgotten, either by its author or in later years by the Air Ministry. Much of Wallis's paper had dealt with attacks on earth dams, and one of the specific targets referred to was the Möhne Dam. He continued to seek alternative methods of destroying Germany's dams, and in 1942 produced provisional designs for a bouncing bomb. Subsequently in May 1943 the finished product proved successful when both the Möhne and Eder Dams were breached. The story of the development of this particular weapon is outlined in the next chapter.

Concurrent with the final development and deployment of the bouncing bomb, demonstrating, as Mr Wallis had predicted, the effects of underwater pressure, serious consideration was given to the use of deep penetration bombs against a number of specific targets. At an Air Staff meeting held on 8 June 1943 to discuss future air operations, a request was made by the Air Officer Commanding No 5 Group, Bomber Command, that the possibilities of Wallis's deep penetration bomb should be reconsidered, with particular reference to a possible attack on the Rothensee Ship-lift at the junction of the Mitteland Canal and the River Elbe north of Magdeburg. The destruction or crippling of this vital lift would stop river and canal traffic between Berlin and the rest of Germany.

Mr Wallis, who attended the meeting, agreed to produce a report on the estimated penetration and effect of the bomb if released from 22,000 ft. On receipt of the report, the Director of Bomber Operations (DB Ops) undertook to evaluate the weapon's possibilities. Wallis's report was presented to DB Ops 18 days later. Mr Wallis suggested using a 12,000 lb compromise bomb, know-

Eighth-scale Tallboy model used for wind tunnel experiments.

ing full well there was no current aircraft capable of carrying anything larger. The 12,000 lb bomb was a scaled-down version of his original ten ton one.

After some discussion the concept was agreed and Air Staff approval was given for the production of twelve 4,000 lb models for ballistic trials and development of the 12,000 lb bomb. The Controller of Research and Development, Ministry of Aircraft Production was given a requirement on 18 July 1943 to produce twelve 4,000 lb models and 60 12,000 lb bomb cases. Fortunately, as events subsequently proved, but for some reason inexplicable at the time, the Ministry of Aircraft Production placed orders not only for the trial models but also for 100 12,000 lb and 22,000 lb bombs, all with the codename 'Tallboy', the 4,000 lb trial bomb, 12,000 lb and 22,000 lb operational bombs being identified as Tallboy small (S), medium (M) and large (L) respectively. It was clear that since there was a finite production capacity, the concurrent production of both Tallboy (M) and the Tallboy (L) would slow down the production rate of both, and seriously hinder Bomber Command's urgent requirement for 12,000 lb deep penetration bombs. The problem was finally resolved when the Chief of Air Staff, with the approval of the Prime Minister, ordered work to stop on the production of Tallboy (L). At this stage, nine empty cases for the Tallboy (L) had been manufactured. The reason quoted, in addition to the pressing need for the medium bombs, was that specialized aircraft would be required for the larger bombs, which could be used for no other purpose and would only have a range of about 140 miles, within which range there were no known targets.

The order to stop work on the Tallboy (L) was given to the Ministry of Aircraft Production on 30 September 1943, together with an increased production order for the Tallboy (M). With the onset of new commitments, the shelving of the full development and production of the large bomb was in fact only of a temporary nature. The need for a Tallboy (L) was restated in July 1944, when it was given the codename 'Grand Slam'.

The decision having been made, production of the Tallboy (M) went ahead concurrently with the production and testing of the 4,000 lb trial models. After a number of difficulties the final design was accepted. At the end of 1943, of the 325 bombs currently ordered (200 to be manufactured in the United Kingdom and 125 under licence in the United States of America) 10 were completed ready for filling, and it was expected that all would be ready for filling by May 1944.

However, trials using the Tallboy (S) highlighted two existing problems, one being a certain lack of stability in free flight and the other a tendency for the bomb to break up on impact. Both problems were largely overcome, although Tallboy breakups were occasionally experienced later. Stability was vastly improved by providing the four tail fins with a five degree offset to the axis of the light alloy tail, thus causing the bomb to rotate as it fell. To achieve the success expected of it, stability and accurate bomb sighting was of paramount importance with these one-chance weapons. Released from the optimum height of 18,000 ft at an air speed of 169 mph, the bomb took 37 seconds to reach the ground, impacting at just over 1,100 ft per sec (750 mph).

Air Vice-Marshal the Hon. R A Cochrane, Air Officer Commanding No 5 Group, Bomber Command, a man of action who brooked no delay, was delighted that his request for a Tallboy-type bomb, made in June 1943, took less than a year to reach fruition and its first operational target. Bearing in mind that the task involved some complex bomb trials, including that of providing a safe and reliable fuzing system, aircraft loading and release gear, it was indeed a remarkable performance, a credit to all those involved. Like all bombs required to penetrate before detonating, fuzing was effected at the tail end. Three similar pistols were fitted to ensure against possible malfunctions. Delays from 0.025 sec to an hour could be incorporated, the first to form shallow craters, the other, not to harras the enemy bomb disposal men, but to ensure that smoke and debris from the first bombs to fall did not obscure the target from following aircraft.

The first Tallboys to be dropped operationally were deployed on the night of 8-9 June 1944. 617 Squadron, based at Woodhall Spa, Lincolnshire, dropped 19 on a railway tunnel near Saumur on the River Loire between Tours and Angers in France, and only 125 miles south of the newly established Allied beachhead in Normandy. This was a hastily-mounted raid with the aim of blocking the tunnel and preventing the movement of a German tank unit expected to move through the tunnel *en route* to the beachhead. The attack was led by Wing-Commander Leonard Cheshire flying one of the three 627 Squadron Mosquitoes also from Woodhall Spa, who from 100 ft accurately marked the target already illuminated by four flare-carrying Lancasters of 83 Squadron based at Coningsby, Lincolnshire. The Tallboys were delivered with great accuracy from heights between 6,000 and 10,000 ft. The whole target area was pitted with craters, some 85 ft in diameter and 25 ft deep. These were the results expected from 0.025 sec delay fuzing, which caused practically instantaneous detonation on impact. One bomb fell on the tunnel 30 yd from the entrance, piercing the roof, bringing down tons of rock, another blocked the tunnel mouth. The debris took weeks to clear and consequently the tank unit was badly delayed and prevented from taking an active part in the attack upon the Allied bridgehead, then only three days old.

Following this successful attack the Air Staff increased the existing order for 325 Tallboys to 2,000 (1,000 of which would be manufactured under licence in the United States). Vickers Armstrong and the English Steel Corporation carried the main burden of Tallboy production in the United Kingdom. However, increasing the order did not immediately increase the availability of these bombs, and on occasions during late 1944 Bomber Command pressed hard for more as targets became available quicker than the specialist bombs with which to attack them. On one very important occasion, two weeks passed before a sufficient number of Tallboys could be gathered together to attack the German battleship *Tirpitz*.

By the end of 1944, 900 cases had been manufactured, but many were still unfilled. It is not known how many were finally manufactured and filled, but it is known that 854 Tallboys were dropped between June 1944 and April 1945 on such diverse targets as shipping, V-weapon launching and storage sites, submarine pens, bridges, dams, viaducts, aqueducts, oil preparation and storage plants, and finally Hitler's mountain retreat at Berchtesgaden. Some details of these attacks are listed below and others are described in the narrative.

Summary of 12,000 lb MC (Tallboy) attacks

Type of target	No. bombs dropped
Shipping	95
Tunnels	30
Submarine and E-boat pens	199
Viaducts and bridges	160
Dams, canals and aqueducts	89
V-weapon sites	107
Oil storage	26
Misc. targets	148
Total	854

Initially, only 617 Squadron (of dam-busting fame) was equipped with Lancasters capable of carrying the Tallboy, but with the demand for a greater production of the bombs and increase of operational commitments, the Air Staff decided that 9 Squadron based at Bardney, Lincolnshire should supplement 617 on Tallboy-carrying operations. Three more squadrons were equipped with modified aircraft before the end of 1944, but in the event, were not required for Tallboy operations.

In September 1944, the Tallboy (M) was officially named 'Bomb, HE, Aircraft DP, 12,000 lb'. Bomber Command, however, pointed out that DP (deep penetration) also meant in service jargon 'drill pattern', and that in any case the delay fuzing of the Tallboy could be as short as 0.025 seconds, which was practically instantaneous. Thus the description was at times inaccurate, as deep penetration was deliberately prevented. Bomber Command argued that the charge-to-weight ratio was about 50 per cent, and therefore the bomb should be in the MC (medium capacity) category. This was agreed, and the correct nomenclature for the Tallboy (M) was and is 'Bomb, HE, Aircraft, MC, 12,000 lb' although to most people it will always remain the Tallboy.

During June and July 1944 the main Tallboy targets attacked were the V-weapon launching, storage or assembly sites in France at Watten, Wizernes, Siracourt, Mimoyecques and Rilly La Montagne. In all, 107 were dropped, together with other types of bomb. There is little doubt that Tallboys caused comprehensive damage which put a stop to or delayed construction of these sites, thus reducing the number of V-weapons available to attack London and South East England.

Perhaps two examples will adequately demonstrate Tallboy's power and destructiveness. The first concerns the underground assembly and V-1 launching site at Wizernes, a few miles south of St Omer. In two raids, on 24 June and 17 July 1944, Lancasters of 617 Squadron dropped 32 bombs fitted for 11 second delays. On 24 June, one Tallboy caused a landslide, completely blocking an entrance to the underground store, and on the second raid, further landslides were caused, completely blocking the remaining four entrances.

The second example was a 14-bomb attack by 617 Squadron aimed at the Mimoyecques site on 6 July 1944. One bomb exploded alongside the main installation, destroying a corner of the massive concrete structure and forming a crater approximately 35 ft deep and 100 ft in diameter. At the bottom of the crater a cavity extended beneath the platform, making it totally inoperable. Once again, the Squadron was led by Wing Commander Leonard Cheshire. However, the Commander of 5 Group, Bomber Command decided enough was enough, and ordered him to leave the Squadron and rest. He had completed four traumatic tours, completing a hundred operations. The attack on the Mimoyecques site was his last operational flight, and two months later he was awarded the Victoria Cross for his sustained courage and skill, particularly in the art of low-level marking. At the same time his three flight commanders (all survivors of the dam raid), Squadron Leaders JC McCarthy, KL Munro and DJ Shannon, were also ordered to take a well-earned rest.

To a large extent this series of attacks substantiated Barnes Wallis's theories that direct hits rarely breached reinforced concrete, whereas craters from near misses undermined the structures, inflicting serious and difficult-to-repair damage. It must be remembered, however, that the attacks upon the V-weapon sites during June and July 1944 were not restricted to a small number of élite crews carrying a special bomb. For example, on 6 July when the Mimoyecques site was attacked, a total of 551 aircraft–314 Halifaxes, 210 Lancasters, 26 Mosquitoes and 1 Mustang–attacked five V-weapon sites, whilst only 14 of the Lancasters carried Tallboys. Additionally, the V-weapon sites were being con-

Left *The Sorpe Dam. This air photograph shows nine Tallboy craters including some direct hits on the dam crest. Two rows of anti-torpedo nets can be seen running parallel to the wall. Also in view are a number of barrage balloons. The power house and compensating basin, centre left, lay some 200 ft below the dam.*

Below *Tallboy being defuzed at Sorpe Dam on 6 January 1959 by Herr Walter Mitzke and Flight Lieutenant J. M. Waters RAF.*

stantly attacked by the US Eighth Air Force and the British 2nd Tactical Air Force.

Other targets close to Barnes Wallis's heart, the German dams, were attacked with Tallboys during October 1944, with mixed success. On 7 October, 617 Squadron attacked the substantial sluice gates in the Kembs Canal on the Rhine near the Swiss frontier to aid an American Army push across the Rhine. One of the eleven bombs, fitted with a half-hour delay pistol, released from only 600 ft finally breached the gates. A massive torrent poured through the gap and the headwaters of the Rhine dropped so much that barges were left stranded on the mud for many miles. Not only did this cut off a valuable German supply route, but it frustrated a German plan to flood the area ahead of the rapidly-advancing Americans. As frequently happened in Bomber Command, this achievement was won at considerable personal sacrifice. Two Lancasters, skippered by Squadron Leader DRC Wyness and Flight Lieutenant C Howard, were shot down in the target area.

Just over a week later on 15 October, 18 Lancasters, armed with 12 bombs having 11 second and six with half-hour delays attacked the Sorpe Dam from between 13,000 and 15,000 ft. Two direct hits on the substantial dam face and a number of very near misses were photographed, but although it sprang a leak, the dam was not breached. Once again, the Sorpe Dam had defeated the latest weapons that could be thrown at it. On this occasion it defeated Tallboy, and as will be seen in the next chapter, it had failed to succumb to Barnes Wallis's bouncing bombs earlier in 1943. At least one Tallboy failed to detonate, and remarkably was recovered from the foot of the dam in December 1958. Subsequently it was rendered safe by a joint German/Royal Air Force bomb disposal team in January 1959. Its half-hour delay pistols were safely extracted after lurking under water for over 14 years.

This was not, however, the first unexploded Tallboy to be recovered. Indeed as the illustration shows, a German draughtsman, Siegfried Werner, produced an excellent drawing of the bomb for use by German bomb disposal teams, within six weeks of its début. The drawing shows the position of the three No 58 pistols (*Aufschlag-Zunder*) over the detonator in turn fitted in the exploder pocket (*Zünderbuchse für Übertragungsladung*) in close contact with the Torpex. As the bomb impacted, the strikers should have overcome the brass cross-piece and struck the detonator to initiate the bomb–obviously they had failed to do so. Perhaps the detonators were defective, or more likely, the pistol-arming wires were not extracted as the bomb left the aircraft, so that it fell safe, the wires preventing the strikers from operating.

The alternative pistol, No 47, provided for delays of half or one hour, depending upon the thickness of a celluloid disc. As the bomb left the aircraft, a cable pulley wound in the pistol-arming screw, crushing an acetone-filled ampoule and releasing its contents. The acetone softened the celluloid disc, such that after the prescribed time it gave way, releasing a cocked striker which impinged upon the detonator, initiating bomb detonation.

Throughout late 1944 and early 1945, Lancasters of No 5 Group continued to drop Tallboys, in conjuction with other bombs, on to specific targets,

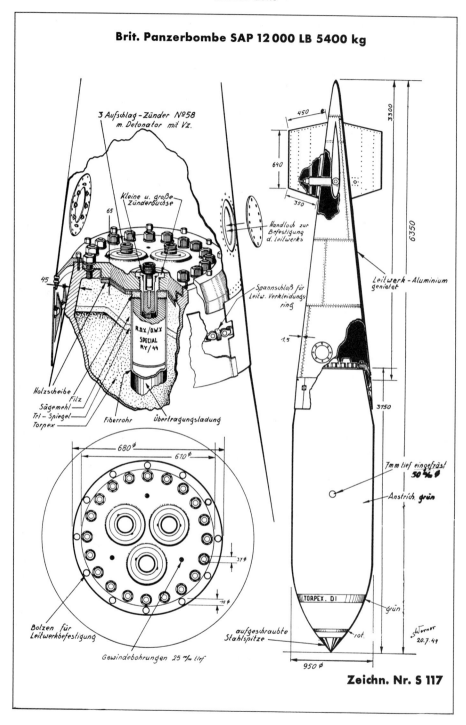

Brit. Panzerbombe SAP 12 000 LB 5400 kg

3 Aufschlag-Zünder No 58
m. Detonator mit Vz.

Kleine u. große
Zünderbüchse

65

Handloch zur
Befestigung
d. Leitwerks

45

Spannschloß für
Leitw. Verkleidungs-
ring

R.D.X./D.W.Y.
SPECIAL
RY/44

Holzscheibe
Filz
Sägemehl
Tri-Spiegel
Torpex

Fiberrohr   Übertragungsladung

Leitwerk-Aluminium
genietet

450

640

350

1,5

3300

6350

3750

680 ⌀
670 ⌀

37 ⌀

75 ⌀

Bolzen für
Leitwerkbefestigung

Gewindebohrungen 25 m/m tief

aufgeschraubte
Stahlspitze

7mm tief eingefräst
50 % ⌀

Anstrich grün

grün

TORPEX DI

grün

rot.

950 ⌀

Werner
20.7.44

Zeichn. Nr. S 117

Bomb, HE 12,000 lb MC (as drawn by the Germans on 20 July 1944).

although as might be expected it was the Tallboy which produced the more devastating results. One significant attack was that carried out against the Ladbergen aqueduct near Munster on the Dortmund-Ems Canal, by 212 Lancasters and 10 Mosquitoes. Six Lancasters of 617 Squadron carried Tallboys, and the remainder 1,000 lb bombs or target markers. The aqueduct was breached in two places, one at least caused by a direct Tallboy hit on the banking. The water flooded out and the canal was completely neutralized. This was a severe blow to the Germans, who were desperately attempting to move U-boat assemblies to their northern shipyards. During the course of this raid, what was thought to be a first was scored by the gunners in a 619 Squadron Lancaster flown by Wing Commander SG Birch, who claimed to have shot down a V-1 flying bomb whilst returning from the raid.

The results claimed for many bombing attacks are often open to considerable argument; nevertheless, unlike many, the neutralization of the Dortmund-Ems Canal was clear for all to see, as were the eminently successful Tallboy attacks directed at the German battleship *Tirpitz* by 9 and 617 Squadrons.

The early attacks upon the 42,900 ton battleship are recounted elsewhere in this book, but it should be remembered that in all she suffered seven major Royal Air Force attacks, eight by the Fleet Air Arm (seven in the Norwegian fjords and one with torpedoes at sea), together with a remarkable assault by Royal Navy 'X' craft. However, it was the 9 and 617 Squadron Tallboys which finally incapacitated and capsized her. Technically she was never sunk, because the water was too shallow to allow complete submersion, but any ship sitting upside down on the bottom of the sea (fjord) bed is most definitely *hors de combat*.

In early September 1944 the *Tirpitz* was at anchor in the Kaa Fjord in Northern Norway, over 1,500 miles from the only viable advanced operational air bases in Northern Scotland, well beyond the range of heavily-loaded Lancaster bombers. However, Yagodnik airfield, on an island in the Dvina River 20 miles south of Archangel in Russia, was only 600 miles from the *Tirpitz's* anchorage. It was therefore decided, with Russia's agreement, that the Tallboy squadrons would launch their attack from there.

Subsequently, on 11 September 1944, 38 Lancasters of 9 and 617 Squadrons and a Mosquito for weather reconnaissance set out to fly to Yagodnik. One Lancaster aborted with technical defects and returned to base. In appalling weather conditions six crash-landed in Russia, but without serious injury to the crews. Despite many servicing problems 28 Lancasters set off on 15 September 1944 to seek out their prey; 20 carried Tallboys, one a camera crew, and the remainder were carrying 'Johnny Walker' bombs. The latter, described in some detail elsewhere in the book, were to prove ineffectual, so no further mention will be made of their contribution in this raid.

On arrival in the target area, the *Tirpitz* was found to be partially obscured by a dense black smokescreen, consequently only 15 Tallboys were released, from heights between 11,350 and 17,500 ft. No serious damage to the *Tirpitz* was claimed or observed. No aircraft were lost, but whilst returning to Lossiemouth in Scotland on 17 September, one aircraft, a 617 Squadron Lancaster skippered by Flying Officer F Levy, crashed in Norway with 11 men on board.

Unknown to the attackers or the Air Staff in the United Kingdom, the *Tirpitz* had in fact been very seriously damaged. One of the Tallboys had hit her bows, almost completely destroying them from the stem to the forward gun turret. The impact and shock waves had also crippled her main engines. It was later learnt that the Germans estimated that repairs, if they were carried out without interruption, would take at least nine months. Whose bomb actually caused the damage is open to question, but an independent witness claimed that a 'hit' had been scored by Flying Officer W Daniel, the Canadian bomb-aimer with Wing Commander W Tait commanding 617 Squadron. However, other reports credit Squadron Leader D Melrose and crew of 9 Squadron with the vital hit. Inter-squadron rivalry apart, the important thing was that the *Tirpitz* was crippled, but nobody in the United Kingdom realized it.

Following a conference in Norway on 20 September 1944, at which the German Commander-in-Chief and Naval War Staff were present, it was decided that it was no long possible to make the *Tirpitz* ready for active sea-going operations. It was further decided that, as far as possible, she should be moved to the area west of Lyngenfjord, for mooring in shallow water, and employed as a floating gun battery. Accordingly the stricken vessel was moved on 15 October 1944 to a berth three miles west of Tromsö, Norway's northernmost port, on the 70th parallel. She was protected against underwater attack and aerial torpedoes by a double net barrage, supplemented by shore anti-aircraft gun and smokescreen units transferred from Kaa Fjord. In anticipation of further bombing attacks, dredgers were used to move 14,000 cubic metres (10,704 cubic yards) of fill to build up the fjord bottom under the *Tirpitz's* hull to ensure that if the worst came to the worst, their 'unsinkable' ship would still be usable as a gun platform.

Still unaware of the *Tirpitz's* condition, Prime Minister Churchill, the General Staff, and the Admiralty still considered her a major menace, and urged Bomber Command to 'get on with the job'. Fortunately, the battleship now lay within range of the Scottish air base, so Lancasters fitted with more powerful Merlin 34 engines, special overload fuel tanks capable of carrying 2,406 gallons, and stripped of the mid upper gun turrets and excess armour plating could just make the 2,250 mile round trip. All these modifications took time, but the aircraft were ready to renew the onslaught on 29 October 1944. Thirty-seven Lancasters took part, 9 and 617 Squadrons each providing 18 aircraft whilst a 463 (Australian) Squadron Lancaster carried a film crew to record events.

Unfortunately, contrary to optimistic weather forecasts the *Tirpitz* was found to be obscured by thick cloud. The bombs were dropped on the estimated position of the battleship. No hits were claimed; however, the Germans later admitted some minor damage from a near miss and congratulated themselves on driving off a determined attack with no casualties to themselves – something of a morale booster for a crew understandably suffering considerable stress and strain. One Lancaster was damaged by anti-aircraft fire and force-landed in Sweden. None of its crew was seriously hurt, and they later returned home.

Above *A view of the stricken* Tirpitz *from the stern.*

Right *Another view of the massive giant, capsized and sitting on the bottom.*

The final blow was struck 14 days later, on Sunday 12 November 1944 when 29 Tallboy carrying Lancasters of 9 and 617 Squadrons, accompanied by the camera-carrying Lancaster of 463 (Australian) Squadron, set out once again from Lossiemouth. Taking off shortly after 3 a.m. they arrived in the target area just after 9.30 a.m. (the time of sunrise in those northern latitudes at that time of the year).

The aircraft were flying at approximately 14,000 ft in an open formation, enjoying excellent visibility, so good indeed that according to a contemporary German report the *Tirpitz* opened fire with its forward main armament at 9.40 a.m. at a range of 13.1 miles. This was followed up shortly after by its secondary armament and heavy anti-aircraft weapons, supplemented by the shore installations. For some reason no smoke-screen was deployed and the fighter aircraft requested by the *Tirpitz* as early as 8.25 a.m. failed to appear. Despite heavy anti-aircraft fire, the Squadrons pressed on with their attack. In just five minutes, 18 Tallboys were dropped, 16 falling very close to the ship, 11 at least within the anti-torpedo netting.

Subsequent German reports indicated that two direct hits were observed on the port side, one on the aircraft catapult and another abreast 'B' turret, causing the battleship to list some 15 or 20 degress to port. At 9.45 a.m. the *Tirpitz*'s commander Captain Weber ordered the abandonment of all lower decks. By 9.50 a.m. the huge vessel had a list of 70 degrees, when suddenly a violent explosion blew 'C' turret, weighing in excess of 700 tons, overboard. No direct hits were reported near 'C' turret, so the Germans supposed that the raging fires below deck had reached the explosives stored in the magazine beneath the turret, so causing the massive explosion. Within two minutes the ship capsized at an angle of about 135 degrees, entombing many of her crew. The captain and a number of senior officers died in the armoured control room, unable to open the blast buckled doors. Out of a total complement of 1,600 men, approximately 100 were ashore, 800, (many seriously injured) were rescued, and 700 perished. One 9 Squadron Lancaster was seriously damaged, but just managed to land safely in Sweden.

During the latter days of the war what remained of the German Fleet played little more than a passive role, nevertheless the Royal Air Force and the Royal Navy vigorously continued to seek and destroy enemy warships wherever they could be found. An example of this policy related to the last surviving pocket-battleship, the *Lützow* (alias the *Deutschland*), which was detected at Swinemünde on the Baltic coast. Eighteen Lancasters of 617 Squadron attacked her on 16 April 1945, with a mixture of Tallboys and 1,000 lb bombs. She was straddled by three Tallboys and sank at her moorings in shallow water, her bottom torn out. During this attack, concentrated anti-aircraft fire struck the Lancaster flown by Squadron Leader J Powell. It lost a wing and went down trailing flames; only one parachute was seen. This aircraft was the last total loss suffered by the Squadron, although on this occasion 15 aircraft received varying degrees of damage. After hasty repairs 617 Squadron plastered the island fortress gun emplacements of Heligoland on two successive days with a mixture of Tallboys and Grand Slams.

Heligoland before and after being hit with a mixture of Tallboys and Grand Slams.

Appropriately the squadron's final attack of the Second World War, and the final operational use of Tallboys, was launched against Hitler's Bavarian retreat at Berchtesgaden on 25 April in the final days of the Third Reich. On that day 359 Lancasters and 16 Mosquitoes of Nos 1, 5 and 8 Groups, Bomber Command attacked the 'Eagle's Nest' chalet and the local SS guards barracks. Among this fleet of aircraft were 16 Lancasters of 617 Squadron, four carrying Tallboys and the remainder 1,000 lb bombs. Although Hitler was not at home, the attack was a success, the SS Barracks was destroyed and houses owned by Hitler, Goering and Martin Bormann all received direct hits. Whether this final fling was cost effective or necessary will never be resolved.

During the last year of the war, what of the 22,000 lb bomb, the Tallboy (L) or Grand Slam referred to earlier? As with the Tallboy (M), the introduction and production of the Grand Slam was initially hindered by misunderstanding. After the Normandy invasion in June 1944 opportunities quickly presented themselves to inspect some of the massive concrete structures built on the Cherbourg peninsula. Examination of these targets made it clear that the Tallboy was not powerful enough to destroy this type of target, particularly with the 18,000 ft limit of operational height. The Commander-in-Chief Bomber Command (Air Marshal Sir Arthur Harris) began to press the Ministry of Aircraft Production to produce some large Tallboys (Grand Slams). The Chief Executive of the Ministry of Aircraft Production wrote to the Chief of Air Staff on 14 July 1944, stating that he was under pressure from 'Bomber' Harris and felt that he could produce 50 of the large bombs per month without detriment to Tallboy (M) production. At the Chief of Staff's meeting the following day it was agreed that a production run of 600 should start as soon as possible, 400 in the United Kingdom and 200 in the United States. It was also agreed that 50 Lancaster aircraft should be converted to carry the bomb. This conversion would eventually involve strengthening the airframe, fitting more powerful Merlin 24 engines, and in an effort to reduce weight the removal of all unnecessary equipment. This included the removal of the mid upper gun turret, one of the two guns from the nose turret, two of four from the rear turret, and of armour plate beneath the pilot and in some cases that of wireless sets and the wireless operator.

However, immediately after the Chief of Staff's meeting, the Air Staff reconsidered the matter in the light of the War Cabinet forecast that the European war would be over by the end of the year (i.e. December 1944), and cancelled all new bomb production and aircraft modifications. This brought an immediate response from the British Staff in Washington who, having used all their influence to obtain agreement from the Americans to manufacture 200 Grand Slam cases, were now required to cancel the order. They suggested that an order for perhaps 50 bomb cases might alleviate the position. After some debate it was agreed that 50 bombs of US manufacture and 10 modified aircraft should hastily be provided. This decision was soon overtaken by events, and not only did it seem that the war in Europe was likely to be prolonged beyond December, but more and more targets likely to be vulnerable to Grand Slam were being identified. Consequently the Chief of Air Staff (Sir Charles Portal)

Above *A temporary crossing over the centre spans of Arnsberg railway viaduct in June 1945. Chunks of the original spans destroyed by the Tallboy/Grand Slam attack of 19 March 1945 can be seen lying in the River Rühr below.*

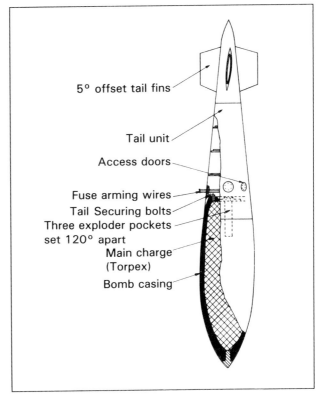

5° offset tail fins

Tail unit

Access doors

Fuse arming wires

Tail Securing bolts

Three exploder pockets set 120° apart

Main charge (Torpex)

Bomb casing

Right *Bomb HE 22,000 lb MC.*

agreed on 18 October 1944 that the original production programme of 600 bombs and 50 modified aircraft should be implemented. Between August and October, development work on the original nine bombs manufactured in 1943 progressed, and one aircraft had been modified to carry a Grand Slam.

By November the first inert-filled Grand Slam was dropped from a height of 20,000 ft, resulting in minor modifications to other bombs but otherwise a successful drop. The first live Grand Slam was released over Ashley Walk range in Hampshire on 13 March 1945 from a height of 16,000 ft, producing a crater 124 ft in diameter and 30 ft deep. On the very next day Squadron Leader C C Calder of 617 Squadron carried one over Germany and dropped it on the Bielefeld viaducts from 16,000 ft.

These viaducts had been attacked several times previously, but until the advent of Tallboy and Grand Slam, with no significant success. Two piers supporting one viaduct were shattered by 18 near misses on 22 February 1945. On 14 March, along with Squadron Leader Calder and his Grand Slam, were 13 Tallboy-carrying Lancasters of 617 Squadron, together with a pathfinder Mosquito. To say the least, the results were spectacular. Seven spans of each viaduct were destroyed. (The whole viaduct consisted of two parallel viaducts, each carrying a main railway line.) Five piers of one viaduct were completely destroyed, and only the stumps of five piers of the other viaduct remained in the gap. Later the German authorities estimated that 20,000 tons of concrete and masonry had fallen.

A number of Grand Slams were deployed against U-boat pens and other reinforced concrete structures. These attacks are discussed elsewhere, but of the 41 dropped during its comparatively short lifespan, some of the most effective damage was inflicted, in conjunction with the Tallboy, when used against vital viaducts and bridges previously immune to air attack. Seven of these were destroyed in the course of ten days during March 1945, virtually paralysing German communication links. In addition to the Bielefeld viaducts these were:

Date Attacked	Target	Tallboys dropped	Grand Slams dropped
19 March 1945	Arnsberg viaduct	12	6
21 March 1945	Arbegen railway bridge	17	2
22 March 1945	Nienburg railway bridge	12	5
22 March 1945	Altenbeken viaduct	16	–
23 March 1945	Bad Oeynhausen railway bridge	10	–
23 March 1945	Bremen railway bridge	11	5

From mid March, the 'earthquake' bomb onslaught reached its peak. Both 9 and 617 Squadrons were heavily committed, the former using Tallboys only and the latter a mixture of Tallboys and Grand Slams. Not all attacks were immediately successful but in the end most of the targets selected succumbed to Tallboy and its big brother.

Sixteen Lancasters of 9 and 617 Squadrons attacked the Arnsberg viaduct on 15 March 1945, dropping six Tallboys and two Grand Slams, but visibility was poor and the viaduct was temporarily reprieved. Its luck ran out four days later when six Grand Slams and twelve Tallboys caused two spans to collapse and the abutments to be seriously undermined. Two days later, twenty Lancasters of 617 Squadron crippled the railway bridge at Arbergen just outside Bremen. Two spans extending to 180 ft were breached; one of these was completely destroyed and the other one dislodged from its piers.

The Altenbeken viaduct and the railway bridges at Bad Oeynhausen and Bremen suffered a very similar fate. If not completely paralysed, road and rail communications in this part of Germany were certainly badly disrupted. During post-war interrogation, Herr Kehrl, head of the German Economic Planning Department, admitted that 'Chaotic communications were responsible for 90 per cent of the decline in industrial production during the final three months of the conflict.' The 'earthquake' bombs were not entirely responsible for this disruption, many other types helped, but there is little doubt that they played a significant role in that part of North West Germany which later became the British Zone of Occupation.

Subsequently in April 1945 the Grand Slam was understandably formally approved for Royal Air Force use. Later still its name was changed to 'Bomb, HE, Aircraft, MC, 22,000 lb', those of British manufacture being nominated the Mark I, and the American counterpart the Mark II.

The vital statistics of the Tallboy and the Grand Slam were:

	Tallboy	**Grand Slam**
Weight	12,000 lb	22,000 lb
Overall length	21 ft	25 ft 5 in
Maximum diameter	38 in	46 in
Case thickness:		
(a) Near tail	1.25 in	1.75 in
(b) Near nose	4.1 in	7.75 in
Weight of explosive	5,200 lb	9,135 lb
Type of explosive	Torpex	Torpex

Size apart, the bombs looked identical, the perfectly streamlined bodies being manufactured of high-quality steel with specially hardened nose portions in the

Above *Example of a Tallboy which broke up on impact. Tail and base plate are missing clearly showing the HE filling and the three exploders.*

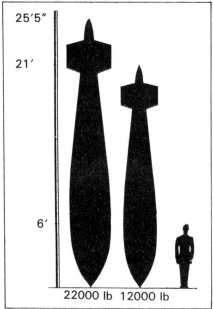

25'5"

21'

6'

22000 lb   12000 lb

Left *Relative sizes of Grand Slam and Tallboy.*

Right *Another Tallboy which broke up as it penetrated a massive concrete structure.*

form of a plug. To counter some of the impact breakups experienced with the smaller bomb, the casing of the Grand Slam was thickened and a number were subjected to a special oil-hardening process to ensure additional robustness.

Both bombs amply justified Mr Barnes Wallis's revolutionary ideas for huge bombs capable of tackling massive and otherwise invulnerable targets. However the 22,000 lb Grand Slam was never used to destroy or cripple subterranean targets from 40,000 ft, so one can only conjecture on how well it might have performed had it been used as its designer had intended.

Despite height limitations, one or both of the bombs performed effectively against capital ships, viaducts, bridges, canals, tunnels and reinforced concrete roofs up to about 10 ft thick. They were less successful when faced with 23 ft of reinforced concrete, which was often used to protect U-boat pens. Nevertheless, even then occasional successes were achieved, not so much by penetration, but by the shock waves induced in the concrete.

Tallboy in particular suffered a number of break-ups on impact before the fuze could detonate the explosive, or occasionally detonated prematurely due to the sensitivity of the torpex filling. Near misses of up to about 40 ft were extremely effective in breaching bridges, viaducts, canals and sluice gates. Not only did they destroy spans and embankments, they also shattered the foundations of the piers, making repairs that much more difficult. For instance, a near miss of 60 ft was sufficient to collapse the railway bridge at Bad Oeynhausen by the earthquake effect.

Clearly, if the war in Europe had continued beyond May 1945 there would have been a need to provide Grand Slams with even stronger bodies to tackle thicker reinforced concrete, without reducing the explosive content but perhaps desensitising it to some degree. Tallboy would have required similar treatment, because Grand Slam was likely to overkill some of the less substantial targets.

Among the many bombs produced during the Second World War, it can be said with certainty that, atom bombs apart, the Tallboy and Grand Slam were the most effective air-dropped weapons deployed. They achieved what other bombs, even in considerable numbers, could not, However, they would have been useless without the ruggedness of the Lancaster bombers and the skill of their crews. Both bombs were expensive to produce, but more than repaid their cost, and some would say they were worth their weight in gold.

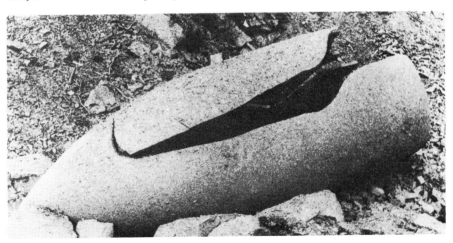

CHAPTER SEVEN

BOUNCING BOMBS, ATTACK ON THE DAMS

Enemy dams, and particularly those in Germany like the Möhne, stood high on the Air Ministry priority target list from the very first days of the Second World War. As early as 1939 Sir William Halcrow, a Member of the Institute of Civil Engineers, was asked by the Air Ministry to prepare a technical report on the construction of the Möhne Dam. Regrettably the bombs then available to the Royal Air Force were totally impotent against the massive structures which dammed Westphalian waters. Suggestions for deploying airborne torpedoes, sea mines and a number of unorthodox weapons were all considerered and rejected, because they lacked either punch or operational practicability.

The water pressure on the face of a gravity dam tends to support and close cracks, rather than weaken the structure; consequently, nothing less than punching a large hole through the ramparts would suffice. It was generally agreed that gravity dams such as the Möhne and Eder, along with earth and rubble types like the Sorpe, were exceptionally hard nuts to crack. The latter consisted of two sloping earth and rubble banks with a vertical concrete core not susceptible to direct hits or shock waves – practically impossible to shift. The other two, and more like them, were massive masonry or concrete structures with a broad base and a high wall, triangular in cross-section to increase strength. However, provided the wall could be seriously ruptured by shock waves emanating from an underwater detonation, there was every chance that it could be overwhelmed by inherent water pressure.

The vexing problem was how to accurately place sufficient explosive to destroy a gravity dam and at least cause serious leakages in the earth type, necessitating emptying its reservoir to effect repairs.

The prizes were most attractive if this could be accomplished. All the dams in southern Westphalia east of the Ruhr industrial area supported hydro-electric schemes and provided water, an essential commodity for the industrial Ruhr. This area consumed nearly a quarter of all Germany's water reserves, and the Möhne provided by far the largest proportion. Consequently, in selecting targets, the Möhne Dam was given priority for destruction. Additionally the Eder Dam helped to maintain the navigable waters in the River Weser and the Mittelland Canal. Enormous physical and morale damage could be inflicted on the German war effort if a number of these dams were simultaneously breached, causing initially a surfeit of unwanted floodwater, and then not enough to support industrial output or civilian needs. For these reasons, the need to find a viable means of destroying the dams at the earliest opportunity became increasingly pressing.

As was seen in the previous chapter, Mr Barnes Wallis, working independently of the Air Ministry, produced some novel ideas for tackling massive invulnerable surface, underground or underwater targets. He had the German dams very much in mind, having read Sir William Halcrow's report and original German reports on the construction of the dams. These reports were all held by the Institute of Civil Engineers. Wallis's initial proposal failed to find favour, because the size of his 'earthquake' bomb and the height from which it had to be dropped were far in excess of current or proposed capabilities of the Royal Air Force.

However, he was not a man easily deflected from what he opined to be a worthwhile idea, and indeed his ultimate successes bear adequate testimony to his doggedness, shrewdness and above all his technical brilliance. In any event he approached Dr Pye, the Director of Scientific Research (DSR), who was impressed by his ideas and authorized the use of the Road Research Laboratory for a series of trials to determine the effect of varying charges against or near the wall of a gravity-type dam. In furtherance of the Wallis proposals, an informal committee entitled the Air Attack on Dams Committee (AAD) was formed on 10 March 1941 to consider and co-ordinate further development with the DSR as chairman.

The trials were complex, involving numerous ideas, all of which were faithfully recorded in the Road Research Laboratory Reports of 1940-43. One noteworthy trial involved the construction of a one-fiftieth scale model of the Möhne Dam. This entailed the manufacture of hundreds of cement blocks, each measuring $0.4 \times 0.3 \times 0.2$ in and laying them in courses of fine cement mortar with a thin coating of rendering. The subsequent trials on the miniature dam, supplemented by a full-size trial against the redundant Nant-y-Gro Dam in Radnorshire, Wales, confirmed that the Möhne Dam should probably be breached if about 6,500 lb of high explosive were detonated hard against the dam wall. It also indicated that a charge detonated 50 ft from the wall would require something like 30,000 lb of high explosive.

The prospect of providing a bomb to contain the latter 'near miss' amount of explosive was for all practicable purposes entirely out of the question, so the main problem was how to plant the smaller amount right up against the wall face. Fortunately, Mr Wallis was already directing his inventive brain to a possible solution.

In April 1942, he published a revised proposal calling for a spherical bomb which could be dropped from very low level some 400-500 yds from the dam face, to bounce its way across the surface to the wall, where it would sink and detonate at a depth of 30 ft. He specified that the sphere should be back spun before release, thus extending its range and momentum, whilst ensuring it would rebound from the wall and crawl down the face before detonating. The extra speed would also help the sphere tear its way through anti-torpedo nets, if necessary.

This paper was first seen by his very good friend Professor Blackett, Scientific Adviser to the Board of Admiralty, who was suitably impressed. He passed the paper to Sir Henry Tizard, Scientific Adviser to the Chief of the Air Staff, who within 48 hours arranged for the Shipping Research Tanks at the National Physical Laboratory, Teddington to be used for further trials. In anticipation, Mr Wallis constructed a number of two-inch model mines, a model dam and ship's hull, along with an apparatus for projecting the mines to simulate an aircraft launch. The comprehensive resources at Teddington enabled him to light and film the miniature mine's trajectory and behaviour after it struck the dam wall. In each of the early experiments the mine hit the dam wall and ran down it, before its simulated detonation just as predicted. As determined by the earlier Road Research Laboratory trials, this was vitally important, because to be effective the mine had to be in contact with the dam wall at the moment of detonation.

A formal demonstration was held at Teddington on 21 June 1942 attended by service and scientific staff of the Air Ministry, Admiralty and Ministry of Aircraft Production. Fortunately at about the same time the more destructive explosive Torpex was supplanting Amatol, so that the desired effect could be achieved with less explosive, consequently the overall size of the mine could be reduced. At about the same time the Admiralty found it had a need for a Wallis type bomb/mine, but smaller, to tackle enemy warships, such as the *Tirpitz* then hiding in the Norwegian fjords. Fortuitously, too, the Royal Air Force now had Lancasters capable of carrying the larger mine well beyond the Ruhr to the dams.

All present on the 21st were most impressed with the mine's potential, and approval was readily given for full-scale live trials. Thus, theories were turned into action, which eventually led to the development of the 9,150 lb 'bouncing bomb', codenamed 'Upkeep', and the 1,280 lb spherical mine 'Highball'. The former was more correctly a mine, but became colloquially known as a bomb, and as such was designed specifically for use against the German dams. The saga of the latter, sponsored by the Admiralty initially to attack the *Tirpitz* but later the Japanese Fleet, is recounted in Chapter Twelve.

Highball's significance is that the Admiralty's enthusiasm for the project did much to spur on the development of Upkeep; indeed, many of the initial trials ran concurrently. As a result of the 21 June demonstration, action was initiated to modify a number of Wellingtons for the aerial trials and to produce six half-size inert prototype bombs (approximately 4,000 lb) for experimental purposes – the Wellington could not accommodate anything bigger. By the end of November it was established that the arming systems would operate satisfactorily at the required depth. At that stage, however, no aircraft drops had taken place. The first scaled-down inert spherical weapon was dropped from a

Wellington on 3 December 1942 off Chesil Beach, near Portland, Dorset with Captain M Summers, the Vickers test pilot, at the controls and Barnes Wallis crouched in the bomb-aiming position to release it. Initial results were not very encouraging; even with strengthened cases the mines shattered on impact with the sea. However, they doggedly continued, and at a final trial in Janaury 1943, by now using dummy mines of solid wood, highly satisfactory results were achieved, proving the weapon system to be a practical proposition and not just a scientist's dream.

The results were formally passed to the Air Staff by the Controller of Research and Development (CRD), Ministry of Aircraft Production in a memoradum dated 12 February 1943. In this he analysed the results and the technical possibilities of producing the full-scale operational version in time to meet Mr Wallis's proposal that the dams should be attacked in May 1943, when they held the greatest volume of water following the winter snow and rain. CRD did not feel this date could be met, and favoured delaying deployment until the Highball/Mosquito trials were completed. (It was proposed that Highball should be carried by Mosquitoes.) Clearly the risk of one project compromising the security and surprise of the other was also a consideration.

However, after lengthy discussion between various members of his staff, the Chief of Air Staff decided that the dam project should proceed with all possible haste. Instructions were issued on 26 February for the immediate conversion of three Lancasters for operational trial purposes, and for another thirty to be converted as soon as possible for operational use. One hundred and fifty bombs were also placed on order. A V Roe were tasked to manufacture the bomb-carrying and release equipment, and Vickers the bombs. However, it soon became apparent that the installation of the bombing and ancilliary equipment was not the simple conversion envisaged, and that it would be necessary to build it in on the basic aircraft production line. Unfortunately, this limited the modified aircraft to the one specialist task, and consequently it was agreed that the number of Upkeep Lancasters ordered should be reduced to 20. During this period the closest co-operation was maintained between Mr Wallis and Mr Chadwick of A V Roe (later Sir Roy, Chief Designer at A V Roe).

There now followed a period of intense activity for all concerned. Aircraft and mine manufacturers worked continuous shifts 24 hours a day, 7 days a week. 5 Group, Bomber Command was notified on 17 March that a new weapon was being produced for use against 'a large dam in Germany' and a new squadron with specially-designed Lancasters was to be formed within the group to undertake the operation. Four days later 617 Squadron came into being at Royal Air Force Scampton, Lincolnshire, under the command of Wing Commander G P Gibson and manned by specially-selected aircrews. Without delay or waiting for the special aircraft to be delivered, the squadron began low flying and navigational exercises, many of them over water at 120 ft, the then optimum height for Upkeep's release determined by the Chesil Beach Wellington trials. A series of daylight flights over the Derwent Water reservoir in what is now Cumbria clearly indicated the difficulty of maintaining this exacting height even in the best conditions, let alone during the dark hours under real operational conditions. The problem was solved by simple mathematics and the use of two spotlights, one mounted in the nose and the other on the belly of the aircraft. They were trained downwards so that the beams formed a single spot at their intersection on the water when flying at precisely 120 ft.

At this particular time, the still experimental bombs consisted of a steel cylinder 60 in (1,530 mm) long and 50 in (1,270 mm) in diameter, clad in wooden slats to form a sphere. The intention had been that, like Highball, the cladding would be of high quality steel but, owing to other priorities and the haste with which the bombs were manufactured, the metal was not readily available. During the earliest Lancaster trial on 13 April at Reculver, Herne Bay, Kent, the wooden cladding shattered on sea impact. What at first sight appeared disastrous turned out to be a blessing. Fortuitously the cylindrical core bounced across the water admirably, so Mr Wallis, to his considerable relief, was able to abandon cladding altogether, thus saving manufacture time and weight.

The best results were obtained when the cylinder was back spun in the bomb bay at 500 rpm and released from about 60 ft at 210-220 mph. Launched at between 400 and 500 yds from the target, in its revised form Upkeep bounced four or five times as it sped over the surface to the trial target, before sinking below the surface. This was considered very satisfactory and established the pattern for all remaining training exercises, and ultimately the actual attack upon the dams. The revised flight height of 60 ft was exactly half of that previously envisaged and practised. Without the spotlights it would have been impossible to fly over water at night at that constant low level.

The air crew would now be exposed to the twin hazards of near-suicidal low-level flying, and at the same time betraying their precise position to the enemy gunners as they flew in over the dams.

Up to this point the inert-weapon Lancaster air drops had been undertaken by Vickers' test-pilot Captain M Summers, and Squadron Leader M V Longbottom on loan to the firm. Then on 12 May 1943, as the trials neared conclusion, three key crews of 617 Squadron selected for the dam raids and temporarily detached to Royal Air Force Manston, Kent, successfully launched three inert bombs. Next day a live bomb was released well out to sea off Broadstairs to confirm the launching technique and weapon functioning. All went well – it bounced along the water as expected, before disappearing below the surface and detonating. Finally another was dropped into the sea unarmed on the 15th, just to prove it would not detonate if it became necessary to jettison a bomb safe in an emergency. On that same day a signal was sent to Bomber Command by the Assistant Chief of Air Staff (Operations), advising 'Operation "CHASTISE" approved. Execute at first suitable opportunity.' Air Marshal Sir Arthur Harris at Bomber Command and Air Vice-Marshall The Hon. R Cochrane at 5 Group wasted no time in deciding the attack should be launched the following night (16/17 May 1943).

On the 15th there was feverish activity at Scampton ensuring that the 56 live bombs held would rotate smoothly in the bomb-bays of the newly-arrived Lancaster specials. Last-minute preparations were also in hand to effect the

Top *The front wall of the Möhne Dam as it was.*
Above *The rear wall of the Möhne Dam.*

bombing-up of the 19 aircraft selected for operations, plus one reserve. Take-off was planned for 9.30 p.m. the following night to attack the Möhne, Eder, Sorpe, and if possible Ennepe Dams. Only on seeing scale models of the dams at final briefing did the aircrews know the real purpose of their intensive low-flying training and the destination for the strange-shaped bombs they were about to deliver.

They were briefed to rotate the bombs at 500 rpm at least ten minutes before release, and launch them at the optimum height, speed and distance from the target established during the Reculver trials and rehearsed many times over the lakes and reservoirs of England and Wales. Priority was given to the destruction of the Möhne, Eder and Sorpe Dams. Any bombs remaining were to be directed at lesser dams as circumstances permitted.

The conduct of the operation and the heroism displayed by the aircrews is now history and recorded in great detail in a number of publications, including a first-hand account by Wing Commander Gibson himself. It is therefore unnecessary to provide a detailed account here. It is sufficient to say that during the early hours of 17 May 1943, four dams were attacked, the Möhne, Eder, Sorpe and Ennepe, although there is some doubt concerning the latter. Each presented a formidable target both to the bomb inventor and the crews dedicated to their destruction. Not only were they massive, but lying in remote valleys they were very dfficult to get at except in fine moonlight conditions, circumstances most favourable to the defenders but fraught with danger for the low-flying attackers. The loss of eight Lancasters with 53 aircrew killed and three taken prisoner bears testimony to the inherent dangers faced by those who participated.

It would be appropriate, however, before considering the results achieved, to consider target construction and to say something about the aircraft bomb installation and the workings of the bomb.

The best known of the dams, the Möhne, was ceremonially opened on 13 July 1913 – an ill omen, in the light of events 30 years on. Located above the Möhne-Hever river valleys, leading to the River Ruhr approximately 26 miles south-east of Dortmund, the imposing rubble limestone masonry wall was 2,133 ft (650 m) long, 132 ft (40.3 m) high, 112 ft (34.2 m) thick at the base and at the top 24.6 ft (7.5 m). It held back 135 million cubic metres of water (just under 30,000 million gallons). The lake covered an area of 3,300 acres and had a 25-mile shoreline. The compensating basin below the dam accommodated two electrical power stations, the larger of the two having an annual output of 10 million kilowatt hours. At the time of the attack the depth of water was approaching its maximum.

The largest of the dams attacked was the Eder, which held back 205 million cubic metres of water (just over 45,000 million gallons). It is situated well to the east of the Ruhr, 20 miles (32 km) south-west of Kassel. The 1,289 ft (393 m) long masonry wall stood 143.75 ft (43.8 m) above the Eder Valley. It measured 113 ft (34.5 m) thick at the base and 18.7 ft (5.7 m) at the crest and served at least four local power stations and helped to maintain water flow in the River Weser and the Mittelland Canal connecting with the Dortmund–Ems Canal. When attacked, the water depth at the dam was approximately 100 ft (30.48 m).

The Sorpe Dam, unlike the others, was a rubble and earth dam buttressed by a reinforced concrete core. It is situated about ten miles (16 km) south west of the Möhne, and its sloping banks stood about 160 ft (48 m) above the Sorpe Valley leading to the Ruhr. Barnes Wallis saw little hope of breaching this massive structure, but at best hoped for serious leakages.

Finally the Ennepe Dam; this gravity dam was one of the subsidiary targets. Built between 1903 and 1905 it is located about 33 miles (53 km) south-west of

Above *The earth-rubble concrete cored wall of the Sorpe Dam.*

Below *The masonry wall of the Ennepe Dam.*

the Möhne in the Schwelm region. The masonry wall was 1,063 ft (324 m) long and 162 ft (49.5 m) high.

But what of the bombs themselves? During their hasty and traumatic development the design changed in some detail almost every week, as did the design of the release and suspension gear in the Lancaster specials allocated for the task. Consequently no standard in-service manuals were published in the short time available. In any case, the bomb was used only on one occasion, so the need for such documentation did not arise. With the passage of time it has become virtually impossible to provide accurate drawings of British origin, so use must be made of the meticulous records maintained by the Germans to describe the bomb and the Lancaster installation. A number of aircraft were

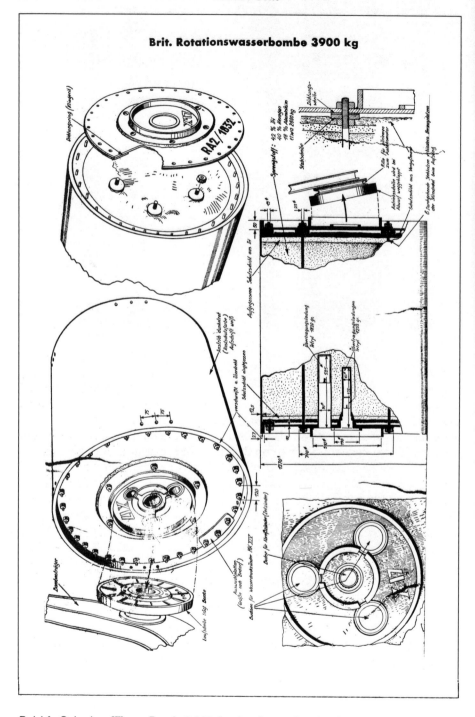

British Spinning Water Bomb 3,900 kg (as drawn by the German Bomb Disposal Organization).

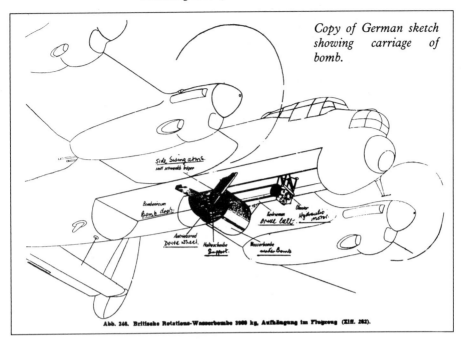

Copy of German sketch showing carriage of bomb.

Abb. 246. Britische Rotations-Wasserbombe 3900 kg, Aufhängung im Flugzeug (Zif. 282).

lost *en route* to the target, and one in particular, Lancaster E-Easy, skippered by Flight Lieutenant N G Barlow, hit power cables near Haldern-on-Rhine and crashed, killing all of the crew. The Germans did, however, recover the bomb practically intact. From it and the wreckage of other dambuster aircraft they were able to produce realistic diagrams depicting the bomb and the method of carriage. These diagrams, drawn on 26 May 1943, just nine days after the attack, were intended for use by the Luftwaffe bomb disposal teams, but they will serve 46 years later to describe how Upkeep was carried and functioned.

The aircraft mounting consisted of two side-swing calliper arms (*Schwenk Träger*) fitted with disc-like wheels (*Antriebsscheibe*). These matched up with two 20 in diameter circular tracks *(Laufscheibe),* one on each end of the bomb *(Wasserbombe).* The external diameter of the discs were minimally smaller than the circular tracks, back spin being transmitted by friction between the driven disc and corresponding bomb track. Power for rotation was supplied by an aircraft inboard engine through the medium of a variable-gear hydraulic motor *(Ölmotor)* and a fan belt *(Keilriemen)* running in a groove *(Rille)* in the driven disc. When the bomb-aimer pressed the release button, the calliper arms moved outwards, freeing the spinning cylinder, at the same time arming the hydrostatic pistols. Having bounced a number of times over the surface *en route* to the dam wall, hopefully clearing or barging through anti-torpedo nets (two sets protected the Möhne) it rebounded off the wall and crawled down its face to a depth of 30 ft, where 5,720 lb (2,600 kg) of Torpex explosive *(Sprengstoff)* detonated.

Detonation was initiated when the three hydrostatic pistols *(Wasser-*

Above *Photograph of the Möhne Dam taken 4 hours after it was breached.*

Below *Reconnaissance photograph of the breached Eder Dam.* (IWM)

Bottom *Captain Heinz Schweizer of the Luftwaffe bomb disposal organization (centre with Iron Cross at neck) shows Nazi leaders the bomb from Lancaster E for Easy which he recovered and defuzed.*

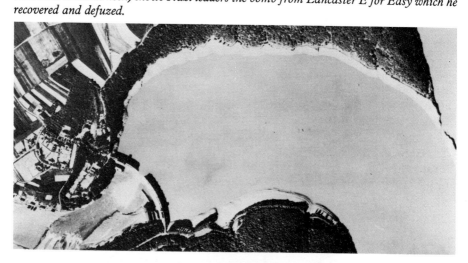

druckzünder) Mark XIV sensed the correct water pressure to function the firing mechanisms – one pistol could do the job, but three provided insurance against defects. The strikers were freed at the appropriate depth, firing in turn the detonators, exploders *(Übertragungsladung)* and Torpex instantaneously.

To prevent defective bombs falling into enemy hands, a self-destruct time fuze was activated at the point of release. It detonated the bomb some 60-90 sec later, allowing sufficient time for normal pistol operation. None of the pistols or the time-fuze in the bomb recovered by the Germans would have been armed – the crew perished long before it would have been necessary to put the bomb into its active mode.

Of the nineteen bombs which left Scampton, eleven were dropped on or near one or other of the dams; five on the Möhne, three on the Eder, two on the Sorpe and one on either the Ennepe or the Bever. Bits and pieces picked up in later years suggested that the latter, lying a few miles south, may have received the bomb intended for the Ennepe. In any event, no damage was done to either. Of the remainder, two were brought back to Scampton. One was dragged off an aircraft *en route* flying low (too low) over the Zuider Zee (IJsselmeer), four detonated as aircraft crashed or were shot down, and as already mentioned, one was recovered by a *Luftwaffe* bomb disposal team.

Details of how each aircraft and bomb fared during the night of 16/17 May are shown in Appendix 4. The cost in aircraft and men was high, but for strategic wartime reasons they were to a great extent offset by the major result achieved. Both the Möhne and Eder dams were breached, each losing about two-thirds of its contents in a raging torrent through gaps 66 ft (20 m) deep and 246 ft (75 m) wide, and 72 ft (22 m) deep and 230 ft (70 m) wide respectively. This represented a loss of between 25,000 and 30,000 tons of masonry at each. Unlike the others, the Sorpe bombs were dropped conventionally from 60 ft just like depth charges, in the knowledge that the 'bouncing' technique was unlikely to be effective against the robust immovable earthworks. Two craters below the water line adjacent to the dam crest caused crumbling and leakages, which forced the Germans to partially drain and effect repairs.

The devastation in the narrow Möhne Valley and along the River Ruhr can be gauged from the text of a German report issued some weeks after the catastrophe (see Appendix 5). The immediate effects in the much wider Eder Valley were not nearly so devastating. Nevertheless, at least 29 people lost their lives when the local villages and four power-generating stations were inundated. Tank and U-boat component factories in Kassel were flooded, as was the important *Luftwaffe* air base at Fritzlar, ten miles downstream. Bridges and roads were washed away and serious damage was inflicted on the banks of the Weser; farmland was devastated or made unworkable.

The Germans had repaired both breaches by late October 1943. Work on the Möhne commenced just five days after the attack, involving over 2,000 workers, among them numerous specialists and slave labourers – unfortunately, many foreign 'workers' had perished in the earlier floods. Much of the damage was left untouched; for instance, the Möhne electrical power stations were not rebuilt until 1955.

Undoubtedly the bombs on the Möhne and Eder dams caused widespread damage and confusion out of all proportion to the numbers used. The blow was not a mortal one, but coming on top of the increasingly heavy Bomber Command assaults on the Ruhr, Upkeep contributed significantly to making life almost intolerable for industrialists and workers alike. The bomb was never used again, although consideration was given to its deployment against the Mittelland Canal and Italian dams. However, when Tallboy gained favour in 1944, the remaining 'bouncing' bombs were sea-dumped.

In this short chapter it has been possible only to recount a small portion of the thought and effort which led to the perfection of a weapon which differed from all others not only in design, but also in the fact that it was limited to one objective. Among special weapons, the 'Dambuster' must take pride of place. Of ingenious design, and highly successful, it was produced in a remarkably short time. The story of its development and production is an epic in the history of aerial bombs. Not only was it a credit to Mr Barnes Wallis, its designer, but to all who took part in the development and production. Furthermore, the courage and aggressive spirit displayed by the aircrews of 617 Squadron who delivered it, is unlikely ever to be surpassed or forgotten. Many of them, already highly decorated, received new awards, including that of a Victoria Cross to the leader, Wing Commander G P (Guy) Gibson DSO, DFC, who personally directed the successful operations over the Möhne and Eder Dams, as well as flying alongside at least three of the attacking aircraft in turn in an attempt to draw the defenders' fire from the aircraft actually on a bomb run. Individual bomb runs had to be done at spaced intervals to allow the water to settle after each explosion, and to determine if major damage had been inflicted.

Sadly, as with many brave men, he was killed on yet another operational sortie, along with his navigator Squadron Leader J B Warwick on 19–20 September 1944 whilst returning from a successful target-marking raid on Rheydt and Mönchengladbach in the Rhineland. Their Mosquito crashed near Bergen-op-Zoom on the East Scheldt estuary. Both are buried in the cemetery at Steenbergen-en-Kruisland, eight miles north of Bergen-op-Zoom.

CHAPTER EIGHT

BOMBS VERSUS THE GERMAN FLEET

The main aim of this chapter is to show how the semi-armour-piercing (SAP) and armour-piercing (AP) bombs, designed for attacking enemy warships and their associated port installations, fared during the course of the Second World War. However, circumstances often demanded that other bombs in the general bombardment range had also to be used for the purpose: consequently, they too are included in the story. Other air-dropped weapons used for anti-shipping purposes, such as the 12,000 lb Tallboy, torpedoes, sea mines and anti-submarine weapons, have been allocated chapters in their own right, although cross reference to some will be included.

With the exception of some very special bombs/weapons, similar bombs were deployed against Axis shipping in the Middle East, particularly the Mediterranean, and the Japanese in the Indian and Pacific Oceans. The story of the successes and failures of these bombing campaigns is beyond the scope of this book.

The anti-shipping formations contributed substantially to the enemy defeat in every theatre of operation, especially in the Middle East. There, from 1940 to 1943, the Royal Air Force and Fleet Air Arm, operating from the Nile Delta, Malta, the Western Desert and from aircraft carriers, practically starved the Italians and Germans of ammunition, fuel and other vital supplies essential to their North Africa campaigns. This was reflected in the sinking of 769 ships (1,234,200 tons) at sea or in port, including a number of warships. The Italian battleship *San Giorgia* was sunk by the Royal Air Force in June 1940, and the destroyers *Sauro Manio*, *Pantera* and *Tigre* were sunk by combined Naval and Royal Air Force action in April 1941.

The sinkings of warships, large and small, and merchantmen armed and unarmed, in North West European waters were no less creditable, as shown in the table overleaf. The story of successes against capital ships will be covered in more detail, but the tonnages are included in the table.

Over and above the Royal Air Force figures, the Fleet Air Arm, sometimes

RAF Coastal Command			RAF Bomber Command	
Type	No	Tonnage (long)	No	Tonnage
Warships at sea	150	86,300	4	1,650
Merchantmen at sea	193	427,500	21	29,500
Warships in port	—	—	152*	166,580
Merchantmen in port	—	—	127*	163,600
* A small proportion of these were sunk by Coastal Command				

under the control of Coastal Command, sank 12 warships (10,944 tons) and 29 merchantmen (58,557 tons).

Coastal and Bomber Command flew approximately 40,000 and 2,700 sorties against ships at sea, and lost 800 and 126 aircraft respectively. Many more were lost attacking vessels in port. Attacking ships at sea or in port was extremely hazardous, be they individual merchantmen, convoys protected by armed escorts, or warships with their in-built defences and, frequently, fighter escorts. Many attacks were delivered at mast level against stiff opposition, requiring considerable skill, determination and courage. This was never lacking, whether in home waters, the Mediterranean or the Far East war zones, in the latter case often ill-reported and largely forgotten.

It was there that Lieutenant R H Gray, a Canadian of 1841 Squadron, HMS *Formidable*, won a Victoria Cross on 9 August 1945. Flying a Corsair carrying two 500 lb bombs, he attacked the Japanese destroyer *Amakusa* in harbour at Onagawa Wan Bay, Honshu on Japan's Eastern coast. Ground fire set his Corsair ablaze, but Gray pressed home his attack and sank the vessel with a direct hit, before crashing to his death. His courage reflected that of the many others who met an anonymous fate during the years after 3 September 1939 when Bomber Command first crossed swords with the German fleet.

On that day at 11.15 a.m. the Prime Minister, Neville Chamberlain, announced that the country was in a state of war with Germany. Three-quarters of an hour later, a Blenheim of 139 Squadron, crewed by Flying Officer A McPherson, Commander Thompson RN and Corporal V Arrowsmith, took off to photograph units of the German Fleet at Wilhelmshaven and Brunsbüttel at the western end of the Kiel Canal.

Coastal Command had 11 squadrons of Ansons and one squadron of Hudsons for general reconnaissance work, with two strike squadrons of obsolescent Vildebeeste torpedo bombers and six squadrons of flying-boats. None was in any way suitable for attacking capital ships, the Ansons and Hudsons having neither the range nor the bomb load for the purpose. The former carried 200 lb for a range of 250 miles; the latter could go twice as far, with 750 lb. The Vildebeestes and flying-boats were entirely unsuitable.

Consequently, the Bomber Command Blenheims, Hampdens and Wellingtons were earmarked for the task of locating and striking the German Fleet. However, in the first flush of war no one knew for certain where the enemy capital ships were based, and even if they did, there was little intelligence to say where they were on this, the first day of the Second World War. The purpose of McPherson's flight was to try and find out. It was believed, however, that the 17,490 ton pocket battleship *Admiral Scheer* and the 5,600 ton light cruisers *Nürnberg*, *Leipzig*, *Königsberg* and *Emden* were anchored in the Wilhelmshaven area, and the 31,800 ton battle cruisers *Scharnhorst* and *Gneisenau* lay at Brünsbuttel. Intelligence believed that the 12,750 ton heavy cruiser *Admiral Hipper* was at Kiel with the light cruiser *Köln*. The veteran battleship *Schleswig-Holstein* was thought to be at Swinemünde on the Baltic coast, and it was known that the pocket battleships *Graf Spee* and *Deutschland* were already in the Atlantic. The former was scuttled off Montevideo on 17 December 1939 during the Battle of the River Plate, and the latter was remaned *Lützow* when she returned to her home port in November. Most of these warships, as well as the 42,800 ton battleships *Bismarck* and *Tirpitz*, still under construction, and the heavy cruiser *Prinz Eugen*, were to suffer Royal Air Force, and in some cases Fleet Air Arm, bombs, mines or torpedoes.

As a result of McPherson's photographs and a further single Blenheim reconnaissance next day, the *Leipzig* with four destroyers was spotted near Wilhelmshaven in the Jade Estuary. Two large warships, presumed to be the *Scharnhorst* and *Gneisenau*, were spotted at Brünsbuttel. The chance of a first strike fell to the Blenheims which were standing by each with two 250 lb SAPs, but were forced to change to 500 lb GP bombs at the last minute because cloudy weather over the target area demanded a low-level attack. The SAP bombs (described in Chapter Two) had to be dropped from at least 3,500 ft to stand any chance of penetrating armour; the GPs, with more explosive and less metal, might just damage the superstructure and gun turrets. Hitting a moving ship from any height was difficult and the higher the aircraft the greater the difficulty. Even when motionless, the largest ship presented a small area to aim at. On this occasion, the GPs were fitted with 11-second delay detonators to allow the Blenheim crews to escape from the blast and splinters. Unfortunately, these delays had the serious disadvantage that the bombs could bounce off the armour plating before detonating.

On the afternoon of the 4th, 15 Blenheims, five each from 107 and 110 Squadrons Wattisham and 139 Squadron Wyton, were tasked to search for and attack warships in the Schillig Roads off Wilhelmshaven. Because of the very poor visibility the latter failed to spot any ships. However, most of the others sighted either the *Admiral Scheer* or the *Emden*, and made low-level attacks. Some, led by Flight Lieutenant K C Doran of 110 Squadron, attacked the *Admiral Scheer* and scored two near misses and one hit, shattering the ship's aircraft catapult gear. German reports indicated that three other bombs hit the pocket battleship but bounced off without detonating. Nevertheless, she was non-operational for several weeks. One Blenheim crashed on the deck of the *Emden*, causing some damage and casualties. Five Blenheims failed to return, four from 107 Squadron and one from 110 Squadron.

Later that day, 14 Wellingtons of 9 and 149 Squadrons carrying 500 lb SAPs set out to attack warships lying off Brunsbüttel. Four only claimed to have found a target and bombed it. It is believed one merchantman was damaged but, because of a navigational error, two bombs were dropped on the Danish town of Esbjerg, over 100 miles north of Brunsbüttel, killing two Danish civilians. Two Wellingtons failed to return. One fell to flak and the other to a fighter, the *Luftwaffe's* first victory over the Royal Air Force.

Thus, on the second day of war, Bomber Command flew 30 sorties and lost 7 aircraft (23.3 per cent) but on the credit side one pocket battleship was prevented from sailing for four weeks. (Bomber Command eventually sank her in April 1945.) These initial losses and navigational problems set the pattern for what was going to be a hazardous occupation. The determination and courage of the crews indicated they were up to the job, even if the GPs were not. The bombs were good enough for merchant ships but certainly not for heavily armoured warships. No judgement could be passed on the SAP bombs at this stage, because none so far had struck a warship.

Apart from reconnaissance flights over the North Sea, there were no aggressive operations for the next 25 days. Then, on 29 September, 11 Hampdens carrying SAP bombs set out in two formations of six and five aircraft to search the Heligoland area. One formation attacked two destroyers but scored no hits; the other, from 144 Squadron, did not return. Post-war records show that this formation was shot down by a swarm of Me 109s. Eighteen aircrew were killed, including the Squadron Commander, Wing Commander J C Cunningham. At the time, the Royal Air Force was unaware that their bombers' movements were being detected by Freya radar installations on Heligoland and Wangerooge islands. These plotted their course and directed the fighters, based on the Frisian Islands and on the mainland. The Me 109, with two 7.9 mm machine guns and up to three 20 mm cannon, and the Me 110 with six machine guns and two cannon, vastly out-gunned the Wellington, the best of the British bombers then available, with its three gun-turrets; rear, front and ventral (under the fuselage)*, each with two .303 in Brownings. All these turrets had blind spots; they could not traverse sufficiently to confront beam attacks, and the guns could neither compete with the cannon's range nor its ammunition's destructive qualities. The Blenheim and Hampden armament was even less satisfactory.

Appropriately, the bomber crews having experienced the sting in Heligoland Bight, rapidly named it the Hornet's Nest. The sting became more poweful as time went by. Overshadowed by the flak organization and the *Luftwaffe*, they were hamstrung by Government edicts strictly warning them not to seek out warships in anchorages at naval bases, to avoid causing civilian casualties. Aircraft were not to infringe Danish or Dutch territorial waters, nor to attack warships escorting merchantmen, if there was any chance of damaging the latter. In the circumstances, perhaps this was carrying the rules of war, drawn up at the Hague Convention in 1923, a bit too far for the exasperated aircrews.

* (In Mark I form).

Nevertheless, 24 Wellingtons of 38, 139 and 115 Squadrons set off in formation on the morning of 3 December and attacked two cruisers off Heligoland. To give the 500 lb SAPs a chance of penetrating the decks, they were dropped from between 7,000–10,000 ft. One stick of three straddled an unnamed warship, later seen being towed into port down at the stern.

One Wellington from 115 Squadron, suffered a bomb hang-up which later accidentally (?) fell on to the Island of Heligoland, the first to be dropped on German soil during the Second World War. Flak from Heligoland was fierce and enemy fighters intervened, one of which was shot down by Leading Aircraftman J Copley, a 38 Squadron rear gunner. He and his colleagues, nearly all Aircraftmen, repulsed the fighters, and all the Wellingtons returned safely.

On 14 December 1939, 42 aircraft set out to search for the cruisers *Nürnberg* and *Leipzig,* which had been torpedoed by a British submarine and were limping back to the Jade Estuary. This was the largest bomber force yet deployed and consisted of 23 Hampdens, 12 Wellingtons and 7 Whitleys. The Hampdens and Whitleys found nothing, but the Wellingtons of 99 Squadron had a running battle with flak-ships (converted trawlers) and fighters, when they penetrated the Schillig Roads under the 800 ft cloud base to attack a small convoy. Five bombers fell to fighters, and another crashed on landing back at its base. One fighter was shot down but, as far as can be ascertained, no ships were hit.

Worse was to follow four days later, on the last raid of this series of attacks on the German Fleet. Twenty-four Wellingtons from 9, 37 and 149 Squadrons, each carrying three 500 lb SAPs, formated over King's Lynn about 9.30 a.m. Minutes later they set off, led by Wing Commander R Kellet, 149 Squadron, to scour the north-west German coast for warships, once again inhibited by the Government restrictions. Two aircraft turned back with technical problems, but 22 made landfall just off the Danish-German border, flying at 10,000 ft in an attempt to put themselves above the flak-ceiling and the hazards encountered earlier that month.

They flew along the coast towards Wilhelmshaven, where they were greeted by ineffectual flak bursting below. Mindful of their specific instructions, no bombs were dropped on a battleship and a cruiser lying close in. Soon after clearing the flak barrage and heading west for the open sea, they were set upon by a swarm of radar-controlled Me 109 and 110s. The air gunners put up a gallant fight, struggling to manipulate the guns in their ice-cold turrets, but the .303 in Brownings were no match for the speedy heavily-armed opponents. Unable to traverse the gun turrets sufficiently to confront beam attacks, the bombers started to go down in flames, partially because of the lack of fuel-tank protection. Within the hour, ten bombers were lost, along with two German fighters. By this time most of the bomb loads had been jettisoned to enhance manoeuvrability. Ten of the 22 survived, including that of the formation leader. Some made forced landings, others arrived home with wounded crew members, mostly air gunners. Two others just failed to make the English coast and had to ditch. One went in 40 miles East of Cromer, the crew clambered out but they were never seen again. Sergeant Ramshaw and his 9 Squadron crew were somewhat luckier; hit repeatedly by the German fighters, the aircraft ditched just off Grimsby. With the exception of the mortally-wounded rear gunner, Leading Aircraftman Dilley, the others were picked up by a trawler and transferred to a local hospital.

This action, in which 12 Wellingtons were lost, together with the Wellington losses four days earlier, meant that 50 per cent of the 34 Wellingtons deployed had been shot down, without once crossing the German mainland. This put serious doubt on the existing theory that a bomber formation could adequately defend itself in daylight against fighter aircraft. The initial offensive against the German Fleet produced no significant results. Some 860 sorties were flown, 41 bombers were lost in dropping 61 tons of bombs which caused relatively minor damage to the *Admiral Scheer* and *Emden,* the destruction of a minesweeper and ten fighter aircraft. As a result of the Wellington mauling, Bomber Command staff decided to abandon similar forays until fuel tanks could be self-sealing or armour plated. However, in April 1940 it was decreed that, for self-preservation if nothing else, the 3 Group Wellingtons and 5 Group Hampdens (1 Group Battles were in France and 2 Group Blenheims were otherwise engaged) should be converted to a night bomber force. This was a recognition that they could not safely penetrate Germany, singly or in formation during daylight.

Despite these losses, attempts to find and bomb German warships continued through the winter months, with little success and only minor losses, mainly because the aircraft avoided the Hornets' Nest whenever possible.

At dawn on 9 April 1940, German forces invaded Denmark and Norway. The overland invasion of Denmark was practically unopposed and the country was quickly occupied. Norway, however, had to be invaded by sea and air, both of which were vigorously opposed by the Norwegian forces supported by an Anglo-French expeditionary force at Narvik in the North. The campaign lasted just two months, and for more than half that period, until 15 May, the embargo on attacking the German mainland remained; consequently many vital targets such as ports and communications in North Germany were out of bounds. Therefore the most obvious target for the Royal Air Force was the shipping supporting the Norwegian invasion.

On 7 April a Coastal Command Hudson spotted a sizeable force of German warships, including the *Scharnhorst, Gneisenau and Admiral Hipper* steaming North beyond Heligoland. It turned out that the mini-fleet was on its way to support the invasion of Norway. That afternoon, 12 Bomber Command, 107 Squadron Blenheims, each carrying four 250 lb SAP bombs made a determined attack on the warships. Bombs straddled one of the larger ships but caused no damage. Later that day two Wellingtons, each armed with three 500 lb SAPs, failed to make contact.

Now that the worst was known, Coastal Command's reconnaissance aircraft did their utmost to track down enemy warships and on the 9th confirmed the presence of the light cruisers *Köln* and *Königsberg* at Bergen. Twelve Wellingtons (9 and 115 Squadrons temporarily attached to Coastal Command) and 12 Hampdens (5 Group, Bomber Command) set out to attack the warships.

The Coastal Command aircraft were recalled, but the Hampdens continued and attacked the ships with 250 and 500 lb SAPs. Two hits were claimed and minor damage inflicted on one of the cruisers.

The single-engined Fleet Air Arm Skuas did much better early next morning. Seven belonging to 800 Squadron, led by Captain R T Partridge RM and another nine from 830 led by Lieutenant W P Lucy RN took off from Hatson in the Orkneys just after dawn, armed with a single 500 lb SAP each, and headed 300 miles east to Bergen. They dive-bombed the *Königsberg* which lay immobilized alongside a jetty, scoring three direct hits and a number of near misses. She burst into flames, than a magazine exploded, shattering the hull. One of the Skuas was lost in the face of stiff anti-aircraft fire. Thus, the Fleet Air Arm had the distinction of sinking the first warship ever with bombs, and with the relatively small 500 lb SAPs, at that. Dive-bombing was something of a lottery when confronted by alert gunners; nevertheless, this was a fine morale-booster, at a time when there was little else to cheer, and perhaps showed how the job should be done.

Lack of cloud cover on 11 April prevented a force of Hampdens attacking warships known to be in Trondheim Fjord, but that night 23 Whitleys and 20 Hampdens attacked ships at various locations in the Skagerrak and Kattegat, *en route* from Kiel to Oslo. Results were difficult to determine by night, but a blinding flash signalled the end of at least one vessel, believed to have been an ammunition ship. Next day, 83 Wellingtons, Hampdens and Blenheims carried out an armed reconnaissance, once again armed with SAP bombs, searching for the *Scharnhorst, Gneisenau* and a cruiser, along with a destroyer screen reported steaming south in the Skagerrak. In the prevailing foggy conditions, nothing was found, but the bombers were set upon by a host of Me 109 and 110s. In a fierce running battle, nine bombers, and maybe ten, were shot down at a cost of five German fighters, although the raiders claimed seven; this operation was the last major daylight foray by Hampdens and Wellingtons.

Most of the British air operations during the Norwegian campaign were carried out at extreme aircraft range, more often than not in appalling flying conditions without fighter support and with little information to go on, more or less flying blindly into the unknown. Nevertheless, the crews stuck to their formidable task. One Wellington crew's experience speaks for many. They flew from their Scottish base at 300 ft through fierce snowstorms, reconnoitred the Norwegian coast from north to south and back again for over ten hours in the perishing cold. Such conditions were quite familiar to the Coastal Command men as they actively harried the German fleet during this particular campaign. On the morning of 11 June, 12 Hudsons of 233 Squadron based at Wick in Northern Scotland penetrated Trondheim Fjord and aimed 36 250 SAPs at the *Scharnhorst;* dropped from 15,000 feet in misty conditions, perhaps it is not surprising that no strikes were recorded. The Skuas from HMS *Ark Royal* were unlucky on the following day when a bomb struck the deck but failed to detonate, or perhaps it bounced off. About this time, the British campaign in Norway was ending in virtual disaster. Three days earlier, *Scharnhorst* and *Gneisenau* attacked the withdrawal fleet, sinking the aircraft carrier HMS

Glorious and her escorting destroyers HMS *Ardent* and *Acasta* just off Narvik. This was a painful loss for the Navy, and no less so for the Fleet Air Arm, which lost the Swordfish of HMS *Glorious* and for the Royal Air Force too, which lost ten Hurricanes together with their pilots and the ground crews of 46 (Hurricane) and 263 (Gladiator) Squadrons.

All were desperate for revenge, but although further aerial sorties were deployed, it was yet to come. *Scharnhorst* left Trondheim for Kiel and she was spotted by a 233 Squadron Hudson on the 21st, steaming south near Bergen, accompanied by the two destroyers and four torpedo boats. By mid afternoon, nine Beaufort torpedo bombers of 42 Squadron, led by Squadron Leader G Smith, were on their way from Wick armed with two 500 lb SAPs each on the Squadron's first operational strike since it was established in Coastal Command. They came upon *Scharnhorst,* her escorts and an umbrella of Me 109s just south of Bergen, and the guns of the combined mini-fleet opened up with murderous fire. The Beauforts dived into the hail of gun-fire and released their bombs from about 1,500 ft. It was reported, but not confirmed, that three detonated on *Scharnhorst*'s stern and gun turrets. In the confusion, the crews may have been deceived, and it may have been that the relatively small bombs, all fitted with a delay detonator, just skidded or bounced off the armour and detonated harmlessly alongside. Indeed they had little chance of penetrating the two-inch upper decks, let alone the main decks over four inches thick, unless of course dropped from a very high altitude. The 500 lb SAP would then come down vertically at about 1,100 ft per second. The chances of getting a strike with the contemporary aircraft and bombs sights were somewhat remote.

Having survived the gun barrage, the Beauforts were attacked by the Me 109s, and soon those skippered by Flying Officer Barrie-Smith, Pilot Officer Rigg and Flying Officer Seagrim were shot down. The balance was adjusted marginally when Leading Aircraftman Begbie shot down a Me 109 with his .303 in Vickers 'K' gun, virtually a pop-gun compared with the superior enemy armament. So ended the third attack of the afternoon on *Scharnhorst* and her escorts. Half an hour earlier, six Swordfish from Hatson had delivered a torpedo attack; five of the torpedoes had run true, but the big ship was able to evade them; two Swordfish failed to return. Just minutes later, four Hudsons from 224 and 233 Squadrons, Leuchars, attacked with eight 500 lb SAPs. Dropped from high level it is not surprising that they fell wide. However, the Hudsons were not high enough to avoid the flak and the Me 109s, which shot two down and seriously damaged the others.

No sooner had the Beauforts left the scene than six more Hudsons, this time from 269 Squadron Wick, took up the attack from high level. Again the SAPs fell very wide and every aircraft was damaged by flak. The *Scharnhorst* reached Kiel safely, but this was hardly a safe haven. On the night of 1–2 July 1940, she was hit by a 2,000 lb AP bomb delivered by an 83 Squadron Hampden. As already recounted in Chapter Two, this was the same night that the first 2,000 lb bomb dropped on the German mainland, killing ten Kiel citizens. This new bomb, first used by a Beaufort when it sighted a cruiser off the Frisian Island of Norderney on 7 May, had a fine sleek heavy-forged steel case, wherein lay its weakness. There was too much metal and only 166 lb of explosive. Hits were difficult to achieve from heights which would ensure penetration, and the current aircraft could not carry enough to drop sticks of bombs to compensate for aiming errors.

After an inauspicious start, bombers became an increasingly important factor in keeping enemy capital ships in port, ultimately sinking some and crippling others so that they took no further part in the war. In the meantime, Bomber Command, and to a lesser extent Coastal Command, had to direct their efforts at much smaller but at that time equally important prey, namely the 'invasion fleet' being amassed in Germany's newly-acquired Channel ports. For the purpose of this chapter, the barges and other vessels could hardly be classified as warships of the German Fleet, but because they came under control of the German Navy and their destruction was of vital importance to the British cause, the story is worth briefly recounting.

Having overrun France, Belgium and the Netherlands during May and June 1940, the Germans acquired a number of ports with superb facilities. To undertake Operation Sealion, Hitler's plan to invade Southern England on or about 15 September 1940, the Germans began to assemble large numbers of men and materials in what were to become known as the invasion ports. Some of them were only a night's sailing-time for motorized barges, and less for the larger transports from England's southern shores. The implications of these preparations caused the British Government great trepidation and well-justified concern, because it was believed that some 26,000 barges of between 300 and 3,000 ton were registered in Belgium and the Netherlands alone. In fact this was an over-estimation of those actually available. On 4 September the German naval staff advised Hitler that 1,910 barges, 419 tugs, 1,600 motorized barges and 168 transports, with a total capacity of 700,000 tons, were available and that more were to be added. By the third week of September some 3,000 self-propelled barges were reported in Dutch, Belgian and French ports and estuaries.

Meanwhile, during July and August, Bomber Command concentrated mainly on those ports capable of embarking large numbers of troops and supplies, such as Calais, Boulogne and Cherbourg, and others housing barges, Rotterdam, Flushing, Ghent, Antwerp and Dunkirk among these. During the same period, sea mining of the Channel coasts continued, and operations were mounted against German airfields in France and the Low Countries in support of Fighter Command's battle over southern England.

Most of the contemporary bombs on the Royal Air Force inventory were launched at the invasion fleet. Although relatively small, they were quite capable of dealing with thin-skinned targets such as barges, and indeed a significant portion of the fleet was immobilized. Among others, 250 and 500 lb GPs were used to shatter the vessels and their surroundings, 40 lb GPs and still smaller 20 lb fragmentation bombs were deployed as an anti-personnel measure and 4 and 25 lb incendiaries were included to set wreckage and spilt oil ablaze.

Many tons of bombs were dropped during that historic summer, but the main onslaught on the enemy invasion fleet took place at the height of the Battle of Britain and continued into May 1941, just to make sure. The events were largely overshadowed by the fateful battle going on above Britain. Thus the contribution of the bombers was largely overlooked in favour of the sterling work being done by the fighters; nevertheless, the former made a significant contribution to the outcome. Some 500 full-scale attacks were delivered on the various ports; for instance, Den Helder received 26, Amsterdam 24, Rotterdam 28, Flushing 55, Ostend 75, Dunkirk 62, Boulogne 89, Le Havre 40 and Cherbourg 16. By 1 September, 150 barges were reported at Boulogne, 266 at Calais and a week later it was estimated that the channel ports alone accommodated more than a thousand. The effective bombing of the invasion ports, allied with Fighter Command's victory over the *Luftwaffe*, raised serious doubts in Hitler's mind. By October he postponed Operation Sealion until the spring and forever, although at the time he thought the job could still be done. One of the reasons given for not invading the South Coast was the bad weather (it was a reasonable summer) and another was the constant bombing of the docks, ships and barges. Undoubtedly, the bombing attacks threw the preparations into a permanent state of confusion, but just as important, Hitler's naval and military chiefs greatly feared the powerful British naval forces which were likely to confront any invasion force.

The northern dockyards of Germany were also attacked between July and October 1940, as an adjunct to the anti-Sealion operations. Hampdens, Whitleys and Wellingtons dropped some 680 tons of bombs on Kiel and Wilhelmshaven, the former housing the *Scharnhorst, Gneisenau, Admiral Hipper* and *Prinz Eugen*, and the latter the still uncompleted *Tirpitz*, with the *Lützow* berthed nearby. No significant damage was done, at least no mortal blows were struck, but undoubtedly the raids delayed construction and repair work on these capital ships. Indeed the *Tirpitz* did not venture forth until January 1942, but three of the others most certainly did much earlier.

At the beginning of 1941, Hitler announced that within nine months Great Britain would be starved of food and ammunition from America by the combined efforts of the U-boats, surface raiders such as *Scharnhorst, Gneisenau, Admiral Hipper* and her sister *Prinz Eugen*, along with the *Bismarck* and *Tirpitz* when commissioned, and lastly the four-engined Focke-Wolf 200 C Kondors. During 1941 Coastal Command was mainly preoccupied with U-boats, so the 2 Group Blenheims were deployed to assist in harrying surface shipping in daylight, to combat a German boast that thanks to the *Luftwaffe* their shipping had the free run of the seas from the Norwegian fjords down to the Spanish border. The Blenheims and the Coastal Command aircraft allocated to the task were soon to find out that the job was no sinecure; losses were heavy. For instance the Blenheims made 1,750 sorties between 12 March and 14 July, during which time they saw over 1,000 enemy ships of various types, including destroyers, armed naval auxiliaries, flak ships, minesweepers and armed merchantmen. Over 400 were attacked, nearly all at mast-head level with 250 and 500 lb GP bombs. The Blenheims claimed to have despatched some 300,000 tons of shipping, but confirmed figures reduced this figure considerably. Sixty-eight Blenheims paid the price of low-level flying; the work was indeed hazardous, calling for special qualities of determination. Undoubtedly, the loss of just over 1,000 aircraft on direct shipping attacks (876 of them by Coastal Command) throughout the war is worthy of more comprehensive coverage, but space prohibits.

Between April 1941 and March 1942, Bomber Command deployed nearly 50 per cent of its effort against naval associated targets, much of it directed at four German capital ships in French ports. In late 1940 Winston Churchill said 'The Navy can lose us the war, but only the Air Force can win it. The fighters are our salvation, but the bombers alone provide the means of victory.' He was thoroughly convinced that battles might be won or lost, enterprises might succeed or miscarry, territories might be gained or quitted but, dominating all, the British power to carry on the war, and even keep the people alive, lay in mastery of the ocean routes and the free approach and entry to the seaports. Early in 1941, the pressure was growing increasingly; shipping losses were greater than the numbers which could be constructed, hence the need to sink or at least cripple the large surface raiders, as well as the U-boats and the Kondors. Churchill also stated quite categorically that 'if the presence of enemy battle cruisers in Biscayan ports is confirmed, every effort by the Royal Navy and the Royal Air Force should be made to destroy them there and for this purpose serious risks and sacrifices must be faced.'

The heavy cruiser *Admiral Hipper* was the first German warship to use the excellent dock facilities in Brest. Damaged by the Royal Navy after destroying seven ships in a convoy, she took refuge on 27 December 1940. She made one further foray from Brest between 1 and 15 February 1941 and ultimately left for Kiel on 15 March of the same year. She therefore fell under the Churchillian dictate, and during her stay, Bomber Command launched some 250 bombing sorties at Brest dockyard and the heavy cruiser in particular, together with many mining operations off the port to prevent, or at any rate, delay her escape. By then it had become clear that Brest, with its strong defences supplemented by search-lights, barrage balloons, smoke-screen equipment and an effective fighter aircraft screen, together with the warship's own armament, was going to be a difficult target to attack, and thus it proved to be. Churchill, despite his admiration for the Royal Air Force, showed some displeasure at its inability to dispose of the menaces lying there. However, considering the hazards of flying in 1941, the inadequacies of navigational and bombing equipment and the contemporary bombs, plus the exceptionally stiff opposition from enemy fighters and ground gunners, it is understandable why more was not achieved.

During the course of the attacks on the *Admiral Hipper*, the *Scharnhorst* and *Gneisenau* were having a successful foray in the Atlantic, sinking 22 ships (115,600 tons) before taking refuge in Brest on 22 March 1941 for servicing and repair. The first bomber attack against them was delivered on the night of 30–31 March; 109 aircraft took part using 500 lb SAPs, among other types. Although no hits were recorded, it was only the first instalment of some 3,000 tons of high explosive and 30 of incendiary bombs to be dropped, until they escaped north in February 1942. Some 275 mines were also dropped during this period to help keep the Atlantic raiders cooped up. They were joined on 1 June by the *Prinz Eugen* which limped into port with a defective engine, having left the *Bismarck* to be sunk by the Royal Navy on 27 May some 500 miles off Brest, after being damaged by Swordfish torpedo bombers (see Chapter Nine).

During the bombing campaign directed at the three warships, a number of significant strikes were achieved. These apart, the constant bombing made life almost intolerable for shipyard workers and ships crews. The situation in Brest was quite chaotic, with servicing and repair plans thrown into complete confusion. Every attack on the warships was a traumatic experience for the aircrews involved; none was routine and many stories will never be told. However, details of a few of the more noteworthy events, particularly those which focus on a particular ship, are provided as an indication of the ordeals faced by the aircrews and indeed the German sailors and the French port workers.

On the night of 4–5 April 1941, 54 aircraft attacked the general dock area. A Wellington claimed a hit on the *Scharnhorst* with a 1,900 lb GP bomb, but this was not confirmed by the Germans. However, they did report that a 250 lb SAP bomb had fallen in the water between the *Gneisenau* and the dock side, failing to detonate. They also confirmed that several bombs fell on the Continental Hotel, killing a number of naval officers, including some from both the *Scharnhorst* and *Gneisenau*. During the morning *Gneisenau*'s Captain, fearing the 250 lb SAP to be a delayed-action type, moved his vessel into the outer harbour. There, early next morning 6 April, she was torpedoed by a 22 Squadron Beaufort and seriously damaged (see Chapter Nine for further details). Further damage was inflicted during a major bombing attack four nights later, when four bombs struck home, setting her on fire, killing 50 members of the crew and injuring a further 90. *Gneisenau* was now holed above and below the water line.

The *Prinz Eugen* was next to suffer. During a 52 aircraft attack on the night of 1–2 July, a 500 lb SAP seriously damaged the compass platform, the gun control room and the radio transmitter. About the same time, a Wellington crashed on the quay alongside, adding to her immediate problems, killing the Executive Officer and approximately 60 ratings. The ship, like the *Gneisenau*, remained out of action until the end of the year.

Three weeks later at midday on the 22nd, a Coastal Command reconnaissance aircraft reported that the *Scharnhorst* was no longer in Brest. At 8.30 a.m. next day a Spitfire found her at anchor 240 miles South in La Pallice. Having completed minor repairs and a refit in Brest, she was hoping to carry out sea trials in comparative peace, having left a large tanker covered in camouflage nets in her old berth at Brest. Fortunately, Coastal Command's keen-eyed airmen spotted the difference. Response to the Spitfire's report was immediate. That same afternoon, 23 July, six Stirlings, three each from 7 and 15 Squadrons, each armed with three 2,000 lb APs, set out for La Pallice. 15 Squadron fared badly, only one aircraft reaching the target, where it was attacked by fighters, and on the return flight had to ditch in the sea 50 miles off Milford Haven. The other aircraft reached the target area, and at least one hit on *Scharnhorst*'s stern was reported.

Continuing the attack during the night, some 30 Whitleys bombed the dock area, causing a number of fires which were still smouldering the next morning, when a force of 15 Halifaxes made a determined attack upon the ship. The bombers of 35 and 76 Squadrons, each carrying fifteen 250 lb SAPs, scored five direct hits from between 10,000 and 12,000 ft. Three penetrated the ship's bottom without detonating, but the other two caused serious damage and flooding in the dynamo section and a propeller shaft tunnel. Despite some 4,000 tons of sea water within her hull she sailed for Brest that night, where she was to undergo lengthy repairs. A third of the Halifaxes were shot down, but despite this proportionally high loss, the raid was rightly deemed a success because the *Scharnhorst* was immobilized for six months while she was again made battle-worthy – the aircraft losses had to be offset against the enormous havoc the *Scharnhorst* might have caused to merchant shipping if let loose on the high seas.

On that same day, 24 July 1941, 100 bombers attacked her compatriots in Brest, and 36 Blenheims, escorted by three squadrons of Spitfires, attacked Cherbourg to draw off the expected German fighters. The main force, made up of 18 Hampdens and 79 Wellingtons, each carrying five 500 lb SAPs, together with three Royal Air Force Flying Fortresses from 90 Squadron, Polebrook were given a fierce reception by 20 to 30 fighters. Two Hampdens and eight Wellingtons were shot down, and two others crashed on landing. Hits on the *Gneisenau* and *Prinz Eugen*, with another on a tanker, were claimed but never confirmed. Interestingly enough, a Fortress flying at about twice the height of the other aircraft, over 30,000 ft, claimed to have struck *Prinz Eugen* with an 1,100 lb (American) bomb. In any event, all three warships were already immobilized with repair programmes for the rest of the year. On that eventful day, 151 bombing sorties were flown with a loss of 17 aircraft (11.3 per cent) but as previously stated the losses were justified by the need to keep the warships cooped up.

On 16 December it was noted that the *Prinz Eugen* had left dry dock; consequently on the following night over 100 aircraft attacked Brest yet again, but with little success and no damage to the warships. However, a daylight raid on 18 December was more successful. A mixed group of 47 Manchesters, Halifaxes and Stirlings claimed to have bombed accurately, and the *Gneisenau* was seen to be on fire after the attack. Six bombers failed to return, but set against that, *Gneisenau*'s hull plating was buckled by blast, along with a set of dock gates, which imprisoned the *Scharnhorst* for a month beyond the planned completion date for her repairs. Between 18 December 1941 and 12 February 1942, over 850 bombing sorties were mounted by Bomber Command against Brest and her, by now, unwelcome guests. The only successful one in respect of the warships was that on the night of 6–7 January when a bomb detonated alongside the *Gneisenau* and tore a gash 20 ft long in her hull, flooding two compartments. This was the final straw, and the German naval authorities decided to move all three ships to the greater protection (it was thought) of a German port. Hasty repairs to the *Gneisenau* were carried out and detailed plans made to move the ships to Wilhelmshaven and Kiel.

Thus it was that the battle cruisers *Scharnhorst* and *Gneisenau* and the light cruiser *Prinz Eugen* slipped quietly out of Brest at 9.45 pm on 11 February, met up with a destroyer escort and headed for the English Channel. The Germans had chosen the timing well, journeying in typical February weather with poor visibility, low cloud and often driving rain. Indeed, on 12 February most of Bomber Command was stood down for the day. It was not until 11.00 am on the 12th, by which time the mini-fleet had collected its fighter escort, that it was spotted by a Fighter Command Spitfire – then the alert was sounded.

The heroic story of the Fleet Air Arm and Coastal Command torpedo bombers on that day is told in the next chapter. Here we are only interested in the bomb-carrying aircraft of Bomber and Coastal Commands. To most it was a day imbued with a sense of urgency, but for many of the aircrew it was also one of frustration. Of the 256 sorties flown, only 39 crews claimed to have seen anything of the three larger warships and six escorting destroyers. Undoubtedly some of those who failed to return, two Hudsons, nine Hampdens, five Wellingtons and two Blenheims, did press home attacks, and suffered for it. In any event, no hits were claimed by those who did survive close contact, and the German Navy admitted none.

With the weather going from bad to worse throughout the day, it was essential that the bombers be prepared at their Lincolnshire, Yorkshire and East Anglian bases with the utmost haste and at very short notice. Even then the bombing-up and fuelling would take some hours, so that none were likely to confront the enemy before about 3 p.m. By then the February day would be closing in. The situation was further complicated because 100 of the 242 bombers earmaked needed a complete change of load – 500 lb SAPs had to be substituted by 500 and 1,000 lb GPs, for use at lower levels. The cloud ceiling of about 700 ft meant that the former could not be dropped from sufficient height to effect penetration, and their small explosive content would be somewhat ineffectual on ships' decks. It was recognized that the GPs could at least damage superstructures and gun positions, perhaps helping at the same time to detract enemy attention from the torpedo bombers who looked more likely to inflict crippling blows below deck. Load changes were not permitted to delay take-off deadlines; if the job could not be done, the original load was carried.

A first wave of 5 Group Hampdens came upon the mini-fleet at about 3 p.m. as it continued to push northwards off Walcheren in the Scheldt Estuary. To the enemy, these veteran bombers must have looked like sitting ducks, so they took full advantage. In no time at all four aircraft were shot down, one at least by a fighter. Of those who returned, only three claimed to have bombed one ship or another. The same reception met each of the successive waves; the second wave of 5 Group Hampdens fared slightly worse than their colleagues who led the attack, five being shot down. Two were seen going down in flames at about 4 p.m. whilst attacking *Gneisenau* and *Prinz Eugen* off the Hook of Holland. The destroyer *Z-29* claimed another of the five.

The 2 Group Bostons and Blenheims went into action at about the same time. Few of them bombed; many aborted, having failed to locate targets; fuel loads permitted them little or no leeway for search purposes. Those that did sight the warships experienced stiff opposition, and two Blenheims were shot down. In rapidly deteriorating weather, amidst the all-pervading murk and darkness, the heavier bombers fared no better, being entirely unsuited to the low-level tactics forced upon them in unrealistic circumstances. A mixed force of 4 Group Halifaxes and Wellingtons put in three claimed attacks only, all returning safely to their Yorkshire bases, unlike the Lincolnshire Hampdens. From the East Anglian bases, 1 Group deployed 37 Wellingtons and 3 Group 54 Wellingtons and 7 Stirlings. Four Wellingtons failed to return and one Stirling crashed on return to base.

The day's events reflect quite clearly what Churchill had meant when he said '... risks and sacrifices must be faced'; it was just a pity that the bombing paid no great dividends. However, as recounted in Chapter Ten, all was not lost. *Scharnhorst* and *Gneisenau* received crippling damage from airborne sea-mines during the voyage, the former hitting two mines and the latter one.

Although the day proved successful for the Germans, and something of a disaster for their opponents, the sailing of the mini-fleet from Brest finally released Bomber Command from its almost nightly presence over Brest. During the past ten months some 1,900 aircraft, over 1,700 from Bomber Command, dropped some 3,500 tons of bombs and lost 127 aircraft. The cost in men and aircraft was substantial, but relatively small in comparison with the havoc the three warships might have wreaked had they been let loose on the open seas.

However, Bomber Command's confrontation with the warships still had some way to go. *Scharnhorst* was now in Wilhelmshaven, shortly moving to Kiel, and *Gneisenau* was already in Kiel. On the night of 25–26 February, 61 aircraft bombed Kiel, with the huge floating dock containing the *Gneisenau* as the main aiming point. A huge accommodation ship was hit and burnt out, with considerable loss of life, but the battle cruiser survived. On the following night another 49 aircraft – 33 Wellingtons, 10 Hampdens and 6 Halifaxes attacked the floating dock. On this occasion at least one 2,000 lb AP bomb hit the *Gneisenau*. Her forecastle was shattered, the fore magazine burnt out, 116 of her crew killed and she was officially recorded as being severely damaged. Indeed this damage, together with the mine damage suffered during her 'Channel dash' had now proved terminal. She was decommissioned on 1 July 1942 and all rehabilitation attempts were abandoned in January 1943. She spent the remainder of the war partially dismantled at Gdynia, a useless hulk with about 150 ft of her forepart and all her guns removed.

The *Scharnhorst* escaped any significant bomb damage, both in Wilhelmshaven and Kiel, although it was not through want of trying on Bomber Command's part. In the depth of winter 1943 she put out to sea from Gdynia, where she was now based, to attack British convoy JW 55 B *en route* to Russia. Instead she was confronted by a Royal Navy battle force off the North Cape of Norway on 26 December 1943. After being reduced to a floating hulk by the heavy guns of the battleship HMS *Duke of York*, a number of destroyers closed in and put an end to her with eleven torpedo hits. Only 36 men out of a ship's company of 1,968 survived the pounding and the icy cold of the northern waters.

Nearly a year earlier, Bomber Command's attention focused on the *Tirpitz*, then based in Fottenfjord near Trondheim. The Prime Minister considered the *Tirpitz* a vital enemy target; the very threat she posed tied up a number of British and American battleships which were vitally needed in the Mediterranean and Far East. His concern was reflected in an urgent instruction to General Ismay for the Chiefs of Staff Committee, on 25 January 1942. After stating that the presence of *Tirpitz* at Trondheim had been known for the past three days, he went on:

> ... the destruction or even crippling of this ship would be the greatest event at sea at the present time. No other target is comparable to it. She cannot have ack-ack protection comparable to Brest or the German home ports. If she were only crippled it would be difficult to get her back to Germany. No doubt it is better to wait for moonlight for a night attack but night attacks are not comparable with day attacks. The entire naval situation throughout the World would be altered and naval command in the Pacific would be regained. There must be no lack of co-operation between Bomber Command, the Fleet Air Arm and aircraft carriers. A plan should be made to attack both with torpedo bombers and heavy bombers by daylight or at dawn. The whole strategy of the war turns at this period on this ship which is holding four times the number of British capital ships paralysed to say nothing of two new American battleships retained in the Atlantic. I regard the matter of the highest urgency and importance. I shall mention it in Cabinet tomorrow and it should be considered in detail at the Defence Committee on Tuesday night.

His concern was well justified: fitted with eight 15 in guns supplemented by 95 of smaller calibre, cocooned by a 15 in armoured crust to protect her vitals, and manned by 2,500 fervent seamen, she was going to be a difficult target, and so it proved. Numerous aircraft and a number of midget submarines had a go at one time or another, before the 'unsinkable' ship succumbed to the 12,000 lb Tallboys dropped by Bomber Command in November 1944, as recounted in Chapter Six. However, on the run-up to her demise she suffered a number of near misses. One, with torpedoes, is described in Chapter Nine, and others with the 1,000 lb Spherical Mine and the Johnny Walker bomb in Chapter Twelve.

Little was achieved before September 1943, mainly because *Tirpitz* was well protected by natural cover in the Norwegian fjords. Not only was she difficult to spot close to a hillside, but the problem for the night attackers was compounded by cloud, darkness and enemy smoke-screens. Four full-scale attacks by a total of 96 Halifaxes, 7 Stirlings and 23 Lancasters during 1942, with the loss of 10, caused Captain Karl Topp and his crew little more than passing inconvenience. However, such sorties as *Tirpitz* made to sea were also pretty ineffectual, so that by the time she sailed for Kaa Fjord in Norway's far north on 15 March 1943, the new Captain, Hans Meyer, inherited little sense of achievement. If he had any satisfaction at all it was in the knowledge that his ship was

Action pictures showing Fleet Air Arm Barracudas flying over Kaa Fjord and attacking the Tirpitz on 3 April 1944. Pictures taken by Sub-Lieutenant R. Eveleigh, later Captain RN.

now beyond the range of land-based bombers.

However, on the morning of 22 September 1943 the Royal Navy midget submarines *X6* and *X7*, commanded by Lieutenants Donald Cameron and Geoffrey Place, penetrated the elaborate defences and planted their 2,000 lb Amatex-filled mines, with clockwork fuzes, adjacent to *Tirpitz*'s vulnerable bottom. Severe damage was inflicted throughout the battleship. Besides taking on about 800 cubic metres of floodwater, three main engines were damaged, electrical and communication systems were put out of action, and two 9 in gun turrets were knocked out of alignment. Quite appropriately, both Lieutenants were awarded Victoria Crosses, some compensation for a job extremely well done and the loss of a number of X-craft and crews. After working day and night, the specialist repair teams finally declared the Tirpitz seaworthy again on 15 March 1944, just in time for the next onslaught, this time by the Fleet Air Arm.

It mounted a number of concentrated dive-bombing attacks during the spring and summer, deploying Fairey Barracudas in the bombing role, escorted by fighters to fend off the *Luftwaffe* and keep down the heads of the *Tirpitz*'s gunners with a hail of machine gun fire. The most successful attack was delivered in the early morning of 3 April by 40 Barracudas of 827, 829, 830 and 831 Squadrons from the aircraft carriers HMS *Victorious* and *Furious*. They were supported by 51 Corsairs, Hellcats and Wildcats, some from the main carriers and others from the escort carriers *Searcher, Emperor, Pursuer* and *Fencer,* all of which were cruising about 120 miles west of Kaa Fjord.

The Barracudas carried mixed bomb loads of either a single American 1,600 lb AP bomb, or three 500 lb SAPs, or three 500 lb MCs, or even two 600 lb Anti-Submarine (AS) bombs. The intent was to penetrate the main armoured crust with the slightly delayed APs, and the lighter upper decks with the SAPs. To do so it was necessary to release the loads from above 3,000 feet in a high-speed dive at angles between 45 and 60 degrees, to provide sufficient impetus. The other bombs were fuzed to function on impact, so as to blast the superstructure, the upper decks and gun positions. In the event of near misses the anti-submarine bombs were also programmed to detonate underwater, hopefully damaging the more vulnerable bottom. The fighters having vigorously played their part, the first wave of 21 Barracudas led by Lieutenant-Commander R Baker-Faulkner, dived at the planned 210 knots in the face of fierce enemy gunfire and caught the *Tirpitz* just as she weighed anchor for sea trials in Alten Fjord. Considerable damage was inflicted from stem to stern; many men were killed or wounded, but there was little respite. The second wave of 19 Barracudas, led by Lieutenant-Commander V Rance, repeated the treatment despite vigorous opposition from the shore batteries and the eighteen 37 mm and fifty 20 mm guns mounted on the battleship.

Some bombs did not detonate, including a 1,600 lb AP, requiring attention by a *Luftwaffe* bomb-disposal team. However, 14 struck home, four 1,600 lb APs and ten 500 lb SAPs; none penetrated *Tirpitz*'s vitals. Nevertheless, severe damage was inflicted on the upper decks and superstructure, steam pipes were shattered, light armour was penetrated and badly twisted, and gun positions were dislocated. One near miss, most probably a 600 lb anti-submarine bomb, sprang the side plating, causing an influx of 875 tons of seawater to the bilges. In all, 112 seamen were killed and 316 wounded. Among the more seriously wounded was the Captain, Hans Meyer. *Tirpitz* underwent weeks of feverish rehabilitation before she was again declared seaworthy on 22 June under a new Captain, Wolf Junge, promoted from within the crew.

Following this successful attack, HM King George VI sent the following message: 'Hearty congratulations on your gallant and successful operation yesterday. George RI.'

Above *The* Admiral Scheer, *capsized at her berth after the attack by Bomber* *Command on Kiel, 9/10 April 1945.*

Below *The cumulative effect of Allied bombing attacks on Kiel Dockyard. Apart from* *the damage to dockyard buildings and plant the capsized* Admiral Scheer *can be seen at* *A. The badly damaged* Emden *and* Admiral Hipper *can be seen at B and C respectively.*

Other Barracuda raids mounted from the carriers HMS *Victorious, Furious, Formidable* and *Indefatigable* proved somewhat ineffectual, but two hits were achieved on 24 August by a 500 lb SAP and a 1,600 lb AP. The first detonated under a 9 in gun turret, and the other penetrated the ship's bowels without detonating. The *Luftwaffe* bomb-disposal team reported that it only contained half the prescribed amount of high explosive. If so, the loose packing had probably broken the detonation chain; a costly defect indeed – *Tirpitz* still menaced the Arctic convoys and tied up Allied battleships which could have been used to better effect in the Far East.

It was now recognized that the Fleet Air Arm had neither the aircraft nor the bombs to sink her, whereas the Royal Air Force now had both, if only the *Tirpitz* could be reached by land-based bombers. The Lancaster/12,000 lb Tallboy combination had already proved itself against hardened targets during the past two months and the question of putting the *Tirpitz* within range could be overcome by using a Russian airfield. So began the final attacks on the *Tirpitz*, the story of which has already been told in Chapter Six.

During the final months of the war Bomber Command continued its offensive against the remaining German capital ships. The *Lützow* was found at Swinemünde on the Baltic coast and sunk on 16 April 1945. A week earlier the *Admiral Scheer* was turned over on her side by massed Lancaster bombing whilst at anchorage in Kiel, and nearby the cruisers *Admiral Hipper* and *Emden* lay stranded and heavily damaged by previous successive Bomber Command attacks. The battleship *Schleswig-Holstein* was severely bomb-damaged at Gotenhafen in Danzig Bay on 18 December 1944, and was subsequently scuttled by the Germans just before VE-Day. The *Gneisenau*'s bombed-out hulk fell into Russian hands and was finally broken up in 1951. The American Eighth Air Force sank the light cruiser *Köln* at Wilhelmshaven on 30 March 1945.

When the Allies took over Germany's northern naval ports, at least six bombed-out destroyers, torpedo boats and mine layers were found. The *Prinz Eugen, Nürnberg* and *Leipzig,* together with 15 destroyers, capitulated in Danish ports. At one of these, Abenraa, the *Leipzig* was discovered, badly damaged. Therefore, out of the 15 major warships referred to at the beginning of the chapter, only the *Prinz Eugen* and the *Nürnberg* remained intact and seaworthy. The former was finally sunk during American atom bomb trials at Bikini Atoll in the Pacific during November 1947.

The evidence produced so far, and that yet to be dealt with, clearly indicates that the Royal Air Force and the Fleet Air Arm played a very significant role in ensuring that the German Fleet spent more time in port than at sea. It also proves that no ships are immune from air-delivered bombs, mines or torpedoes, whether they be mighty battleships or sleek modern vessels such as those deployed to the Falkland Islands by the Royal Navy in 1982. However, the stories told so far, and others to be told in succeeding chapters, also clearly show that some aerial weapons were much more effective than others.

CHAPTER NINE

AIRBORNE TORPEDOES

The torpedo was designed specifically to enable ships at sea to attack enemy vessels at or well below the waterline, where protection was frequently non-existent or at its weakest. During the First World War some torpedoes were adapted for airborne use, but very few were used. However, during the Second World War airborne torpedoes were used extensively. By far the most devastating and successful torpedo attack was launched by the Japanese on the United States Fleet at Pearl Harbor in December 1941, bringing that shocked nation into the war. In more honourable circumstances, thoughout the war years the Royal Air Force and the Fleet Air Arm achieved a number of notable successes and some heroic failures.

The inventor of the first torpedo was Robert Whitehead, the English manager of a marine engine factory in the Austrian port of Fiume (now in Yugoslavia). In co-operation with Captain G Luppis of the Austrian Navy, he produced a small weapon in 1867 during the Austro-Italian War. It contained only 18 lb of dynamite, but established the mechanical principles upon which future torpedo development was based.

Whitehead came to England in 1869-70 to demonstrate his 14-in model to the Royal Navy. Generally, torpedoes were categorized thereafter by the diameter of their cylindrical bodies. For example, the main surface types used by the Royal Navy during the First and Second World Wars were the 18 and 21-in models, whereas only the 14 and 18-in versions were adapted for airborne launching.

The Admiralty was suitably impressed by Whitehead's demonstration firing at an old warship off the Isle of Sheppey, Kent, and gave the Royal Laboratory, Woolwich, the task of further developing what was deemed to be an admirable concept. By 1911 Woolwich had produced a 17 ft long, 18-in torpedo capable of speeding through the water at 35 knots (39.7 mph) to a target 2,000 yd distant. In earlier days, the torpedo was propelled though the sea by an engine powered by compressed air, but as time went on a semi-diesel engine was developed. Driving power was achieved by a mixture of steam and gas, water being evaporated and superheated in a generator by a jet of burning shale oil. Except for some updating, the propulsion system remained the same well into the Second World War.

To cater for early seaplanes, an 810 lb 14-in torpedo was adapted and successfully launched into the Solent from a Short Folder aircraft by Lieutenant A M Longmore RNAS (later Air Chief Marshal Sir Arthur, RAF) on 28 July 1914, just six days before the start of the First World War. Previously, in 1913, he had taken to the air with a similar torpedo suspended from a Sopwith seaplane powered by a 200 hp Salmson engine, but he had not been allowed to drop the precariously-slung cargo. An Italian, Captain A Guidoni, launched the very first airborne torpedo, albeit a 350 lb dummy one, way back in 1911.

During the First World War, 14 and 18-in torpedoes were available to the Royal Naval Air Service (RNAS), and later to the Royal Air Force. However, only three, as far as can be determined, were used in anger, all of them 14-in, and that during the Dardanelles campaign against the Turks in 1915. Later in the war when the Short 320 seaplane carried the 18-in torpedo, suitable targets were hard to come upon. Indeed, no real opportunities presented themselves. In any case, the larger torpedo proved an onerous burden for the relatively flimsy and underpowered seaplanes.

The successes claimed for the three 14-in weapons dropped from Short 184 seaplanes in August 1915 were marginal, and debate still continues as to who actually carried out the first successful airborne attack against an enemy vessel at sea. Flight Commander C H K Edmonds RNAS certainly achieved the first airborne torpedo strike in an operational setting when on 12 August he launched his torpedo and hit and damaged a 5,000 ton Turkish merchantman close inshore off Injeh Burna (in the Dardanelles). His understandable delight was somewhat dampened when on return to the seaplane carrier *Ben-My-Chree*, an ex-Isle of Man packet boat, he learned that his target had already been beached and abandoned by its Turkish crew, following a gun attack by two British submarines. However, five days later on the 17th he discovered a Turkish supply ship underway off Ak-Bashi-Liman and, as on the previous occasion, he dived to about 15 ft above the water and released the torpedo at a range of 350 yd, hitting the vessel and setting it on fire. She did not sink, however, and was later towed to safety by the Turks.

The third attack, again on the 17th, was more bizarre. When Edmonds took off from the carrier *Ben-My-Chree* he was accompanied by Flight Lieutenant G B Dacre, also flying a Short 184 seaplane. Because of technical problems Dacre was forced to make an emergency landing upon the water. Having partially rectified the fault, he found he could not take off weighed down by the torpedo. Rather than abandon it he taxied along the water looking for a suitable target. He eventually sighted a small, 300 ton Turkish tug. He closed to within striking range, released his torpedo and sank it. Relieved of its burden, the seaplane was able to get airborne and return safely to the carrier. This was undoubtedly the first sinking of an enemy vessel at sea by an airborne torpedo, although ironically the torpedo was not airborne at the time of release.

Aircraft development progressed slowly during the inter-war years, and torpedoes were carried on a succession of aircraft types, including the Blackburn Cuckoo, Dart, Ripon, Baffin and Shark, followed by the Fairey Swordfish. Thus at the onset of the Second World War in 1939, the standard torpedo aircraft of the Fleet Air Arm was the Swordfish, with a top speed of up to 130 mph and a flight duration of approximately seven hours.

At this time, Royal Air Force Coastal Command was no better equipped, operating only the already obsolescent Vickers Wildebeeste torpedo bomber. However, it was soon replaced in the United Kingdom by the Bristol Beaufort, which commenced torpedo patrols in September 1940, at the height of the Battle of Britain. Sadly, but not surprisingly, two squadrons of Wildebeestes operating in the Far East were annihilated by the Japanese in 1941–42. By that time, the Beaufort was supplemented by Handley Page Hampdens and Vickers Wellingtons adapted for the torpedo role, having been declared by Bomber Command as surplus to requirements with the coming of the more sophisticated heavy bombers. By the end of 1942, the Beauforts were supplanted by the Torbeau, a converted Beaufighter. Together with the Wellingtons they were then deployed to the Middle or Far East.

Torpedo development too, progressed slowly during the inter-war years. With various improvements the 18-in model graduated from the Mark I to the Mark XII by 1940. At that stage most torpedo bombers used the latter, but later in the war some deployed with the updated Mark XV and from 1943 some aircraft carried the American Mark 24 designed specifically to destroy submerged submarines.

But what of the torpedo itself? The weight and size of the weapon depended on the type of warhead and components fitted for a particular operation; generally it was between 1,446 and 1,801 lb, with the high explosive content ranging from 319 lb of TNT to 545 lb of the much more powerful Torpex. The metal cylindrical body containing the propulsion and control systems, and the warhead incorporating the explosive and firing devices, were approximately 204 in (17 ft) long when fully assembled. For example the 18-in Mark XII had a total length of 203 in, the warhead taking up 56.4 in. Fitted with an impact pistol and containing 545 lb of Torpex, the overall weight was 1,801 lb. Speed through the water could be preselected at 27 or 40 knots (30.6 or 45.4 mph), permitting a maximum target range of 3,500 or 1,500 yd respectively. The latter distance was more realistic and effective – obviously, the chances of a strike diminished as the range increased.

The internal mechanism of a typical torpedo is somewhat complex, but a simplified description is offered to assist in understanding the various problems faced by the designers and those who carried them to their selected targets. When launched from the aircraft, a starting lever opened a valve admitting compressed air to the engine, turning it over and lighting a mixture of fuel and air, thus providing gas and steam to rotate the driving shaft and two propellers. These were mounted one behind the other revolving in opposite directions, an arrangement which enhanced running evenness and balance. Once running at the selected speed, the torpedo was kept on course by a gyroscope together with vertical and horizontal rudders, the appropriate depth being maintained by a hydrostatic control device.

Firing pistols (or exploders, in naval parlance) were fitted in the warhead to initiate detonation on impact. In the early days of the Second World War a magnetic type was used, with varied success. Inherent magnetism within the target ship triggered the firing device as the torpedo passed below the intended victim, thus attacking the ship at its weakest point, directly underneath. At least that was the intention, but for one reason or another, it was not always achieved. There were also three direct impact types one purely mechanical and two electrically fired.

All pistols were fitted with safety devices to ensure safe handling or jettisoning in an emergency. Furthermore, they were programmed not to arm until the torpedo had travelled a selected distance through the water. This distance could range from 100 to 1,000 yd. Like the torpedo, the pistol action too was complex, but it can be explained in relatively simple terms. Before an aircraft took off, a safety clip was removed; this together with a preventer ensured the vanes did not rotate during handling or flight. On impact with the water, the preventer lever between the vanes was forced back, out of contact. Travel through the sea caused the impeller to rotate, enabling the internal mechanism to push the detonators into contact with the primers, cock the strikers, and push aside three safety bolts to clear the strikers' path to the detonators. Should the boss of the pistol or any one of the six vanes now impact with the target, the strikers would be forced on to the detonators, thus initiating the practically instantaneous detonation chain. Failing to achieve a strike, the torpedo ran out of steam (literally) and sank. Most aircraft carried only a single torpedo, so it was important to get everything right – good opportunities presented themselves infrequently.

When attacking a heavily-armed ship or fleet of ships, getting everything right was an exceedingly chancy operation. There were so many variables, not least of which was the torpedo itself. This had not been primarily developed for air use, and yet it was expected to fly unaided for at least 250 yd before even reaching its intended environment. To have any chance at all it had to be launched from extremely low level in a straight and level flight. In the case of the Beaufort flying at about 140 mph, the optimum height was about 80 ft. To reduce aim-off errors to an absolute minimum, it was often necessary to launch the torpedo at point blank range, allowing only enough distance for the pistol to arm.

Nevertheless, with all its vagaries, it was considerably more effective than the contemporary bombs. As a naval worthy was heard to say 'It is better to let water in at the bottom with a torpedo than to let air in at the top with a bomb.' This was indeed a truism. A single detonation under a vulnerable hull could break the back of a large merchantman, and severely damage the strongest warship. On the other hand, it needed a number of side-on strikes even to temporarily incapacitate the hardened ships. However, a great deal depended on the point of impact; a strike on the steering gear, for instance, could be devastating, as the *Bismarck* found to her cost.

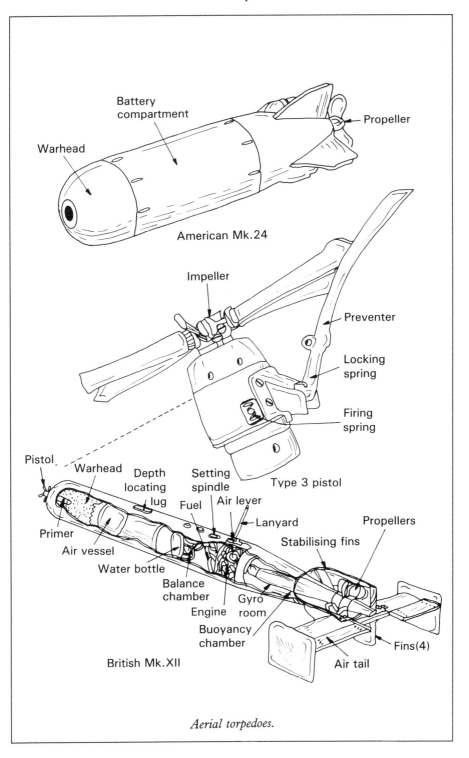

Aerial torpedoes.

A consistently efficient magnetic pistol would almost certainly have produced more sinkings, triggering as it did below the victim. Consequently, less torpedoes would have been needed at a time of chronic shortage in 1940–41. They were difficult and expensive weapons to produce, requiring a good kill rate to justify their existence. Unfortunately, despite some significant successes, the magnetic pistol proved alarmingly fickle, quite often functioning prematurely, due in some measure to the torpedo's own inherent magnetism. It was also suspect in large sea swells or in the presence of extraneous pick up. In any event, rectification proved almost insuperable, leading to its abandonment in favour of the direct impact types.

The problems associated with torpedo instability included a natural tendency for them to hit the water tail-first, thus frequently damaging the steering and propulsion mechanism. These problems were ovecome by fitting a 42-in air tail, which broke away on impact with the sea surface. Trials with a gyroscopically-controlled wing-tail 'Toroplane' in 1941 were abandoned in favour of the simple air tail. Additionally, a special mechanism was built into the Beaufort release gear which assisted the torpedo to hit the water at such an angle as to prevent the possibility of ricochet, and limited the initial plunge to less than 45 ft. After porpoising for one or two cycles, the torpedo assumed the appropriate depth, speed and course to the target. Many targets were missed because one or other of these parameters were not achieved and, of course, skilful enemy evasion added to the problems.

So much for the torpedo, but just how effective was it in actual operations? This can only be judged by considering some of its operational uses. Both the Fleet Air Arm and the Royal Air Force achieved a number of successes, along with some notable failures. That is if not succeeding, despite great dedication and courage, often in very adverse conditions, can be termed failure.

Probably the most notable, early success was the attack by Swordfish aircraft of the Fleet Air Arm against the Italian fleet at Taranto harbour on the night of 11–12 November 1940. A force of 20 aircraft from 813, 815, 819 and 824 Squadrons took part. The weapon loads consisted of Mark XII torpedoes, and 250 lb SAP bombs, supplemented by 4.5 in Reconnaissance Flares to light up the target area. The torpedoes were fitted with magnetically-operated pistols set to run at a depth of 33 ft to avoid anti-torpedo nets. The anchorage at Taranto, the Italian Fleet's main base in Southern Italy, was also protected by barrage balloons and anti-aircraft batteries, so this was to be no easy ride for the 130 mph Swordfish.

The attack was executed in two waves, the first led by Lieutenant-Commander N W Williamson and the other by Lieutenant-Commander J W Hale. Each of the pilots selected his own target, and in the face of violent opposition launched his torpedo from between mast height and about 500 ft at ranges of 300 to 1,000 yd. The much maligned magnetic pistol behaved admirably in the calm water of the harbour, only one out of the eleven failing to detonate. Five hits were achieved on three battleships. The 35,000 ton *Littorio* suffered three, and the 28,700 ton *Caio Diulio* and *Conte di Cavour* one each. The 10,000 ton heavy cruiser *Trento* and the destroyers *Libeccio* and *Passagno* received significant damage from direct bomb hits or near-misses. On top of all that, a seaplane hangar and oil installations were substantially damaged by bombs. Surprisingly, this feat was achieved with the loss of only two Sword-fish. The crew of one of these, that flown by Lieutenant-Commander Williamson, survived – the warships did not fare so well. The *Littorio* suffered substantial damage to her hull and was out of action for six months. The *Caio Diulio*, with two magazines flooded, had to be beached to prevent her sinking, and repairs were not completed until May 1941. The *Conte di Cavour* suffered such damage that her operational career was abruptly ended.

By any standards this was an important naval victory, which shattered Italian morale as well as the pride of her fleet. Post-war archives indicate that this attack had still further repercussions – it demonstrated to the Japanese that a torpedo attack was possible against a well-protected harbour where the water was less than 45 ft deep.

Japanese planning for a surprise attack against the US Fleet at Pearl Harbor began in the spring of 1940, and was intended to be a high-altitude bombing operation supported by dive bombing and torpedo attacks by midget submarines. The successful results at Taranto prompted significant changes to Japanese planning.

The Japanese naval attachés in London and Rome reported, among other things, that the water at Taranto was only 42 ft deep and that at Pearl Harbor 45 ft; both depths at that time considered too shallow for airborne torpedo attacks. Consequently, the plan of attack against Pearl Harbor was amended to include a large number of airborne torpedoes, modified to accord with the British version used at Taranto. The results of the Japanese attack on that fateful day in December 1941 are well documented and need no further comment.

Mention should also be made of the Fleet Air Arm Albacore, permanently over-shadowed by the more famous Swordfish, but also having its moments against enemy warships. One of these came on 28 March 1941 at Greece's southern tip during the all-day Battle of Cape Matapan. In support of the surface naval element, a mixed force of Albacores and Swordfish from 815, 826 and 829 Squadrons, operating from the carrier HMS *Formidable* and Malenme airfield, Crete, took part, as did Royal Air Force Blenheim bombers, of 84, 113 and 211 Squadrons, based at Menedi, near Athens.

Airborne torpedo attacks were made on a number of Italian warships. An Albacore of 829 Squadron struck the battleship *Vittorio Veneto* above the port outer screw and brought her to a stop. It seemed likely that Lieutenant-Commander J Dalyell-Stead and crew, all of whom perished, scored the hit. Later, she was able to proceed at reduced speed; the 8,000 ton cruiser *Pola* was not so fortunate. A well-directed Mark XII, set to run at 28 ft and launched by Sub-Lieutenant C P C Williams from an Albacore, stopped the cruiser in her tracks, where she was sent to the bottom by surface ships, which also accounted for three cruisers and two destroyers, some of them Taranto survivors. Williams had to ditch, but he and his two crewmen were picked up by HMS *Juno*.

German capital warships were also the victims of some of the early airborne torpedo attacks by the Royal Air Force and the Fleet Air Arm, and must be includ-

Fleet Air Arm Albacores.

ed among the success stories, although the successes were bought at great cost. By mid 1941, the German battle cruiser *Gneisenau*, the battleship *Bismarck* and the pocket battleship *Lützow* (alias *Deutschland*) had been crippled by airborne torpedoes.

Some ten months before she escaped north to Kiel, the *Gneisenau* was severely damaged at Brest by a 22 Squadron Beaufort on detachment to St Eval, Cornwall. She had just been moved out of dry dock to avoid possible damage from an unexploded 250 lb SAP bomb. Just after dawn on 6 April 1941, Flying Officer K Campbell and crew made a spectacular low-level attack on the heavily-defended warship, defying gunfire from three flak ships, numerous shore anti-aircraft batteries and *Gneisenau*'s own guns. The Beaufort was destroyed and its captain and crew of Sergeants J P Scott, W Mullis and R W Hillman perished, but the torpedo ran straight and true, tearing a hole 40 ft wide in the battle cruiser's side. Seawater flooded two turbines, and a propeller shaft was severely distorted, damage which took some eight months to repair. Two other Beauforts, piloted by Flying Officer J Hyde and Sergeant A Camp either failed to see the warship, or were driven away by heavy flak. Flying Officer Campbell was awarded a well-deserved Victoria Cross, the first torpedo airman to be so honoured. It brought considerable credit to 22 Squadron, which had made its torpedo début on 15 September 1940, sinking the 5,000 ton transport *IJmuiden* near Flushing.

In company with the heavy cruiser *Prinz Eugen*, the battleship *Bismarck* left Gotenhafen (now Gdynia) on 19 May 1941, to attack allied North Atlantic convoys. Whilst some of the lesser escorts were being refuelled in Grimstad Fjord near Bergen on the 22nd, *Bismarck* and the others were photographed during the afternoon by a Coastal Command reconnaissance Spitfire, piloted by Flying Officer M Suckling and based at Wick. Unfortunately, the mini-fleet sailed later in the evening before a bomber attack could be mounted. Early next morning the *Bismarck* and the *Prinz Eugen* entered the Denmark Straits (between Iceland and Greenland).

Just after 8.00 p.m. the same day (23 May 1941), in very poor visibility, battle was joined with the heavy cruisers HMS *Norfolk* and HMS *Suffolk,* who reported details to the now-alerted main British fleet. At dawn the following day, the German ships met up with the battleship HMS *Prince of Wales* and the 48,000 ton battle cruiser HMS *Hood.* In the ensuing action, following a massive explosion, the *Hood* sank 300 miles south-west of Iceland, with only three survivors. More than 1,500 men were lost including, Vice-Admiral L Holland. The *Prince of Wales* was badly damaged and forced to withdraw from the scene of action.

Hit three times, the *Bismarck's* captain decided to head for St Nazaire, some 1,600 miles distant on the Bay of Biscay. She was hampered by two large holes in the hull, flooded compartments, two boilers behaving erratically, a persistent oil leak and 1,000 tons of oil inaccessible in the forward storage tanks. Later, it was recognized that she had insufficient fuel to reach St Nazaire, so plans were made to receive her in Brest. She proceeded south at reduced speed, suffering some loss of electrical power and knowing that the forward radar was not functioning. Just after 6.00 p.m. the *Prinz Eugen* left the *Bismarck* and headed directly into the North Atlantic to pursue her original task of harrying the Allied convoys, – though she was to limp into Brest eight days later with defective engines.

Around midnight on 24–25 May, the *Bismarck* came under another determined attack; this time it was the turn of 825 Squadron from the aircraft-carrier HMS *Victorious.* Flying in from all directions, just above the waves, a technique perfected by the Fleet Air Arm, the eight Swordfish ignored the hail of anti-aircraft fire from the zigzagging battleship and the massive water spouts produced from shells deliberately fired into the sea by the big guns. They released their 1,600 lb torpedoes at point blank range. One struck home at the waterline on the armoured belt amidships, doing little material damage. Perhaps because of the short range it failed to assume the proper running depth of 31 ft to get at the vulnerable below-water hull. Nevertheless, it had the distinction of killing one of the crew and injuring six more by concussion – *Bismarck's* first war casualties, inflicted by Sub-Lieutenant Lawson's well-directed torpedo. This attack further aggravated the warship's problems, and her speed was reduced to 20 knots (22.7 mph). The Squadron Commander of 825 Squadron, Lieutenant-Commander E K Esmonde was awarded the Distinguished Service Order (DSO) for his courageous leadership during the attack. He actually received the award at Buckingham Palace on 11 February 1942, just one day before he was to die trying to prevent the passage of the *Scharnhorst, Gneisenau* and *Prinz Eugen* through the English Channel, an action for which he was subsequently awarded a posthumous Victoria Cross.

Swordfish torpedo bomber taking off from an aircraft carrier.

After the attack by 825 Squadron, the Royal Navy lost contact with the *Bismarck* and it was not regained until Flying Officer D Briggs and his American co-pilot, Ensign L B Smith US Navy, on reconnaissance with a 209 Squadron Catalina flying boat from Lough Erne in Northern Ireland, spotted her from 2,000 ft at 500 yd in very poor visibility about 400 miles West of Ireland – it was now 10.15 am on 26 May 1941. As a result, two separate operations were mounted by the carrier HMS *Ark Royal* deploying Swordfish of 810, 818 and 820 Squadrons. The first foray in mid-afternoon proved nearly disastrous, in that some of the torpedoes were inadvertently launched at the cruiser HMS *Sheffield*. Fortunately, she successfully evaded a number, whilst others, all fitted with magnetic pistols and set at 30 ft, functioned prematurely in the swell. Nothing was lost except some brotherly love and esteem. *Sheffield* got some good practice in torpedo evasion and it became patently obvious that the magnetic pistols were highly unreliable.

The same 15 aircraft, led by Lieutenant-Commander T P Coode, made up for the earlier *faux pas* between 8.00 and 9.30 pm. This time the 15 torpedoes were fitted with direct-contact pistols and set for a running depth of 22 ft. They approached *Bismarck* through the blistering firepower, just as reckless of personal safety as their colleagues from HMS *Victorious* two days earlier. One hit was scored on the rudder just after 9.00 p.m. and another amidships ten minutes later. The first of these was the vital (perhaps mortal) blow, the rudder jamming 15 degrees to port. The battleship was no longer steerable – indeed, she was forced on to a course away from the safety of a French port. Sub-Lieutenant A Beale scored the hit on the *Bismarck*'s port side, amidships, and it seems likely from contemporary reports that either Lieutenant Godfrey-Fausett or Sub-Lieutenant K Pattinson, who flew in at wave-top level doing 90 knots (102.3 mph), struck the vital blow on the rudder. No aircraft were lost, but many were seriously damaged. Sub-Lieutenant A W D Beale DSC was to die less than a year later on 5 April 1942 when his torpedo-carrying Swordfish, with five others of 788 Squadron, were shot down by Japanese fighters over Colombo, Ceylon (Sri Lanka).

Harried by destroyers all night, the *Bismarck* could neither choose her course nor evade the final British pounding, inflicted by the battleships HMS *King George V* and HMS *Rodney*, which started at about 8.45 a.m. on the 27th. Ultimately, the helpless hulk, full of dead or dying men, was despatched by three torpedoes from the cruiser HMS *Dorsetshire*. She sank at 10.40 a.m. 400 miles west of Brest.

The gallant crew had put up a tremendous fight in the face of fearful odds – 2,085 men were lost, including the Captain Ernst Lindemann and Fleet Commander, Admiral Gunther Lutzens; 115 men survived. Given a few more hours she would have escaped to the safety of a strong *Luftwaffe* umbrella; consequently, one Fleet Air Arm torpedo played a significant part in ensuring that she did not, apart from revenging the loss of the *Hood*. Perhaps things might also have turned out vastly different but for the fortuitous sighting by Flying Officer Dennis Briggs and the crew of Catalina 'Z' Zebra 209 Squadron, Royal Air Force. Perhaps too, Korvettenkapitän Schneider, who directed *Bismarck*'s guns which sank *Hood*, would have lived to enjoy the Knight's Cross of the Iron Cross bestowed upon him by Adolf Hitler.

Some three weeks later on 12 June 1941, *Lützow* attempted to break out into the Atlantic. She was sighted towards midnight in the Skagerrak with five escorting destroyers and pin-pointed by Flight Sergeant R H Loveitt in a 42 Squadron Beaufort. Coming in low he torpedoed her just off Lindesnes, Southern Norway – no doubt to the chagrin of her escorts. The torpedo struck amidships, partially crippling her. The listing pocket battleship had to be towed to Kiel for repairs, which were not completed until January 1943.

In the Mediterranean on the morning of 15 June 1942, nine Beauforts of 39, 85 and 217 Squadrons Royal Air Force set out from Malta to attack elements of the Italian fleet sailing south from Taranto to attack a Malta-bound British convoy. When sighted, the heavy cruiser *Trento* was heading three cruisers in line astern surrounded by four destroyers. Flight Lieutenant A H Aldridge of 217 Squadron selected *Trento* as his victim. Flying in at 80 ft across the leading destroyer he launched his Mark XII torpedo from about 850 yd. It struck the target on the bow below the water line and soon the crippled cruiser was burning furiously, abandoned by her consorts and escorts, and left to the mercy of the enemy, who called up the submarine HMS *Umbra*, which sank her with a well-directed torpedo. Six days later Aldridge also torpedoed the 7,700 ton

German merchantman *Reichenfel,* which was carrying fuel and ammunition to Rommel's hard-pressed army in the western desert.

On the day following the *Trento*'s demise, the battleship *Littorio* was torpedoed in the same waters by Pilot Officer Hawes in a 38 Squadron Wellington. Badly damaged, she was out of action for at least two months. The Wellingtons, along with the Hampdens and Torbeaus, had few brushes with the larger German and Italian warships, but the Torbeau in particular did exceedingly good work among armed auxiliaries and merchantmen in European waters. Whilst stationed in Russia during the latter part of 1942, the Hampdens were instrumental in encouraging the German warships in the Norwegian fjords to stay in port.

Such then were some of the airborne torpedo success stories, but what of the near misses and the glorious failures referred to earlier? One classic near-miss was the Albacores' brush with the *Tirpitz* beyond the Arctic Circle in March 1942. Twelve aircraft, led by Lieutenant-Commander W J Lucas flying from the carrier HMS *Victorious* intercepted the 42,800 ton warship on 9 March off the Lofoten Islands as she steamed south to her base in Trondheim Fjord after an unsuccessful foray against the Arctic convoys to Russia. The Germans subsequently admitted that a number of the well-directed torpedoes passed within yards of the ship's stem and stern. The Albacores launched their weapons at point blank range, despite a hail of anti-aircraft shells, and two were shot down. It was later claimed that this attack gave the *Tirpitz* a fright and almost succeeded in crippling her. Unfortunately, frightening or almost crippling a ship does not win naval battles.

Turning now to the glorious failures, the operations on 12 February 1942 with both the Fleet Air Arm and the Royal Air Force deployed, must surely come within this category. This was the bleak winter's day when the German warships *Scharnhorst, Gneisenau* and *Prinz Eugen* escaped from Brest, through the straits of Dover and the North Sea to their home ports at Wilhelmshaven and Kiel, having dodged the Mark XII airborne torpedoes aimed at one or other of them.

Six Fleet Air Arm Swordfish of 825 Squadron based at Lee-on-Solent, but detached to RAF Manston earlier in the month, set out just after noon in two echelons of three each. They were supported by ten Spitfires, who had difficulty in keeping in touch with the slow-flying 'Stringbags'. The Swordfish sighted the enemy warships sailing in line ahead, with the *Prinz Eugen* leading. The first three aircraft, led by the Squadron Commander, Lieutenant-Commander E K Esmonde, swooped down to 50 ft and flew towards the enemy. At a range of 2,000 yd every anti-aircraft gun in the fleet opened fire, whilst enemy fighters engaged the Spitfires. Holes were torn in the fabric of the aircraft, but on they flew. The *Gneisenau* and *Scharnhorst* opened fire with their main guns raising a solid wall of water in front of the aircraft, and still they flew on. The aircraft flying alongside Esmonde were piloted by Sub-Lieutenants B W Rose and C M Kingsmill. All three managed to release their torpedoes, but almost immediately Esmonde's aircraft crashed and sank, and Rose and Kingsmill managed to fly a short distance before ditching in the sea. Leading Airman

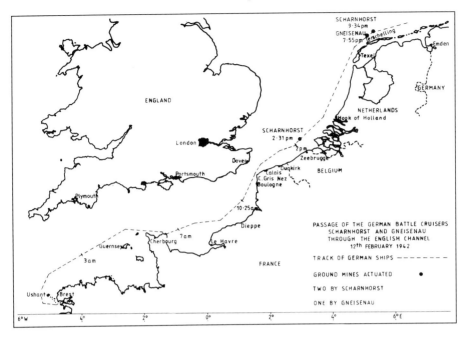

Track of German battle cruisers, 12 February 1942.

Johnson, the air gunner in Rose's aircraft was killed but the remaining five crew of the two aircraft were rescued.

Of the second wave of three aircraft little is known; piloted by Lieutenant J C Thompson and Sub-Lieutenants C R Wood and P Bligh, they were last seen taking violent evasive action but still heading towards their targets. Nothing further was seen of them or their crews. Of eighteen men who took off from Manston, only five survived, and of those only Sub-Lieutenant E Lee, Rose's observer was unwounded. Lieutenant-Commander Esmonde was subsequently awarded a posthumous Victoria Cross for supreme gallantry against fearful odds. The four surviving officers were awarded Distinguished Service Orders (DSOs), and the surviving air gunner, Leading Airman Bunce, the Conspicuous Gallantry Medal (CGM). The officers and men who lost their lives were mentioned in despatches, the only posthumous award then available other than the Victoria Cross. Admiral Ramsay reported to the Admiralty, 'In my opinion the gallant sortie of these six Swordfish constitutes one of the finest exhibitions of self sacrifice and devotion that the war has yet witnessed' (despatch dated 16 February 1942). Esmonde's body was later recovered and buried in Gillingham (Kent) cemetery.

825 Squadron personnel were not the only gallant men on this fateful day. At least 28 torpedo-armed Beauforts of 42, 86 and 217 Squadrons attacked the warships between 3.40 and 6.30 p.m. in failing light and atrocious weather conditions. Latterly, the clouds were down to 600 ft and visibility was less than 1,000 yd, conditions which suited the Germans admirably. Nevertheless, a few

of the Mark XIIs ran close to all three ships, and the Germans admitted later that only smart steering frustrated the efforts of the Beauforts which had had to be hurriedly deployed to East-coast airfields to bring them within striking distance of the mini-fleet sailing up the Dutch coast. Things might have been different if the bulk of the Beaufort force had been alerted sooner at their home bases, St Eval, Cornwall and Thorney Island, Hampshire. Not only were they within reasonable striking distance, but the weather conditions were marginally better earlier in the day. Heavy coastal batteries, Royal Navy surface craft and Bomber Command fared no better. Of 240 bombers deployed, only 39 even caught a momentary glimpse of the warships, through low cloud and rain. Not surprisingly, no hits were claimed. However, not all was lost, both *Scharnhorst* and *Gneisenau* suffered considerable damage from airborne mines laid by Bomber Command some days earlier (see Chapter Ten).

This action, on one of the foulest days of the year, favoured the Germans and cost the Fleet Air Arm and the Royal Air Force dearly. The former lost six Swordfish, and the latter two Blenheims, two Hudsons, three Beauforts, five Wellingtons and nine Hampdens, along with some fighters. Many more were

Preparing to load a Mk XII airborne torpedo with whiskered contact pistol on to a Bristol Beaufort. (IWM)

damaged. For the Germans, this was an epic voyage, demonstrating great opportunism, fine seamanship and great gallantry.

The *Prinz Eugen* thwarted the Beauforts again four months later. She was spotted on 17 June steaming south towards Kristiansand in the Skagerrak, accompanied by four destroyers. Nine aircraft from 42 Squadron launched torpedoes, but no strikes were achieved to mitigate the loss of three aircraft shot down.

From mid-1943 there was a dramatic change in the use of airborne torpedoes with the advent in the Fleet Air Arm and the Royal Air Force of the American Mark 24 torpedo. This weapon, designed specifically to kill submerged submarines, was first obtained from America in May 1943 for use by airborne submarine hunters. The 680 lb Mark 24, acoustic homing torpedo – known to some as 'Wandering Annie' – sought out engine noises, with deadly accuracy. This was manifested in the many U-boat kills recorded.

The torpedo, 84-in long, 19-in diameter, contained a nose warhead with 92 lb of RDX/TNT fitted with a direct contact fuze, and a battery-powered electric propulsion system and guidance equipment. Dropped from the optimum height of 250 ft it was capable of running and searching for ten minutes or more in a preselected circle of 4,000 yd range at a speed of 12 knots (13.6 mph). It homed directly on to an engine noise, the fuze detonating the high explosive warhead on impact. Normally, it was aimed at freshly submerged U-boats trying to escape the attentions of the hunters. This weapon was available to the Fleet Air Arm and, for instance, the Swordfish of 835 Squadron on the escort carrier *Nairana*, had it on the inventory, whilst shepherding Arctic convoys to Russia. However, there is no evidence that it was used. On the other hand, success came quickly to the Royal Air Force Coastal Command Liberators, each capable of carrying ten of the torpedoes.

On 13 May 1943, just after the Mark 24 was introduced, the German submarine *U-456* was severely damaged by Flight Lieutenant J Wright and crew of 86 Squadron, in the vicinity of convoy HX 237, eight days out of Newfoundland. The *coup de gras* was given to the doomed U-boat by a Royal Navy escort ship. The Squadron, operating from Aldergrove near Belfast, had another successful encounter next day when Pilot Officer F F Gaston and crew sank *U-266* in the North Atlantic. Two more were accounted for in July. Squadron Leader T M Bulloch of 224 Squadron sank *U-514* off Northern Spain on the 4th, and Flying Officer J Moffat of 120 Squadron sank *U-338* in the North Atlantic on the 20th. Many more were to follow them to the bottom.

American records claim that the US Forces used 142 Mark 24s in combat, sinking 31 submarines and damaging 15. They further claim that the Allied Forces, principally British, expended 204 in sinking 37 U-boats and damaging 18. In all, this represented a 20 per cent kill rate, or a 30 per cent hit rate, far superior to that achieved by most of the other contemporary weapons. Used in very different circumstances, which militated against them (submerged U-boats do not fire back), the British airborne torpedoes achieved nothing like those figures. The British designers half hoped for a kill, the Americans expected one, and quite often got it.

Undoubtedly the British Mark XII and Mark XV torpedoes could be most effective provided they were well directed and ran true. Unfortunately too many missed, perhaps not surprisingly when one considers what the low-level torpedo bombers had to face. However, having braved all and released the torpedo correctly it is sad that many functioned erratically or failed to detonate on reaching the target. The inconsistency of the torpedo was also present in the surface or sub-surface launched types, so it is not surprising that they sometimes functioned less well when air-dropped. Indeed Robert Whitehead was most upset when the Royal Navy began to fire his beloved weapon from deck tubes – it is hard to imagine what he would have thought of launching heights in excess of 300 ft.

The adverse operational environment militated significantly against the airborne torpedo and those who directed it at the enemy. Nevertheless, the weapon contributed substantially in destroying or temporarily crippling Italian and German warships at a critical time in the earlier years of the Second World War. The cost in men and machines was high, but in assessing the torpedo's cost effectiveness in retrospect, it can perhaps be said that the successes outweighed the failures. What cannot be disputed is the dedication and gallantry of the torpedo airmen, who not only challenged the might of the Italian and German Fleets operating sometimes with obsolescent, if not obsolete equipment, but daily faced the rigours of adverse weather conditions and the prospect of being forced down into what was indeed a cruel sea.

CHAPTER TEN

AIRBORNE SEA MINES

Initially, the sea mine was seen purely as a defensive weapon. Its development and use during the Crimean War, closely followed by its use in the American Civil War, firmly established it as a major weapon of war, but still in the defensive role. However, the Russo-Japanese War of 1905–6, saw its first offensive use. The Japanese lost two battleships and three cruisers to offensive mines, and the Russians one battleship. Mines also badly damaged a number of capital ships on both sides. These successes, or disasters, as the case might be, established the sea mine as an essential weapon of major maritime powers.

Prior to and during the First World War most of the Royal Navy mines were of the spherical, moored, horned type. Direct ship contact with any one of the horns initiated an electrical current which detonated the mine. Credit for first inventing the magnetic mine and using it operationally fell to the British, who laid 472 off the Belgian coast in August and September 1918. They were not a great success, many of them inadvertently detonating shortly after deployment. They were categorized as influence ground mines, because they were laid on the sea bed in shallow inshore waters where they lurked until the firing system was triggered by the inherent magnetism of an unsuspecting enemy vessel.

Development practically ceased when the war ended two months later, and little progress was achieved until rearmament pressures in 1936 influenced the Admiralty to authorize development work on a moored magnetic mine for use against submarines. Posing a major threat during the First World War, these were seen as a similar threat in any future war. Ultimately, it was introduced for naval use in 1941 as the M Mk I. However, the need for ground mines was also considered, and the first order for 30 aircraft-dropped, trial, magnetic mines was placed by the Admiralty in July 1939. This type was intended to be free-dropped from torpedo-bomber aircraft. As a result of the trials and repeated meetings of the Naval and Air Staffs, it became clear that neither the Beaufort torpedo-bomber, earmarked by Royal Air Force Coastal Command as a minelayer, nor the Royal Navy Fleet Air Arm Swordfish and Albacore aircraft, had the range to reach many of the areas selected for minelaying. Consequently it was decided to give the longer-range Bomber Command Hampden aircraft a mining capability. This necessitated a major mine modification to fit it for the increased speed and height of dropping likely to be adopted by the Hampden. Therefore, to reduce impact damage it was fitted with a nose fairing and a drogue parachute which slowed its rate of descent.

The trial programme was completed in March 1940, and production models of the modified mine, nominated as the 1,500 lb 'A' (airborne) Mk I, were made available to the Royal Air Force in early April. The first British aerial minelaying operation was carried out by the Hampdens of 5 Group, Bomber Command on the night of 13–14 April 1940, when they laid 14 mines off the Danish coast, some five months after the *Luftwaffe* had dropped its first magnetic mines in British waters.

The availability of these airborne mines was indeed timely. The so-called phoney war was at an end; the Germans invaded Norway during that month and the Low Countries and France in May. By the end of June 1940, they occupied 1,600 miles of coast and inland water stretching from northern Norway down to Biaritz on the Franco-Spanish border.

The need to restrict enemy shipping by minelaying now became a matter of the utmost urgency. Unfortunately, many of the mineable waters were either inaccessible, or were too exposed for Royal Naval vessels. Consequently, the increased burden had to be borne by aircraft, although the Admiralty retained responsibility for target selection.

Taking full account of individual aircraft capabilities, the Naval and Air staffs agreed that initially Bomber Command Hampdens would be responsible for mining operations in the more distant western Baltic, the Kattegat (that arm of the North Sea linked to the Baltic which separates Denmark from Sweden), the Great and Little Belts (the two straits either side of Fyn Island off the Danish East coast), Kiel Bay and the approaches to the Elbe River. The shorter-range Coastal Command and Fleet Air Arm aircraft (operating under Royal Air Force control at Royal Air Force bases) would operate off the Ems and Weser Rivers and in the Huibert Gat (a gap between the Dutch Frisian Islands). Subsequently, when the Germans overran France and the Low Countries, Coastal Command directed much of its effort to the Belgium and Channel ports. From August onwards it concentrated on laying mines off those Biscay ports now in use by U-boats.

Nearly 4,000 mines were laid during 1940, 1,167 of which were laid by aircraft, each carrying a single mine. The air-delivered mines accounted for the sinking of 137 enemy vessels, representing 74 per cent of all vessels sunk by mines, but at a cost of 31 aircraft.

Airborne minelaying operations in North West European waters during 1941 continued at about the same level, although there was a shift of emphasis yet again from the north to the Biscay ports. The shift on this occasion was caused almost entirely by the arrival of the German battlecruisers *Scharnhorst* and *Gneisenau* at Brest on 22 March. Between March and June 1941 that port's approaches received an average of 70 mines a month, to dissuade the trapped high seas raiders from leaving port.

By the end of the year, Coastal Command abandoned the minelaying role and its Beaufort aircraft were reassigned to the torpedo-bomber role, thus leaving Bomber Command with sole responsibility for the minelaying task. However, from time to time until March 1943 the Fleet Air Arm Swordfish heroically supplemented their Royal Air Force colleagues.

Officially, Bomber Command assumed the overall responsibility for airborne mining operations in home waters on 25 March 1942, on the basis that 'such operations are to be carried out as part-training for inexperienced crews and by veterans in so far as it does not prejudice the normal bombing effort.' Thus it was that mining operations by Bomber Command usually took second priority to that of bombing missions. This, despite the fact that the Command was the Admiralty's agent for aerial minelaying, a role previously held by Coastal Command.

To meet its new commitments, Bomber Command deployed its heavier bombers on the minelaying task, thus enabling heavier mine loads to be carried over greater distances. Included were the Wellington (two mines), the Manchester and Halifax (four mines) and the Stirling and Lancaster (six mines).

By 1944–45, the very long range (VLR) Liberators, operating mainly in the Far East, were capable of carrying six mines for a distance of 900 nautical miles at 150 knots (1,036 miles at 172 mph). However, if speed and surprise was essential, the Mosquito XI B could carry two mines at 270 knots (311 mph) to a range of 370 nautical miles (426 miles).

As for the airborne mines themselves, four main British types were used. All were robustly designed for release from aircraft flying at at least 200 mph, and depending upon the type, from a height of between 100 and 15,000 ft, so they would not be damaged by impact with the water or the sea-bed. Within eight months of its introduction, the 1,500 lb A Mk I mine was modified to assist manufacturing processes and strengthen the steel casing. Three modifications progressively upgraded the category to Mk IV. Thus by the beginning of 1941, it was technically the A Mk IV but, because it remained essentially identical to the A Mk I, it was universally known as the 1,500 lb A Mk I–IV. Approximately 750 lb of its total weight was taken up by high explosive. A smaller version, the 1,000 lb A Mk V containing between 625 and 675 lb of high explosive, was introduced during 1940–41. These two were the airborne mines predominantly used throughout the war years. The latter was deployed almost entirely in the magnetic mode, whereas the A Mk I–IV incorporated a number of triggering options. These included magnetic, acoustic and a combination of both, introduced in 1940, 1942 and 1943 respectively. The acoustic system was actuated by the noises and vibrations emanating from a ship's engine and/or its propellers.

The mine could be made to detonate on first sensing a magnetic or acoustic impulse. Alternatively, it could lie dormant for a number of days, permitting ships to pass over unharmed perhaps up to 15 times before detonating. Thus, the enemy was often lulled into a false sense of security, and the minesweepers were in a state of chaotic uncertainty. To suit friendly shipping plans, the trig-

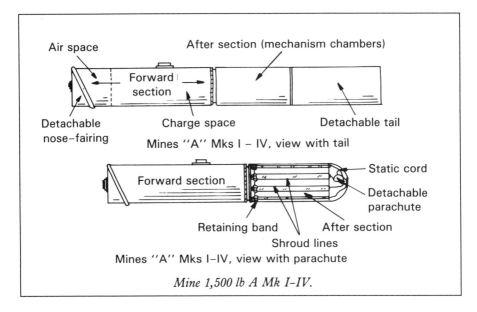

Mine 1,500 lb A Mk I–IV.

gering devices could be set to neutralize after a fixed period. By fitting arming clocks, mines could be programmed to remain inactive for many months on the sea bottom.

The 1,500 lb A Mk I–IV was supplemented in 1944 by the more versatile 2,000 lb A Mk VI. This contained more explosive and was triggered by even more sophisticated devices. At about the same time, improvements were made to the 1,000 lb A Mk V, including the fitting of acoustic devices, upgrading it to the 1,000 lb A Mk VII.

The external shape of the 1,500 lb A Mk I–IV mine and its attachments is illustrated. However, it is neither practical nor wise to describe the triggering devices in detail; many are still in use (see Appendix 6). These mines caused havoc wherever they were used. The cylindrical steel case, 18 in in diameter and 120 in long including the parachute pack and nose fairing, contained the main explosive charge of 750 lb of Amatol or 775 lb of Minol. The case also contained the appropriate triggering devices and a hydrostatic water pressure safety switch, which armed the mine when it sank to an appropriate depth. Lying on the sea or river bed, leaving the parachute and nose fairing discarded on the surface, it lurked awaiting the potentially fatal magnetic or acoustic pulses generated by an unsuspecting victim, or persuading minesweepers into thinking it was not there at all. The smaller 1,000 lb A Mk V, and its successor the A Mk VII, each contained between 625 and 675 lb of explosive.

Both sizes of mine were occasionally converted for use as parachute land-mines, code-named 'Magnum' and 'Tim' respectively. This was achieved by increasing the explosive content by some 46 per cent, fitting a bomb firing system and a domed nose. For example, the explosive in the 'Magnum', the 1,500 lb A Mk I–IV, was increased to 1,100 lb giving the mine an overall weight of 1,850 lb. A large container of explosve, detonated at roof top or ground level, is a most effective way to create blast damage, as was demonstrated by the German use of parachute mines on London and other cities. Their mines, however, were larger and contained some 1,535 lb of high explosive. The same principle was adopted in the range of high capacity British bombs.

The first operational use of converted mines was made on the night 12–13 August 1940 by Hampdens of 49 and 83 Squadrons based at Scampton exactly five weeks before the first German parachute mines were dropped on London. On this occasion Flight Lieutenant R A B Learoyd of 49 Squadron won the Victoria Cross for a valiant low-level attack on the Dortmund-Ems Canal near Münster, where the canal crosses the River Ems by means of an aqueduct. Despite fierce enemy anti-aircraft fire and severe damage to his aircraft, he pressed home the attack, inflicting sufficient damage to severely restrict barge traffic for over four weeks. The cost, however, was not light. Flight Lieutenant Learoyd and his crew of Pilot Officer J Lewis, Sergeant J Ellis and Leading Aircraftman Rich, managed to struggle home. So did Pilot Officer Matthews and crew and the formation commander Squadron Leader J Pitcairn-Hill, despite having badly damaged aircraft. Others were less fortunate–Pilot Officer E M Ross and crew perished alongside the canal, whilst Flying Officer A R Mulligan and crew baled out in the target area.

During the following years, Coastal Command Beauforts used 'Magnum' and 'Tim' against the German warships lurking in Brest during 1941–42. The heavy cruiser *Admiral Hipper*, which had arrived on 27 December 1940 and left on 15 March 1941, was the first to feel the effects. Little damage was done to the cruiser, but considerable blast damage was done to the dock facilities.

Using mines in this fashion was something of a side issue to the main objective of laying mines in water. These operations were codenamed 'Gardening' and the mines were referred to as 'Vegetables'. These mines were laid, or planted, in individual areas which were given codenames derived from flowers, trees and fish, great care being taken to conceal their geographic location. For example, the Kiel Canal became 'Lettuce', the Kattegat 'Silverthorn' and Brest approaches 'Jellyfish'. Some 80 locations were allocated appropriate codenames. To enable the aircrews to identify target areas and achieve reasonable accuracy, it was generally the practice, up to the end of 1943, to plant the 'Vegetables' from 1,500 ft or preferably lower. This could be extremely hazardous in the face of shore and shipborne anti-aircraft defences. New techniques were successfully tried out on the night of 30/31 December 1943, when three Stirlings laid eleven mines in the Gironde estuary on the West coast of France from a height of 12,000 ft. Some days later, on the night of 3–4 January, six Halifaxes laid some more just off Brest from a similar height, using the navigational aid H2S which gave a rough pictorial view of the coast line. By February, this equipment was increasingly employed in conjunction with pathfinding target-marking techniques. This was a far cry from the rudimentary techniques employed by the Hampdens and Beauforts in 1940.

Mine warfare by its very nature is clandestine, and some tend to think of airborne minelaying operations as a rather underhand affair, utilizing a small number of aircraft sneaking into an area, laying a few mines and disappearing into the night. This is far from the truth; aircrews naturally prefer not to be spotted, but a very large percentage of operations were carried out in the face of extremely heavy anti-aircraft fire from both flak ships and shore batteries, to say nothing of enemy night-fighters. Numbers, too, were not insignificant – minelaying operations involving 100 aircraft were relatively common and on one occasion, on the night of 28–29 April 1943, 227 aircraft of Bomber Command laid nearly 600 mines, with the loss of 23 aircraft either *en route* or in the waters around Denmark, Kiel Bay and the Western Baltic.

The largest proportion of mines were laid in North West European waters. The first airborne minelaying operation was mounted on the night of 13–14 April 1940 when Bomber Command Hampdens laid 14 1,500 lb A Mk I magnetic mines in the Great and Little Belts off the east coast of Denmark. A typical sortie was that flown by Flight Lieutenant B Mitchell of 49 Squadron, Scampton, together with his crew of Pilot Officer Matthews (later to skipper one of the first aircraft to drop 'Magnums'), Sergeant Fenner and Leading Aircraftman Dutton. They took off at 7.35 p.m. and dropped their mine as briefed from 700 ft into the Little Belt just off Mittelfart, landing back at base at 2.50 a.m. next morning. The trip for that particular aircraft was uneventful, apart from being a first, and exhausting, having lasted for more than seven hours. Not all sorties were to be quite so routine; indeed, on this occasion one Hampden failed to return. Two more were lost on the following night when 28 Hampdens laid more mines in the same area.

On that same first night, 14–15 April, six Coastal Command Beauforts of 22 Squadron based at North Coates dropped six 1,500 lb mines into the Weser and Elbe estuaries. Among the aircraft captains on this, the Beauforts' first mining foray, was the squadron commander, Wing Commander H V Mellor (later missing on operations 25–26 May 1940). Another, captained by Pilot Officer Fordham, failed to return. These losses between 13 and 15 April 1940 were the first of over 500 Royal Air Force aircraft to be lost mining in North West European waters.

Some days later, the Fleet Air Arm Swordfish of 815 Squadron, also operating from North Coates, mined the Jade and Weser estuaries near Wilhelmshaven. Soon after, 812 Squadron joined them in mining coastal and inland waters in and around the Netherlands and Belgium. They were the first of many Fleet Air Arm squadrons who gallantly supplemented the Royal Air Force minelaying operations.

By the end of 1940 1,167 mines had been planted, in areas stretching from the Baltic to the Bay of Biscay. The annual figures progressively increased, reaching a peak of 17,493 in 1944, as did the number of ships sunk or damaged. Even the larger warships were not immune to the lurking 'A' mines, a number being trapped on more than one occasion. The heavy cruiser *Prinz Eugen*, sister ship to the *Admiral Hipper*, was damaged by an A Mk I-IV mine on 23 March 1941, setting back German plans to launch her at the Atlantic convoys. Nearly a year later, on 12 and 13 February 1942, she formed part of the mini-fleet including the battle cruisers *Scharnhorst* and *Gneisenau* which made the escape from Brest to the northern naval bases. In any event, it was 'A' mines that severely damaged the two battle cruisers when all else failed (see also the chapter on airborne torpedoes).

Towards the end of Janaury, intelligence reports indicated that the German ships might break out at any time. As a precaution 5 Group's Hampdens and Manchesters, among others, were tasked to lay speculative mines off the Frisian Islands, particularly around Terschelling Island, a likely sea route for the warships. Between 6 and 11 February, at least 98 A Mk I-IV mines were laid in the line of possible escape. Later, on 12 February, three of them achieved strikes, two on *Scharnhorst* the other on *Gneisenau.*

Scharnhorst triggered the first mine at about 2.30 p.m. off Zeebrugge, two compartments being flooded through a large hole in the starboard side. Some boilers were damaged and the port engine stopped. After some hasty repairs she set off, carrying 1,000 tons of floodwater and with the echo sounder and direction finder out of action. At about 8.00p.m. *Gneisenau* struck unlucky off Terschelling. Holed in the starboard side with the central turbine out of action, she too was brought to a standstill. After about 25 minutes, she proceeded northwards at a reduced speed with her navigational equipment seriously impaired. This was her second encounter with a Royal Air Force mine. Back on 5 May 1940, she had struck one in the River Jade near Wilshelmshaven, necessitating a 14-day repair in Kiel dockyard.

Scharnhorst suffered a second strike just after 9.30 p.m. north-west of Terschelling Island. A third compartment was flooded and her helm jammed. Listing badly, she drifted for about two miles with engines stopped, but after some temporary repairs and careful engine nursing she proceeded at about 14 knots (15.9 mph). Luckily for both ships, darkness and low clouds obscured their traumatic experiences from marauding Royal Air Force bombers. *Scharnhorst* limped into Wilhelmshaven in the early hours of the 13th, whilst *Gneisenau* and the undamaged *Prinz Eugen* entered the Elbe estuary at Brunsbüttel at about 7.00 a.m., having circumvented 13 more mines laid some hours earlier by Hampdens and Manchesters in the Elbe and Weser estuaries. These mining operations during the period 6–13 February cost No 5 Group the loss of five aircraft.

According to official records, air-laid mines in North West European waters accounted for 152 warships sunk and 340 damaged. These vessels ranged in size from 350 tons right up to the largest warships, and included 16 U-boats. Additionally 300 merchant ships were sunk and a further 165 damaged. These merchant ships included such troop-carrying liners as the 22,117 ton *Hamburg*, the 21,131 ton *Hansa* and the *Berlin* of 15,286 ton.

Large numbers of barges were also sunk in canals, effectively blocking the traffic until removed. Royal Air Force mines took the greatest enemy toll, but although very much a minority force, the Fleet Air Arm Swordfish and Albacores accounted for at least 11 ships off the Low Countries and France. Their successes in the Mediterranean were much more significant.

Although the bulk of minelaying operations were undertaken in enemy coastal waters, some of the more spectacular Royal Air Force attacks were

Armament staff preparing an A Mk VI mine. Naval Officer advisers were provided at Higher Formations and Petty Officers at bomber stations.

launched against canals and other inland waters. These were regularly attacked throughout the war using conventional bombs, in an effort to breach their banks or damage aqueducts. Occasionally, however, they were a target for mine-laying aircraft in an effort to stem these vital means of communication. Such an attack was made on the bright moonlight night of 12–13 May 1944 when 22 Mosquitoes of 692 Squadron (8 Group) made a daring low-level attack on the Kiel Canal, a stretch of water joining the North Sea to the Baltic. Twelve aircraft from the sister squadron (139) marked the selected area and made a 'spoof' or diversionary attack on the lock gates at Brunsbüttel at the canal's western end. The mines laid that night closed the canal for seven days, holding up 63 ships. One Mosquito of 692 Squadron was lost.

Another attack on the same target was carried out by Mosquitoes of 571 Squadron on 30 October 1944 and is a typical example of the individual and collective courage displayed on so many mining operations. The canals was extremely well protected by anti-aircraft guns, but despite this the mines were laid from a height of 700 ft. A number of aircraft were seriously damaged by intense and accurate anti-aircraft fire, and the two-man crews had considerable difficulty in making good their escape. For example, Squadron Leader E J Greenleaf's navigator was killed and one of his own arms was completely immobilized by shrapnel. Despite these misfortunes he laid his mines accurately and flew the badly-damaged Mosquito back to base. He was awarded a well-deserved Distinguished Service Order for actions which typified the courage of those who 'gardened' from dark and hostile skies.

One must not forget, however, the many thousands of armourers who laboured hard and long to prepare and load the 'vegetables' for the 'gardeners'. Mention has already been made of the night 28–29 April 1943, when 227 aircraft of Bomber Command laid 593 mines. Less than a month later, 328 mines were laid in Kiel Bay during the night of 21–22 May. Before that attack the armourers of one Lincolnshire airfield, East Kirby, assisted by their Royal Navy Petty Officer adviser, loaded 26 Lancasters of 57 and 630 Squadrons each with six A Mk VI mines. These mines contained 1,030 lb of explosive and a most sophisticated firing mechanism, and had a total weight of practically 2,000 lb. This meant that the armourers had to load approximately 140 tons of mines before the aircraft could leave. The Air Officer Commanding 5 Group, Air Vice-Marshal The Hon R A Cochrane, clearly understood and appreciated their efforts, for on the next day he sent the following signal:

V GPE 22/22.

TO OFFICER COMMANDING NO. 55 BASE.
FROM A O C 5 GROUP.
BT 22 1515B

A392 22/MAY

PERSONAL FOR OFFICER COMMANDING WISH TO CONGRATULATE THE ARMAMENT STAFF AT EAST KIRKBY ON THEIR REMARKABLE PERFORMANCE YESTERDAY IN FUZING AND LOADING A RECORD NUMBER OF MINES. THE OPERATION HAS BEEN A VERY GREAT SUCCESS TO WHICH THEIR EFFORTS HAVE GREATLY CONTRIBUTED.
BT 22 15 15B

DG K
R 172 U G S

(The signal was annotated 'Noted' and initialled on 23.5.44 by J.A.M., the Station Armament Officer, East Kirkby, and co-author of this book.)

The overall results of the airborne mining campaign in North West European waters were impressive; of all the offensive mines laid in the area, 72 per cent were laid by air and these caused 87 per cent of all vessel hits. This represented a hit for every 33 mines laid.

Undoubtedly, this campaign played a major part in the general offensive against enemy-controlled shipping, providing the only means whereby attacks could be made on many remote and important waters. The results achieved far exceeded those obtained by any other single weapon. Apart from directly damaging or sinking many ships, mines caused severe dislocation to enemy plans and placed an intolerable strain on the already over-stretched ship-repair yards and mine-sweeping organization. Important convoys and U-boat training, particularly in the latter years, were severely curtailed, and neutral merchantmen were provided with considerable incentives not to operate in areas subject to minelaying. Consequently, German industry was slowly, but surely, starved of many of its essential basic commodities.

With hindsight, the cost in men and machines appears high, but in terms of total war and the weapons used, the airborne minelaying success was achieved economically. Coastal Command, supplemented by the Fleet Air Arm, laid 908 mines and lost 40 aircraft, whereas Bomber Command, who undertook the bulk of the task laid 47,152 and lost 467 aircraft.

Other minelaying campaigns were undertaken by the Middle and Far East Air Commands, in which a further 7,344 mines were laid, 1,588 in the Mediterranean area, 1,382 in the Danube and 4,374 in the Far East. A few examples taken from each theatre indicates how the mines were used and by whom.

In the Mediterranean area, the Fleet Air Arm Swordfish and Albacores led the campaign. Following Italy's entry into the war in June 1940 they started mining the North African ports through which passed supplies for Italy's colonial army. Operating from aircraft-carriers and land bases, they laid 32 by the end of the year, most of them the 1,500 A Mk I-IV. One very successful drop occurred on 17 September, when nine strike aircraft and six Swordfish of 819 Squadron flew from the aircraft-carrier HMS *Illustrious*. The target was Benghazi, the strike aircraft provided diversions and the Swordfish laid six A Mk I mines within 600 yd of the harbour entrance. Later the same day the Italian destroyer *Aquilone* and the 1,200 ton cargo ship *Verace* struck mines and sank. Nine days later a further ship, the *Intrepide* was also sunk by these mines. Six mines laid, three ships sunk, must rank amongst the best results in the history of air mining.

Ten months later the Royal Air Force attacked the same target. Four Wellingtons of 38 Squadron, each carrying two 1,000 lb A Mk V mines, set off on the night of 15–16 July 1941 to lay mines off Benghazi harbour, while others carried out a bombing raid on the town and harbour. Three aircraft laid mines successfully, but the fourth was shot down. From then on, more and more aircraft from 38, 40 and 148 Wellington Squadrons from bases in Malta, the Nile Delta and Libya became available for minelaying tasks, ranging far and wide to ports such as Brindisi (Italy). Palermo (Sicily) and even as far as the Corinth Canal (Greece). In August 1941, three out of five Wellingtons were severely damaged by anti-aircraft fire over the canal.

The range of targets was further extended in 1942. Beauforts as well as Liberators and Marauders began to take a hand. During the year, almost 650 mines were laid, with the loss of eight aircraft. Activity was most intense during the successful Eighth Army battles in the latter half of the year and the Tunisian landings in 1943. Mining added significantly to the many supply problems the Germans were already experiencing due to anti-shipping strikes on the high seas and in port. Later in 1943, attention, was focused upon the Sicilian and Italian coasts in preparation for the Allied invasion of Sicily on 10 July.

Bomber Command took part on the nights of 13–14 and 18–19 April, when large forces of Lancasters bombed the dock area and town of La Spezia, an important naval base in North West Italy. On 13–14 April 208 aircraft bombed the target, and on 18–19 a further 173 continued the attack. Under cover of these raids, Lancasters of 49, 50 and 57 Squadrons mined the approaches to the naval base, laying a total of sixty 1,000 lb A Mk V mines. These were the only occasions when aircraft from outside the Middle East Command laid mines in the Mediterranean. Some aircraft in distress were diverted to newly-captured North African bases for attention, before returning to their Lincolnshire bases.

By the end of 1943, 178 Squadron Liberators and 38 Squadron Wellingtons were busily engaged in mining Greek waters. One hundred and twenty-eight A Mk V mines were laid in the seas around Crete and near Salonika and 339 were laid in 1944, mainly in the Aegean Sea, whilst in March 1945, 77 were laid in the Adriatic at the approaches to Venice and Pola.

The concentrated mining of the River Danube in 18 separate operations between 8 April and 4 October 1944 was by far the most successful undertaken by the Mediterranean Air Command, and certainly reaped a rich harvest. The idea of mining the Danube was not new, it had been considered several times during the course of the war, the first as early as June 1940 when the Commander-in-Chief Mediterranean suggested using Naval aircraft. This proved to be impracticable, both because of the limited range of available aircraft and the inability of the A Mk I–IV to function efficiently in water of less than 30 ft deep. Other forms of attack were considered, including the use of the 'W' bomb (referred to in Chapter Twelve). Thus it was not until bases in Italy became available that the proposed mining of the River Danube became a practical proposition.

This great river, the second largest in Europe, rises in the Black Forest and runs through Germany, Austria, Czechoslovakia, Hungary, Yugoslavia, Bulgaria and Rumania, to its mouth in the Black Sea. Altogether it has over 1,500 miles of navigable water stretching from the Black Sea back into Germany. During the Second World War it was a natural link between Germany and the grain areas of Hungary, a strategic route to the Russian front and above all a lifeline to the Rumanian oil fields such as Ploiesti. Whilst the Russian army cut railway links in the East, and Allied bombers progressively dislocated communications in general, the Danube assumed a high-priority role in supporting the German war effort. It was estimated that eight million tons of cargo passed along the waterway annually – at least that was the figure before Royal Air Force minelaying Wellingtons and Liberators went into action from their bases on the Foggia Plain in central Italy.

The force included six Wellington squadrons, 37, 40, 70, 104, 142 and 150, together with three squadrons of Liberators, 178, 31, and 34, the last two belonging to the South African Air Force, In addition there was a squadron of Halifaxes (614) which acted as pathfinders. During the six months of the operation twelve minelaying aircraft were lost, six of each type. This loss was offset by the widespread dislocation and damage caused to high-priority enemy shipping by the 1,382 mines laid. Some 1,500 lb A Mk I-IV mines were laid in sections of the river where the water was deep enough for them to function, but the vast majority were of the 1,000 lb A Mk V magnetic type.

Large stretches of the river between Bratislava (on the Austrian/Hungarian border) to Guirgui about 30 miles south of Bucharest were mined. The approaches to Belgrade, Budapest and Bratislava also received special attention. As a result,156 ships (78,120 tons) were sunk and 120 (90,165 tons) damaged. These included merchantmen, tank barges, tugs, minesweepers and patrol vessels. Traffic was cut by up to 60 per cent, at a time when the Germans were already being starved of vital commodities, including oil for both the *Luftwaffe* and the German armies in the field. The loss of five minesweepers and the difficulty of raising sunken wrecks in remote locations did little to alleviate the predicament before the Russian army overran the eastern end of the river and the Allies took a stranglehold on the western end. There is no doubt that the mining of the River Danube in 1944 was the most successful operation undertaken by the Mediterranean Air Command.

However, as the war progressed, offensive air-dropped mines were also being laid in the Far East. Some of the first were laid by Royal Netherlands Air Force Catalinas during the Japanese attack on Sumatra. On the night 2–3 February 1942 eight British A Mk I-IV mines were laid in the Palembang River and a further sixteen in the Banka Strait. These were, however, a once-off operation, and no other air-mining activity was to take place for another year.

There were no British long-range bombers available in the area until October 1943, and insufficient for mining operations until the end of the year. At that time the Liberators of 159 Squadron at Tigri, together with Wellingtons of 99 and 215 Squadrons at Jessore, were earmaked for the task from their bases in the Calcutta area of Bengal (Eastern India). However, in early 1943, the Tenth United States Army Air Force was relieved of its responsibilities to keep open the air supply route to China, having handed them over to the 14th USAAF, and became available for offensive action in Burma.

Initially, 10th USAAF carried out bombing and offensive air sweeps in the sea approaches to Rangoon, which at that time was the main port of entry for the Japanese army and air force in Burma. These attacks proved ineffective, and no marked decline in the use of Rangoon was noticed. It was decided, therefore, to try long-range mining. The first sortie against the Rangoon approaches was made by the 7th Heavy Bombardment Group, 10th USAAF on the night 22–23 February 1943. The Liberators laid 40 British A Mk V mines, the first of 125 to be laid by the Americans during 1943. They also laid 272 of their own Mk 13 ground mines. The effect was immediate, and shipping traffic dropped dramatically; during October, November and December only two ships, totalling 16,000 tons, were reported to have used the port. During the same period in 1942 the tonnage using the port was in excess of 100,000 tons.

After the first mine-laying operations the Japanese immediately started work on the construction of a railway link from Bangkok in Siam (Thailand) to a point on the existing railway between Ye and Moulmein in Burma. This was the notorious 'Death Railway', built under the most rigorous conditions by Allied prisoners of war.

Following the formation of South East Asia Command (SEAC) in November 1943, the Supreme Commander, Admiral Lord Louis Mountbatten, integrated all the air forces in his area under an Allied Commander-in-Chief, Air Chief

Marshal Sir Richard Peirse. This resulted in the formation of Eastern Air Command, consisting of the 10th USAAF, and from the Royal Air Force, two squadrons of Wellingtons (99 and 215) and the newly-formed 159 Squadron of Liberators. This latter squadron was soon to become the chief minelaying squadron in the area. 159 Squadron carried out its first minelaying operation on the night 7–8 January 1944. Each aircraft carried six A Mk V mines and laid them in the Irrawaddy estuary close to Rangoon. From February 1943 to January 1944 a total of 519 air-dropped magnetic mines were laid, without the loss of a single aircraft. Attacks upon Japanese-operated ports, river estuaries, and wherever it was possible to aggravate their supply problems, continued throughout 1944.

A second squadron of Liberators (355 Squadron) based at Salbani, also in Bengal, joined 159 Squadron and the two Wellington squadrons in May 1944. There followed a series of wide-ranging operations. A Mk V mines were laid around Mergui Island in the Andaman Sea, Rangoon, Moulmein and Ye, the Sittang and Tavoy Rivers, Bangkok and many other places. During 1944, the Royal Air Force, together with the Americans, laid a total of 1,149 mines, 860 American and 289 British. Since each air force often laid mines belonging to the other country, mainly to ease individual supply problems but also to confuse the Japanese, the ratio of mines by nationality does not necessarily reflect the ratio of mines laid by each nation. During the year the Royal Air Force flew over 40 minelaying operations, and 159 Squadron lost three Liberators due to enemy fire, one each over Port Blair in the Andamans, Moulmein and Rangoon.

From January to July 1945 airborne mining continued, although the 1,000 lb A Mk V mine was being replaced by the more sophisticated A Mk VII and the Very Long Range (VLR) Liberators of 160 Squadron based at Sigiriga in Ceylon (Sri Lanka) were taking a hand in delivering it. They concentrated on far-flung targets such as Sumatra, Singapore and North Malaya. In all, the Squadron laid just over 800 mines on 61 operations. Perhaps, however, the most epic flights were undertaken by 159 Squadron between October 1944 and January 1945. Led by Wing Commander Blackburn, 15 aircraft took off from an advanced base near Calcutta on the night of 27–28 October 1944, each aircraft carrying six mines. The operation involved a round trip of over 3,000 miles to mine the approaches to Georgetown harbour on Penang Island off North West Malaya (Malaysia). Later, photographic reconnaissance showed some ships sunk, so the Japanese were beginning to see the minelayers making real gains in the water they had controlled over the previous three years. This type of operation was repeated again in November and January. The squadron went on to lay 1,178 mines in 1945 without loss.

Due to the remoteness of the waters attacked, and a lack of intelligence common to all Far East operations, it is impossible to determine the overall effects of the 4,374 mines laid by the Royal Air Force in the Far East. Unlike the Germans, renowned record keepers, the Japanese paid scant respect to this aspect; records were for most purposes non-existent. Nevertheless, at least seven sinkings were confirmed in 1945. Two of these, the tankers *Hozan Maru* and *Etsunan Maru* were victims of mines laid by 160 Squadron off Bangkok and Chumphon in the Gulf of Siam. 159 Squadron was credited with the *Kyurgu Maru* off Bangkok, and the *Kyo* off Georgetown. So it seems the Japanese were the first to lose ships to the offensive mine in 1905, and the last to do so in a major war 40 years later.

In conclusion there can be no doubt that during the course of the Second World War, the airborne ground mine became an established and efficient weapon of war. The triggering devices advanced from the simple magnetic form to the sophisticated and complex combination of magnetic and acoustic, becoming ever more devilish and initially unsweepable. As with any nation properly equipped and experienced in mine warfare, Germany invariably found a solution to each new sweeping problem, but on each occasion it took time, and during that period her ships were at increased risk.

In particular, the 13,500 mines laid in the Kattegat, Kiel Bay, the Belts and the Baltic, where mineable waters abounded, reaped a rich harvest. Mining of the Kiel Canal and the River Danube give ample proof of the vulnerability of inland waters to determined minelayers. The long-range aircraft of the Far East showed that even the remotest waters could not be regarded as mine-free. Even if not so productive as those laid elsewhere, these mines proved a considerable thorn in the flesh for the Japanese, at a time when their fortunes were rapidly deteriorating.

Undoubtedly, the expenditure of over 55,000 airborne mines world-wide was well worthwhile. The operations brought considerable credit to all the aircrew who took part in this frequently forgotten aspect of air warfare, starting with Flight Lieutenant Mitchell and his Hampden colleagues on 13–14 April 1940, and finishing with Wing Commander Blackburn and his VLR Liberators in 1945.

CHAPTER ELEVEN

AIRBORNE WEAPONS VERSUS SUBMARINES

At the end of the First World War the threat posed by the submarine to warships, and more especially merchant ships, was well understood and appreciated. Consequently, the Admiralty and Air Ministry agreed to develop new, purpose-designed, anti-submarine bombs. Thus, between 1924 and 1939 the 100, 250 and 500 lb AS Bombs were developed (see Chapter Two).

In the inter-war years, whilst these bombs were being developed, various British Governments rather gullibly believed that, like themselves, the Germans were willing to co-operate in abolishing the submarine as a weapon of war. Consequently, there was little enthusiasm for the development of anti-submarine bombs, and by September 1939, although all three bombs were in service, none had been tested against a real submarine or even a representative target. However, whilst still negotiating, Fregattenkapitän (later Admiral) Karl Dönitz was busy building up a fleet of U-boats.

By 1939, about 100 were commissioned, although not all were ready for immediate operational use. Among those that were was the very effective 700 ton Type VII, which were to take a heavy toll of British shipping throughout the war years. Both the Royal Navy and the Royal Air Force were ill-prepared to meet the very real and immediate threat they posed. Coastal Command did not have adequate resources in aircraft or weaponry. The Command's needs had largely been sacrificed to the hasty pre-war build-up of Bomber and Fighter strength. Consequently, although the best use was made of the limited resources available, the anti-submarine aircraft could do little in the early war years to support the Royal Navy in protecting the merchantmen from the marauding U-boats.

For the purposes of this chapter on anti-submarine aerial weaponry, it is not appropriate to say how the naval ships coped with the U-boat threat, or to go into anything more than brief detail of the tactics employed by Dönitz's men. However, before turning to the aerial weapons developed and deployed to counteract the threat, it is probably appropriate to provide a few examples of the damage wrought and the ordeal faced by the Royal and Merchant Navies. This will show just why the hunting down and destruction of the U-boat fleet was a matter of paramount importance and urgency, affecting the lives of the citizens of the United Kingdom and its war effort, so dependent on the sea lanes being kept open at all costs.

The first shock came when the liner ss *Athenia* was torpedoed and sunk by Leutnant Fritz Julius Lemp in *U-30* west of the Hebrides on the very day war was declared, 3 September 1939. Just 14 days later, *U-29* (Schuhart) sank the 22,500 ton aircraft-carrier HMS *Courageous* in the Western Approaches, with the loss of 519 officers and men. By the end of that, the first month of war, U-boats had sunk 41 merchantmen (153,000 ton), with worse to follow on 14 October, when *U-29* (Prien) sank the battleship HMS *Royal Oak* in the 'safe' anchorage of Scapa Flow, with the loss of Rear Admiral H E C Blagrove and 785 others. Prien was later killed in *U-47* when it was sunk on 7 March 1941 by HMS *Wolverine*.

The crippling losses continued during 1940 and 1941. For instance, the aircraft-carrier HMS *Ark Royal* and the battleship HMS *Barham* were sunk in the Mediterranean on 13 and 25 November 1941 respectively. *U-81* (Guggenberger) torpedoed the carrier, with little loss of life, but 861 officers and men were lost when *U-331* (von Tiesen Hansen) sank the battleship.

Luckily during the early war years the Germans, like the British, were having problems with their magnetic torpedo exploders, causing considerable frustration among the U-boat commanders and particularly so during the Norwegian campaign in April 1940. For instance, five torpedoes fired at the battleship HMS *Warspite* from close range failed to function as she cruised off Narvik. Nevertheless, they did account for 64 merchantmen (260,748 ton) during that month, before the magnetic exploders were ousted by direct-contact types, and later by electrical types.

By May 1941 the U-boats were moving further westwards into the Atlantic to attack convoys to and from the United Kingdon, whereas previous operations were limited to waters not beyond 20 degrees west. They now operated in 'wolf packs' between 32 and 35 degrees west, and had a rich harvest well beyond the range of British anti-submarine aircraft operating from Iceland and United Kingdom bases. Progressively the type VII C U-boats were, with tanker U-boat support, able to stay at sea longer, and along with the 740 ton type IX Cs they were able to range much deeper into the safe gap in mid-Atlantic, well beyond the reach of British, Canadian and later American aircraft.

On the ninth of that month (May) Leutnant Lemp, who had sunk the ss *Athenia* with the loss of 118 lives including 22 Americans, met his end when he was shot by a naval boarding party from HMS *Bulldog* when attempting to scuttle *U-110*. The significance of this particular incident was that, in capturing the U-boat, the Navy recovered her 'Enigma' encoding machine and code books. This enabled the intelligence staff, who developed the 'Ultra' machine at Bletchley Park, Buckinghamshire, to intercept and interpret signal traffic passing between U-boats at sea, and also to and from their controllers at base; this factor great contributed to many of the subsequent U-boat losses.

The 'wolf pack' technique referred to earlier was the idea of Admiral Dönitz. As a First World War submariner, the U-boat chief clearly saw the benefits of concentrating a pack of U-boats against well-escorted convoys, rather than scattering his resources far and wide. He first tried out the technique in October 1939. Convoy HG 3 sailing home from Gibraltar suited his purpose well: naval and airforce cover was meagre, bordering on the non-existent. All went well with the convoy until the 17th, then the mixed bag of 27 merchantmen ran into Commander Hartmann's four-boat 'wolf pack', which stalked them until twilight, before pouncing. In swift succession three ships, totalling 24,200 tons, were sunk by three separate U-boats. The convoy scattered in all directions offering still better targets for the marauding U-boats, but strangely no further attacks took place that night. One ship, however, the *Clan MacBean* proceeded dourly on its planned course but, on the following day, was attacked by *U-37* (Hartmann) and only swift helmsmanship prevented a torpedo strike. Hartmann moved in for a second strike, but the unarmed *Clan MacBean* closed to within 100 ft of the U-boat which, on seeing the intention to ram, crash-dived, leaving two of his gun crew in the water. He later picked them up, but wisely by then his intended victim had sped off at full speed, to fight another day. For many, however, there never was another day. Some 32,000 British merchant seamen were to die during the course of the sea war.

These examples give some idea of the ordeals faced by the seamen, and at the same time point to some of the serious shortcomings, particularly in air cover and the inadequacy of the weapons initially provided to the airborne anti-submarine forces. The Coastal Command Ansons, Hudsons and Sunderland flying-boats had neither the operational range nor the tracking equipment required, and the early anti-submarine (AS) bombs provided were generally ineffective, as already mentioned in Chapter Two.

However, as more suitable aircraft with adequate tracking equipment and weaponry were introduced progressively into service, the anti-U-boat forces gradually got the uppper hand, and by May 1943 Dönitz's losses were increasing alarmingly (for him, at any rate). He was losing the Battle of the Atlantic, and indeed the battle wherever his boats operated. Later in 1944 and 1945 his difficulties were compounded by effective bombing of the U-boat bases, industrial plant and communications, all of which had been contributing to a planned U-boat build-up to offset losses and introduce bigger and better boats. Although U-boat effectiveness, particularly in the Atlantic, was decisively curbed between 1943 and 1945, they continued to pose a real threat as new boats and modified equipment and tactics were introduced.

However, what of the weapons, equipment and tactics used by the aerial anti-submarine forces which brought about this curbing of U-boat activity, and eventual victory in the North Atlantic and elsewhere? The only AS bombs in service at the beginning of the war were the relatively light-cased 100, 250 and 500 lb bombs; by 1940 all three were the Mark IVs, having a solid nose and clip-on tail fin. Whether used by Coastal Command or the Fleet Air Arm, failures on occasions were as high as 40 per cent. The main problem was the impossibility of a guaranteed detonation at a depth of between 20 and 25 ft, the

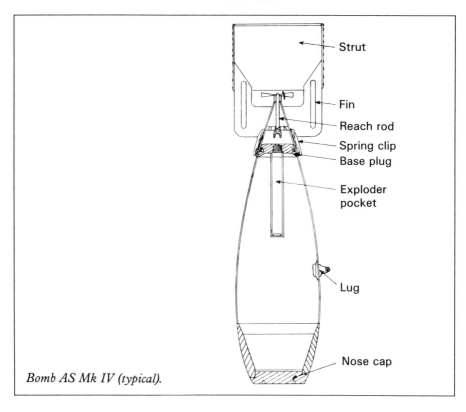

Bomb AS Mk IV (typical).

optimum depth for attacking surfaced submarines. As described previously, they were unpredictable in their underwater path, particularly when dropped from low altitudes and, because of the relatively small lethal range of the charge, low altitude bombing was the only way to achieve accuracy of any sort. The experiences of the Ansons and Skuas mentioned in Chapter Two bear testimony to the hazards posed to low-flying aircraft from bomb splinters, not to mention enemy gunfire.

There is little doubt that these bombs were inefficient; for example during 1939 Coastal Command aircraft spotted 57 U-boats, attacked 40 and damaged eight. In Janaury 1940, six U-boats were sighted, four attacked and one destroyed; during the next month the corresponding figures were 15, 11 and two damaged, and in March six were attacked, with one success. Although other factors contributed to the apparent lack of success, the case against the AS bomb was well substantiated when a number of British submarines were inadvertently attacked, and escaped with little or no damage. HMS *Snapper*, attacked on 5 September 1939, was a case in point: a bomb strike near the conning tower caused only the failure of a number of electric light bulbs!

Saddled with an inadequate range of AS bombs, among many other problems, the Coastal Command Staff at Royal Air Force Northwood began at once to look for a more satisfactory weapon. The only readily-available alternative to the AS bomb was the Naval depth charge, used by the surface fleet for many years as its standard anti-submarine weapon. It appeared to have several very obvious design points in its favour; first a well-tried hydrostatic pistol of relatively simple design and a high charge: weight ratio of approximately 70 per cent, compared with under 50 per cent in AS bombs. It also seemed to have the great advantage that it could be released from low altitude without damage to the aircraft, since there was a longer delay between impact with the water and detonation than that in the AS bombs. Ironically, the longer delay was the main disadvantage of the depth charge, since the surface-launched types were fitted with pistols designed to operate at any depth setting between 50 and 300 ft. So even if set to the minimum, the depth charge would sink to twice the optimum depth (25 ft) for a surface kill before detonating. Another minor disadvantage was that, should the aircraft be lucky enough to score a direct hit, the depth charge would more likely than not break up and fail to detonate. It was hoped, however, that it would roll off the casing and sink beneath the U-boat, and function normally.

However, at this stage this was all conjecture; it was first necessary to determine if the naval depth charge could be dropped safely from an aircraft. To this

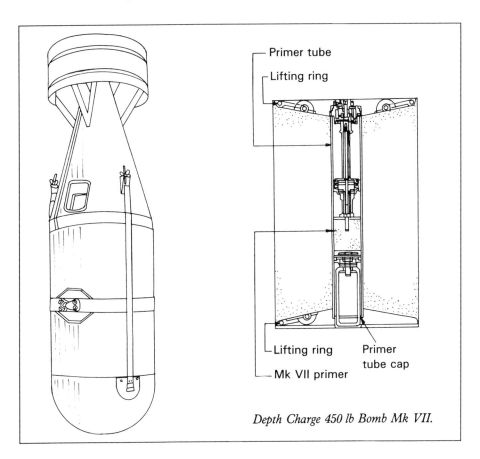

Depth Charge 450 lb Bomb Mk VII.

end, at Coastal Command's request a series of trials was undertaken at the Torpedo Development Unit, Gosport to determine depth charge behaviour when dropped from aircraft. Specially adapted naval 300 lb Mk VII Depth Charges were used, and it was found that limitations of height and airspeed had to be enforced to avoid the possibility of break-up on impact with the sea. Modifications were incorporated to convert the drum-shaped charge into a shape approaching that of a bomb, to improve its ballistics and to reduce drag whilst being carried externally on aircraft. Consequently breakaway tails and nose fairings were designed, and the first live DC bomb was released from a Sunderland flying boat off the Isle of Wight in April 1940.

It functioned satisfactorily, and was immediately adopted as a successor to the existing AS bomb range. One hundred Mk VII Naval depth charges were acquired by Coastal Command and converted under the control of the Command for operational trials. By June a further 700 were procured and the Ordnance Board having approved the modification, production of conversion sets was undertaken by the Ministry of Aircraft Production. Thus, in quick time and perforce of circumstances, a new Royal Air Force anti-submarine weapon was born and christened the 450 lb Depth Charge (DC), complete with a Mark VII hydrostatic pistol. The weapon consisted of little more than a cylindrical, thin-skinned metal drum containing about 290 lb of Amatol high explosive along with detonators and primers to fire it. The detonation chain was initiated by the hydrostatic pistol which released the strikers at the appropriate depth, dependent upon water pressure.

Although a step in the right direction, it did not prove entirely satisfactory, being too bulky for carriage in the Anson and Hudson, and too few could be carried by the Sunderland and Catalina flying boats. Additionally, it was prone to break up if dropped above 500 ft, and presented blast hazards to the aircraft if released below 100 ft. Nevertheless, in the absence of suitable bomb sights, attacks had to be delivered at the lowest possible altitude to have any hope of despatching or damaging an elusive U-boat. Parachute attachments were unsuccessfully tried, to eradicate the possibility of break-up, but they only added to the aiming problems.

One modification, urgently needed, was that to the pistol to enable the depth charge to be dropped safe in case of emergency. Initially this was not considered necessary, because it could be jettisoned over deep water where it could detonate safely, and if released over land the hydrostatic pistol would not function. However, it was foreseen that if an aircraft crashed into the sea while carrying depth charges, they would detonate on reaching the requisite depth, and members of the crew who might possibly escape to the surface would almost certainly be killed. The pistol was therefore modified to provide an extra safety device, and redesignated the Mk X.

Apart from minor modifications to the depth charge body and means of suspension, the 450 pounder, although little used, remained in its original form throughout the war. There were, however, a number of progressive modifications to its pistol.

As already mentioned, the depth charge was too heavy and bulky for some aircraft, consequently it became necessary to design a smaller type. This time the initiative was taken by the Fleet Air Arm who urgently needed a weapon to replace the AS bombs then carried by the Swordfish. Production of the new depth charge was undertaken by the Superintendent of Mine Design, Admiralty and eventually issued as the Depth Charge Type 'F'. It weighed 246 lb and contained 170 lb of Amatol, a charge: weight ratio of just under 70 per cent.

By November 1940 the 'F' Type was available to both the Fleet Air Arm and the Royal Air Force, and redesignated Depth Charge Mk VIII, but better known to its users as the 250 lb DC. The high explosive was contained in a thin-cased cylinder 39 in long and 11 in diameter. To provide better ballistics a plain drum tail was later fitted, increasing the overall length to 56 in. No nose fairings were fitted. Like the 450 lb DC, detonation was initiated by the Mk

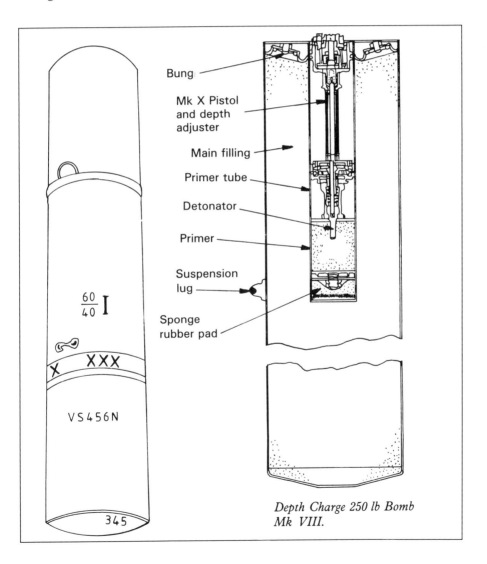

Bung

Mk X Pistol and depth adjuster

Main filling

Primer tube

Detonator

Primer

Suspension lug

Sponge rubber pad

$\frac{60}{40}$ I

XXX

X

VS456N

345

Depth Charge 250 lb Bomb Mk VIII.

VII pistol, quickly replaced by the Mk X. Following a series of trials conducted independently by the Admiralty and Air Ministry, the Mk VIII DC (250 lb) was finally cleared for general operational use on 23 January 1941.

Ultimately, with progressive improvements it became the most effective weapon put into the hands of the airborne U-boat hunters during the Second World War. However, the early versions suffered a number of drawbacks: apart from functioning too deep (50 ft) the 170 lb of Amatol still lacked punch, even if it was some 20 per cent larger than that in the 250 lb AS bomb. By 1942 the existing shortcomings were eradicated by supplanting Amatol with the 30 per cent more powerful and destructive Torpex, and modifying the hydrostatic pistol to function at a depth of between 22 and 25 ft. Alterations were also made to the depth charge exterior. The tail fittings were weakened to ensure rapid breakaway after impact on the sea surface, and the nose profile was reshaped from convex to concave, to slow down the rate of sinking, thus assisting the pistol operation. As a result of the various improvements to enhance effectiveness, the standard of the 250 lb DC was raised to Mk XI and the pistols to Mk XIV and XVI.

By the middle of 1942, production priority concentrated on the 250 lb Mk XI and its pistols, and from that time on this combination proved a formidable weapon against the U-boats in all theatres of war.

Unlike previous anti-submarine weapons, its real worth was recognized when a series of trials were undertaken using a captured U-boat. Fortunately the German U-boat *Graf (U-570)*, renamed HMS *Graph*, fell into British hands, surrendering to a Hudson of 269 Squadron piloted by Squadron Leader J Thompson, south of Iceland on 27 August 1941. Suffering damage from four 250 lb DC near-misses and a few bursts of machine gun fire, Korvettenkapitän Rahmlow hoisted the white flag. The Hudson circled the U-boat for three and a half hours until relieved by a Catalina, and eventually the U-boat and its crew were taken in charge by the Royal Navy. Apart from being a valuable acquisition, this was the first time an underwater vessel surrendered to a land-based aircraft.

Subsequent trials undertaken with HMS *Graph* confirmed that a charge detonated below the hull was significantly more effective than one above it. Furthermore, the effects were considerably magnified if detonation occurred adjacent to a bulkhead or any metal fittings attached to the pressure hull. They also confirmed that substantial damage resulted to sensitive electrical instruments and control equipment from relatively distant detonations. It was deduced that possibly more damage was being inflicted on U-boats than previously suspected. Nevertheless, close inspection and searching trials showed the Type VII U-boats to be robustly constructed and capable of withstanding considerable damage. This was borne out later when a number of them were subjected to vicious aerial poundings with depth charges and would have been expected to succumb, yet escaped to fight another day.

Robust or not, successes with the 250 lb Torpex-filled depth charge were numerous, and none more so than during the early months of 1943 when Dönitz's U-boats were operating at peak strength just prior to their defeat, which virtually drove them from the North Atlantic, a defeat to which the anti-submarine aircraft operating far out in the Atlantic and the Bay of Biscay contributed significantly. Five out of six U-boats had to pass through the latter to and from their French bases.

In the latter months of 1942 and the early months of 1943, Allied shipping losses were horrendous. Convoys of some 60 ships were being attacked by U-boat packs of up to 20 boats. During the first ten days of March, 41 ships were sunk, with the loss of half a million tons of cargo, and a further 73 were lost during April and May. Many merchantseamen perished, and others were cast adrift on the cold waters of the North Atlantic to face appalling hardships.

Most of the early wartime losses were in the so-called North Atlantic gap over 1,000 miles out in mid ocean some 30 degrees west and to the south of Greenland, well beyond the reach of anti-submarine aircraft – an area of death and disaster for the mariners, but a happy hunting ground for the U-boats. However, by late 1942 the more powerful and well-equipped longer range Halifaxes and Liberators were making their presence felt in the Bay of Biscay and in the Gap respectively. The very long range (VLR) Liberators of 120 and later 86 Squadrons operating out of Iceland and Northern Ireland were particularly successful, and often their very presence over a convoy was enough to deter U-boat attacks, especially as the aircraft were now equipped with search radar which enabled them to locate both the convoys and surfaced U-boats; but more of the technological aspects later.

Although shipping losses were exceptionally high, so were U-boat losses. In May 1943 Coastal Command carried out 83 attacks, sinking 16 and damaging a further three. At that time there was thought to be 48 U-boats on station in the North Atlantic, another 44 in transit and a further 60 in their French bases, to say nothing of those in the central and South Atlantic, and the Mediterranean. It would be impracticable to cite and describe each and every victory over the U-boats, so it is hoped that one or two examples will give some idea of the actions involved.

For instance, on 19 May 1943 Flight Sergeant W Stokes, the captain of a 120 Squadron Liberator, sighted the 770 ton Type VII C *U-954* (Löwe) on the surface in the North Atlantic. The Liberator was carrying two Mk 24 homing torpedoes (described in Chapter Nine) and four 250 lb DC. To digress somewhat, this relatively small load became the norm for those Liberators operating in the Gap after the torpedo was introduced earlier in May. Previously, to provide an endurance time of 15 to 16 hours, the weapon load had been reduced from 16 to six 250 lb DCs to provide space in the bomb-bay for an additional fuel tank. This modification distinguished the VLR Liberator from the standard long range type.

In any event, Stokes attacked his quarry near Cape Farewell south-west of Greenland, and for Kapitänleutnant Löwe and his crew the location proved cruelly appropriate, as they were sent to the bottom by three well-aimed 250 lb DCs dropped from a height of 60 ft. This sinking brought personal loss to the German Naval Chief Karl Dönitz, whose youngest son Peter was a member of the ill-fated crew.

Armourers load eight 250 lb depth charges on to a Coastal Command Liberator.

Aircraft losses to the enemy and sea were high, but courage and dedication to the task was never lacking. This was equally true of the U-boat crews, who invariably fought desperately, often still firing as they disappeared below the waves for the last time. With losses rising, in 1943 Dönitz ordered his U-boats to mount increased armament and to fight it out on the surface. Many did so, using multiple 20 mm cannons and even a heavy 3.7 in anti-aircraft gun along with the usual machine guns. An example of this occurred on 11 August 1943 some 200 miles south-west of Dakar, when Flying officer L A Trigg (RNZAF), the captain of a 200 Squadron Liberator based at Yundum Airfield, Bathurst in the Gambia, West Africa, spotted a U-boat on the surface. It turned out to be *U-468* fitted with the latest large calibre anti-aircraft guns, and she was prepared to defend herself vigorously. In all, Trigg made three attacking passes over the U-boat at heights down to 50 ft. In each case the aircraft was hit, and on the final pass, the Liberator, now in flames, released its last 250 lb DCs and crashed into the sea, killing all on board. The U-boat was critically damaged and sank some 20 min later. Seven members of the crew, including the captain, Oberleutnant Schamong, managed to swim clear and reach a rubber dinghy ejected by the Liberator as it crashed.

Next day a Coastal Command aircraft circled the dinghy and dropped supplies – at this stage the Germans were thought to be the Liberator crew. Eventually a British corvette HMS *Clarkia* picked up the survivors. Their generous account of the daring and courage of Trigg and his crew resulted in Flying Officer L A Trigg being awarded a posthumous Victoria Cross.

Many instances occurred of these one-to-one combats between a single aircraft and a surfaced U-boat. Because of the need to attack at low level and the increased weight of the U-boats' anti-aircraft defences, the odds were about even; unfortunately history tends to be written by the victor, and so the true story of those aircraft which failed to return from their lonely patrols will never be known. Instead we know only of the survivors; one real survivor was Flying Officer J A Cruickshank of 210 Catalina Squadron, Sullom Voe (Shetlands). Whilst patrolling beyond the Arctic Circle on 17 July 1944 he sank *U-347* with four 250 lb DCs. The U-boat went down fighting vigorously, the Catalina navigator being killed by intense U-boat fire, and three other crew members wounded, Cruickshank very seriously, receiving multiple injuries to the lungs and legs. He was later found to have been hit in 72 places. Immobilized, and often unconscious for most of the five hour return flight, he insisted on supervising the landing of the badly-damaged flying boat in the Shetlands. The second pilot, Flight Sergeant Garnett, who flew the flying boat most of the way back was also wounded, so it was very much a case of an exceptionally dogged fight by captain and crew, which earned John Cruickshank the Victoria Cross.

Another instance of this one-for-one battle occurred on 4 August 1943, when Flying Officer A A Bishop of 423 Sunderland Squadron (RCAF) pressed home his depth charge attack so vigorously on *U-489* in the Bay of Biscay that not only did he sink the U-boat, but was forced to crash beside the sinking wreck. The survivors from the U-boat and the Sunderland, united in misery, remained together and were eventually rescued by a British destroyer, cold, wet and suffering from exposure. Who was the real victor?

When the U-boats' potential for death and destruction of thousands of tons of vital food, stores and munitions of war is taken into account, the loss of one aircraft and crew, offset against the loss of a U-boat, must be considered a victory for the side deploying the aircraft. That is, if one ignores the individual crews for whom death in the North Atlantic or elsewhere could hardly be termed a victory.

Before leaving the story of the 250 lb DC, reference must be made to trials which continued into 1944 and 1945 to perfect an air-delivered 250 lb depth charge capable of being dropped from high altitude and at relatively high speeds, together with a pistol capable of operating at a depth of either 20 or 60 ft. The latter depth was necessitated by the need to attack U-boats fitted with a Schnorkel, a device which enabled U-boats to obtain fresh air and recharge their batteries whilst still effectively submerged. These prototype depth charges, fitted with two air-armed pistols, increased the mark number of the 250 lb DC to Mk XV. Although accepted into the Fleet Air Arm in January 1945 they were not introduced for service in the Royal Air Force, and little is

U–426 *about to sink surrounded by detonating 250 lb depth charges dropped by a Sunderland of 10 Squadron (RAAF) on 8 January 1944. A U-boat crew member can be seen in the water on the starboard side. (IWM)*

known about their operational prowess.

Obviously the availability of effective depth charges was not in itself sufficient; as always, the major problem of the anit-submarine airmen was to find and position themselves directly above the U-boat at the lowest possible altitude to give the weapons a chance of succeeding. This was only achieved with the introduction of air-to-surface vessel (ASV) radar and a combination of ASV radar and searchlights by night. After early trials on Naval Swordfish, among other aircraft, the first sets of a 1.5 m wavelength ASV Mk 2 (ASV II) radar became available in mid 1940. An ASV I had been tried earlier, but with little success. From a range of about five miles, the radar operator was able to direct the pilot on to a surfaced U-boat. The ASV sent out pulses, and the returning echoes from the U-boat, or any other large object on the surface, were detected by two aerials fitted to the aircraft. From his radar screen display, the operator was able to deduce an object's location, track and range.

Thus in addition to the dangers and inconvenience of direct attack, the U-boats were forced to remain submerged by day, or face the consequences. So in the main they were often unable to shadow convoys from the surface, with the intention of submerging and attacking after dark. However, ASV on its own suffered a serious disadvantage after dark. Although it could pick up a surfaced U-boat from about five miles, it could not guide the aircraft any closer than a mile, before wave echoes distorted the image. In daylight this did not matter because by then it could be spotted visually. At night, however, contact was normally lost. For the record, a Whitley of 502 Squadron, St Eval, achieved the first Royal Air Force radar kill by sinking *U-206* in the Bay of Biscay on 30 November 1941.

The problem of locating U-boats at night was largely overcome with the introduction of the Leigh (Search) Light with a 22 million candle-power beam, invented by Squadron Leader H Leigh of Coastal Command. These were first fitted to the 172 Squadron Wellingtons at Chivenor, Devon. The first successful attack using the potent combination of the ASV II, a Leigh Light and 250 lb DCs was made by Pilot Officer W H Howell and crew when they sank *U-502* in the Bay of Biscay on 5 July 1942. The established technique was to use the ASV to get on the U-boat's track whilst still several miles distant, lower the unlit Leigh Light in the ventral turret below the fuselage pointing ahead and downwards, and then just before the radar image became unreadable switch on the light. If all went well the target should be illuminated some one mile ahead. In Howell's case this is exactly what happened and the depth charges were released upon the floodlit U-boat from 50 ft. During June and July 1942 the number of night interceptions in the Bay of Biscay rose to about 20. A surfaced U-boat was now almost as much at risk by night as by day.

This state of affairs was short lived, however; the Germans countered the ASV with a U-boat equipment known as 'Metox'. This picked up the ASV signals and gave warning to the crew of an aircraft's presence. U-boats could submerge in 27 seconds, thus getting well below the surface before the hunters spotted them. As with all counter-measures, a counter-counter-measure was found; the problem was overcome by the introduction of the ASV III in March 1943. This equipment operated on a ten cm wavelength and was almost identical to H2S used in Bomber Command. Furthermore, it had a forward scan of 12 miles and a side scan of 20, and could detect convoys and surfaced U-boats with great clarity.

This too had a short life, some seven months, before it was countered by 'U-Naxos', a U-boat version of the device used to locate H2S pulses on bomber aircraft. Although this caused problems, by then the major battles in the Atlantic and Bay of Biscay were declining, and the U-boats were on the retreat. However, once again British scientists countered the problem and in 1944 produced ASV IV which operated on a wavelength of three cm, which remained supreme for the remainder of the war.

As recounted earlier, the ineffectiveness of the 100, 250 and 500 lb AS bombs necessitated the hurried but relatively successful development of a range of air-delivered depth charges. However, at the time Coastal Command had some definite reservations. As early as 31 March 1942 the Commander in Chief wrote to the Air Ministry expressing these reservations. He argued that the Mk

VII DC (450 lb), despite modifications, could still not be dropped without risk of break-up on impact from above 150 ft or at an air speed in excess of 150 knots. He felt that the smaller Mk VIII DC (250 lb) was more satisfactory, but because of its size lacked killing power in all but the most accurately delivered attacks. To obtain accuracy it was necessary to release them from very low altitude, thereby negating the safety advantage of being able to release them from a greater height. He finally expressed a priority requirement for a new anti-submarine bomb which among other specifications should be capable of release without risk of break-up from 5,000 ft at an airspeed of 200 knots. Perhaps the advice provided by his advisers was somewhat ill-judged, considering the success achieved by the ubiquitous 250 lb DC (of course he may have been criticizing the Amatol-filled version). In any event, a development programme was instigated at once and despite initial controversy over the exact requirement, a 600 lb AS bomb was supplied to Coastal Command Stations by mid December 1942, albeit with the caveat that, pending further stick safety trials, they should only be dropped singly. This restriction effectively prevented their use on operational patrols, where stick release alone gave some assurance of a kill.

The necessary approval was given by March 1943, permitting release from heights between 1,200 and 5,000 ft at any airspeed. This precluded low-level use, therefore, and at that stage in development of bomb sights, denigrated accuracy. Consequently, the figure was reduced to 500 ft on 6 May, and one month later Bomb Aircraft 600 lb AS Mk I was formally introduced into service. Its vital statistics are tabulated later on in this chapter, together with those of other anti-submarine bombs and depth charges.

Little or no modification was required to the 600 pounder, but the hydrostatic tail fuze was a constant source of experimentation. Indeed by August 1943 over 400 experimental bombs were dropped under trial conditions. Experimental work continued throughout 1943 and 1944, resulting in the introduction of the 895 fuze to replace the 862.

Although it was used from time to time, it never really gained popularity as an anti-submarine weapon. Coastal Command statistics show that a total of only ninety-seven 600 pounders were used, in 28 attacks on U-boats between May 1943 and April 1945. Its very first kill was achieved on 16 May 1943 when a Wellington of 311 (Czech) Squadron from Talbenny Wales sank a U-boat, identity unknown.

Further success was achieved on 30 July 1943 when three U-boats, later identified as *U-504* (Luis), *U-461* (Stiebler) and *U-462* (Vowe), were spotted on the surface in the Bay of Biscay. A number of Halifaxes from 502 Squadron, Holmesley South, attacked *U-462*, dropping six 600 pounders from between 1,600 and 3,000 ft. One of these crippled and brought her to a halt, forcing the crew to abandon ship. The empty hulk was later sunk by Naval surface vessels. Flight Lieutenant Jenson, Flying Officers Van Rossum, Hensow and Biggar all played a part in her destruction, together with Flight Lieutenant W Irving in a 53 Squadron Liberator, who first reported sighting them. For the record, *U-504* was destroyed by the Royal Navy and *U-461* by Flight Lieutenant D Marrows in a Sunderland, coincidentally of 461 Squadron (Royal Australian Air Force). He however, used seven 250 lb DCs for the kill, not 600 pounders.

U-461 and *U-462* were *Milch Kühe* (milk cows) *en route* for the Indian Ocean. Ten of these 1,700 ton Type XIV U-boat tankers were built to replenish the German underwater fleet at sea with fuel, torpedoes, ammunition and other essentials. Their loss was likely to have far-reaching effects on German plans to maintain the U-boat presence in the far oceans. Indeed, *U-468* sunk by Flying Officer Trigg on 11 August was expecting to rendezvous with *U-462*, not knowing she had been sunk 12 days earlier.

Despite the sinking of *U-462*, the 600 pounder had relatively little success in

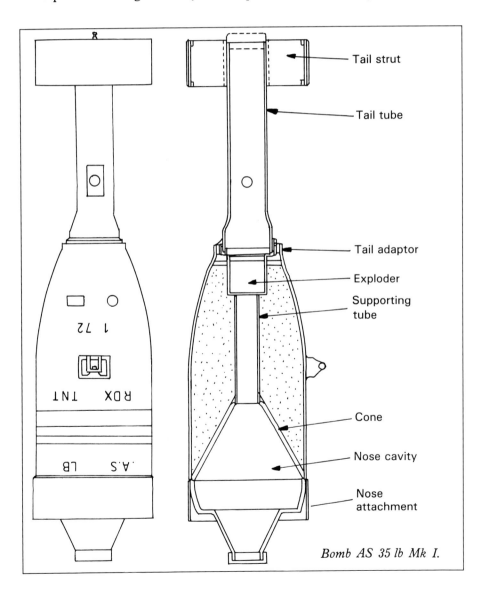

Bomb AS 35 lb Mk I.

the U-boat war, especially if the expense of design and production is taken into account. In fact one wonders if it was ever really needed in the first place, despite Coastal Command's insistence. It had little advantage over the 250 lb DC, other than that it was unlikely to break up before detonating, in the event of a direct strike on a U-boat. Because of its versatility in this respect, it could be used as either a bomb or a depth charge. For this reason, the Fleet Air Arm Barracudas dropped a number, albeit with little success, on the *Tirpitz* in Kaa Fjord on 3 April 1944.

In any event, to produce adequate anti-shipping bombs, other experiments were conducted during 1941–42 to determine the effectiveness of hollow or shaped-charge fillings as a means of penetrating the hulls of submarines or large surface ships. The hollow charge, described fully in Chapter Twelve, is essentially a charge, detonated from the rear, in which the forward portion is hollowed out to form a truncated cone. The effect is to focus the energy of detonation into a fierce jet capable of penetrating thick armour plate and producing on the other side of the plate a slug of molten metal. This technique was deemed to have great potential for attacking submarine pressure hulls and the decking of armoured capital ships.

Following the capture of *U-570* in August 1941, plating representative of that in the U-boat was prepared and tests undertaken with a small shaped-charge bomb of some 35 to 40 lb, containing about 12 lb of high explosive, to determine whether a bomb of this small size could penetrate or damage a U-boat pressure hull. The results were considered satisfactory, and full development trials went ahead. By April 1943 the greater part of the trials were complete, and in June the Bomb Aircraft 35 lb AS with fuze 866 was cleared for operational trials.

By mid September, full-scale operational trials of the new bomb were started by 224 Liberator Squadron, which had six aircraft specially modified to carry 72 bombs apiece. Mk III low-level bomb sights were used and the loads released from not less than 350 ft. Three attacks were delivered against surfaced U-boats, but the results were inconclusive. The first, on 2 July, was confused by pilot error, in that 24 of the small AS bombs were released accidentally, together with a stick of 250 lb DCs. The U-boat was damaged, but it was impossible to determine by which weapon. On the following day 24 bombs were released on the first pass over a second U-boat, followed by another with a stick of depth charges. The pilot ensured that the U-boat was sunk, but was again unable to determine which weapon had caused the mortal damage. In early September, two sticks of 24 bombs were aimed at a third U-boat and a single hit was obtained, but there was no apparent damage. However, it was noted that many of the other bombs detonated on striking the water. This was disturbing, because the design of the bomb mechanism was evolved to ensure that this should not happen. Detonation was intended to occur only if the bomb struck the submarine, above or below the water.

Coastal Command crews were far from happy with this turn of events and the bombs' performance in general. Consequently, even when they were carried in mixed loads for operational trial purposes, the 250 lb DC was the weapon selected on sighting a U-boat. Compounding the Command's dissatisfaction with the shaped-charge bomb was the fact that loading a full complement took two and a half times as long as that for 250 lb DCs. Additionally, 72 exposed fuzes were far more vulnerable to gun fire attack than a full load of depth charges.

Not surprisingly, the 35 lb AS bomb was discredited, and Coastal Command discontinued its use in its original role. However, when the U-boats started fighting back on the surface, some use was made of it from high level, but with no success. The Naval Staff too decided on 1 December 1943 that it had no requirement for this bomb, so its demise was complete. In all, 3,289 were manufactured and filled, but only the 96 referred to earlier were released against U-boats. One wonders whether it should have been relegated to the next chapter, dealing with the also rans.

So much for the main air-dropped weapons used to counter the U-boat menace at sea. The problems of attacking them in port or under construction is considered later. Undoubtedly the 250 lb DC was the most effective weapon until the advent of the American Mk 24 homing torpedo, but it was the airborne depth charges in particular, supplemented by the better types of AS bombs, which swung the balance towards the defeat of Admiral Dönitz's men in the North Atlantic and the Bay of Biscay. The vital statistics of all these weapons are given in the table on page 238.

Despite the defeat of the U-boats in the North Atlantic in May 1943 (of which some more later), the anti-submarine war continued at high tempo until the final cease-fire. The last U-boat to be sunk in action, *U-320* (Emmrich), was depth-charged by Flight Lieutenant K Murray in a 210 Squadron Catalina off the Shetlands on 7 May 1945. She foundered with all hands just after the cease-fire on the following day.

One of the fears of the planners when preparing for Operation Overlord, the Allied invasion of Europe on 6 June 1944, was the threat posed by U-boats. The invasion fleet of just under 7,000 ships of all kinds, 1,213 being warships, made a tempting target for some 40 U-boats deployed specifically along the routes likely to be used by it. To counter the expected U-boat threat, 30 squadrons of anti-submarine aircraft, armed with the full range of AS weapons, were deployed to protect the fleet. These included Liberators, Sunderlands, Wellingtons, Catalinas, Halifaxes and Swordfish. 'Ultra' intelligence (based on 'Enigma' code breaking) provided the anti-submarine aircraft with the U-boats' general locations, whilst ASV III, supplemented by Leigh Lights when necessary, pinpointed exact locations. Consequently the U-boats, under constant harassment from aircraft and surface escort vessels, achieved little. During the period 6 to 10 June 1944, six U-boats were sunk by aerial weapons, one on the 6th, three during the night of 7–8th and one each on the 9th and 10th.

In the course of the war a number of airmen sank more than one U-boat, but none more quickly than Flying Officer K Moore, RCAF, in a 224 Squadron Libertor. He sank two in the English Channel in less than half an hour during the early hours of 8 June 1944. His 250 lb DCs accounted for *U-629* (Bug) and *U-413* (von Lehsten). The captain of the latter and over 40 of the crew survived,

Vital statistics – AS bombs					
Bomb Statistics	*35 lb*	*100 lb*	*250 lb*	*500 lb*	*600 lb*
Overall length in inches	29.2	45	58	76	56.7
Greatest diameter in inches	7	8.05	11.3	14.2	17.5
Weight and type of explosive	16 lb of TNT or Torpex	44 lb of TNT or RDX/TNT or Torpex	149 lb of Baratol or 134 lb of RDX/TNT	308 lb of Baratol or 282 lb of RDX/TNT	432 lb of Minol or 439 lb of Torpex

Vital statistics – depth charges			
Depth charge Statistics	*450 lb Mk VII*	*250 lb Mk VIII*	*250 lb Mk XI*
Overall length in inches	62.75	39 or 56	54.8
Diameter in inches	17.5	11	11
Weight of explosive	290	160	175
Type of explosive	Amatol	Amatol	Torpex

Note: Dimensions varied slightly with the different marks of both bombs and depth charges.

frustrated in their attempt to attack the Normandy invasion fleet.

The conventional U-boat types, ranging from 700 to 1,700 tons, were not the only manned underwater threat; in the early days of 1945 they were supplemented by midget submarines. These harassed ships carrying supplies to Continental ports, Antwerp in particular. Three types were deployed, the two-man 15-ton *Seehund* (Seal), the one-man ten-ton *Molch* (Salamandar) and six-ton *Biber* (Beaver), carrying mixtures of torpedoes and sea mines. Aircraft accounted for at least 16 sunk and ten damaged. All types of aircraft were involved, using depth charges, bombs, rockets, the six-pounder Molins Gun and 20 mm cannon. A Coastal Command 119 Squadron Albacore probably damaged a Seehund with six depth charges off the Dutch coast on 23 January 1945, and a Swordfish of the same unit sunk another on 11 March. Two more midget submarines were sunk by the Barracudas of 810 Squadron, Fleet Air Arm, Beccles, and the cannon-firing Spitfires of 91 Squadron Wouldham on 13 and 26 April respectively.

Similar weapons were deployed against the main U-boat fleet, and although they do not come under the general category of air-dropped anti-submarine weapons, the three-inch rocket and Molins Gun, in particular, were designed with U-boats in mind. Therefore, this range of weaponry is worthy of mention, because their use by Coastal Command and the Fleet Air Arm added considerably to the number of U-boat sinkings.

The heaviest airborne gun deployed was the 57 mm Molins fitted to Coastal Command's Mk XVIII Mosquitoes. It fired some 25 AP shells in 20 seconds and was effective up to about 2,000 yd. Among other Mosquito squadrons 248, based at Predannack and Portreath in Cornwall, had a number of successes with it. The first, on 7 November 1943 when Flying Officer A Bonnet (RCAF) damaged *U-123* (Schröter) near Lorient; and *U-976* (Tiesler), homeward-bound to St Nazaire, was sunk by Molins' firepower on 25 March 1944.

A number of Coastal Command anti-submarine and strike aircraft were adapted in 1943 to carry eight underwing three-inch rockets. These included the Hudson, Liberator, Beaufighter and Mosquito. The Fleet Air Arm adapted the ever-versatile Swordfish, and it was one of these which achieved the first rocket success on 23 May 1943. Operating from the escort carrier HMS *Archer*, Sub-Lieutenant H Horrocks seriously damaged *U-752* in the North Atlantic, whilst escorting a Liverpool-bound convoy. Three of the armour-piercing 25 lb heads, launched from 300 yd, smashed into the hull on the waterline about 20 ft ahead of the rudder. Kapitänleutnant Schrouter died on the bridge defending his vessel from further attack by an 892 Squadron Martlet (American Wildcat). The survivors scuttled the boat before taking to their life rafts. Escort carrier Swordfish achieved other successes; for instance, Sub-Lieutenant J F Mason, 816 Squadron from HMS *Chaser* sank *U-366* with four rockets on 5 March 1944, whilst shepherding convoy RA 57 homeward-bound from Russia.

The Royal Air Force achieved its first rocket success in the Western Mediterranean on 28 May 1943 when Flying Officer G Ogilvie, 608 Hudson Squadron, obtained six direct hits on *U-755* (Going). The crew just managed to leap overboard before she sank stern first. The second, *U-418*, was sunk on 1 June by Flight Lieutenant M C Bateman, 236 Beaufighter Squadron. Another, *U-389* went down to the rockets of Flight Sergeant C Alsop, 269 Hudson Squadron on 5 October whilst patrolling south of Iceland.

The rocket consisted of a light metal tube some 55 in long and 3 in diameter, packed with a quick-burning rocket propellant, initiated electrically. For use against U-boats, it was fitted with a 25 lb solid-shot AP warhead, whilst for general purposes a 60 lb high explosive head was fitted. The 25 lb head was capable of piercing a U-boat hull or shattering the bridge or gun positions. Not only could it sink a U-boat in its own right, but holes punched in the hull often prevented the vessel from diving, making it a sitting duck for surface warships or marauding aircraft. The best results were obtained if rocket salvoes were aimed to strike the sea at an angle of about 15 degrees from the surface 20 yd

short of the submarine. After an initial plunge to 10 ft or so, they started turning upwards to impact with the vulnerable hull below the waterline at about
half of their original speed of sound.

Little so far has been said in this chapter regarding Bomber Command's role
in the anti-submarine war, because it rarely destroyed U-boats at sea. However,
some successes were achieved in the Command's own right, and others whilst
particular squadrons were temporarily detached under Coastal Command control. Perhaps somewhat fortuitously, Squadron Leader M V Delap in an 82
Squadron Blenheim scored Bomber Command's very first U-boat sinking on
11 March 1940. He came across *U-31* surfaced in the North Sea and promptly
despatched it with four 250 lb GP bombs. Among successes scored by detached
squadrons was the sinking of *U-751* by Flight Lieutenant P R Casement, 61
Lancaster Squadron in the Bay of Biscay on 17 July 1942. Irrefutable
photographic evidence showed the crew swimming away from the doomed
vessel. Six months later, on 14 January, a No 10 OTU (Operational Training
Unit) Whitley flown by Sgt A Benson sank *U-564* (Suhren) with 250 lb DCs off
Cape Ortegal, Portugal. Survivors from the U-boat were picked up, but later
the aircraft, already damaged by the U-boat's gun fire, was shot down by
German fighters.

Bomber Command's main contribution to the U-boat war was the attacking
of U-boat bases, assembly docks, component manufacturing plants and
transportation facilities between the factories and the assembly areas. As indicated in Chapter Four, much of the bombing directed at U-boat bases and
supply sources during the earlier years of the war was largely ineffectual.
Ironically, the attacks on the French Bay of Biscay U-boat bases in early 1941
had long-lasting and adverse effects upon the U-boat war, because they encouraged the Germans to build reinforced shelters (pens) in which to service
their boats. These pens were practically impervious to air attack, until the advent of the 12,000 lb MC Tallboy in 1944.

Following the attacks in 1941, Dönitz, with sound foresight and alacrity, set
about providing massive structures of reinforced concrete with huge sliding
doors through which the U-boats could enter and leave. They were built not
only in the French Atlantic bases, but wherever the U-boat fleet was likely to
operate. Considering the immense threat posed by the U-boats in 1941–42,
justifiably it might have been expected that the building sites would have
presented very vulnerable and worthwhile targets in the early stages of construction. Yet, although construction was monitored by photographic reconnaissance, Bomber Command's attention was directed elsewhere, to satisfy
other competing priorities. Thus, by January 1942 the pens at Brest and
Lorient, and the bulk of those at St Nazaire and La Pallice, had passed the stage
when bombing would be effective. The opportunity missed in the latter half of
1941 was missed for good. By the time U-boat facilities again became a priority
target in January 1943 it was too late; over 4,000 tons of bombs did little to
deter U-boats going to sea or being serviced in their home bases (see Chapter
Four).

Back in 1941, the raids on shipyards building U-boats were more fruitful.

For example, 906 sorties flown to Kiel between mid-March and the end of May caused worthwhile production losses at three establishments, the Deutschewerke, Kregmarenwerft and Krupps Germanic Werft. However, compared with attacks to come in 1944 these were mere pinpricks, and recovery time was quick. Overall, the damage inflicted during 1941 was disappointing; frequently, lack of adequate navigational equipment prevented the aircrews reaching and identifying the selected target, and as recounted previously, the GP range of bombs was ineffectual.

Things did improve somewhat in 1942 with the advent of the four-engined heavy bombers and more adequate bombs, but problems associated with target identification and marking were still largely unresolved. By then, too, the emphasis had changed to other industrial targets, although some spectacular attacks were delivered against U-boat associated targets. Perhaps the most spectacular was the low-level daylight raid on the M.A.N. Maschinen plant at Augsburg in southern Germany on 17 April. The plant produced something like half of the U-boat diesel engine requirements, so its destruction was a matter of the utmost urgency. This raid was one of Bomber Command's experimental attacks, an attempt to achieve accurate bombing on a pinpoint target using a small force of the recently-introduced Lancaster bombers flying at low level in daylight. Carrying four 1,000 lb GP bombs apiece, 12 aircraft, six each from 44 Squadron Waddington and 97 Squadron Woodhall Spa, set out in two waves of six led by Squadron Leader J D Nettleton, 44 Squadron, to negotiate the 1,100 mile round-trip over very hostile territory. Four were shot down on the outward journey and three more near the target on the homeward journey. Nettleton and his crew were the only 44 Squadron survivors. He was later awarded the Victoria Cross for valiant leadership on what turned out to be a near suicidal mission which was justified only by the importance of the target in the U-boat war. Later reports indicated that 18 bombs, all fuzed with an 11 second delay, hit the target but five failed to detonate, perhaps having been dropped from too low a level. Machinery and buildings were damaged, but output was soon back to normal. John Nettleton, by then a Wing Commander, was killed when his Lancaster was shot down by a German night fighter over the English Channel whilst returning from a raid on Turin on the night of 12–13 July 1943.

Spectacular and heroic as it was, this attack on Augsburg was not a great strategic success, nor did it do much for the reputation of daylight bombing at low level. Subsequently, it was not until February 1944 that the M.A.N. diesel engine plant, together with most of the old town, was destroyed. By then Bomber Command, with an effective range of bombs, sophisticated navigational aids and well-practised target identification and marking techniques, was causing vast damage, not least to facilities related to the German Fleet and to U-boats in particular.

From the second half of 1944 onwards, when 617 Squadron's Lancasters started to deploy the giant 12,000 lb Tallboy, and later the 22,000 Grand Slam earthquake bombs, U-boats were no longer safe in their 'impregnable' pens. These bombs were not designed specifically to penetrate heavy reinforced conrete (see Chapter Six); they relied mainly on the shock waves transmitted through the concrete, or from the 'earthquake' effect emanating from near misses close to the building foundations. For instance, hits on the pens at Hamburg brought down 1,000 tons of débris, crushing two U-boats and crippling another six. Three near misses at Bergen (Norway) on 12 January 1945 tore a large hole in the pen wall, sank two U-boats, and threw another on to the dock wall. Sailings from most of the ports were seriously disrupted, sometimes because the huge armoured pen doors jammed, preventing vessels getting in or out. On top of that, the morale of the crews and servicing personnel dwindled alarmingly with each new attack on the lairs.

From September 1944 onwards, bombing intensity progressively increased, and widespread chaos became the order of the day in factories, on supply routes, in assembly yards, dockyards and operational ports. As the German Controller of Submarines admitted during post-war interrogation in 1945:

> By the end of 1944, conditions for the U-boat industry were chaotic everywhere, components and main assemblies for pre-fabricated boats could not be moved. Lack of electrical motors and batteries caused severe bottlenecks, the Accumulateron Fabrik plant at Hanover was the only battery producer still functioning. Furthermore, main electric motors were practically unobtainable. Destruction of floating cranes almost brought assembly of the more powerful pre-fabricated U-boats (1,600 Ton Type XXI) to a stop even when sections did manage to reach the assembly yards in the North. Transportation along the canal systems at last came to a grinding halt in early 1945 after the RAF attacks on the Dortmund-Ems in particular.

Post-war research revealed that the biggest factor delaying production of the new and vastly sophisticated Type XXI U-boats was the breaching of the Dortmund-Ems and Mittelland Canals between September 1944 and January 1945. The former canal fed at least nine other important canals on its way north to Emden. In fact, very few of these new all-powerful submarines went to sea, other than for trials, and thanks to Bomber Command only one, *U-2511* (Schnee), was fully operational when Admiral Dönitz issued the cease-fire to his U-boat fleet on 4 May 1945. Most of the damage to the Dortmund-Ems Canal was inflicted by 5 Group Lancasters using Tallboys and 1,000 pounders. As recounted in Chapter Six, two of the former caused a serious breach in the embankments at Ladbergen on the night of 23–24 September 1944. A six-mile stretch was drained, leaving many loaded barges stranded, while others were thrown bodily on to the banks. These attacks were repeated from time to time, and immediately after the war, many rusted sections of the 1,600 ton Type XXI U-boats could be seen lying in the mud, victims of Air Marshal Sir Arthur Harris's onslaught. From the foregoing, and accounts elsewhere in the book, it can be seen that, particularly in the latter part of the war, Bomber Command contributed significantly to the victory over the U-boats. Some of the effects were clearly manifested, but it is doubtful if the overall effects on the production of U-boats and their components can ever be fully established, nor can the many setbacks to Dönitz's operational and training schedules be assessed with any certainty.

What is fairly certain is that few industrial plants associated with U-boat production, like those at Hanover, Augsburg and Danzig, to name but a few, escaped the bombers. Much the same can be said for U-boat building/assembly yards and pens located from St Nazaire in the south to Bergen (Norway) in the far north. All came under heavy and very often effective attack. It is difficult to say exactly how many U-boats Bomber Command accounted for but, apart from those sunk at sea and mentioned earlier, it is believed that between 1943 and 1945 it destroyed 111 in production and another 42 in port.

This said, however, as far as the British were concerned, the Fleet Air Arm, Royal Navy and Coastal Command, Royal Air Force bore the brunt of the aerial war against the U-boats at sea. The latter started as something of a cinderella force, short of suitable anti-submarine aircraft, with little or no specialist equipment to hunt its quarry and an insufferable inadequacy of suitable weaponry. Progressively the anti-submarine resources began to improve, and with the coming of longer range aircraft fitted with sophisticated tracking and spotting equipment supplemented by a reasonably effective range of weaponry, particularly the 250 lb DC and the American homing torpedo, U-boat kills accelerated from 1942 onwards.

By May 1943 Coastal Command, under Admiralty operational control, had become a potent anti-submarine force; indeed, the bulk of U-boat sinkings after that time were credited to aircraft. Apart from technological improvements, some other factors contributed to the success. Three in particular are worth mentioning. First, Coastal Command was able to swamp the Bay of Biscay with regular anti-submarine patrols, and as already mentioned, five out of six U-boats passed through it to and from their French bases, so the detection and killing rate was high. Similar tactics were employed in the Skagerrak and Norwegian waters in late 1944 and 1945 after the U-boats evacuated the French ports. Secondly, instead of patrolling wide expanses of the North Atlantic hoping to find the enemy, the patrols were concentrated around particular convoys where U-boats were more likely to be found. Once in the convoy area, the aircraft came under control of the surface escort commander using radio communications. In this way the surface and aerial anti-submarine forces were able to supplement each other's efforts. Not only did the success rate improve, but the U-boat commanders were forced to submerge for longer and longer periods, or even to withdraw from the battle scene. Thirdly, operational research indicated that the stick spacing between individual depth charges was too small, so consequently from March 1943 onwards it was standardized at an optimum figure of 100 ft, which undoubtedly improved the effectiveness of the 250 lb DC in particular.

To emphasize the Coastal Command effort, it is appropriate to indicate the intensity of the battle scene in the bridged gap during 1943 and just before the U-boats were virtually driven from the North Atlantic. The experience of two convoys, HX 229 and SC 122, making for the United Kingdom and sailing through the Gap between 17 and 19 March, should serve the purpose. In all, during those three days there were 75 engagements with U-boats. Thirty-two of these were attributed to the VLR Liberators of 86 and 120 Squadrons operating out of Northern Ireland and Iceland. They sighted 24 U-boats and attacked 13, expending 65 250 lb DCs. At least one was sunk and another damaged, but the main benefit to the convoy during the hours of daylight was that the U-boat commanders began to find the situation intolerable. It just seems a pity that these particular Liberators did not have the benefit of Leigh Lights, when a round-the-clock assault might have been mounted. Nevertheless, in his book *Crisis Convoy*, describing critical battles in the North Atlantic, particularly in the notorious Gap, Vice Admiral Sir Peter Gretton DSO, CBE, DSC, a veteran escort commander, in paying tribute to the Liberators wrote:

> Air cover showed itself to be the key to the problem. The Liberators from Iceland and Northern Ireland cannot be too highly praised. They were quick to appreciate the requirements and effective in their execution. ... Out of the many factors contributing to the victory, the provision of air escorts for convoys threatened or under attack was the most important of all.

This tribute to the Liberators was well deserved; in all they sank 71 U-boats and damaged another 27. Of course, the VLR Liberators caught the eye because they were the only aircraft capable of operating way out in mid North Atlantic; many other types of aircraft contributed significantly. In this context, and bearing in mind the part played by the 250 lb DC, a few more of its successes are tabulated in Appendix 7.

For the record, Coastal Command aircraft accounted for 169 German U-boats and four Italian submarines, two in the Atlantic. In addition, another 40 U-boats were credited to other formations coming under the Command's control, and a further 120 U-boats and at least one Italian submarine were damaged by Coastal Command aircraft and its attached units. Undoubtedly the best results were achieved in 1943 when in all, 219 U-boats were sunk, 84 falling to Coastal Command units.

Perhaps of all the battles of the Second World War, the victory over the U-boats in the Bay of Biscay, the North Atlantic and elsewhere, was the most significant. Had it been lost, Britain would have been starved of food supplies and, much more importantly, would have been deprived of critical resources vital to the war effort. Not only was it a battle against an implacable enemy but also against the cruel seas, often in the most appalling weather far out in the Atlantic or up in the icy northern waters. Unless rescued quickly, crews forced down stood little chance of survival. A case in point was the experience of a Canadian Canso crew belonging to 162 Squadron, attached to Wick in Northern Scotland and captained by Flight Lieutenant D E Hornell. They sank *U-1125* (Sauerberg) with four 250 lb DCs north of the Shetlands on 24 June 1944, but in the course of the gun fire battle the amphibian was seriously damaged and set alight, forcing it to ditch. The crew took turns in the dinghy, escaping temporarily from the ice-old water. Two of the crew died quickly from exhaustion and exposure, followed later by David Hornell, who suffered long hours of intolerable hardship before expiring. For his courage and stoicism he was awarded a well-deserved Victoria Cross. This drama took place in high summer; one can just imagine the conditions in mid winter. It cannot be said with any certainty how many men lost their lives in aerial operations specifically directed at U-boats, but in all, Coastal Command lost 1,777 aircraft and 5,866 aircrew engaged in anti-shipping operations during the course of the war, a large proportion on anti-submarine duties.

The Germans, too, suffered high losses, some 785 U-boats were sunk out of the 1,162 commissioned, with the loss of 28,000 crewmen. During the last week of the War, 221 U-boats were also scuttled off the North Sea and Baltic ports – an ignominious end for a proud and very often gallant fleet.

CHAPTER TWELVE

THE ALSO RANS

Any record of the development of British air-dropped weapons must include details of the 'also rans'. Since the first inception of air-dropped weapons before the First World War, many designs of such weapons were conceived, tried and failed, and others had only limited success. In this chapter, six only are being considered, all of which came to fruition during the Second World War. These had a great deal of time and effort expended upon their development, and a few had the potential to become as well known as the bouncing bomb of dambuster fame, or the Tallboy. On the other hand, with hindsight, some were doomed to failure almost from conception, and those that were used in anger in no way reflected their potential for greatness.

Without exception the 'also rans' described are anti-ship weapons. The start of the Second World War hastened the need for a new range of weapons to attack Germany's inland waterways and hardened naval capital ships. British surface vessels could already lay standard buoyant mines in German coastal waters and broad river estuaries whilst, as described earlier, the Royal Air Force and the Fleet Air Arm were preparing to lay air-dropped magnetic mines in those same waters.

In the case of inland waters, such as the important canals and navigable rivers, the only possible approach was by air. The standard buoyant mine could not be laid from the air, and the 1,500 lb air-dropped magnetic mine did not come into service until April 1940. Consequently a special weapon had to be devised with all possible haste, and such a weapon was the 35 lb W (water) Bomb, designed to float down rivers and, on contact, to destroy barges or pontoon bridges. Alternatively, it could be moored in canals to await passing shipping.

The primary object of the other five was to sink enemy warships. The weapons were the 1,000 lb Spherical Mine, the 250 lb Buoyant (B) Bomb, the Johnny Walker (JW) Bomb, the Capital Ship (CS) Bomb and finally the 1,280 lb Spherical Spinning Mine 'Highball' designed by Mr Barnes Wallis and a contemporary of the dambuster bomb 'Upkeep'.

It had long been recognized that ordinary high explosive bombs were unlikely to be fully effective against hardened ships, protected as they were by armoured decks and sides, and there was an urgent need for a weapon to attack the weakest part, namely the vulnerable underwater hull, which was provided with no special protection.

The debate on the vulnerability of capital ships to air attack was at its peak in the 1930s. In November 1936 a report by the Sub-Committee of the Committee of Imperial Defence was published and presented to Parliament. It was titled *Report on the Vulnerability of Capital Ships to Air Attack* and expressed the Admiralty view that:

> ...the Admiralty makes no claim that a ship, however designed, can be invulnerable in all circumstances to every form of attack. But they do think that the capital ship of the future can be so designed as to distribution of her armour on decks and sides, and as to interior sub-division, that she will not be subject to fatal damage from the air.

The view expressed in the second sentence was also reflected in the views of the German Naval Command, hence their faith in capital ships such as the *Scharnhorst, Gneisenau* and *Tirpitz*. The members of the Committee writing the report, however, concluded that:

> ...it is plain to us that capital ships cannot be constructed so as to be indestructible by bombing from the air.

The Air Ministry clearly supported this view, but in actuality had no specialist weapons to attack capital ships, either at sea or in port.

Returning to the 35 lb W Bomb, which was conceived in September 1939 and first used operationally in May 1940, although 6,000 bombs were ready for use a month earlier. This gestation period was one of feverish activity, changes of design, changes of size, changes of purpose and the need to build in extra safety devices to prevent charges of indiscriminate bombing; all added to the pressure of production. The war scene also added to the pressures. At this time Germany was threatening to invade her neighbours, consequently there was a desperate need to stop or at least restrict traffic flow in her important inland waters. Among these were the Dortmund-Ems and Mittelland Canals, and the rivers Rhine, Elbe and Weser. The most important of these, as seen by the First Lord of the Admiralty (Mr Winston Churchill) was the Rhine, described by him as 'the main artery of German trade and life'. The need increased when the invasion of the Low Countries and France became a reality in May 1940, and Hitler began to assemble his invasion fleet of barges during the summer of the same year, with the intention of mounting an invasion of southern England at the earliest possible date.

The initial requirement was specified by Mr Churchill, who wished to retaliate against the German mining of British estuaries and coastal waters, which began within hours of the Second World War starting. His idea was to heavily mine the Rhine, both by dropping airborne mines directly into the German Rhine, and other types of mine which could be cast adrift into the

Rhine from French soil. The latter would be fed into the river anywhere between Strasbourg and the Lauter near the Swiss/French border, to drift
downstream into Germany. He also planned to air-drop mines into other German inland waterways. As with most Churchillian plans, this was to be no
small operation. This was reflected in a minute dated 19 November 1939:

> Finally, as very large numbers of these mines would be used and the process kept
> up night after night for months on end, so as to deny the use of the waterway, it is
> necessary to bear in mind the simplification required for mass production.*

The requirement therefore for this small bomb/mine was that it should float
freely at either one or three feet below the surface of the water, if necessary it
should moor itself in this configuration, and it should be capable of remaining
at the bottom of a canal for up to seven days, after which it should rise into its
selected position below the surface. Additionally it had to be self-sinking after a
pre-arranged period, so that it would not travel downriver into neutral water –
the Rhine runs through the Netherlands to the sea and, at this stage of design
that country was still neutral. A final requirement was that the construction
must be such that if it fell on to a hard surface, such as river or canal banks, it
would not detonate. The Air Staff were of the opinion that should the air-
dropped weapons inadvertently detonate on the banks or in adjacent towns,
Britain might possibly be accused of indiscriminate bombing. (During the first
few months of the war no bombing of land targets had taken place because of
this restricted bombing policy.)

Having decided on the requirement, it was necessary to determine whether
such a device existed or could be manufactured. As it happened, Major M R
Jefferis of the Royal Engineers (later Brigadier Sir Millis Jefferis, Chief
Superintendent of the Military Engineering Experimental Establishment) had,
in September 1939, been considering, amongst other weapons, an anti-pontoon
bridge mine to be dropped from aircraft. He was in the War Office MIR
(Military Intelligence Research) branch, one of whose tasks was the design of
special weapons, and was assisted by Captain (later Colonel) R S Macrae of the
Intelligence Corps. Major Jefferis had discussed this project with Professor
A M Low, who not only suggested a form of fuze mechanism, but also
introduced him to Mr Albert Midgley of Messrs Midgley Harmer, builders
of pipeless organs. Mr Midgley was a well-known inventor and designer of
many fuzes used during the First World War, and went on to design many
more during the Second. As a result of this collaboration a small inert mine
weighing between 2 and 3 lb was designed and built in Mr Midgley's factory.

Churchill heard of this design in November 1939, and the pressure was on to
produce an operational version. Since it was to be air dropped as well as placed
in the water, the development of the weapon was taken over by the Directorate
of Armament Development (D Arm D) Ministry of Aircraft Production, whose
Director was Air Commodore P Huskinson. Although both Jefferis and
Macrae continued to play a major part in its development, much of the design

* Churchill's *The Second World War*, Volume 1.

work and all the production was undertaken by Mr Midgley and his company. Additionally, a wide range of service organizations were involved in the development and subsequent trials. For example, the Royal Aircraft Establishment was responsible for several modifications to the drogue parachute which were found to be necessary. Professor Low's suggested fuzing system for the original prototype was not used in subsequent versions or the production model, and he appears to have taken no further active part in the project, although he did receive a financial commission from Midgley Harmer in respect of his initial introduction of Mr Midgley to Major Jefferis.

Explosive trials carried out at HMS *Vernon* (Portsmouth) during November determined that the mine needed to contain a minimum of 8 lb of explosive to sink a barge or pontoon. Midgley redesigned the mine, assisted by Jefferis and Macrae, to accommodate just under 10 lb of high explosive. The mine was now cylindrical in shape and equipped with radial whiskers like the ribs of an umbrella. These ribs would normally be compressed, but when released sprang out to form electrical contacts, which closed a circuit to a small battery when touched, thus initiating detonation of the mine. Woolwich Arsenal was ordered to manufacture 100 to enable dropping trials to be carried out at Staines reservoir. Some were dropped on 21, 27 and 29 December 1939 but the ballistics were bad and the bombs, as they were now classified, received extensive damage on impact. None functioned as intended. However, this was of little importance because further trials at HMS *Vernon* had already determined that the previous figure of 8 lb was incorrect, and at least 20 lb of high explosive would be needed to sink a barge.

As might be expected, this caused considerable consternation, and the cancellation of the 100 smaller bombs previously ordered.

At a meeting in the Air Ministry on 29 December Mr Midgley produced a revised design for a 35 lb bomb containing 20 lb of high explosive and fitted with a small retarding drogue parachute. Additionally he prepared a complete production programme detailing the materials, tools and manpower required for large-scale production of the bomb in his own factory and those of subcontractors. Air Vice-Marshal Tedder who was chairing the meeting was so impressed that he agreed, subject to satisfactory trials, that Midgley Harmer should be given a contract for 10,000 W Bombs, as they were then named.

These 10,000 formed the Mk I model of the bomb intended for use in rivers. It consisted of a cylindrical casing ten in in diameter and approximately 15 in long, filled with a charge of 20 lb of TNT. The bomb had a negative buoyancy (i.e. it would not float), and attached to it by cords were a number of cork floats. These corks were accommodated in a small chamber at the top of the bomb, together with the compressed firing whiskers. Both the firing contacts and the corks were held in place by a lid which after two or three minutes in the water was released by the action of the dissolving of a soluble plug. These corks suspended the bomb at a depth of 3 ft below the surface. A second soluble plug initiated action to sink the bomb after a lapse of 6, 18 or 48 hrs, depending upon the type of plug, thus preventing it from drifting into neutral waters.

A very similar Mk II model was designed for use in the still waters of canals.

W Bombs, from left to right, first inert prototype, second and third prototypes and Mk II Service model. Note that in the service model, top of photograph is bottom of mine.

The bottom of this bomb was fitted with a 5 lb sinker and 6 ft of mooring cable. After entry the bomb sank to the bottom of the canal, and after a variable period of up to seven days a soluble plug released the bomb from the sinker, allowing the former to rise up 6 ft to the end of the mooring cable. Since the average depth of most canals was approximately 9 ft, this system positioned it 3 ft below the surface in a static position. The Mk III bomb was identical to the Mk I except that the cork floats were attached directly to it so that it drifted just below the surface, hopefully hitting a pontoon bridge having a very shallow draught. A small number of a further variant were manufactured which had a diameter of 18 in, as compared with the standard 10 in, and were intended for release immediately above those pontoon bridges protected by heavy steel nets. They do not appear to have been particularly effective as they are the only designs recorded in the German bomb disposal manuals.

A series of trials of all three types were carried out to determine their effectiveness in water, their ballistic qualities and ability not to detonate if dropped on hard ground. These were conducted at Staines reservoir, in the Thames at Reading and Wallingford, at Kempton Park and Porton. Subsequently they were declared fit for air service in April 1940 and it was decided that the 23,000 required should be manufactured by Midgley Harmer Limited; 14,000 Mk I,

6,000 Mk II and 3,000 Mk III.

Once they were declared fit for operational use, the bombs were released to eighteen Bomber and eight Coastal Command Stations, and to at least two Fleet Air Arm Squadrons. By 11 June 1940, 21,910 bombs in all were delivered to the Royal Navy and the Royal Air Force, the remainder having been expended on trials.

In accordance with Churchill's original plan the bombs were first deployed operationally by setting them adrift in the Rhine. However, operations were neither on the massive scale he originally envisaged, nor were they immediately supported by nightly air deliveries. During March, 1,750 bombs were made available to a Royal Navy contingent in France, with the intention of launching them into the French Rhine at Strasbourg. The French, however, objected and nothing was done until Germany invaded the country on 10 May 1940. They were then cast into the river causing considerable confusion in the upper reaches within German territory. Practically all river traffic between Karlsruhe and Mainz was suspended, and extensive damage was done to the Karlsruhe barrage and a number of bridges. Unfortunately this relatively minor damage was overshadowed by the greater confusion caused by the rapidly advancing German armies *en route* to the Channel ports.

Official histories indicate that the W Bombs were never dropped operationally, yet unit records and bombing diaries show this to be incorrect. In fact Mr Churchill, now Prime Minister, sent a minute to the Secretary of State for Air and Chief of the Air Staff on 11 June 1940 saying that he would be glad if the Chief of Air Staff would infest the reaches of the Rhine mentioned the day before and that he should act as soon as he could.

Bomber Command reacted at once and a number of W Bomb-laying sorties were carried out during June. Five Whitleys of 10 Squadron, Dishforth, took off on the night of 14–15 June, each carrying 72 W Bombs in three containers of 24. Only two, captained by Flying Officers Paterson and Smith, found their targets on the Rhine between Worms and Oppenheim, and dropped their bombs from 500 ft. Three nights later Flying Officer Paterson again made a successful attack on the same target, as did Flying Officer French-Mullen and Sgt Johnson. Four other aircraft failed to bomb the target, but it should be emphasized that when carrying W Bombs the crews were explicitly briefed not to drop their bomb loads unless they could positively identify their targets.

The Fleet Air Arm joined in too and four Albacores of 826 Squadron operating out of Bircham Newton dropped 240 W Bombs in the mouth of the River Maas on various nights between 25 June and 2 July 1940. A few days later on the night of 6–7 July, five Coastal Command Blenheims of 53 Squadron, Detling, dropped their full loads of 48 bombs each in the IJmuiden-Amsterdam Canal. The captains of these aircraft were Squadron Leader Murray, Flight Lieutenants Brown and Bartlett, and Pilot Officers Stewart-Richardson and Starky.

They followed this up on the night of 26–27, when four aircraft, carrying a mixture of W Bombs and 250 lb General Purpose bombs, found their targets in the Haarlem Basin and related waterways. This attack was led by Squadron

Leader Oliver and supported by Flight Lieutenant Bartlett and Pilot Officers Corbett and Massey.

There is no proof that the W Bomb caused any lasting damage, although clearly they were a confounded nuisance to the Germans at the time. In any event, priorities changed and at the same time increasing use was made of the newly introduced 1,500 lb A Mine. Consequently the W Bomb was shelved in late 1940 and scrapped a year later.

This bomb was an example of a promising weapon conceived in great haste to meet a temporary operational requirement. This necessitated overlooking certain weak points in design, its greatest disadvantage being that it could not be stored for any great length of time. Its small batteries and soluble plugs deteriorated extremely quickly, and were intended for early use. The bomb was never completely safe; under damp conditions the soluble plugs could deteriorate, and since they formed part of the safety system there was a constant risk of detonation during storage or routine handling. Indeed, on 22 June 1940 a bomb inadvertently functioned at Royal Air Force Dishforth, killing two armourers and injuring three others.

Perhaps one of the most surprising things about the W Bomb was the number of people who claimed to have invented it, or who applied for patents on it. During 1939 and 1940, when presumably both serving officers and civilians alike had the survival of the nation at heart, it is interesting to note that nearly all concerned in its development were filing patent applications. The first was by Professor Low on 2 November 1939 for his idea relating to the fuzing system of the first prototype. The second, on 11 January 1940, was made jointly by Major Jefferis, Captain Macrae and Mr Midgley for the design of the mine, which was basically the first production model. Three months later Jefferis and Macrae were presenting another application, this time in respect of improvements to the mine mechanism. Finally, on 27 March 1940, Mr Midgley and for the first time Air Commodore P Huskinson, presented a joint application in respect of the design of the sinker release mechanism.

With the exception of Professor Low, whose application was accepted in October 1942, all the other applicants had to wait until after the war for their applications to be accepted, thus making them available to the general public. The story did not end even then; the Royal Commission on Awards to Inventors, sitting at Somerset House, London on 13 April 1953, began the hearing of claims for awards from Professor A M Low and Colonel R S Macrae in respect of their work on the W Bomb. The statements and claims put before the Commission during the next four days were both contradictory and antagonistic. For a bomb which was very much an 'also ran', it all seems rather sad that such distinguished men should become so involved and self-seeking.

Turning to the 'also rans' designed to attack capital ships, the one with the longest gestation period was undoubtedly the 250 lb B (Buoyant) Bomb, more frequently referred to as the Buoyancy Bomb. Its primary objective was to attack the bottoms of enemy warships on the high seas. Proposals for its development were first made by Lieutenant H A Williamson RN in late 1914 but no serious action ensued. The proposal was resurrected in 1923 when Wing Commander T R Cave-Brown-Cave, commanding the Marine and Armament Experimental Establishment on the Isle of Grain, Kent, made suggestions to the Director of Research at the Air Ministry for the development of what he called a buoyancy bomb.

The idea was to suspend a bomb under water in the path of an oncoming warship, to detonate on contact or after a fixed delay period. The Air Ministry found this too much like a mine, of which there were plenty. However, the notion of having a bomb which could be dropped in front of a ship and rise to strike the bottom was most appealing. It was decided to follow this line of development in conjunction with the Admiralty.

There followed during the next decade, with little sense of urgency, a series of learned papers and trials reports relating to underwater trajectories, aerodynamic tests, tests of fuzing mechanisms and a variety of sizes and designs of bomb ranging from 250 lb to over 1,000 lb. By the early 1930s action had been concentrated upon a 250 lb version, and as early as 1925 at a meeting held at the Admiralty on 13 February the bomb was given its official name of B (Buoyant) Bomb. The 250 lb version was known amongst the research establishments as the B2, and all the experience of the previous years was built into the redesigned system. At last a mechanical fuzing system was used instead of the electrical one which had posed endless problems during the years of experimentation.

The late half of the 1930s was taken up with experiments and modifications to bring the weapon up to the necessary operational standards. Ultimately 540 Mk I bombs were made available to Bomber and Coastal Commands at the end of 1939. At that time the intention was that the Hampden, Wellington and Beaufort should carry four apiece. The proposed technique was to drop them from about 6,000 ft in the direct path of advancing enemy warships, particularly capital ships, but there is no record to show that they were ever used. A proposal by Coastal Command, in late 1940, that the bomb should be used as a floating mine in confined waters was considered, and although a few bombs were modified for that purpose, none were ever deployed.

In time, the weapon was modified and improved, and when the Mks II to IV became available, additional aircraft were earmarked to carry them. These improved versions could be released from between 1,500 and 15,000 ft into a minimum water depth of 75 ft. Theoretically, the bomb would initially plunge to about 50 ft, rise at 3.5 ft per sec and detonate against the last two-thirds of the ship's hull.

Attempts were still being made to perfect the as yet unused bomb in the latter half of 1943. Records show that Fleet Air Arm Swordfish from 835 Squadron were doing trial drops in reaches of the Clyde on 22 September. About this time, 150 bombs were stocked in the Mediterranean area, and a year later 500 were sent to the Far East with the Japanese Fleet in mind. The stock at home were held mostly by Coastal Command.

Despite the time, energy and money spent on this bomb, none was ever used operationally so it had no opportunity to show its worth, perhaps because the Air Staff, unlike the Admiralty, were never keen to use it. By the time the Mark

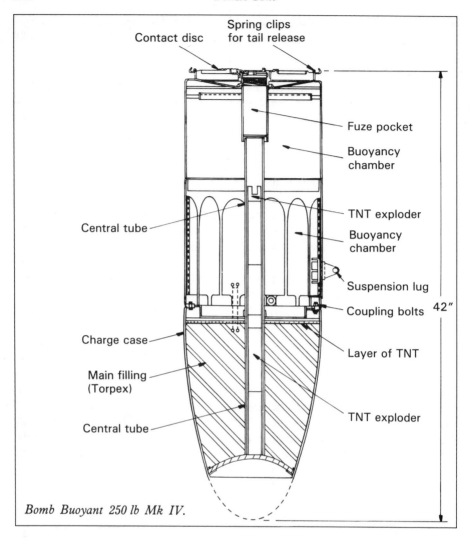

Bomb Buoyant 250 lb Mk IV.

I became available it was competing with the airborne torpedo, and within a few months the airborne mine. Furthermore, the operational staff at Head-quarters Bomber Command were not too happy at the prospect of attacking enemy warships in broad daylight – since the opening days of the Second World War, in brushes with the German Fleet and its *Luftwaffe* escorts, the bombers had usually come off second best. By 1943, when the bomber aircraft themselves, along with much improved tracking, identification and target-marking techniques might have been able to deal with warships at sea, few op-portunities were presented, because the German Fleet rarely went to sea. Many of the well-known ships were either undergoing war damage repair or simply dared not venture out.

Consequently, one does not know how the Buoyant bomb would have fared operationally. Nevertheless, it is worth describing the Mk IV version (illustrated) to show what might have been a successful weapon, given the right opportunity.

It was 72 in long and just over 14 in in diameter. The explosive charge of just over 113 lb of Torpex was contained in a truncated cone charge case with a concave nose. To this was fitted a breakaway nose fairing. Behind the charge case a buoyancy chamber and a small tail unit were fitted. The nose fairing and tail unit provided the necessary aerodynamics during its initial drop. Detonation was initiated by a hydrostatically-armed tail fuze.

On striking the sea surface, the nose fairing shattered and the tail unit broke away, releasing a wheel-shaped disc tethered to the bomb base. Having plunged to about 50 ft, the bomb ascended slowly under its own buoyancy. If all went according to plan, the wheeled disc, rising slightly ahead of the bomb body, performed two vital functions: it armed the hydostatic fuze at the appropriate depth and on impact, hopefully with the ship's bottom, initiated the detonation chain via the hydrostatic fuze. Failing contact, the bomb sank after ten minutes when sufficient water entered the buoyancy chamber, thus avoiding possible damage to friendly shipping. Needless to say, the whole process demanded immaculate timing and accuracy from the bomb-aimer, most probably in the face of violent opposition from the intended victim and its escorts. It would be a triumph indeed to have the bomb eventually impact on the last two-thirds of the ships's bottom. Dropped in sticks, the chances would certainly be more realistic, but still very chancy.

Altogether, over 20 years of research and development went into this bomb and in the end suitable targets no longer existed and, not surprisingly, the Air Staff were loath to deploy it, even if it had been available. The 250 lb Buoyant Bomb was not only an 'also ran', it barely qualified for entry at the starting gate!

From 20 years down to three months, such was the change in development time expended on the next 'also ran'. Early in 1942, the 'unsinkable' 42,900 ton German battleship *Tirpitz* was lurking in the Norwegian fjords, together with other elements of the German Navy. The *Tirpitz* in particular posed an enormous threat to the Atlantic and Arctic convoys, so it was decided that she must at all costs be prevented from going to sea. It was recognized that the contemporary bombs such as the 2,000 lb armour-piercing and the 500 lb semi-armour-piercing bombs and others, designed purely for general bombardment purposes, could at best probably only superficially damage her.

Since arriving from Kiel on 15 January, she had been moored close inshore in the half-mile-wide Fottenfjord, approximately 20 miles from Trondheim and 35 from the Swedish frontier. She lay under overhanging rocks surrounded by wooded slopes up to about 250 ft high, protected by wire cables between the crests, anti-torpedo nets on three sides, ship and shore anti-aircraft batteries and smoke screening equipment both on the ship and the surrounding shores. All in all, the *Tirpitz* was an extremely difficult target to hit, even without the vagaries of Norwegian weather and man-made smoke screens. High level attacks stood little chance of success, whilst the environment and opposition made those at low level extremely hazardous.

For these reasons high-level bombing attacks during March proved ineffectual. One such attack made by 33 Halifaxes on the night of 30–31 March 1942 came to nothing, foiled by bad weather and extensive smoke screening. Six aircraft were lost and only one bomb load, consisting of a single 4,000 lb HC Bomb plus four 500 lb bombs dropped from a medium altitude fell anywhere near the *Tirpitz*. This and similar attacks confirmed the desperate need for an underwater weapon, in the form of a mine, dropped at extremely low-level with sufficient accuracy to get at the battleship's bottom.

The situation demanded urgent resolution. It certainly could not await development of an entirely new airborne mine. The next best thing was to effect some sort of improvization and, to this end, the 290 lb Naval Mark XIX Spherical Contact Mine was selected for adaption. The Royal Air Force procured 100, each being modified by strengthening the case and removing the mooring mechanism together with the eight external contact firing-switch horns. Most of the inside was also removed and the body filled with approximately 770 lb of the high explosive Amatol. Lastly the modified weapon was equipped with a Mk XIV hydrostatic pistol and a suspension lug to enable its carriage on an aircraft. Rechristened the 1,000 lb Spherical Mine, the 31 in diameter sphere was ready for the *Tirpitz*, having been conceived and completed in under three months.

The workings were relatively simple. On release from the aircraft a safety clip was extracted from the pistol and retained on the bomb carrier. After sinking to a depth of 14-18 ft (some thought 30 ft would have been more suitable) a rubber diaphragm in the hydrostatic pistol expanded, thus releasing the striker mechanism and detonating the Amatol through the medium of a detonator and exploder, hopefully adjacent to the ship's bottom. Alternatively, it could be dropped safe in the event of an emergency. In such circumstances, the safety clip would not be extracted, thus preventing water from entering the pistol to expand the diaphragm and free the striker.

Records show that the mines were used on only two occasions, on successive nights, at the end of April 1942 when the *Tirpitz* was still moored close inshore near Trondheim. The operations were mounted by 4 Group Halifaxes and 5 Group Lancasters, although the latter did not carry mines, operating only in a bomb supporting role, as did some of the Halifaxes. To bring the battleship within striking range the attackers were deployed from their home bases in England to Lossiemouth, Kinloss and Tain in northern Scotland. The plan on both occasions was that the supporting aircraft should lead the way and attack the defences from about 6,000 ft with 4,000 lb HC blast bombs and 500 lb bombs to distract attention from the mine-laying aircraft. In turn, the minelayers would take advantage of the confusion to sneak in at very low level, mast height if need be, and drop their loads of four or five mines apiece.

At about 10.30 p.m. on 27 April 1942, 26 Halifaxes and ten Lancasters took off heading for Trondheim and the *Tirpitz*. The Halifaxes of 10 and 35 Squadrons were loaded with mines, whilst the Halifaxes of 76 Squadron and the 5 Group Lancasters carried bombs in the supporting role. Some three hours later, the plan was executed in the face of vicious anti-aircraft fire, with the

Tirpitz practically obscured by a dense smoke screen. Those who saw her got only momentary glimpses amidst the general confusion. None of the mines detonated sufficiently close to trouble the battleship – some even fell on the steep slopes alongside. Four Halifaxes and one Lancaster failed to return, a number had to abort before they reached the target, and another brought back four mines which hung-up over the ship.

One of the lost Halifaxes was piloted by the commander of 10 Squadron, Wing Commander D C T Bennett, who escaped to neutral Sweden and returned to England five weeks later. As recounted in Chapter Four he was later appointed Air Officer Commanding 8 Group, the élite Bomber Command Pathfinder Force.

Another Halifax, the brand new S for Sugar No W 1048 of 35 Squadron, on its first mission, was piloted by Pilot Officer D McIntyre. On completing the bombing run the aircraft was hit several times and its starboard outer engine set on fire. McIntyre, with careful nursing, managed to crash-land on the frozen Lake Hoklingen, 30 miles north-east of Trondheim. With the exception of the flight engineer, Sergeant V Stevens, who injured a foot and was taken prisoner, the crew escaped to Sweden. The aircraft sank into 90 ft of water, where it remained until 1973. In that year it was recovered in a reasonably sound condition. As the only known nearly complete Halifax in existence, it was partially restored by the men of the Royal Air Force Wyton and is now on public display in the Royal Air Force Museum at Hendon.

The raid was repeated on the following night, 23 Halifaxes and 11 Lancasters taking part. The *Tirpitz* again escaped damage, but two Halifaxes were lost.

The Germans picked up some mines among the birch trees and conifers on the slopes above the Tirpitz, leading to a belief that they had been deliberately dropped there to roll down and sink below the ship. This was not the main intention, but it certainly would have given the bomb-aimers a second string to their bows. In any event, the Germans took the possibility very seriously and erected netting to protect the ship. Within days of the attack the Germans picked up a number of unexploded mines and published a very good diagram of the mine for use by their bomb disposal teams. The illustration of what they called the Britische Kugelwasserbombe, and the British called the 1,000 lb Spherical bomb alias the Mark XIX Contact Mine, is illustrated.

This 'also ran' was a simple idea, developed in a remarkably short time to fill a gap in air-dropped weaponry. It deserved to succeed, but depended upon a low-level attack and accurate placement in the face of extremely efficient defences. These two were rarely compatible and it was not until Mr Barnes Wallis designed Highball that the problems of accurate low-level attacks on protected capital ships and accurate placement appeared to be solved.

Meanwhile, concurrent with the development of the Buoyant Bomb during the early months of 1942, other minds too were wrestling with the problems of defeating heavily-armoured capital ships. Once again, *Tirpitz* was uppermost in the designers' minds. At this stage of the war it was considered essential that she should, at all costs, be prevented from going to sea and possibly attacking the Arctic or Atlantic convoys.

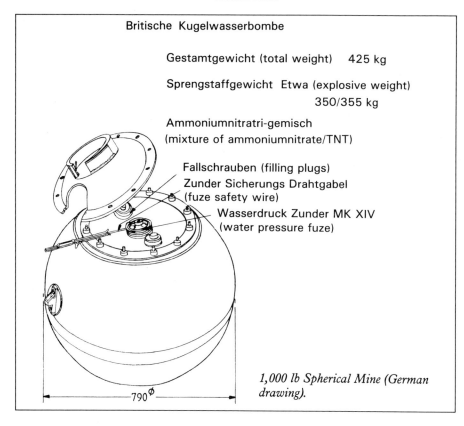

Britische Kugelwasserbombe

Gestamtgewicht (total weight)   425 kg

Sprengstaffgewicht Etwa (explosive weight)
350/355 kg

Ammoniumnitratri-gemisch
(mixture of ammoniumnitrate/TNT)

Fallschrauben (filling plugs)
Zunder Sicherungs Drahtgabel
(fuze safety wire)
Wasserdruck Zunder MK XIV
(water pressure fuze)

1,000 lb Spherical Mine (German drawing).

790 ⌀

Development was therefore started on what was later to become known as the Capital Ship (CS) Bomb. Development action was initiated, and spurred on, by Lord Cherwell (Professor F A Lindemann), Scientific Advisor to the War Cabinet and close friend of Prime Minister Churchill. Perhaps, too, it was at his insistence the development continued long after Air Staff enthusiasm had cooled to what was basically an admirable concept.

At that time, January 1942, it was widely recognized that the orthodox weapons for attacking warships, the 2,000 lb armour-piercing and 250–500 lb semi-armour-piercing bombs, had to be dropped from a considerable height to achieve the necessary striking velocity. The chances of hitting a moored ship, let alone a moving one, lessened alarmingly as the height increased. This apart, explosive content of these heavy-cased bombs was far too small to inflict lethal damage to a hardened battleship like the *Tirpitz*. She was protected by some 15 in of side armour and covered with a tortoise-like armoured crust five to ten in thick, designed to prevent bomb penetration from above. This armoured deck was supplemented by two-inch plating on the upper and main decks which confronted any bomb even before it reached the armoured crust. Understandably, but incorrectly as future events were to prove, the Germans thought the *Tirpitz* could scarcely be holed, far less be sunk by bombs.

Lord Cherwell postulated that the main armour of ships like the *Tirpitz* might be defeated by a large light-cased bomb packed with high explosive and using, in his words 'the shaped charge principle'. This principle, better known as the Munroe Effect and discovered by Doctor Charles Monroe in 1889, focuses the energy of detonation directly in front of the bomb, rather than dissipating it in all directions. Such a bomb would have to be dropped from low level to increase the chances of hitting the target; the risk to the attacker would have to be accepted. This was a fine concept from the laboratory standpoint, but a traumatic one for those who would have to deliver it.

However, Lord Cherwell's proposals were accepted, and a number of static trials were commenced using layers of armoured plate to simulate the decks of proposed targets. Three separate forms of 'shaped charge' were experimented with, the first was the hollow charge, the second the plastic nose and the third the disc or ring charge.

The hollow charge achieves the true Munroe Effect; a hollow portion is provided in the nose of the bomb, in the form of a truncated cone. As with all these charges, the explosive is detonated from the rear, and in this case generates a jet which will pierce the armoured plate in front of it. If the inner cone is lined with soft metal, then a molten slug of metal also is driven through the target plate.

The action of the plastic nose bomb, or as it is now known the squash head, was somewhat different. On impacting with the target the nose flattens against the target and spreads the explosive in close contact with and over a relatively large area of the impact point. On detonation, the energy released either cuts out a large piece of the armour plating, or because of the shock wave set up in the armour, a scab of it is blown off on the inside. In either case a large lump of metal, propelled at speeds approaching 4,000 ft per sec (2,725 mph) is driven through the ship, and perhaps even out through the bottom.

The disc or ring charge method took account of the possibility that the bomb might first impact on the lighter superstructure, so it was provided with its own projectile. This took the form of a steel disc strengthened by a ring round the periphery located in the bomb nose in front of the explosive. This method required more explosive to ensure sufficient energy was imparted to the disc. This method is known as the Miznay Schardin Effect. In the case of the last two methods, apart from the damage caused by the projectile, high blast effects were expected to sweep the decks and superstructure.

Trials continued throughout 1942 and by March were concentrated only on the plastic nose and disc ring type. Problems arose over the size of the bomb. From small-scale trials using the plastic nose, it was calculated that to drive a lump of metal through a capital ship the bomb needed to be 36 in in diameter and weigh approximately 3,000 lb, with the proviso that it would first hit at least $1\frac{1}{2}$ in of deck armour. Should it first hit the lightly-armoured superstructure, much of the projectile effect would be lost. In the case of the disc ring type, it was calculated the bomb would need to be 36 in in diameter and weigh up to 5,000 lb. Further trials indicated that the bomb should be increased to 45 in diameter, but only the Lancaster was capable of carrying a bomb of this size, and even then the bomb doors would not fully close. However, a reduction of 7 in to 38 in diameter would enable the bomb to be carried in the Halifax as well – indeed, it could carry two of the modified size. Consequently it was agreed that the first full-size bombs should be manufactured in two sizes, 45 and 38 in diameters. It was also agreed that, because of its greater versatility, the disc ring method should be used, and the bomb then officially became known as Bomb CS Type DR.

Full-scale trials started at Shoeburyness in April 1942. During these it became clear that to be effective the bombs had to strike the target armour at not more than 30 degrees from the vertical, and preferably at less than 15. To achieve this, bombs had either to be dropped from a height of about 20,000 ft or they had to be stabilized with a drogue parachute. The use of drogues proved impractical with bombs of that size, and consequently a smaller 30 in diameter bomb, which could be stabilized, was selected for development in November 1942. Its trials were completed in early 1943 and it was shown that it could penetrate a succession of seven armoured steel plates, ranging in thickness from one to four inches.

The need to drop the larger CS Bombs from greater heights had now put them in direct competition with the 2,000 lb armour-piercing bomb already well established and which could, if dropped from 10,000 ft, achieve the same degree of penetration as the CS Bombs but with less damage, assuming of course that they could hit the target in the first place. The Air Staff felt that the chances of achieving a direct hit from high level were somewhat remote, whilst there was no wish to put the bomber crews in jeopardy at low level with only marginal chances of success. The Commander-in-Chief Bomber Command supported these sentiments, having been advised that the Lancaster could only carry a single CS Bomb, as opposed to six 2,000 lb armour-piercing bombs. Making all allowances for the increased damage expected from the CS Bombs, he was further advised that, by virtue of the larger load of 2,000 lb bombs, the relative chance of damage from a direct hit or near miss was 2.7 to 1 in favour of the armour-piercing type. This swung the balance, and most probably denied the CS Bomb further opportunities of proving its worth, or otherwise.

By mid 1943, components for 50 bombs of each size, 30, 38 and 45 in, had been manufactured but not all had been filled with explosive. However, some had already been dropped upon the enemy, probably as part of operational trials. Some of the earliest 38 in trial bombs were dropped on the Polish part of Gdynia in Danzig Bay on the night of 27–28 August 1942. In view of the importance of the target, it is perhaps not surprising that even experimental bombs were deployed. The target was the German aircraft-carrier *Graf Zeppelin*, which was reputed to be ready to sail. Nine Lancasters of 106 Squadron, each carrying a single CS Bomb, set off for the nearly 1,000 mile flight to Gdynia. Seven reached Gdynia, but could not locate the *Graf Zeppelin* because of haze, and bombed instead the general harbour area. No damage was claimed or admitted. On at least one other occasion CS Bombs were carried on an operational sortie. A squadron of Lancasters carrying CS Bombs took off early in 1943 with the intention of attacking the *Scharnhorst* reported off Norway. Unfortunately, extreme winter weather caused abandonment of the operation.

Undoubtedly if either of these capital ships had been disabled, if not sunk by a CS Bomb, the time and effort expended in design and development might have been vindicated. In any event it is now difficult to assess the worth of the CS Bombs, and their development appears to have been a waste of time and money. However, a wartime Director of Naval Construction claimed them to be 'the most effective anti-ship weapon yet seen, if operationally practicable'. Clearly, in the eyes of the Air Staff they were not, because to obtain a direct hit with a single bomb was no easy task. Not only did the bomb require a direct hit, but one in the right part of the ship, and in the correct attitude to ensure satisfactory detonation.

The Assistant Chief of Air Staff (Operations) ruled on 19 July 1943 that there was no further operational requirement for the CS Bomb, and no further orders were to be placed. By the middle of 1944, of the 150 bombs manufactured only six 45 in, twenty-four 38 in and forty-five 30 in remained. All were reduced to scrap.

Thus the CS Bomb must remain an 'also ran', although like several of the others it had potential, but chance was against it on the one real opportunity it had for making history and a name for itself.

Just a month before the CS Bomb made its operational début (and finale), the Director of Armament Development, spurred on by Bomber Command, stated a new requirement for a weapon capable of attacking the bottom of a capital ship whilst at anchor. Once again, with the *Tirpitz* uppermost in mind, this ultimately resulted in the production of the 'Johnny Walker' or JW Bomb, which was in effect an air-dropped oscillating mine, with quite a complex action.

On impacting the water it sank to a predetermined depth, armed itself and then rose towards the surface, hopefully hitting the bottom of a ship and detonating as it did so. Should it not hit a ship, just before it reached the surface it sank again and repeated the cycle and in so doing moved laterally 30 ft. In this way it sought out a possible target and continued this cycle for a predetermined period, after which it self-destructed. The bomb was also designed to explode should it achieve a direct hit upon something hard such as a ship's deck or superstructure, upon its first release from the aircraft.

The idea was not original, oscillating mines laid by surface craft dated back certainly as far as 1913, when the Leon mine of Swedish design was experimented with by the Royal Navy. Similarly, a depth bomb which either exploded on impact or after it had reached a predetermined depth of water had been built by Vickers between the two world wars as an anti-surbmarine bomb. However, the combination of all these elements in an air-dropped weapon was new. To assuage Bomber Command's urgent need, from July 1942 onwards there ensued a frantic period of trials and experimentation, until only ten months later a number of JW Bombs were delivered to the Royal Air Force for special operations. Certain limitations were placed on their use, the most important being that to operate successfully they needed a 50 ft minimum depth of water. This excluded using them in the important naval base at Kiel and a

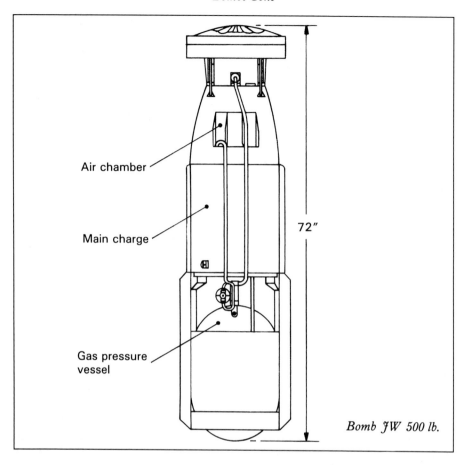

Air chamber

Main charge

72"

Gas pressure
vessel

Bomb JW 500 lb.

number of Baltic ports, but it was perfectly suitable for most of the Norwegian fjords where some of Germany's largest warships lurked during 1942 to 1945.

With the failure of the 1,000 lb Spherical Mine, and doubts concerning the capabilities of the B Bomb, the arrival of the JW Bomb was especially welcome. Despite that, no use was found for it until September 1944, 16 months after its first delivery to Bomber Command. By then, it was in competition with the 12,000 lb Tallboy, capable of destroying a warship by pure brute force rather than sophistication.

With hindsight it is possible to ponder that the design of the bomb might have benefited from a more comprehensive study and continued operational trials. This is supported by the fact that as soon as delivery was made, work started on the production of a Mk II version, but the war ended before it could be perfected.

The early trials on the complex JW Mk I bomb were carried out with Hampden and Beaufort aircraft. The first set out to prove the ballistic feasibility of the new weapons, during a series of trials at Porton range in Wiltshire and others, whilst the Beauforts dropped replica bombs from heights up to 5,000 ft into Gare Loch, Scotland to prove their flight and underwater qualities. A 4 ft breakaway parachute was fitted to ease the bomb into the water, together with a 100 lb cast-iron nose cover cap which was discarded on impact, to ensure the bomb fell nose-first. Not surprisingly, the complexity of the workings produced more than enough headaches. A glance at the illustration will show that the bomb was far from cylindrical or streamlined, with a number of protruberances which badly influenced the air flow. It is not surprising, therefore, that one of the major problems was flight stability.

Much thought was given to the type and form of the explosive which would be required to inflict a crippling if not a mortal blow. The problem was further increased by the fact that the design of the bomb was such that the explosive would be separated from the target by the bomb's buoyancy chamber. Ultimately, the Admiralty advised the use of about 100 lb of Torpex in a shaped charge form, utilizing the Munroe Effect described earlier. They also advised that the Torpex should be supplemented with aluminium to increase the generation of gas and so increase the bubble effect. This is an effect employed in most mines; as the main charge detonates, a large gas bubble is generated which lifts even the largest ship, and as the bubble collapses the ship drops, often causing more damage than the original explosion.

Little technical information on the detailed workings of the JW Bomb are available, but from a contemporary diagram the general idea can be seen. The bomb weighed approximately 500 lb and was 72 in long and just under 20 in in diameter. As already described it was fitted with a discarding nose weight and a parachute. The body contained a 100 lb shaped charge of Torpex/aluminium in the centre chamber with a buoyancy chamber in the tail and a hydrogen gas reservoir in the nose. A hydrostatic trip valve controlled the flow of hydrogen to the buoyancy chamber. The fuzing mechanism situated in the tail was designed to operate on inital nose impact on a hard surface, or after pressurization upon tail impact with the bottom of a ship.

The oscillations as already described continued until the variable amount of hydrogen was expended. The bomb then sank to 50 ft and self-destructed. In addition to the self-destruct mechanism it was also fitted with several anti-handling devices to prevent its secrets falling into enemy hands.

As far as can be determined the JW Bomb was only deployed operationally on one occasion, and that during an attack upon the *Tirpitz* as she lay in the Kaa Fjord in northern Norway. The attack took place on 15 September 1944 when 27 Lancasters of 9 and 617 Squadrons, specially deployed to the Russian airfield at Yagodnik near Archangel, dropped 12,000 lb Tallboys and JW Bombs. The details of this operation are outlined in Chapter Six.

Of the 27 aircraft, seven carried 12 JW Bombs each. The attack took place at approximately 11.00 a.m. and on arrival the target was obscured by a dense smoke screen. The JW Bombs were released somewhat blindly from between 10,000 and 11,000 ft on to where it was thought the *Tirpitz* lay. Flight Lieutenant D MacIntosh, the captain of one of the 9 Squadron Lancasters carrying JW Bombs, reported seeing about 20 bombs falling into the water, and the rest are also thought to have fallen in the anchorage area, wide of the target. The

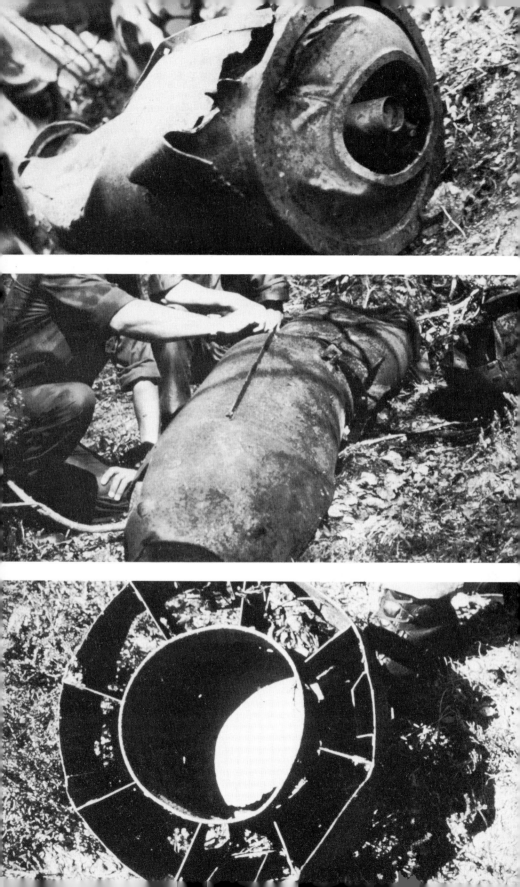

Left *The only known remains of a JW bomb, recovered on the slopes above Kaa Fjord in October 1987.*

Germans never produced a drawing or any other literature on this bomb. It was therefore assumed that the self-destruct mechanism functioned as designed, or that the bombs sank to the bottom without trace – in any event, none were found until October 1987. In that month the Norwegian authorities found an unexploded, although badly damaged, JW Bomb on the slopes above the Kaa Fjord, 43 years after it had originally been dropped.

As recounted earlier, one Tallboy did strike home, signalling the beginning of the end for the *Tirpitz*. Thus as the Tallboys made history, so the JW Bombs were lost in obscurity, so deep a cloud of obscurity that neither the British nor the Germans recorded its detailed design for posterity.

Of all the 'also rans', perhaps the one with real potential to succeed was the weapon codenamed Highball, developed in parallel with Upkeep, the destroyer of the Westphalian dams and, like it, designed by Mr Barnes Wallis. As was seen in Chapter Seven, Mr Wallis demonstrated his idea for a bouncing bomb/mine at Teddington on 21 June 1942 to senior service and scientific staff of the Admiralty, Air Ministry and Ministry of Aircraft Production, using a two-inch diameter model. Those attending were so impressed that full-size trials were ordered in respect of a weapon suitable for the destruction of Germany's dams, and another for anti-shipping purposes sponsored by the Admiralty. The latter, codenamed Highball but more commonly referred to as 'the Naval Weapon' was intended for attack on capital ships at anchor, with the old enemy *Tirpitz* as its prime target.

It had been shown that considerably less explosive would be required to attack a ship's hull than that to breach a huge dam, consequently, two sizes of weapon were developed concurrently. Both were to be spherical in shape, both to be given a back spin before release, but the smaller Highball was designed with a 30 in diameter and to contain 500–600 lb of high explosive. The development of Upkeep has been described earlier, and conveniently that of Highball ran in tandem with this until February 1943.

At that stage, only dummy bombs/mines had been dropped from Wellington aircraft; now operational aircraft were to be used. The original intention, back in November 1942, was to use Beauforts, but the performance of the Mosquito made it a more suitable aircraft. Thus, the first drop of an inert Highball from a Mosquito took place on 24 March 1943, to test the experimental dropping mechanism rather than the weapon. The intention was that two nearly spherical mines should be carried in tandem, with the capability of being released either as a pair or singly. Two sets of caliper arms very similar to those already described to hold Upkeep were mounted in the bomb bay. Unlike the Lancaster, where the back spin was applied hydraulically, Highball was spun by a wind-driven turbine as the Mosquito did not have adequate hydraulic power. Otherwise the release mechanisms were very similar.

As a result of successful trials, and perhaps too optimistically, 15 May was selected as the target date for attacking the *Tirpitz* (well within the optimum period selected by Mr Wallis for the dam attack).

Just 11 days after the formation of 617 Squadron in Bomber Command for the dam operations, 618 Squadron was formed within Coastal Command. This squadron formed up at Royal Air Force Skitten in northern Scotland on 1 April 1943 under the command of Squadron Leader C F Rose, its task being to sink the *Tirpitz* in Alten Fjord near Trondheim, Norway using the new weapon.

Throughout April weapon trials continued, most of them being done by the Royal Air Force test pilot on loan to Vickers, Squadron Leader M V Long-bottom, and occasionally Squadron Leader Rose, the commander of 618 Squadron. Concurrently the crews of 618 Squadron, although not yet equipped with Highball Mosquitoes, flew over 125 low-level sorties against a target ship, *Bonaventure*, moored on Loch Cairnbawn. It had already been shown that to achieve maximum effect, Highball should be dropped from 60 ft whilst the aircraft was travelling at 360 mph. This clearly called for skilled and practiced flying.

The weapon trials in April had perfected dropping and release techniques, but at that stage the Highballs were clad in wood. It was not until 10 May that ten full-size steel-clad weapons were released into Loch Striven. This proved to be a fateful day, because serious problems developed in the release mechanism and clearly the target date of 15 May could not be met. As it happened, this was not the only critical factor, the first two operational Highball Mosquitoes did not reach 618 Squadron until 14 May and by the end of the month they had only 15. The decision by the Chiefs of Staff that Upkeep should be given priority in all aspects of its development was clearly being felt in the Highball project.

However, the problems were overcome, and further trial drops at Reculver, Herne Bay, Kent during June were most successful, including the release of Highballs in tandem. The final design of Highball weighed 1,280 lb, 600 lb of this being made up by the high explosive Torpex. The weapon was completely clad in $\frac{3}{8}$-in thick high quality steel and fuzed with a modified Hydrostatic Pistol Mk XIV, programmed to function by water pressure at a depth of 30 ft in a similar fashion to the pistols used so successfully in Upkeep on the dam raids just a month earlier.

Throughout July, more trials and practices were completed, but were then discontinued because the *Tirpitz* had moved north to Kaa Fjord, well beyond the range of United Kingdom-based Mosquitoes. This was a sad blow to the keyed-up and highly motivated and trained aircrews of 618 Squadron. To give them some operational experience it was suggested that Highball should be used as a depth-charge in the anti-submarine role. A series of trials were undertaken at the end of August, and nine Mosquitoes were actually loaded with live modified Highballs for operational use. This plan was cancelled, and clearly the operational life of 618 Squadron and its Highballs was nearing an end.

Eventually the Squadron was disbanded on 13 September 1943, its specially-equipped aircraft were placed in storage and its aircrew dispersed. Squadron Leader Rose was later killed flying Mosquitoes with 248 Squadron.

This, however, was not the end of the Highball saga. Nine months later on 20 June 1944 at the 201st Joint Chiefs of Staff meeting, its possible use against the Japanese Fleet was debated. It was agreed that in view of the very great military and political advantages which would accrue from a successful Highball attack on the Japanese Fleet, every effort should be made to speed up preparations for such an attack.

In broad terms, these preparations consisted of inviting the Ministry of Aircraft Production to modify and refit 29 Highball Mosquitoes and 3 Photographic Reconnaissance (PR) Mosquitoes for carrier-borne operations. This involved not only the fitting of deck arrester gear, but also the more powerful Merlin 25 engines and larger four bladed propellers. It was agreed that this would take at least five months.

The Air Ministry was invited to undertake a programme of reconstitution and training of 618 Squadron, such that it would be operationally fit by the time the aircraft were available. Finally the Admiralty was invited to provide facilities for the crews of 618 Squadron to undergo the necessary training in deck flying procedures and in due course to give them every facility for the realistic training of crews by allowing dummy attacks on ships in harbour and the dropping of inert Highballs against a capital ship target.

A week later at a meeting chaired by the Director of Operations (Maritime), Air Commodore A D Gillmore, and attended by senior officers from the Air Ministry, Coastal Command including the Commanding Officer designate of 618 Squadron, Wing Commander Hutchinson, the Admiralty and the Ministry of Aircraft Production, a number of decisions were made. For instance it was decided that 618 Squadron would re-form within Coastal Command at Wick under the administration of 18 Group, who would be responsible for its initial training (a number of aircrews would have had no previous Mosquito experience). The squadron would consist of 29 Highball and three PR aircraft, manned by 24 Highball and four PR crews. After initial training it would move down from Scotland to Beccles, close to the Ministry of Aircraft Production range and airfield facilities at Wells-next-the-Sea, Norfolk, where it would be administered by 16 Group. Finally it was decided that the squadron when deployed to the Far East would take with it 150 Highballs.

The next five months was a period of intense concurrent activity in three major fields. First there was the provision of aircraft, then the training of aircrews, and finally the planning of the loading and movement of the squadron and its weapons to its overseas destination. There were problems in all three spheres of action but all were eventually resolved. The aircraft were available on time, but the training period had at times been traumatic. After landing on dummy aircraft-carriers marked out on the runway at Wells-next-the-Sea, the aircrews practised live carrier landings, using Barracuda aircraft. However, to preserve the Mosquitoes from risk of damage, only the PR crews who had to carry out a reconnaissance and return safely to the carrier to report their findings, were permitted to carry out Mosquito landings on an aircraft-carrier. The actual attack training was fraught with difficulties and it was not until 25 September 1944 that the battleship HMS *Malaya,* having just returned from bombarding operations in support of the Allied Armies in France, was available at Invergordon for use as a live target for the dropping of inert Highballs. Thankfully these final trials were a complete success. As far as movement was concerned, a number of plans were considered, but it was finally decided, following a number of loading trials, that the complete squadron together with its aircraft should move in two aircraft-carriers.

618 Squadron reported itself 100 per cent operational in all respects on 21 October 1944. It embarked in the two escort carriers HMS *Striker* and *Fencer*, together with its aircraft, personnel, Highballs and full support facilities, and sailed from the Clyde on the thirty-first bound for Cochin (southern India) and eventually Australia. The carriers were escorted by HMS *Kelvin, Marne, Meteor* and *Muskateer* as far as Gibraltar and from then on by HMS *Undaunted* and *Ursa*.

The squadron had with it 3 PR Mosquitoes and 25 Highball Mosquitoes (two having been retained at the last minute for Highball trials against ships at sea rather than at anchor, and two were damaged during training). Eventually it reached Australia on 23 December, where it waited for a suitable target, previously defined as at least five capital ships at anchor or in harbour in one location.

So 618 waited through January, February, and until June 1945, then on the twenty-ninth it was officially notified that, yet again, the squadron was to be disbanded and that for security reasons its Highballs were to be destroyed. Eleven days later the inhabitants of Sydney heard a massive explosion as the Highballs were destroyed at the Royal Australian Navy Arms Depot at Auburn. The Vice Chief of the Air Staff sent a signal of condolence, but that could not compensate for the disappointment felt by this fully-trained and equipped specialist unit armed with a weapon which, but for the atom bombs in August 1945, possessed the potential of a battle-winner to further substantiate its designer's theories.

Thus ends the stories of just some of the 'also rans'. A few, like the Highball and the CS Bomb, had the potential for greatness, others were doomed from the start, but all were ideas conjured up to help defeat a known enemy. In war, and in the design of bombs in particular, it is pointless to surmise 'if only ...'

CHAPTER THIRTEEN

THE ADVENT OF THE NUCLEAR AGE

The strategic power of Bomber Command was at its peak in May 1945, and as already recounted, it had the capability to mount a massive 1,000-plus heavy bomber attack on almost any town or city in Europe and to virtually destroy it overnight. Yet this form of attack was reduced almost to insignificance on 6 August 1945, signifying in many people's minds the beginning of the end for heavy bombers and air-dropped conventional strategic weapons. In fact, although it was not realized at the time, the first sign of the decline of strategic bombing was the introduction of long-range ballistic missiles, the first being the German V2 rocket. The V1, too, might be considered one of the first cruise missiles.

The date 6 August 1945, indelibly marked on world history, was that on which an atomic bomb was first deployed as a weapon of war. A single uranium bomb, codenamed Little Boy, 10 ft long and 28 in in diameter, and weighing 9,000 lb, detonated 2,000 ft above the centre of the Japanese city of Hiroshima at 8.15 a.m. It was released at 31,600 ft from an American Army Air Force B-29 Super Fortress captained by Colonel Paul Tibbets. Four square miles of the city were totally devastated, and within seconds some 78,000 people were killed and an almost equal number injured – many of the injured becoming sick in subsequent weeks, due to nuclear radiation.

A second atomic bomb, this time a plutonium one, codenamed Fat Man, 10 ft 8 in long, 5 ft in diameter and weighing 10,000 lb, was detonated at 11.02 a.m three days later over the industrial seaport of Nagasaki. It killed some 50,000 people and injured another 10,000. Although Fat Man was more powerful than the Hiroshima type, the casualties were lower because parts of Nagasaki, built in a series of valleys, were protected from the direct effects of blast and heat. On board a B-29 observer aircraft were two British representatives, Doctor, later Sir William Penney, one of the British scientists who worked with the Americans on the Manhattan Project, and Group Captain Leonard Cheshire, a former commander of 617 (Dambuster) Squadron.

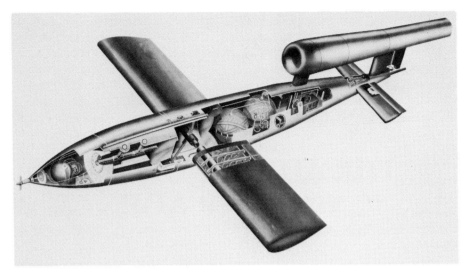

The V1 – one of the first cruise missiles?

Many horrific descriptions have been published on the effect of these weapons upon the buildings and inhabitants of the two Japanese cities, and need not be reiterated. It is sufficient to say that undoubtedly they proved effective and horrific weapons of mass destruction on these their first (and hopefully last) operational sorties.

The first man-made atomic explosion was triggered on 16 July 1945, when the United States detonated a test weapon in New Mexico, the conclusion of the Manhattan Project. Thus, for better or worse, dawned the atomic age. As with all technology, not for long did America remain the sole possessor of atomic weapons; the Soviet Union tested her first device in August 1949, followed by the United Kingdom in October 1952, France in 1960 and China in 1964. Today in the late 1980s it is suspected that other countries too have the will and technology to manufacture nuclear weapons, and may well have done so.

From 1952 onwards, research and trials to produce bigger and better atomic devices, were supplemented by those to produce thermo-nuclear weapons or hydrogen (H) bombs. The spectacular jump from conventional high explosive to atomic weapons was great, but the jump from atomic to thermo-nuclear was even greater. Since the main thrust of this story is directed at development of British weapons, it would be appropriate to consider the fundamental principles of nuclear weapons before covering the development, testing and eventual deployment of these weapons to operational units.

The functioning of atomic devices is based on the fundamental discovery that splitting the nucleus of an atom with neutrons (electrically neutral particles of an atom) releases tremendous energy in a process called fission. The only elements which will split with a relatively small input of energy are the very heavy ones such as naturally-occurring uranium or man-made plutonium. Once the nuclear fission process is initiated it releases more neutrons, which in turn split more nuclei, generating a chain reaction. When controlled, this reaction produces energy like that in a nuclear reactor, whereas if programmed to occur suddenly and unbalanced, it produces an atomic explosion accompanied by a violent release of energy.

The earliest atomic bomb designs employed a conventional explosive charge to force one sub-critical mass (one where there are insufficient free neutrons to start a chain reaction) of uranium 235 or plutonium 239 into another sub-critical mass, thus raising the number of free neutrons to the level required to start a chain reaction. Subsequent to many experiments, it was established that the sub-critical mass in atomic bombs could be more efficiently triggered if it was completely surrounded by a relatively thin-skinned spherical coating of conventional explosive which could be detonated simultaneously at a large number of selected points on the skin.

The resultant fission reactions produced energy or yield expressed as the equivalent yield of tons of TNT. Thus the bomb dropped on Hiroshima was equal to 12,500 tons of TNT, i.e. $12.5 \times 1,000$ tons, described as having a yield of 12.5 kilotons.

In November 1952, just a month after the United Kingdom detonated its first atomic test device, the United States detonated its first hydrogen bomb, and in August 1953 the Soviet Union followed suit. Unlike the atomic type the H-bomb does not use the fission process, but another, known as the fusion process. Instead of splitting the nuclei of heavy element atoms, the fusion process combines or fuses the nuclei of two light element atoms to form the nucleus of a third element. This occurs naturally in the sun and other stars when hydrogen atoms are united under great pressure and heat to form helium, with the release of large quantities of energy. The H-bombs, for which details are available, use a mixture of hydrogen and lithium to form tritium. The trigger generating the heat and shock to initiate the fusion process is in fact a small fission atomic explosion. Once started, the fusion process is sustained by heat rather than neutrons, and consequently is termed a thermo-nuclear reaction.

This reaction has four main advantages over the fission process. Weight-for-weight it generates a far greater release of energy, the only radio-active particles are those produced by the initial fission trigger because the radio-active tritium, being a gaseous substance, disperses in the atmosphere. The materials used are relatively cheaper and are more readily available than uranium 235 and plutonium 239, only small quantities of which are required for the trigger. Finally, because there is no need for a specific sized sub-critical mass, the thermo-nuclear warhead can be designed with dimensions to suit any particular requirement for such diverse weapons as full-scale bombs, long or short-range guided missiles, battlefield shells or even depth charges and mines.

The yield of a thermo-nuclear weapon is measured in equivalent millions of tons of TNT (megatons), as compared to fission weapons measured in kilotons. It is a sobering thought that estimates indicate that the sum total of explosive dropped on Germany in air-dropped weapons during the Second World War would add up to less than the yield of a one megaton nuclear weapon. On 30 October 1961 the Soviet Union detonated an estimated 58 megaton device, the largest man-made explosion recorded on earth – so far.

Having briefly described the basic atomic/nuclear concepts, it would now be appropriate, in similar fashion, to say how the United Kingdom came to develop, test and deploy her very own air-dropped nuclear weapons. The origin of the atomic bomb can probably be traced back to the atom-splitting experiments undertaken by Sir Ernest Rutherford and his colleagues in 1932. However, a number of others contributed, for instance, Otto Hahn split the nucleus of a uranium atom in Berlin during 1938, and a Danish physicist, Niels Bohr, published a learned paper on 1 September 1939. However, not until the spring of 1940 did two physicists, refugees from Germany and Austria working in England, write a paper indicating that ten lb of uranium 235 could yield the energy equivalent of several thouand tons of dynamite. As a result a scientific committee (the Maud Committee) was established to investigate the possibilities of atomic energy and weapons in particular. Soon after the fall of France in 1940 two French physicists previously working in Norway arrived in England, bringing with them the then total world stock of heavy water, at that time an essential ingredient in fission experiments. They joined the Maud Committee working at the Cavendish Laboratory in Cambridge.

By mid 1941 the Maud Committee produced a detailed report showing the possibility and methods of producing an atomic bomb. In true scientific openness (or naïvety), this report was passed to the United States of America, at that time a neutral nation. America reacted by setting up an investigative project which was to form the basis for the Manhattan Project, leading to the production of the first operational atomic bomb. The British Government set up a similar project under the code name Tube Alloys, innocuous enough, but probably recognizing that considerable industrial muscle would be needed to support research and development.

Perhaps not surprisingly, considering the many competing realistic wartime priorities, the Americans, although themselves not at war soon took the technological lead and by mid 1942 were loath to share their secrets. Nevertheless, after considerable negotiations Prime Minister Churchill and President Roosevelt signed the Quebec Agreement in August 1943, which enabled United Kingdom scientists to take part in the Manhattan Project. Perhaps more importantly, each nation agreed not to use any developed bomb without the consent of the other and that neither would share atomic information with a third party, other than by mutual consent. Thus, both nations were privy to the plans to bomb Hiroshima and Nagasaki.

However, the United Kingdom was clearly the junior partner and when the war was over there were hints that sharing of information was perhaps not as frank as it might be. As a result of these doubts, President Truman and Prime Minister Atlee signed the Washington Agreement in November 1945, promising full and effective co-operation in the development of atomic energy for civil and military purposes. It was short-lived because just nine months later in August 1946, the United States Congress passed the Atomic Energy Act (The

McMahon Act) prohibiting the passing of classified atomic information to any foreign country, with penalties for doing so up to and including the death sentence.

Consequently, in January 1947 the United Kingdom Government, or rather an inner circle of Cabinet Ministers, decided that the country should produce its own independent atomic weapons. This decision was not formally released to the public or indeed Parliament until May 1948, although when it was there were no major objections. The reasons for the Atlee Government's decision to manufacture atomic weapons were complex; one was national pride that Britain, after her efforts during the war, should remain a major power and belong to the big league. Another was certainly the perceived need of an independent nuclear deterrent against potential military threats – at this time there was no commitment from the United States to help defend Western Europe against a possible threat from the East. NATO was not established until April 1949. For these reasons, and others outside the scope of this book, the United Kingdom began to build and test her own atomic and later, thermo-nuclear weapons.

At the same time, successive British Governments attempted to reach an acceptable exchange of information agreement with the United States. Talks began in 1949, only to end abruptly when Klaus Fuchs, the British naturalized scientist working at Harwell, was arrested for espionage in January 1950. Not until the United Kingdom demonstrated that she could design and manufacture both fission (1952) and fusion (1957) weapons, and establish a nuclear power plant (1956) did a series of agreements with the United States prove to be possible.

Sufficient has already been said to establish why the British Government decided to produce its own nuclear weapons, so it is unnecessary in the context of this book to dwell on the contents of these agreements. However, it can probably be seen from the information provided that, unlike the procedures adopted before and during the Second World War for stating an operational requirement in respect of a conventional weapon (in which the military staff expressed a requirement for a weapon to be developed against a specific target or group of targets), the nuclear weapon requirement was based mainly on political grounds, although no doubt the military staffs did provide some input.

Testing of British weapons was conducted in two phases, the first from 1952 to 1957 during which a total of 12 atomic explosions took place: three in the Monte Bello Islands, an uninhabited group of islands off the north-west coast of Australia, and nine others on the Australian mainland. The second phase, which slightly overlapped the first, took place in 1957–58 when nine thermo-nuclear devices/weapons were detonated off the Malden and Christmas Islands in the Pacific Ocean.

Details of the 21 detonations are both interesting and important, as they show the development of the United Kingdom's nuclear weapons from the first relatively crude atomic device to the perfected nuclear air-dropped weapon. These perfected weapons, together with the Royal Air Force V bomber force, provided the United Kingdom's independent nuclear deterrent until the responsibility was assumed by the Royal Navy with its missile-carrying submarines.

The Soviet Union carried out her first atomic test in August 1949, thus becoming the second atomic power. This event served only to increase the pressure on Doctor Penney and his staff at HER (High Explosive Research) based at Fort Halstead in Kent, which later moved to Aldermaston and became the AWRE (Atomic Weapons Research Establishment).

The test of Britain's first device, codenamed Operation Hurricane, was scheduled for late 1952. Very similar to the Nagasaki version, it was a nominal 20 kiloton plutonium bomb mounted on a redundant Royal Naval frigate, HMS *Plym* (1,450 tons) anchored close inshore to Trimouille Island in the Monte Bello Group. Because of the location and distance from the United Kingdom it was very much a Royal Navy-backed project, although there were ten Royal Air Force officers on Doctor Penney's staff, including Wing Commander J S Rowlands GC (later Air Vice-Marshal Sir John) who was closely involved in the design aspects of the weapon. The Army, too, was represented, by members of the Royal Engineers who were responsible for the civil engineering aspects of the project.

At about 9.15 a.m. local time on 3 October 1952 the device was detonated; HMS *Plym* ceased to exist and Britain became an atomic power. The Prime Minister made a statement to the House of Commons on the 22nd including the words:

> The object of the test was to investigate the effects of an atomic explosion in a harbour ... Thousands of tons of water and of mud and rock from the sea bottom were thrown many thousands of feet into the air and a high tidal wave was caused. The effects of blast and radio-active contamination extended over a wide area.

As a result of this test many people assumed that the United Kingdom had an operational capability, but this was far from true, much work was still required. In any case, the V bombers ordered in December 1950 were not yet available to carry the bomb.

Less than a month after Hurricane, the United States detonated the world's first thermo-nuclear device, followed by the Soviet Union some nine months later in August 1953. Neither of these devices could in any way be described as weapons, and another four years elapsed before a viable H-bomb was dropped from an aircraft. By 1953, Britain continued with her own trials, this time codenamed Operation Totem. Two test firings were undertaken, the first on 15 October and the second 12 days later. On these occasions the devices were placed on metal towers at Emu Field, a location in the South Australian desert about 300 miles north-west of Woomera. These devices, of ten and eight kilotons respectively, increased Sir William's (Penney was knighted after Operation Hurricane) knowledge of fall-out problems and enabled the effects of heat and blast against military vehicles and tanks to be evaluated.

Perhaps the most interesting and potentially hazardous experiment during the trial was that sponsored by the Air Ministry, and known as Hot Box. This required a specially prepared Royal Air Force Canberra to fly through the mushroom cloud within a few minutes of detonation, to enable the Ministry scientists to investigate the effects of contamination, heat and blast on the aircraft's structure and crew. The Canberra deployed was crewed by Wing Commanders G H Dhenin (Pilot, also a medical doctor and a member of the Royal College of Surgeons), E W Anderson (Navigator and ex-Pathfinder) and Group Captain D A Wilson (Observer, and a consultant in radiology). The aircraft entered the cloud six minutes after detonation on 15 October and reportedly found it rather like a thick London fog, although a lot more hazardous. Not surprisingly, the crew were found to have been exposed to a greater degree of radiation than anyone else on the Totem trials. Fortunately, because the test data obtained was adequate, the crew was not required to fly through the cloud produced during the second test shot, although all were keen and ready to do so. In subsequent trials it became customary for an air-sampling aircraft to fly through the cloud within minutes of detonation, but by then the crews and the aircraft had the benefits of personal protection and aircraft modifications incorporated as a result of the Hot Box trials.

Following the successful Totem experiments there was a pause in British testing, mainly because in June 1954 the Government decided that, like the United States and the Soviet Union, the United Kingdom must have a thermonuclear capability – this fact was announced to Parliament in a White Paper dated February 1955. Now the British scientists had three main tasks, first to build up a stockpile of 'Blue Danube' atomic bombs, which were based on the device tested during Operation Hurricane; secondly, to design a range of efficient atomic bombs to meet the Royal Air Force future requirements, and finally, to begin the research and development of an H-bomb.

During the next two years there were no British tests to grab the headlines; however, there were plenty of others. For example, the United States carried out a further 23, including that of a second thermo-nuclear device at Bikini Atoll on 1 March 1954. Similarly, during this period the Soviet Union detonated at least seven, one of which, triggered in November 1955, was in the megaton range. Incidentally, in the same month the Soviet Union launched its first long-range ballistic missile from a submarine. The world became aware of the hazards emanating from nuclear testing when a Japanese fisherman died from radiation sickness some 72 miles East of Bikini Atoll as a result of the American test on 1 March 1954. Subsequent investigations indicated that the device detonated was not a straightforward thermo-nuclear type as described earlier, but one cased in natural uranium which produced a fission reaction as a result of the fusion process. Therefore, it was a three-stage device, an atomic fission trigger, a light element fusion and a natural uranium fission reaction. In other words, a device of immense power which could be manufactured mainly from relatively cheap components and required only a very small quantity of the highly-priced uranium 235 or plutonium 239. It did, however, produce considerably more fall-out than the relatively clean basic fusion device.

Despite the increasing demands for a nuclear test ban, work continued, and by May 1956 Britain was ready to undertake a further two tests, codenamed

Operation Mosaic, in the Monte Bello Islands. Both devices under test were detonated on steel towers and were the final trials towards producing a thermo-nuclear detonation. Although atomic in nature, and therefore in the kiloton range, both devices were enhanced with light elements, so some fusion elements were present. The first detonation was triggered on 16 May 1956 and the second on 19 June. The second produced a much greater yield than the first, causing considerable speculation in the Australian and indeed the world press. Sir William Penney expressed himself satisfied that they were on the right lines and on course for a series of full thermo-nuclear trials in 1957. Before undertaking these, a series of shots were required to confirm that the proposed United Kingdom atomic bombs were a viable operational proposition.

Code named Operation Buffalo, this series included the dropping of Britain's first operational atomic weapon at the Maralinga Range in South Australia. The first shot on 27 September 1956, was a tower-mounted test of the plutonium warhead intended for the 'Red Beard' bomb. Although its expected yield was about 16 kilotons, it was much smaller in size than the ponderous 40 kiloton 'Blue Danube' then in production, in advance of tests to prove its worth. It was intended for deployment on V-Force aircraft such as the Vickers Valiant, and 'Red Beard' for the lighter Canberra. Progressively they were supplemented or supplanted by more powerful weapons such as 'Yellow Sun', 'Blue Steel' and others for carriage on the Handley-Page Victor and Avro Vulcan of Bomber Command, later reinforced by other Commands to form Strike Command.

Anyway, back in October 1956 the second shot was a 'Blue Danube' device (uranium core) placed at ground level and triggered on the 4th. The weapon for this particular trial was provided with a low yield warhead, some two kilotons, to determine ground shock and cratering effects, should such a weapon be used as an atomic mine. In fact it produced a crater some 150 ft in diameter and 40 ft deep.

The third trial, and perhaps the most important in the context of this story, was the first air drop of a live 'Blue Danube' by the Royal Air Force. The original plan was to use a standard 40 kiloton bomb fuzed to detonate at an altitude of 1,200 ft. However, there was a remote possibility that the fuzing system might fail, and a surface detonation of 40 kilotons was quite unacceptable. For safety reasons, therefore, it was decided to use a low yield (three kilotons) warhead and fuze it to detonate at 500 ft. At 3.30 p.m. on 11 October a Royal Air Force Valiant (WZ 366) of 1321 Flight, 49 Squadron Wittering, piloted by Squadron Leader T Flavell, released the weapon, which functioned perfectly. Both Flavell and his bomb-aimer, Flight Lieutenant E Stacey, were awarded the Air Force Cross for their part in this operation.

The final shot in the series was a variant of the 'Red Beard' warhead, with the addition of some light elements to supplement the information on thermo-nuclear weapons gained during Operation Mosaic. This device was detonated at the top of a 100 ft tower on the 22nd, and produced an estimated yield of 16 kilotons.

The 'Blue Danube' nuclear weapon. (Crown Copyright/RAF Photograph. Reproduced by permission of the Controller of HMSO.)

To perfect the warheads of both 'Blue Danube' and 'Red Beard', three follow-up tests, under the codename Operation Antler, were planned for Maralinga in September/October 1957. However, in the meantime the stage was finally set for the start of the second phase of British nuclear weapon testing, namely the live dropping of the first thermo-nuclear megaton weapons, between May 1957 and September 1958.

These tests, known collectively as Operation Grapple, were not only a prestigious scientific achievement but also a massive logistic and engineering project. The full story of the tests, their support operations and subsidiary experiments is far too diverse for this book; consequently only a record of the actual weapon tests is included. The yields expected from the thermo-nuclear warheads ruled out Maralinga and the Monte Bello Islands as suitable locations for the trials. Consequently, Christmas (Kiritimati) Island, situated just north of the Equator in mid Pacific was selected, together with Malden Island some 400 miles to the south.

The trials were divided into four phases, codenamed Grapple, Grapple X, Grapple Y and Grapple Z, the scope of each test or series of tests depending largely on results achieved progressively during earlier trials. The first series (Grapple) consisted of dropping three separate megaton weapons above Malden Island between 15 May and 19 June 1957, using Bomber Command's first V-type aircraft, the Valiant. On each occasion the weapon was released from 45,000 ft and set to detonate at 8,000, thus avoiding the fireball touching the ground and causing excessive radiation problems.

The original intention was to detonate four weapons, so 49 Squadron Wittering under the command of Wing Commander K G Hubbard deployed four bombers and crews, including his own, to Christmas Island. The first weapon released was carried by Valiant XD 818 captained by Wing Commander Hubbard, who having released it turned on to a set course such that his tail cameras could record the detonation. After about two and a half minutes the shock waves impinged on the aircraft, by now nearly 20 nautical miles from the release point, but they were not excessive and finally after a further five minutes permission was given to remove the anti-flash screens (during the approach and subsequent to weapon release the aircraft had been flown using instruments, all observation areas being covered, except for a small opening for the bomb aimer, who closed it immediately the bomb left reporting 'Bomb gone, shutter closed'). Turning to observe the huge mushroom-shaped cloud, which by now towered to a height of 60,000 ft, the crew saw for the very first time the results of their months of intensive training and years of work by the scientists. Wing Commander Hubbard later said, 'It really was a sight of such majesty and grotesque beauty that it defies adequate description.' No wonder, for it was the first ever live air drop of a megaton weapon; the United States and the Soviet Union had detonated thermo-nuclear devices earlier, but only in static locations either on or under the ground.

The second and third drops, on 31 May and 19 June, were undertaken by Valiants XD 822 and XD 823 flown, by Squadron Leaders D Roberts and A Steele respectively. The release and triggering procedures were similar to the first, but security restrictions still prevent the description of the differences between the three bombs. However, it can be said that for trial purposes each was housed in a 'Blue Danube' casing. These trials demonstrated to the world that the Royal Air Force had the capability to accurately deliver megaton yield nuclear weapons to a target anywhere within the range of a Valiant bomber. The tests were deemed so successful that a fourth was not required, so Squadron Leader B Millet, captain of Valiant XD 824, did not release a weapon although he flew as escort for the first drop. (On each occasion a second aircraft flew 2,000 ft below and one mile behind the dropping aircraft to photograph events from a different angle.)

After each detonation a Canberra from 76 Squadron flew into the cloud to obtain samples. The master sampler was Wing Commander G H Dhenin, referred to earlier as the pilot involved in Operation Hot Box at Emu Field. Geoffrey Dhenin, the Royal Air Force expert on radiation, was a most accomplished and gallant officer. As a Flying Officer he won the George Medal for saving life after an aircraft crash. Not only was he a pilot and a radiation expert but as previously mentioned he was also a qualified physician and surgeon. He ended his career as Air Marshal Sir Geoffrey Dhenin, Director General Medical Services, the top medical post in the Royal Air Force and one of the world's leading exponents of aviation medicine.

In addition to 49 and 76 Squadrons, three others played an important part during these and the following tests. 100 Canberra PR Squadron worked for the Meteorological Team helping to determine when weather conditions were most suitable for weapon detonation, and 206 and 240 Shackleton Squadrons policed the vast exclusion area around the islands to ensure that no one deliberately or accidentally sailed into the exclusion zone.

The remainder of the Grapple tests were conducted over or very close to Christmas Island. Indeed, the single-shot of Grapple X was detonated on 8 November 1957 at 8,000 ft above its south-east tip, some 20 miles from the main airfield and base, and set the standard for all future tests. This particular test enabled Squadron Leader B Millett and his bomb-aimer Flight Lieutenant W Jenkins to gain the experience of releasing a megaton weapon denied to them in the first round of tests. The Task Force Commander for the first two sets of trials was Air Vice-Marshal W E Oulton, last referred to in the book as one of the Halifax pilots who sank two U-boats in May 1943.

The first and only device dropped during the Grapple Y phase of the trials was released in the Christmas Island area on 28 April 1958 by Squadron Leader R Bates and crew of 49 Squadron's Valiant XD 825. It detonated precisely as planned and the scientific results were such that no further drops were required in this series. During the course of 1958 there was increasing political pressure to stop atmospheric nuclear testing, consequently there was correspondingly greater scientific pressure to complete the Grapple Z series of trials as soon as possible.

Thus once again for the fourth time in less than 18 months Wing Commander Hubbard and a detachment of 49 Squadron deployed to Christmas Island. Squadron Leader W Bailey flying Valiant XD 822 dropped the sixth megaton yield bomb of the series on 2 September, followed nine days later by the seventh and last weapon, dropped by Flight Lieutenant T O'Connor in XD 827. Two further detonations were triggered during the month but in both cases the devices were suspended from tethered balloons.

As a result of the successful trials completed in September 1958 Britain's range of thermo-nuclear weapons was fully operational, tested and available to the V Force, thus supplementing the kiloton weapons such as 'Blue Danube' and 'Red Beard' already proved for operational service.

As mentioned earlier Britain's development of the thermo-nuclear weapon in 1957 and a fully-functional nuclear power plant in 1956 led in 1958 to the Americans amending the restrictive McMahon Act and endorsing a new treaty between the United States and the United Kingdom entitled 'Co-operation on the Uses of Atomic Energy for Mutual Defence Purposes'. This treaty included the exchange of weapon designs and other technical information. Later it was extended to include exchange of materials, shared nuclear test facilities (the first United States/United Kingdom joint test took place in Nevada in March 1962) and eventually the American supply of missiles and related technology to which the United Kingdom would fit its own warheads. Thus Britain was accepted as a full member of the, at this stage, small but all-powerful 'nuclear club'.

The V-Force upon which Britain's nuclear capability depended, for what use is any weapon if it cannot be delivered to its target, consisted of three types of heavy bomber. The Vickers Valiant which became operational in Bomber Command in mid 1955, followed by the Avro Vulcan and Handley Page Victor in July 1957 and April 1958 respectively. During 1960–61, the three Valiant Squadrons (49, 148 and 207) based at Marham were assigned to the Supreme

Allied Commander Europe (SACEUR), a senior NATO commander. To provide standardization in the NATO system, an American tactical nuclear weapon was provided for this particular role. However, the three squadrons also had secondary roles armed with British free-fall nuclear weapons and conventional bombs if need be. As a result of the Cuban missile crisis in 1962, when it seemed possible that the V-Force might be forced to make operational deployments, Bomber Command and the NATO-assigned Valiants at Marham introduced a Quick Reaction Alert System. Under this system at least one aircraft from each squadron stood by in the fully-armed nuclear configuration, with the crews at instant readiness.

During its 12 years in existence, Bomber Command's V-Force progressively relied upon British-designed free-fall nuclear weapons, an American free-fall tactical weapon and the British air-to-surface stand-off weapon, Blue Steel. The latter had a range of just over 100 miles so that the releasing aircraft did not have to penetrate right into the target area, thus giving the bomber an enhanced chance of survival. Strike Command, which came into being on 30 April 1968 when Bomber and Fighter Commands amalgamated (with the addition of Coastal Command on 1 January 1969) maintained the British strategic nuclear deterrent role until 1969, when the responsibility was assumed by the Royal Navy Polaris submarines.

Progressively, as the ageing V-Force aircraft became redundant, the Royal Air Force strategic bomber role gradually diminished until it disappeared completely. The bombers were replaced by enormously sophisticated tactical strike aircraft capable of carrying a range of modern conventional and nuclear weapons.

In place of NATO's previous strategy of nuclear retaliation to any attack, the so-called trip wire policy, the Alliance decided in 1967 that a strategy of flexible response should be implemented. This meant that NATO policy would be to counter a conventional weapon attack with equal or better conventional weapons, rather than resorting to nuclear weapons immediately it was attacked, the latter being a procedure thought by many to be suicidal. This policy clearly necessitated the United Kingdom updating its conventional air-dropped weapons.

Between 1945 and 1967 the Royal Air Force used its conventional air-dropped weapons operationally on a number of occasions and some modification and development had taken place, but it was only after the policy change in 1967 that major development took place.

One of the Royal Air Force's longest post-war operations was Operation Fire Dog – the support of ground forces against the Communist insurgents in Malaya during 1948–60. Many types of aircraft were deployed during the 12 years, but the general procedure was to fly over the jungle and simultaneously release the full bomb load of 1,000 lb MC bombs. One Royal Australian Air Force Lincoln squadron permanently based in Malaya claimed to have dropped 33,000 such bombs in eight years. It is not certain how many insurgents were killed or deafened, but it certainly frightened the British, Australian, Malay and Gurkha troops in the jungle.

500 lb low-drag bombs recovered on the Falkland Islands.

During the Mau-Mau troubles in Kenya between April and October 1953, Bomber Command Lincolns of 49, 61, 100 and 214 Squadrons carried out some 500 sorties dropping 500 and 1,000 lb MC bombs. These operations, like those in Malaya, were very reminiscent of the imperial policing actions between the two World Wars described in Chapter Two, and like them were not conducive to the development of new weapons or techniques.

In the United Kingdom too, these early post-war years reflected many of the problems associated with the 1920s. For instance the Culdrose Detachment of the Aerial Torpedo Development Unit was using a Swordfish torpedo bomber in 1952 to experiment with newly-developed torpedoes, and in 1954 Neptune aircraft of 217 Squadron Kinloss were releasing 250 lb depth charges. So until about 1958 the majority of in-service conventional air-dropped weapons were similar to or slightly updated 'left-overs' from the Second World War.

However, with the advent of a nuclear bomber force in more than one country it was clear that one of the priority targets ripe for attack would be enemy airfields. The technique proposed was to approach in fast, low-flying aircraft with the object of achieving surprise by getting in under the enemy's radar screen. However, the advantage gained was offset by the danger of the standard 'iron' 500 and 1,000 lb bombs bouncing off hardened surfaces, and the blast and fragmentation hazards to the low-flying aircraft. In any case, bombs released from very low level were always prone to defects because the safety devices had no time to disengage. The provision of retarding bomb tails to give the aircraft

time to escape did little to overcome the problem. Proximity fuzes, which caused the bomb to detonate some 50 ft above parked aircraft, (the optimum height
to achieve maximum damage) were of little use because the bomber had to fly at
an altitude making it unacceptably vulnerable to the ground defences.

Another problem resulting from low-level high-speed bombing techniques
was the disappearance of the bomb-bay and the resulting external carriage of
bombs. Greater attention had to be paid to bombs' aero dynamic shapes to prevent aircraft drag and unacceptable strain on the suspension gear. This resulted
in the development of improved long, thin-shaped 540 and 1,000 lb bombs.
Despite the improved shape, high-speed external carriage tended to cause
bomb overheating. In May 1964 a committee with the unforgettable name of
TEACASE (Thermal Effects on Airborne Conventional Armament Stores and
Equipment) was formed within the Ordnance Board to advise on the effect and
limitations imposed by aerodynamic heating. This heating tended to melt
existing explosive fillings, or at least make them viscous, and if this occurred in
the vicinity of the fuze it could reduce the power of detonation, or even prevent
it from happening. Trials with high melting-point explosives were undertaken,
but the final solution was to lag the inside casing of the bomb.

Thus by 1967 the Royal Air Force and the Fleet Air Arm had a new generation of bombs suitable for external high-speed carriage fitted with a variety of
fuzes, together with a range of air-to-air and air-to-ground missiles; the latter,

*Tornado aircraft dispensing JP 233 concrete piercing sub-munitions and area denial
mines.*

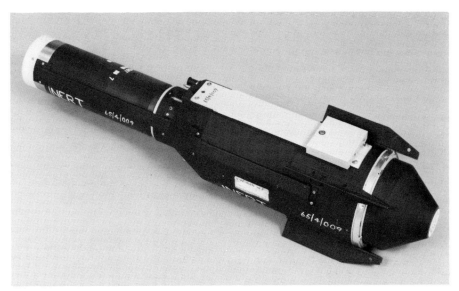

SG 357 concrete piercing sub-munition.

however, do not come within the range of this book. Resulting from the 1967 nuclear policy change there was a general need within NATO to obtain a greater range of air-dropped conventional weapons capable of attacking enemy armour, logistic installations and airfields. This resulted in the development of a series of cluster munitions, that is a single bomb or dispenser (or several, depending on aircraft capability) which ejects a shower of 'child stores', or in common jargon, sub-munitions, to produce a wide spread in the target area during a single pass over the target. The concept was not new, the bomb containers and clusters used during the Second World War dispensed small fragmentation or incendiary bombs. However, cluster munitions of the 1970s and early 1980s were more sophisticated at least in their fuzing actions, and undoubtedly more deadly in operation, although like all new weapon development some needed further research and modification to perfect the range.

At the time of writing the most current and efficient dispenser weapon deployed with the Royal Air Force which can be briefly described, is the Hunting Engineering JP 233 Low-Level Airfield Attack Weapon System designed for use by the Tornado and other NATO aircraft. Flight trials of JP 233 began in 1978, and testing on that aircraft began in 1980. As its name implies, it is designed to attack airfields and this it does by deploying a number of concrete-piercing sub-munitions (SG 357) which crater runways, taxiways and other hard standings. Simultaneously it spreads a carpet of mines (HB 876), accurately overlapping the craters, thus severely hampering repair operations. Each weapon system contains 30 cratering sub-munitions and 215 area-denial mines. Two such systems are carried on one aircraft which will normaly dispense both sets in a single pass across or along the target runway flying at about 500 knots and as low as 200 ft.

HB 876 area denial mine.

Occasionally it may not be advisable to fly at such low levels, so a number of free-fall cluster munitions exist. The Royal Air Force's 600 lb Cluster Weapon BL 755 is an example – this falls to a predetermined height and then dispenses 147 anti-armour bomblets. HADES (Hunting Area Denial System) is another example, this is basically a BL 755 free-fall bomb containing 49 JP 233 mines.

These developments indicate that the nuclear weapon did not, as predicted by many over 30 years ago, spell the immediate end of air-dropped conventional weapons. Certainly the main strategic role as employed against Germany during the Second World War has finally disappeared from the Royal Air Force, but today's strike aircraft are capable of carrying a wide range of nuclear and conventional weapons and can be deployed in a variety of attack roles. The air-dropped bomb may now be terminally guided by radar or infra red seeking guidance systems, but as recently as 1982, Argentinian aircraft demonstrated very forcibly to the Royal Navy the effectiveness of conventional unguided free-fall bombs released from low level. Indeed, if those that failed to detonate had functioned, the outcome of the operation may well have been very different.

The Falklands Conflict also saw the last Royal Air Force long-distance bombing attack when a single Vulcan, fitted with flight refuelling equipment and carrying 21 1,000 lb free-fall bombs, flew 3,800 miles from Ascension Island to bomb the Port Stanley airfield. The main British air attacks during the conflict were mounted by Royal Air Force Harriers and Royal Navy Sea Harriers, each capable of carrying a load of three 1,000 lb bombs or cluster weapons.

Air dropped or air-launched weapons designed to counter surface and subsurface vessels have advanced in the past decade in both concept and function. As always, mines, torpedoes and related weapons are clandestine in operation so it would be improper to describe the current range. Suffice to say there is still a role for aircraft and their weapons in the hunting, locating and sinking of naval vessels.

British bombs and other aerial weapons have come a long way since the vintage days in 1914 when the diminutive Hales bomb and a number of improvised missiles were delivered from equally primitive aircraft. At no other time in history has the dubious means of mass destruction made such enormous strides as that during the last 75 years. It is hoped that the information in this book, although brief at times, will do something to enhance the layman's knowledge of the types of weapon made available for the purpose, giving some idea of how it all came about, particularly as far as the British were concerned. Much of the development was forced on a sometimes reluctant nation by others who posed a direct or indirect threat. However, when the people were aroused the 'goods' were produced with great determination and delivered to those posing the threat, with considerable dedication and, more often than not, great courage. Perhaps, despite its poor reputation, the nuclear weapon with its deterrent effect will ironically put an end to the need for mass destruction or even to the possibility of international wars.

APPENDICES

1   FIRST WORLD WAR AERIAL BOMBS

Bomb type	Year intro-duced	Type of case	Filling		Dimensions (inches)	
			wt (lbs)	type	length	diameter
HE						
16 lb RL	1914	mild steel	7.0	TNT	19.5	5.0
20 lb Hales	1914	cast/forged steel	4.5	Amatol	23.25	5.0
20 lb Cooper	1917	cast/heavy steel	4.5 or 5.4	Amatol TNT	24.5	5.1
50 lb RL	1917	heavy/cast iron	10.0	Amatol	28.25	7.0
65 lb RL	1915	light/mild steel	37.0	Amatol	29.75	9.0
100 lb RL	1914	light/mild steel	60.0	Amatol	29.75	11.5
112 lb RL	1914	heavy/cast steel	35.0 or 40.0	Amatol TNT	29.0	9.0
180 lb RL (AP)	1915	heavy/cast steel	21.0	Amatol	29.0	9.4
230 lb RFC	1916	light/mild steel	110.0 or 140.0	Amatol TNT	50.5	10.0
250 lb RL	1916	heavy/cast steel	110.0	Amatol	36.3	12.5
336 lb RAF	1916	heavy/cast steel	70.0	TNT	59.5 or 53.25	14.0
520 lb RL	1917	light/mild steel	273.0 or 354.0	Amatol TNT	61.0	19.0

Bomb type	Year intro-duced	Type of case	Filling		Dimensions (inches)	
			wt (lbs)	type	length	diameter
520 lb RAF	1917	light/mild steel	280.0 or 356.0	Amatol TNT	61.0	19.0
550 lb RL } 550 lb RAF }	1917	heavy/cast steel	157.0 or 200.0	Amatol TNT	61.0	15.0
1650 lb SN	1918	light/mild steel plate	800.0	Amatol	132.0	18.5
3300 lb SN	1918	light/mild steel plate	1500.0	Amatol	171.0	22.5
Incendiary Incd 6.5 oz	1918	aluminium tube	2.5 oz	Cendite	6.0	0.75
Incd 3.45 in with Hooks	1915	tin plate		Carcass Compo-sition	8.2	3.45
Incd Carcass 10 lb	1915	tin plate	8.5	Carcass Compo-sition	19.25	5.0
Incd 40 lb	1916	tin plate	30.0	Phos-phorus	20.6	8.0
Bomb Petrol Small	1914	tin plate	6.0 pints	Petrol	–	–
Bomb Petrol Large	1915	tin plate	18.0 pints	Petrol	–	–
Ranken Dart		tin plate			5.25	1.0

Notes:
1. Dimensions, shapes and fillings varied slightly in different marks of bomb.
2. RL = Royal Laboratory.
3. RAF = Royal Aircraft Factory.
4. There was also a Hales 10 and 100 lb bomb, scaled up or down versions of the 20 lb bomb.
5. The 336 lb RAF bomb had a shortened version to fit particular bomb racks.
6. There was also a smaller version of the Bomb Incendiary Carcass.

2   BRITISH BOMB PISTOLS AND FUZES

Bomb pistols and fuzes, the basic concepts of which are described in Chapter Two, were developed for a very wide variety of operational purposes, thus, some were simple in design and operation, others more complex, whilst

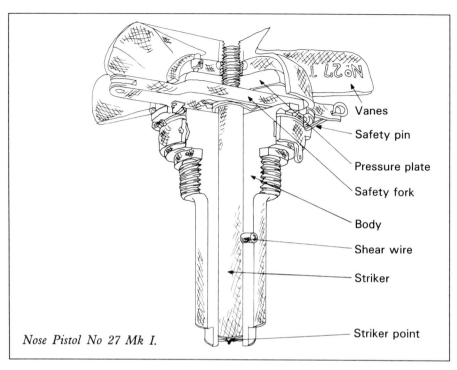

Vanes
Safety pin
Pressure plate
Safety fork
Body
Shear wire
Striker
Striker point

Nose Pistol No 27 Mk I.

modern fuzes are frequently a mass of complex electronics. However, all have one thing in common, they are designed to detonate the bomb. This may be on or after direct impact with a hard surface, at a predetermined height or depth in the air or under water, or in the case of anti-disturbance devices, if interfered with or moved.

Innumerable pistols and fuzes have been designed and used for many diverse purposes, consequently it would be impracticable to attempt to describe each and every one. In any case many tend to be variations on a theme, for example, the No 30 tail pistol is only marginally different to the No 28 but the differences, usually incorporated to improve performance, were sufficient to rename the pistol rather than up grade the mark number. Therefore, to obviate the need for a mass of technical detail, descriptions of the types and their workings will be limited to some simple typical nose and tail pistols used during the Second World War. It is hoped that this information combined with some more detailed information about specific pistols and fuzes mentioned earlier in the book will suffice to provide all that is necessary to give the general idea of their construction and operation.

In the early war years, up to 25 per cent of an aircraft bomb load included long delay pistols or fuzes with anti-removal devices, but the figure diminished significantly as the war progressed and more and more targets were saturated by more powerful, instantaneously detonating bombs. German bomb disposal teams became more adept in neutralisation procedures, but the bombs fitted with chemical long delay pistols always presented problems and even today, when they are occasionally found, require very careful handling. In 1944/1945 long delay pistols with 30 or 60 minute delays (Nos 53 and 53A) were used not so much to harass the enemy but to ensure detonation smoke and debris did not obscure the target as the raid progressed. This applied also to the No 47, occasionally fitted in the 12,000 lb MC Tallboy.

The No 27 pistol illustrated opposite is a typical example of the nose type used in general bombardment bombs.

As the bomb was loaded, the safety fork was fitted with an arming wire which was clipped to the aircraft but capable of being released from it electrically. The safety pin at the opposite end of the safety fork was then removed. When the bomb was released, the safety fork was withdrawn by the arming wire and retained on the bomb carrier. The freed vanes rapidly spun off, exposing the pressure plate attached to the striker. On impact the pressure plate and striker were forced inwards breaking the shear wire, and forcing the striker point on to the detonator percussion cap, thus, initiating the detonation chain. When necessary to jettison the bomb in an emergency over friendly territory, the arming wire and clip was dropped with the bomb so that the in-situ vanes and safety fork prevented detonation. By selecting 'safe' or 'live' fuzing switches, the bomb aimer could determine whether the bombs fell safe by releasing the arming wire and clip or live by retaining it.

In the case of most tail pistols the arming vanes formed part of the tail unit

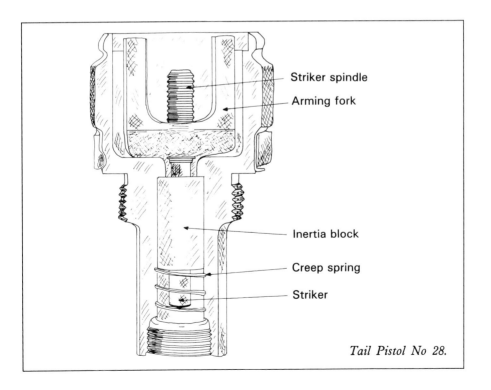

Striker spindle

Arming fork

Inertia block

Creep spring

Striker

Tail Pistol No 28.

rather than the pistol. During bomb preparation, the arming vanes were linked to the already fitted tail pistol by a forked rod which engaged the arming fork on the pistol. Consequently, when the arming vanes rotated so did the pistol arming fork.

The No 28 illustrated on Page 289 is typical of the general range of tail pistols.

When the bomb was released, the arming wire withdrew the safety clip permitting the arming vanes to spin and unscrew the pistol arming fork from the striker spindle, leaving the striker freely floating on the creep spring until on solid impact the inertia block overcame the spring and the attached striker impinged on the detonator percussion cap initiating the detonating chain. Sometimes, short delay trains were incorporated in the detonators to allow a modicum of bomb penetration.

Like the shear wire in the nose pistol, the creep spring was strong enough to ensure that bomb strikes on light superstructures, trees and shrubs did not set the detonation chain in action too soon.

Perhaps one of the most diabolical devices deployed in bombs during the Second World War was the No 37 Long Delay/Anti Removal Tail Pistol illustrated opposite. For good reason it caused trepidation among friend and foe alike. Delays of 6 to 144 hours could be achieved with a combination of acetone and celluloid discs. Any attempt to unscrew the pistol from the bomb pocket triggered instant detonation.

For its time, the construction of the pistol was somewhat complex, nevertheless, a study of the diagram should aid an understanding of the functioning process. When the safety devices were withdrawn as the bomb fell away from the aircraft, the arming vanes, unlike those on the No 28, wound the arming fork and the arming screw *into* the pistol body and crushed the ampoule of acetone. At the same time the head of the arming screw compressed the soft rubber washer effectively sealing the spreading acetone in the pistol body. Slowly and surely, the acetone softened the celluloid disc until the combined countersunk screwhead and striker was thrust down on to the detonator by the compressed striker spring. The length of delay was determined by the thickness of the celluloid disc.

Alternatively, at the lower end of the pistol a soft rubber washer locked the retaining sleeve inside the detonator head. Any attempt to unscrew the pistol body from the bomb resulted in the body unscrewing from the retaining sleeve. After approximately a quarter of a turn, the retaining balls were released and the whole striker assembly moved forward under the action of the striker sleeve spring forcing the striker against the detonator cap.

Later versions were provided without the anti removal device, perhaps due to a recognition of the dangers to Royal Air Force armourers. Not only was it a menace to enemy bomb disposal men, but also to those responsible for fuzing the bombs. One thoughtless back turn to clear a crossed thread usually proved fatal. For this reason, the job was entrusted to no one below senior non-commissioned officer rank. Nevertheless, some nasty accidents occurred so the 37s were handled with the greatest respect and utmost caution.

Another fiendish device, the No 845 Anti-Disturbance Nose Fuze was often

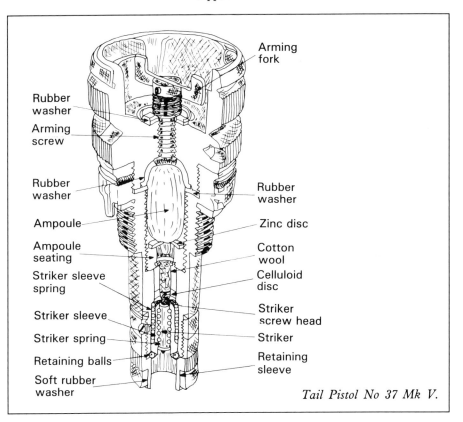

Arming fork

Rubber washer

Arming screw

Rubber washer

Ampoule

Ampoule seating

Striker sleeve spring

Striker sleeve

Striker spring

Retaining balls

Soft rubber washer

Rubber washer

Zinc disc

Cotton wool

Celluloid disc

Striker screw head

Striker

Retaining sleeve

Tail Pistol No 37 Mk V.

used in conjunction with the No 37 in 500 and 1,000 lb GP bombs. When fully armed this electrically initiated device would, at the slightest movement of the bomb, perhaps to examine the No 37 pistol, trigger instant detonation.

The use of this fuze, illustrated overleaf, was abandoned by 1943, consequently it was rarely found in MC bombs. On the whole, the mechanism was too complex for the rough and tumble of intensive operations and in any case manufacturing costs were higher and marginal results hardly justified the expenditure. Since the Germans had a similar fuze their bomb disposal teams were aware that freezing the fuze would temporarily cut off the battery power leaving them only with the tricky problem of handling the No 37 before it functioned.

As was the case with the pistols already described the 845s safety pin was removed during loading and an arming wire and clips fitted in lieu. As the bomb fell clear the safety clip was withdrawn permitting the fuze vane spring to force the vanes free from their stops and commence rotating. This threaded the arming spindle up into the body of the fuze (being a nose type) until its enlarged end engaged the internal shoulder of the fuze body. At this point, the spindle snapped at the weakened annular groove and the upper portion of the spindle and the vanes fell away. The cone below the arming spindle was now held downwards only by its seating spring. On impact, the cone and attached pin

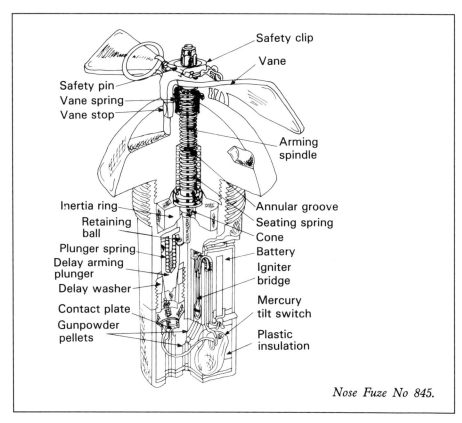

Nose Fuze No 845.

were driven forward by the inertia ring overcoming the seating spring. This forward movement released the retaining ball permitting the delay arming plunger to impinge on the delay washer under the power of the plunger spring. After 20 seconds, by which time the bomb reached its final resting place, the arming plunger forced its way through the delay washer contacted the contact plate completing the firing circuit except for a mercury tilt switch. Any subsequent movement caused the blob of mercury to move and so complete the firing circuit which triggered detonation.

Other fuzes were equally or more complex, for example the Nose Fuzes Nos 860 and 896, and the Tail Fuzes Nos 867, 885 and 886, all barometric air burst types used extensively in flares, target indicators and pyrotechnic clusters.

To describe them would serve little purpose, suffice it to say they were programmed to trigger the particular store at a selected height as air pressure built up on the downward trajectory. Thus, functioning height was independent of aircraft altitudes.

However, one other very simple and effective tail pistol deserves description because it was fitted to the two largest bombs dropped by the Royal Air Force, the 12,000 lb Tallboy and the 22,000 lb Grand Slam – namely the No 58 described opposite.

Its operation was simplicity itself and for this reason it functioned reliably. It consisted of a brass body with a central channel to accommodate a heavy striker. The striker was retained by a small brass cross fastened to the top of the striker. This cross prevented it from moving downwards. In addition the striker was restrained by a safety pin and an arming wire through one of the two arming wire holes.

Just as with other pistols the safety pin was removed when the bomb was loaded on the aircraft. As it fell away, the arming wire was withdrawn leaving the striker supported only by the brass cross. On impact, the inertia of the striker bent the arms of the cross allowing it to impinge on the detonator which could be instantaneous, or more often than not included delays of up to 11 seconds to permit adequate penetration. Using a No 47 pistol, delays of 30 to 60 minutes could be obtained thus ensuring the smoke and debris from one bomb did not adversely effect target sighting of following aircraft.

Details of only a very few simple or specialist pistols and fuzes have been described or mentioned, but it should be said that, quite appropriately, as much if not more design and development effort went into the many diverse types, as that put into the weapons which they activated. Nevertheless, a substantial proportion of the unexploded bomb rate, something between 10 and 13 percent, could probably be traced to defective pistols or fuzes which had to function in very adverse circumstances.

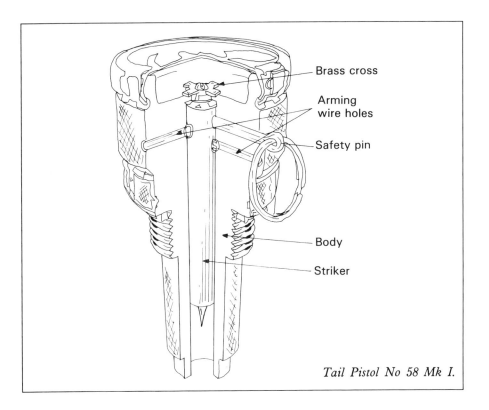

Brass cross

Arming wire holes

Safety pin

Body

Striker

Tail Pistol No 58 Mk I.

3   PATHFINDER FORCE ORDER OF BATTLE AND MARKING INSTRUCTION FOR AN ATTACK ON HAMBURG – CODENAMED DACE (NOTE 1) 24–25 JULY 1943

From Pathfinders

A.   Form B No 295
B.   Date 23 July 1943
C.   85 Mediums and 610 Heavies of 1, 3, 4, 5 and 6 Groups + 110 PFF aircraft will take part in the main attack on DACE (Note 2). T.O.T. zero-zero + 50 (Note 3)
D.   Intention. To groundmark the Aiming Point.

Method

Routemarkers T.I. yellow will be dropped by Blind Markers of 7 and 405 Sqdn at position A. 5411N 0850E as an aid to navigation. These will be backed up by Backers Up of 7, 97 and 405 Sqdn.

Blind Marker aircraft will then act as Finders and will drop their red T.I. in salvo on the Aiming Point. They will also drop Release Point flares, red with green stars, in such a position that Main Force aircraft aiming their bombs at them on an exact heading of 156 magnetic at a speed of 143 kts I.A.S. (Note 4) with bomb sights set for true height and airspeed and zero wind will hit the Aiming Point.

Other Pathfinder aircraft will act as Backers Up, aiming their green T.I. at the estimated centre of all the red T.I.s visible. 'Y' (Note 5) Backers Up are spread evenly throughout the attack and these aircraft are to use their special equipment to check the accuracy of previous T.I.s and Release Point flares. If their 'Y' equipment is functioning properly and if they are thereby certain that the attack has crept off the target they will re-centre it, dropping their Skymarkers and their green T.Is by means of their 'Y' equipment. If however, their equipment is unserviceable they will act as normal Backers Up, repeat Backers Up, of 83 and 156 and are to scatter their anti-personnel bombs on target defences on the way out.

Non Marker (Supporters) Aircraft. Lancasters and Halifaxes will aim their heavy bombs at the centre of the T.I. red or Release Point flares. They will scatter their anti-personnel bombs on target defences on the way into and out from the target. Stirlings will aim their incendiaries at the centre of the pattern of T.I. green or Release Point flares on a heading of 156 magnetic.

Routemarker T.I yellow will be dropped by Blind Markers of 7 and 405 Sqdn at position B. 5343N 0836E, as an aid to navigation on the route home. These will be backed up by Backers Up of 7, 97 and 405 Sqdn.

E.   Night of 23–24 July 1943 [operation was delayed 24 hours].

Bomb loads

Blind Markers.   4 L/7 (Note 6) × 2 T.I yellow LB + 2 TI LB (Note 7) + 3 TI red + 1 × 4,000 HC + 3 × 1,000 MC + 1,600 Gals (Note 8).

7 H/35 (Note 6) × 2 TI red LB + 3 TI red + 3 × 1,000 MC + 1 × 1,000 GP (LD) + 1,775 Gals

2H/405 × 2 TI yellow LB + 2 TI red LB + 3 TI red + 3 × 1,000 MC + 1 × 1,000 GP (LD) (Note 7) + 1,775 Gals

4 L/83 + 3 L/156 × 2 TI red LB + 3 TI red + 1 × 4,000 HC + 3 × 1,000 MC + 1 × 8 × 40 GP (Note 9) + 1,600 Gals

Backers Up.   8 S/7 (Note 6) × 2 TI yellow LB + 2 TI green LB + 3 TI green + 5 × 500 MC + 1,875 Gals

6 H/35 × 2 TI green LB + 3 TI green + 3 × 1,000 MC + 1 × 1,000 GP (LD) + 1,775 Gals

10 H/405 × 2 TI yellow LB + 2 TI green LB + 3 TI red + 3 × 1,000 MC + 1 × 1,000 GP (LD) + 1,775 Gals

3 L/7 + 15 L/97 × 2 TI yellow LB + 2 TI green LB + 3 TI green + 1 × 4,000 HC + 3 × 1,000 MC + 1,600 Gals

6 L/83 + 13 L/156 × 2 TI green LB + 3 TI green + 1 × 4,000 HC + 3 × 1,000 MC + 1 × 8 × 40 GP (Note 9) + 1,600 Gals

Non Markers.   3 S/7 × 16 × 8 × 30 (Note 9) + 1,875 Gals
1 L/7 + 5 L/83 + 3 L/97 + 5 L/156 × 1 × 4,000 HC + 4 × 1,000 MC + 1 × 12 × 20 (Note 9) + 1,600 Gals

10 H/35 + 2 H/405 × 3 × 1,000 MC + 7 × 8 × 40 GP (Note 9) + 1,775 Gals

All 'Y' aircraft to carry 1 flare red/green stars internally and 1 (cluster) × 4 flares red/green stars on bomb carriers in the bomb bay.

Navigation route

Base – 5400N 0300E – 5445N 0700E – 5355N 0945E – Target – 5315N 1000E – 5435N 0600E – 5400N 0300E – Base

Jays (Note 10)

A = 0857, B = 0557, C = 0727, D = 0557
(Remainder of instruction contains detailed orders for the use of radio and methods of reporting weather conditions and wind speeds and deployment details for Window. None of which is directly relevant to this Appendix intended to show the type of complex marking used by Bomber Command).

Notes

1. Bombing targets were usually code named after fish, thus Dace = Hamburg.
2. Number of aircraft are those planned and not necessarily those that actually took part.
3. TOT – Time on Target. Attack will therefore commence at 0050 hr (50 min past midnight).
4. IAS – Indicated Air Speed.
5. 'Y' aircraft. Those fitted with H2S.
6. 4 L/7   4 Lancasters of 7 Squadron.
   7 H/35 – 7 Halifaxes of 35 Squadron.
   8 S/7   – 8 Stirlings of 7 Squadron.
7. LB – Long Burning
   LD – Long Delay
8. 1,600 Gals – Aircraft fuel loads.
9. 1 × 8 × 40 GP – 1 small bomb container of 8 × 40 lb GP bombs
   16 × 8 × 30   – 16 small bomb containers each of 8 × 30 lb incendiary bombs
   1 × 12 × 20   – 1 small bomb container of 12 × 20 lb Fragmentation bombs
10. JAYS. Bogus radio beams intended for deception but throughout the war provided a useful navigational/homing service when more sophisticated aids were jammed.

4   SUMMARY OF ATTACK AGAINST THE DAMS

On 16 May 1943 at exactly 9.28 p.m. the first of 19 Lancasters took off on what was to become one of the best known air attacks of the Second World War. Their target was the dams which supplied the water to the Ruhr industrial area.

The aircraft were split into three groups. The plan was that the first group of nine aircraft would fly directly to the Möhne Dam and if it was breached before all their weapons had been dropped, those with bombs still remaining would fly on to the Eder. The second group of five aircraft were to fly directly to the Sorpe Dam where the intention was that they should attack at the same time as the attack upon the Möhne Dam. The remaining five aircraft were to act as a reserve and fill in any gaps as directed by the leader. It did not work quite as planned, but the 19 bombs and aircraft were accounted for as shown below:

Lancaster A/C Letter	Aircraft Captain	Primary target	Target bombed	Approximate time of release	Results of bomb	Remarks
(a)	(b)	(c)	(d)	(e)	(f)	(g)
G	Wg Cdr G.P. Gibson	Möhne	Möhne	0027	Detonated on bank, left of dam wall.	A/C returned to base.

Lan-caster A/C Letter	Aircraft Captain	Primary target	Target bombed	Approxi-mate time of release	Results of bomb	Remarks
(a)	*(b)*	*(c)*	*(d)*	*(e)*	*(f)*	*(g)*
M	Flt Lt J.V. Hopgood	Möhne	Möhne	0032	Bomb overshot dam and detonated. Destroyed power station.	A/C damaged and crashed 3 to 4 miles NW of target. Captain plus 4 crew killed 2 taken prisoner.
P	Flt Lt H.B. Martin	Möhne	Möhne	0037	Detonated 100 yards short left of dam wall.	A/C returned to base.
A	Sqn Ldr H.M. Young	Möhne	Möhne	0043	Detonated close to dam wall–some damage.	A/C crashed off Ijmuiden (Netherlands) Crew all killed.
J	Flt Lt D.J. Maltby	Möhne	Möhne	0049	Detonated against dam. Dam breached–assisted by previous bomb.	A/C returned to base.
L	P/O D.J. Shannon	Möhne	Eder	0139	Detonated on eastern side of dam.	A/C returned to base.
Z	Sqn Ldr H.E. Maudsley	Möhne	Eder	0145	Detonated on top of dam. Both aircraft and dam damaged.	A/C shot down near Emmerich (Netherlands) Crew all killed.
N	P/O L.G. Knight	Möhne	Eder	0152	Detonated against dam. Dam breached.	A/C returned to base.
B	Flt Lt W. Astell	Möhne	–	–	Detonated as A/C crashed	A/C hit power cable near Borken (Germany) en route to the dam. Crew all killed.
T	Flt Lt J.C. McCarthy	Sorpe	Sorpe	0046	Detonated against dam. Earth wall cratered below water line.	A/C returned to base.
W	Flt Lt J.L. Munro	Sorpe	–	–	Bomb not dropped. Returned to base.	A/C damaged by AA fire near Texel (Netherlands) and returned to base.
H	F/O G. Rice	Sorpe	–	–	Bomb dragged from A/C whilst low flying over Zuider Zee. (IJsselmeer).	Damaged A/C returned to base.
E	Flt Lt N.G. Barlow	Sorpe	–	–	Bomb recovered intact by German bomb disposal organization.	A/C hit power cables near Haldern-on-Rhine en route to dam. Crew all killed.
K	Sgt V.M. Byers	Sorpe	–	–	Bomb lost with A/C in sea.	Shot down by AA fire near Texel (Netherlands) A/C crashed in sea, crew all killed.
F	Flt Sgt K.W. Brown	Reserve	Sorpe	0315	Detonated on dam. Crest damaged for about 250 ft. Some water escaped.	A/C returned to base.
O	Flt Sgt W.C. Townsend	Reserve	Ennepe	0337	No damage–possibly dropped bomb on Bever Dam.	A/C returned to base.

Lancaster A/C Letter	Aircraft Captain	Primary target	Target bombed	Approximate time of release	Results of bomb	Remarks
(a)	(b)	(c)	(d)	(e)	(f)	(g)
S	P/O E.J. Burpee	Reserve	–	–	Detonated as A/C crashed.	A/C hit by AA fire and crashed on Gilze-Reijen airfield (NL). Crew all killed.
C	P/O W. Ottley	Reserve	–	–	Detonated as A/C crashed.	A/C shot down by AA fire North of Hamm (Germany) 6 crew killed 1 taken prisoner.
Y	Flt Sgt C.T. Anderson	Reserve	–	–	Bomb returned to base visibility poor over target area.	A/C returned to base.

Casualties: 8 Aircraft (A/C) failed to return; 53 aircrew killed, 3 taken prisoner.
4 Aircraft damaged by anti aircraft (AA) fire.
1 Aircraft damaged as it struck Zuider Zee.

5 THE ATTACK ON THE MÖHNE DAM, 17 MAY 1943

(Extracts from two German official reports on the effects of the attack)

Report from the Regierungspräsident Arnsberg, Westphalia, to the Minister for Home Affairs, dated 24 June 1943

During the night of 16/17 May 1943 an air raid warning was sounded at 00.23 hours. At about 00.30 hours–00.45 hours the Möhne Dam, which was protected by six 2 cm Anti-Aircraft guns, was attacked by enemy aircraft with large calibre bombs. There was no balloon barrage and the attack was carried out from a very low level. A number of bombs fell into the reservoir immediately in front of the Dam, thereby weakening the structure and probably causing a number of fissures. A further bomb hit the Dam itself and aided by the pressure of the contained water mass made a breach 76 metres wide and 21–23 metres deep. It is now impossible to ascertain whether this breach was caused by the bomb itself, or whether the original hole was later enlarged by the escaping water.

An immense floodwave poured through the Dam into the Möhne and Ruhr valleys. The main wave, carrying about 6,000 cubic metres of water at a height of 8 metres (up to Neheim), reached a speed of more than 6 metres per second. Below Lake Hengstey it still had a speed of 3 metres per second and then slowly spent itself. At 07.30 hours, 1,500–2,000 cubic metres per second were still flowing through the Dam...

Report from the Regierungspräsident Arnsberg, Westphalia, to the Minister of Labour, dated 22 June 1943

DAMAGE TO RIVER AND RIVERBEDS: The bed of the Möhne and the Ruhr is silted up below Neheim and has moved in many places, the river having changed its course slightly. The Möhne, from the Dam to where it flows into the Ruhr, and the latter up to 1.5 km below that point, will have to have its banks completely reconstructed. Below Neheim, in the "Ohl", large gravel banks have been formed and are cutting off the valley. They hinder the drainage of the floodwaters and are the reason why large areas of the Möhne valley are today still flooded. The so-called Mill, or Upper Canal, which branches off from the Möhne above Neheim and supplies water to a number of industrial concerns and to the hydro-electric installation of the firm F. W. Brökelmann, is completely silted up. Works dependent on this water supply are therefore idle.

DAMAGE TO HYDRO AND ELECTRIC INSTALLATIONS: On the Möhne, the power station Möhnesee – capacity 120,000 kVA (kilovolt-amperes) – has been completely destroyed, including the compensating reservoir. All large machinery, with the exception of a transformer which was recovered 100 m. downstream, has disappeared. The small power station situated further south is so heavily damaged that it will probably be impossible to repair it again. Heavy damage has also been caused to the water-works at Schulte in Günne, Hennecke in Himmelpforten and those of the Vew with a transformer station in Niederense and of the firm of Brökelmann in Neheim. The buildings and plant of the small power station Möhnesee have remained intact. In the Ruhr valley, the power station of the water-works at Echthausen has escaped structural damage, but the weir and mechanical installations have been destroyed. At Wickede, weirs have been destroyed at the local power station, the Soest water-works, and the Vereinigte Stahlwerke (Steel Works), and also at the local power station at Fröndenberg, where large portions of the banks of the Upper Canal have caved in. The dam of the water-works at Gelsenkirchen in Langschede has been similarly destroyed. The Hengsen weir of the Dortmund water-works and the power installation Westhofen of the same company have also been badly damaged. In all these cases, works of great economic importance are involved.

The dams of the Ruhrverband on the Hengsteysee, by the Stiftmühle between Hengstey and Harkotsee and the power installations on the Harkotsee have also been damaged due to mud, silt and the undermining of its structure.

The water-gauge installations at Neheim, Fröndenberg, Echthausen and Villingst have suffered fairly heavy damage.

The following damage was caused to overhead and underground electric cables:

100 kV Overhead cable Unna-Neheim destroyed for 3 km.
25 kV Overhead cable Fröndenberg-Neheim destroyed for 3 km.
10 kV Overhead cable Niederense-Honningen destroyed for 2 km.

10 kV Overhead cable Echthausen-Bremen destroyed for 2 km.

10 kV Underground cable Niederense-Volbringen destroyed for 1 km.

25 kV Overhead cable Neheim-Möhne power station is destroyed in a number of places, altogether for about 2 km.

DAMAGE TO WATER-WORKS AND PURIFICATION PLANT: The water-works of the town of Neheim-Hüsten, situated in the Mohne valley, which served the whole town district of Neheim, have been completely destroyed. A second works, further downstream has also been put out of action. That part of the town which is affected is being supplied from Husten by means of a temporary pipeline, laid above ground.

The water-works along the Ruhr, i.e., Gelsenkirchen, Hamm and Dortmund as well as those at Hagen, Witten and Bochum have already been reopened, after flood damage had been repaired, and are now in a position to supply, quantitatively, the most urgent needs of the area. As the quality is uncertain, chlorination has been ordered, and the population told to boil all water before use. The water-works supplying the town of Soest and Gelsenkirchen have both been put out of action.

Of the purification plants, those at Neheim and Fröndenberg have been rendered unserviceable.

DAMAGE TO RAILWAYS: The main line Hagen-Kassel is heavily damaged between Neheim and Wickede and slightly damaged between Wickede and Fröndenberg. The lines were in places completely undermined and at Wickede both rails had been lifted bodily off the embankment and washed on to a lower-lying field. Traffic has been resumed for local trains since the 8 June and for express trains since the 11 June. The southern part of the station at Fröndenberg and the branch line to Menden have been completely wrecked. On the line from Wetter to Witten, one rail has been undermined in parts.

The narrow gauge railway Ruhr-Lippe has not been able to resume operations on the Möhne valley line. The rails from about 1.5 km above the station at Niederense to the Mossfelde estate some way below have been washed away or covered in mud.

DAMAGE TO BRIDGES AND ROADS: All road and narrow-gauge railway bridges have been destroyed in the Möhne valley. The work of reconstruction has been taken in hand. In the Ruhr valley, the following damage has been reported: The road bridge by House Füchten is threatened by high water but not damaged otherwise. The two at Neheim have completely disappeared. Of the ferro-concrete bridge, not even the piles have remained. The upper part of the iron bridge has been washed 100 m downstream and deposited in the river bed. Of the railway bridge above Wickede the flood bridge and that over the upper canal have been destroyed and the bridge over the Ruhr heavily damaged. At Wickede the road bridge has been completely destroyed, likewise the road and the railway bridge of the Frondenberg-Menden line. The flood-bridge at Langschede had been destroyed and the foot bridge is threatened by high water and damaged. The road bridge in Giesecke is slightly damaged, that over the Mill channel more heavily. The road bridges at Schwerte and Westhofen are also threatened by high water and damaged. One of the supporting pillars of the railway viaduct over Lake Harkort has collapsed.

The damage to roads varies from the appearance of pot holes to the complete destruction of the road bed and surface. The worst damage occurred to a stretch of road in Wickede.

DAMAGE TO INDUSTRIAL UNDERTAKINGS: Numerous industrial installations have been hard hit as a result of the attack. In many cases materials, buildings and machinery have been swept away by the floodwaters or damaged extensively by mud. Also they have been hindered indirectly by the damage to electric and water supplies. Worst hit of all were the firms situated in the lower Möhne valley around Neheim.

The camp for workers from the East, which had been erected for the Neheim industries at a cost of nearly a million marks, has completely disappeared. A number of factories further downstream have been damaged too and have had to suspend production, but I have not included them in my survey, since their damage consists less of that caused to buildings, as loss of tools, machinery and stocks of material. I will however mention the steel works at Hagen-Kabel and the steel works Harkort-Eicken in Wetter. In both cases the smelting ovens and rolling mills were working at full pressure when the disaster occurred and damage was so heavy that it cannot yet be assessed.

CASUALTIES: Our investigation into the exact number of deaths have not yet been completed as may be seen from the number of missing. The picture on 1 June was as follows:

| | Germans | | Foreigners | |
Kreis	*Dead*	*Missing*	*Dead*	*Missing*
Arnsberg	160	34	557	155
Soest	224	32	–	–
Iserlohn	49	–	6	–
Total	433	66	563	155

The heaviest losses of life occurred in Neheim and Wickede. The rescue and identification service was handicapped by the fact that the bodies were covered in mud, badly mutilated and had, in the hot weather, rapidly decomposed. Rapid burial was insisted upon to avoid the danger of epidemics. In actual fact no such outbreaks have been reported.

EMERGENCY SERVICES: At first the emergency services were under the direction of the Councils of the three districts concerned. I personally took command of the situation on 25 May. In order to meet the immediate public emergency, strong military and civil help was organized. In the town of Neheim for example, the following personnel were employed up to the 22 May:-

1,250 military personnel.
380 men of the technical emergency service.
42 men and 60 women of the Red Cross.
150 men of the fire service.

Outside the town, the railways have mobilized some of their own manpower with the help of the R.A.D. (Labour Corps) and Pioneer Units. Detachments of the Organization Todt were utilized for bridge and road repair and for work in connection with the rebuilding of purification plant. According to the Group Leader of the O.T. about 2,000 men would be required for the rebuilding of the dam itself. The Council at Arnsberg estimates the labour requirements as follows: 800 as replacement for the drowned personnel, 700 for clearance work and 200 for rebuilding. In addition, 300 men would be needed for the repair of water-works, water system, roads and houses, making a total of 2,000 in all.

Estimates from the other Councils have not yet been received.

As has been said, and can be seen from the above survey of the damage caused by the disaster, industrial and agricultural undertakings have been badly hampered in their production for a shorter or longer period, as the case may be. This was occasioned through the damage sustained by water and mud. Apart from that, water-works, power stations, etc., have been made unserviceable, either permanently or temporarily. The losses in human lives, of materials, tools and machinery, interruption of communications, water and electric supplies were contributing factors.

The effects of the attack were felt far into the Düsseldorf district.

The anticipated damage to the water supply system is of the most far-reaching importance. The Möhne dam is the backbone of this system, serving the whole right Rhine-Westphalia industrial area, which is inhabited by about $4\frac{1}{2}$ million people. With the loss of the Möhne Dame, the available reservoir space has been halved. The result will be that the additional supply of water to the Ruhr will have to be curtailed. The quality of the water will be adversely affected and consumption, unless supplies can be got from other sources such as the Lippe, will have to be cut down, even for industrial consumers. It will depend largely on the speed with which repair work can be carried out and also on the weather during the autumn, to what extent industrial—in part war industrial—production will be affected.

6 SIMPLE DESCRIPTION OF 'A' MINE FIRING CIRCUITS AND ANTI-SWEEPING DEVICES

'A' Mines are ground (sea bottom), non-contact mines laid by aircraft. They are very similar in operation to the naval 'M' Mine deployed by surface ships or submarines.

'A' Mines detonate as the result of influences received from ships passing overhead. These influences may be either magnetic or acoustic. The magnetic mine reacts to the magnetic field inherent in a ships structure due to hammering and rivetting during construction whilst lying in the earths magnetic field. In other words all steel hulled ships become permanent magnets during construction. There is also induced magnetism produced within a ship due to its presence and movement through the lines of force of the earths magnetic field.

A magnetic influence mine contains a magnetic sensing unit known as a coiled rod unit (CRU). The CRU consists of a rod of nickel/copper/iron alloy wound with at least 30,000 turns of fine insulated copper wire. A current is generated within this copper wire coil whenever there is a movement of magnetic lines of force across the coil. The faster the movement the stronger the current, even at its strongest this current is not strong enough to fire a detonator but it is strong enough to close a sensitive relay. The closing of the relay completes the firing circuit which include a small dry battery and detonators. In this way the magnetic lines of force from a passing ship generate a small current in the CRU which closes the firing circuit and detonates the mine. In some mines a short delay is incorporated to ensure that the ship is directly overhead before the main filling detonates.

Anti-countermining devices are incorporated to ensure that the shock of an individual mine detonating does not set off others in the vicinity.

The acoustic influence mine detects the noise vibration generated by a ship and uses these vibrations to detonate the mine. A ship in motion generates a variety of noises but the main ones are caused by its main engines, and its propellors turning in the water. The acoustic mine contains an acoustic vibrator, which at rest is closed conducting a current of about 1.5 volts. Sound waves emanating from a ship reach the mine shell and cause the vibrator lever to vibrate and constantly open and close the circuit producing a pulsating current as opposed to a steady current. These pulsations are received by one leg of a resistor circuit or 'Wheatstone Bridge'. As the sound waves gradually build up as the ship approaches, voltage surges between the contacts increase in strength until finally the firing ciruit is triggered and the mine detonates. Further circuits are included to discriminate between voltage surges due to a ship and those produced by countermining shock.

The magnetic mine because of its inbuilt delay tended to be less effective against small fast ships, whereas the acoustic mine was more successful against fast ships than slower ones. Thus the really effective mine was the one that combined both acoustic and magnetic firing circuits.

Anti-sweeping devices (ASD) and sterilisers were also fitted to 'A' Mines. Apart from sinking ships, mine laying had other purposes. For example, forcing the enemy to employ more mine sweepers and generally to dislocate its war machine to the maximum extent. Several types of ASD were used. Among them, arming clocks which made the mine 'live' after a selected time period. For instance, mines were deployed in the Danube and the Baltic a few weeks before they iced over with time delays of 26 weeks. Nothing happened when the area was swept but a number of unsuspecting victims were sunk or damaged months later after the ice had cleared. For very different reasons, sterilisers, mostly electric clocks, were fitted to mines laid in waters the Allies wished to use later. They caused a dead short across the dry batteries after a selected period. For example, many mines were laid off the Normandy Coast in 1944 to give the Germans the impression that this would not be the jumping off point for the expected Allied invasion. Unbeknown to them, the mines sterilised themselves in good time for D-Day on 6 June.

7 ADDITIONAL U-BOATS SUNK BY 250 lb DEPTH CHARGES

Date	U-Boat	Aircraft	Sqn	Aircraft captain	Base	Location sunk
3 Sep 41	U–705	Whitley	77	–	Chivenor	Bay of Biscay
12 Oct 42	U–597	Liberator	120	Sqn Ldr.T Bulloch	Reykjavik (Iceland)	SW of Iceland
15 Oct 42	U–259	Hudson	500	Sqn Ldr.M Ensor	Blida (Algeria)	W Mediterranean
21 Nov 42	U–517	Albacore	817	–	HMS Victorious	Mediterranean
20 Mar 43	U–384	Sunderland	201	–	Castle-Archdale	N Atlantic
22 Mar 43	U–665	Wellington	172	F/O PH Stembridge	Chivenor	Bay of Biscay
25 Mar 43	U–469	Fortress	206	–	Benbecula	S of Iceland
27 Mar 43	U–169	Fortress	206	–	Benbecula	N Atlantic
10 Apr 43	U–376	Wellington	172	–	Chivenor	Bay of Biscay
2 May 43	U–332	Sunderland	461 (RAAF)	–	Hamsworth	Bay of Biscay
3 May 43	U–440	Sunderland	201	Flt. Lt.D Gall	Castle-Archdale	Bay of Biscay
4 May 43	U–109	Liberator	86	P/O J Green	Aldergrove	N Atlantic
7 May 43	U–663	Halifax	58	Wg. Cdr. W E Oulton	Holmesley South	Bay of Biscay
7 May 43	U–465	Sunderland	10 (RAAF)	Flt. Lt. G C Rossiter	Mountbatten	Bay of Biscay
7 May 43	U–447	Hudson	223	Sgt. Holland	Gibraltar	Off Cape Vincent
15 May 43	U–463	Halifax	58	Wg. Cdr. W E Oulton	Holmesley South	Bay of Biscay
17 May 43	U–646	Hudson	269	Sgt F. James	Kaladarnes (Iceland)	W of Faroes
18 May 43	U–258	Liberator	120	Sqn. Ldr.JRE Proctor	Reykjavik	N Atlantic
19 May 43	U–273	Hudson	269	F/O J Bell	Kaladarnes	S of Iceland

Date	U-Boat	Aircraft	Sqn	Aircraft captain	Base	Location sunk
24 May 43	*U–304*	Liberator	120	F/O D Fleming-Williams	Reykjavik	S of Cape Farewell
8 Jan 44	*U–426*	Sunderland	10 (RAAF)	F/O P J Roberts	Pembroke Dock	Bay of Biscay
6 May 44	*U–765*	Swordfish	825	Lt. Cdr. FGB Sheffield	HMS Vindex	N Atlantic
18 Jun 44	*U–441*	Wellington	304 (Polish)	Flt. Lt. Antonewicz	Dale	English Channel

Notes:
1. This is not an exhaustive list but does indicate the wide range of aircraft, units and bases involved in the anti-submarine war.
2. Rank abbreviations are as follows:
   Sgt.   — Sergeant   Lt. Cdr.   — Lieutenant Commander
   P/O   — Pilot Officer   Sqn. Ldr. — Squadron Leader
   F/O   — Flying Officer   Wg. Cdr.   — Wing Commander
   Flt. Lt. — Flight Lieutenant
3. Sqn. Ldr. TM Bulloch referred to above sank four U-Boats in all, *U-132*, *U-254*, *U-514* and *U-597*, believed to be more than any other pilot during the Second World War.

8 BRITISH NUCLEAR TESTING 1952–58

	Atomic testing (fission)			
Date (local)	Location	Weapon	Yield	Comments
3 Oct 52	Monte Bello Islands	Device on HMS Plym	25 kT	Operation Hurricane
15 Oct 53	Emu Field South Australia	Device on metal tower	10 kT	Operation Totem
27 Oct 53	Emu Field South Australia	Device on metal tower	8 kT	

Atomic testing (fission)				
Date (local)	Location	Weapon	Yield	Comments
16 May 56	Monte Bello Islands (Trimouille Island)	Device on metal tower	15 kT	Operation Mosaic
19 Jun 56	Monte Bello Islands (Alpha Island)	Device on metal tower	60 kT	
27 Sep 56	Maralinga Range South Australia	Red Beard on tower	15 kT	Operation Buffalo
4 Oct 56	Maralinga Range South Australia	Blue Danube (low yield) surface burst	2 kT	
11 Oct 56	Maralinga Range South Australia	Blue Danube (low yield) 500 ft air burst	3 kT	First free-fall weapon drop
22 Oct 56	Maralinga Range South Australia	Red Beard on metal tower	10 kT	
14 Sep 57	Maralinga Range South Australia	Device on tower	1 kT	Operation Antler
25 Sep 57	Maralinga Range South Australia	Device on tower	6 kT	
9 Oct 57	Maralinga Range South Australia	1,000 ft air-burst. Device suspended from balloons	25 kT	

Thermo-nuclear testing (fusion)				
Date (local)	Location	Weapon	Yield	Comments
15 May 57	Malden Island			Operation Grapple
31 May 57	Malden Island			
19 Jun 57	Malden Island			
8 Nov 57	Christmas Island	Blue Danube Free-fall 8,000 ft air burst	Megaton range, exact detail not known	Operation Grapple X
28 Apr 58	Christmas Island			Operation Grapple Y
2 Sep 58	Christmas Island			
11 Sep 58	Christmas Island			Operation Grapple Z

Two further low yield air burst trials were completed in September 1958 with the devices suspended from balloons

INDEX

This index consists of a general index, supplemented by a specialist one. The specialist index lists separately personnel, place names by country (United Kingdom, Germany, Belgium, France, Italy, the Netherlands, Norway and miscellaneous), ships (British, German and Italian), air Squadrons (RN, RAF and RFC) and air-dropped weapons.

GENERAL INDEX

SPECIALIST INDEX

People

(U-boat commanders are listed separately)

U-Boat Commanders

Place names UK

Place names Germany

Place names Belgium

Place names France

Place names Italy

Place names Netherlands

Place names Norway

Place names miscellaneous

Ships British

Ships German

Ships Italian

Squadrons (Royal Air Force)

Squadrons (Royal Navy)

Air-dropped weapons